Woman
In A
Man-Made
World

Woman
In A
Man-Made
World

A Socioeconomic Handbook

Edited by
Nona Glazer-Malbin
and
Helen Youngelson Waehrer

RAND McNALLY & COMPANY / Chicago

RAND McNALLY SOCIOLOGY SERIES

Edgar F. Borgatta, Advisory Editor

Second Printing, 1972

Just as in America there is no Negro problem, but rather a white problem; just as "anti-semitism is not a Jewish problem: it is our problem," so the woman problem has always been a man's problem.

Simone de Beauvoir

PREFACE

A sociologist and an economist—both women—have organized this reader around selected issues related to the contemporary social position of women in the United States. The book originated in the frustration of trying to provide easily accessible and varied readings for courses on women's position in the economy, and on the sociology of women. But, as the book evolved, we felt it might be of equal interest to a wider audience. Myriad issues are raised, the full understanding of which cuts across traditional disciplines. Experiences in recent civil rights and anti-war activities, combined with rising job opportunities and the sexual freedom made possible by improved birth control techniques, reawakened interest in women as oppressed members of society. The question of woman's role in contemporary culture is all-encompassing and, suddenly, imperative. The sociologist C. Wright Mills believed that a meaningful social science must deal with how biography and history intersect within social structures. We share his belief. This viewpoint dictated the choice of most of the selections included in this volume.

We have tried to provide an interdisciplinary introduction to some of the problems facing modern women; it may serve as a base for later, more specialized study. Since interdisciplinary work is necessary for a comprehensive understanding of the subject, these selections will help to prevent researchers from using invalid and narrow bases for their own theories. For the social condition of women is so fraught with bias, so embedded in a complex of ideas and social institutions that it defies easy separation into the tidy compartments of the academy.

This volume is organized into five parts, each of which is prefaced by an introduction. This should provide the reader with a historical or conceptual background for understanding and evaluating the selections. Part One is divided into two sections: readings in the first section provide a historical background for the present condition of women, surveying ideological and structural changes in the family, the economy, and the political system. Readings in the second half discuss two alternative theories analyzing the position of women in society. Various theories which deal with particular aspects of women are presented in other appropriate parts of the volume. Part Two includes readings which propose or evaluate psychobiological, sociocultural, and economic explanations of the differences between the sexes. These writings also illustrate the complexity of the relationships among the biological, psychological, and social levels of experience. The readings in Part Three present theories and empirical studies of the family, the economy, and the school, studies germane to the problems of the contemporary American woman. Part Four includes documentation which may dispel myths perpetuating women's subordinate position. Finally, in Part Five, the selections consider alternatives for the future, ranging from changes in interpersonal relationships to changes in basic social structures. That change is imminent has become part of twentieth century truth, and possible solutions to apparently insoluble dilemmas have become grist for the mill of the social pioneer.

This book is intended for use in undergraduate courses, workshops or institutes which are concerned with the social and economic experiences of women; it may serve, as well, to inform the generally curious.

In selecting readings and writing the introductory comments, we realized our points of view differed considerably. One of us had a special interest in theoretical and empirical analysis derived from Freud and Marx and a propensity to apply the sociology of knowledge to sociology; the other was especially interested in theoretical and empirical analysis derived from the mainstream of traditional economic thought. This contrast should stimulate both teacher and student to many arguments. Certainly, we expect them to explore further alternatives to our contrasting positions.

Many colleagues, students, and friends helped in the preparation of this manuscript. Special thanks are due to Nancy Porter of the Department of English and the Women's Studies program for comments on the readings, and organizational and stylistic suggestions. David L. Cressler of the Departments of Sociology and Psychology, and Harold G. Vatter and John F. Walker of the Department of Economics at Portland State University made helpful comments. Jane Middlehurst Glazer labored patiently over the style and grammar to increase the readability of the book. The women who took part in a graduate seminar on the sociology of women in the spring of 1970, and those in the undergraduate course the next fall, provided much stimulation in their reactions, criticisms, and encouragement. Catherine Lynde, a graduate assistant in the Department of Economics, did an outstanding job in surveying materials relevant to the economic selections, and in preparing many of the readings for publication. Our special thanks to Patricia Chapman, who worked hard and long on the preparation of the reader, handling the massive and at times confused correspondence, showing great patience throughout. Helen Y. Waehrer, whose idea it was to edit this reader, assumed the responsibility for the selection and editing of the readings and introductory comments on the economy and education. Nona Glazer-Malbin assumed the responsibility for materials about woman's social roles from a sociocultural and psychobiological perspective, and the major responsibility for the introductory comments. We share responsibility for the limitations of this book and the frustration that space limitations did not permit us to include many more articles. We appreciate the moral support of Laurette Hupman of Rand McNally as she skillfully moved the book through the editorial stages. The problems of women and of our college editor are illustrated by one of the difficulties encountered in moving this book from manuscript to printed page. The printer found his men hung up on the Sherfey article, and ultimately resolved the problem by assigning the job to his only woman typesetter.

We debated whether we should publicly acknowledge the support of our spouses, perhaps because such acknowledgements sometimes seem condescending. Finally, we decided that women's liberation (and our husbands) needed the recognition that men as well as women could accept that background helpmeet role. Thus, we thank our spouses who, in helping us, received a rapid education in sex-role differences, especially through their domestic experiences when we were in the throes of final manuscript preparation.

We gratefully acknowledge the permission of authors and publishers to reprint the selections in this reader, and Nona Glazer-Malbin acknowledges the help of the staff and the use of the British Museum library during the winter of 1971.

Portland State University
Portland, Oregon
October, 1971

Nona Glazer-Malbin
Helen Youngelson Waehrer

CONTENTS

PART THREE: SEX AND SOCIAL ROLES

PART FOUR: MYTHS ABOUT WOMEN

PART FIVE: TOWARD SEX EQUALITY

PART ONE: GENERAL PERSPECTIVES

> I thank thee, O Lord, that thou hast not created me a woman.
>
> Orthodox Hebrew Prayer

The long thread of cultural ethos which weaves through our current beliefs and behaviors can be unravelled back to Biblical teachings. Not only was Eve created from a mere rib of Adam's, but also, the Old Testament woman functioned only as a vessel for the chosen seed or a chattel of the prospering husbandman. Virtually excluded from religious ritual, she became the negative symbol in this prayer, uttered by devout Jewish men. Thousands of years have elapsed since God spoke to Abraham; oppression has been reduced as more and more people have believed in and gained individual freedoms. Yet, as man advances, woman lags behind. Along with other minority groups such as blacks, homosexuals, political dissidents, and children, American women remain in a subordinate position. Why? Literature, religious doctrine, social science, and folk sayings refer to her biological inferiority, her intellectual incompetence, her destructive sexuality, her moral pettiness and—the final indignity—her enjoyment of subordination and childish dependency.

A HISTORICAL OVERVIEW

Since the social condition of women has its roots in the past, an accurate analysis requires some knowledge of that past. This introduction surveys the changing position of women since the beginning of the industrial revolution in the seventeenth century, with particular emphasis on the Anglo-Saxon experience. The survey interrelates women's work and family life with ideology, type of economy, technology, and social crises.

Ideology refers to "systems of ideas, opinions, perceptions, and interpretations" as influenced particularly by social class position and contemporary social organization rather than as they derive from objective analysis.[1] It provides people with a rationale for their behavior regardless of the conflict or contradictions in their actions. Although *technology* and *type of economy* are partly related, the latter means a system within which a society decides what goods and services should be produced and how these should be produced and distributed; *technology* means both the machines and the ensemble of practices used to attain narrowly defined ends.[2]

The following discussion considers the early effects of those changes in ideology, technology, and economy which decreased the already low status of women; the second section considers subsequent changes in these factors as well as the social crises which accompanied her improving status.

Declining Social Status.

> The first division of labor is that between man and woman for child breeding. The first class antagonism in history begins with the development of the antagonism between man and woman in individual marriage, and the first class oppression is that of women by men. The individual marriage is the cell of civilized society in which we can study the antagonism and contradictions which develop fully in the society.
>
> Friedrich Engels

The fate of women has always been especially tied to the organization of the family while the fate of the family has been interwoven with the organization of the rest of society. The family is the unit of social organization through which men and women experience much of society. This is particularly true of women. It is true whether or not the family is a large extended one with a combination of productive political, educational, and religious activities, or a nuclear family with restricted activities. Traditionally, in the Western world women are subordinate in the family: in childhood, to the father; in adulthood, to the husband, though legally single adult women are often just about the equal of single adult men. In the English-speaking world, married women are subject to laws

---

[1] Karl Mannheim, *Ideology and Utopia* (New York: Harcourt Brace and Company, n.d.).

[2] Jacques Ellul, *The Technological Society* (New York: Vintage Books, 1967).

which derive from the legal fiction that a man and woman become one upon marriage, that "one" being the husband.[3]

The origins of women's social and legal subordination are much debated and it is difficult to reach well-supported conclusions. Some factors most often discussed are (1) the lesser physical strength of women; (2) the physical limitations of frequent pregnancy; (3) the traditional responsibility of women for early child care. The physical advantages of men over women are incorporated into social structure, most importantly in the economic, familial, and government institutions; women and men, through the process of socialization, learn to accept such institutions as "natural" while religious and/or secular ideology provides the rationale. A monopoly by men of the technology of coercion (skills in fighting, guns, knives) further supports the inequality, even long after the initial physical advantage has lost its importance.

Woman's place had not always been in the home. That doctrine was a creation of the period when men were being displaced from their homes as their workplace.[4] In spite of woman's supposed physical disadvantage, she has always played a vital and necessary role in the production of goods and services, not only for family use but also for exchange in the market. Before the seventeenth century and the beginnings of the industrial revolution, she was usually a co-worker with her husband in farm work, or home-centered crafts. (All family members worked together, and quite hard at that, to meet the needs of the family.) Women were frequently members of guilds, along with their husbands, and earned income as traders, domestic workers, tavern-keepers; they ran farm estates, breweries, and even an occasional newspaper and blacksmith shop.[5] With the introduction of machinery, single women[6] as well as married and single men, and youngsters of both sexes left the household for factory wage work. Married women, except among the very poor, remained in the household since their labor was needed there. The incomes which married women once could have earned within the household were lost as the guilds dissolved and most such work was transferred to the factory.[7]

---

[3] Leo Kanowitz, *Women and the Law* (Albuquerque: University of New Mexico, 1965).

[4] Henry Hamilton, *History of Homeland* (London: George Allen and Unwin, Ltd., 1917).

[5] Elisabeth A. Dexter, *Colonial Women of Affairs* (New York: Houghton Mifflin Company, 1924); Alice Clark, *Working Life of Women in the Seventeenth Century* (New York: E. P. Dutton & Company, 1919); Hamilton, *History of Homeland.*

[6] In 1850, the first complete industrial census showed that 24 percent of the total number of persons employed were women. See Edith Abbott's excellent study of the employment of women in the eighteenth and nineteenth century United States, *Women in Industry* (New York: Appleton & Company, 1909), reprint edition by Arno Press, Inc., 1969.

[7] Alice Clark, *Working Life of Women.*

Religious doctrine as well as necessity may have supported the concept of women's inferiority. Judaism and Catholicism were both quite anti-woman—the Bible, the Talmud, and canon law are saturated with allusions to the disgraceful state of being a woman and she remains excluded from complete participation in religious life to the present. No women have been rabbis or priests.[8] Though nuns were common enough among Catholics, Judaism did not offer its woman even second-rank position among the clergy. The Mary-cult of medieval Europe may have softened the life of women, but this is hardly reflected in either civil or canonical law. On the contrary, with the breakdown of feudalism, women lost many of the rights they had acquired. The courtly love and chivalry of the period may have helped the lady of the castle to pass her leisure hours with the comforts of verse and song, but neither she nor her lowly sisters ever seem to have benefited.[9] This is not to deny that the court lady sometimes had the advantage over her husband of being able to read and to run his estates while he was on a crusade.

Protestantism radically rewrote the Catholic version of man's relation to God, and redefined the relation of the devout to economic activity. The Reformation theoretically made women and men equal before God; however, the leading heretics did not have favorable attitudes toward women: "weak, frail, impatient, feeble, inconstant, variable, cruel" described the feminine sex while the abolishment of monastic orders made marriage the only possible means of survival for most women, depriving them of their only profession—and of their only place of learning.[10] Heightened economic activity, which was already beginning to be acceptable to the faithful Catholic without the onus that success would endanger his soul, under Protestantism became, first, an obligation to God, and then was interpreted as a possible sign of grace. Woman's calling was as wife and mother. Man's "calling" was gradually transformed from an initial broadness which included all varieties of statuses into the narrowness of vocation. The remnant of that transformation is visible in the notion that a few special occupations with a religious or humanitarian aspect—minister, nurse, family doctor—were "callings" well into the twentieth century.

As economic gain became a sign of God's possible grace, where were women? When the European and American world shifted from a household to a market economy, women usually remained in the household, partly because their labor was needed. But, perhaps this staying in the household was reinforced by the traditional exclusion of women from

---

[8] Hebrew Union College-Jewish Institute of Religion, Cincinnati, Ohio, expects to ordain women beginning June, 1972.

[9] Emily James Putney, *The Lady* (London: G. P. Putnam's Sons, 1910).

[10] Hamilton, *History of Homeland.*

full participation in religious life—in this case, economic activity which could be taken as a sign of grace.

During the late eighteenth and nineteenth centuries, secular ideology, too, may have contributed to women remaining in the home. Just as menial work gradually came to be considered degrading to the man of rising affluence, by extension it was also considered degrading to his wife, who, while she was his inferior was also his intimate, the mother of his children, and herself the offspring of a high status father. Work outside of the home was seen as a threat to womanly virtue, bad for a woman's physical well-being, and emotional health, and even more important, possible evidence of her husband's failure to earn sufficiently to support a family.[11] Idle wives and idle daughters rarely meant idle men.

The industrial revolution had other important and long-lasting effects. Migration from the farm to the factory encouraged the development of the conjugal family system; except for some earnings from work which married women did in the home, they were economically dependent on their husbands. A woman's work became so restricted to meeting the everyday needs of her family that some historians have suggested she came close to being a high-status family servant.

The change for women from household drudge and near chattel, under Anglo-Saxon law, to the legal rights, and now, nominal economic rights that American women have was exceedingly slow. By the end of the eighteenth century, the American woman had made some gains in property rights though she, along with her English sisters, was still considered the virtual property of her husband. Her body, her services, her domicile, her children, and her earnings belonged to her husband. In contrast, the unmarried woman at least had a chance to earn a living and the right to her earnings.

While in many ways, the industrial revolution eventually improved the standard of living of both women and men, its initial effect was to decrease the social status of women. Women were stripped of a degree of economic independence and prestige that had resulted from working with their husbands and other family members. From being surrounded and supported by an extended family system, woman found herself in the conjugal family. And what legal rights she had gained under feudalism were eroded by juridical opinion originating in England, from where it was brought to the United States.

Toward Improving Social Status. Women do not willingly accept their subordination to men. Legend has Lilith as the first woman and the first feminist, banished from earth, and replaced by Eve, for her

---

[11] Robert W. Smuts, *Women and Work in America* (New York: Columbia University Press, 1959).

presumptive refusal to submit herself to Adam.[12] While religious liberal Anne Hutchinson was no Lilith, since colonial days American women have been involved in social movements for human and women's rights: the seventeenth century rationalist movements for the rights of man raised the aspirations of women: education for women was advocated by such prominent men as Daniel Defoe, Benjamin Franklin, and Dr. Benjamin Rush. But, it was really in the fight to abolish slavery that women learned the depths of their inferiority, and how to organize to expand their own social rights. Women were also prominent in the social reform movement, in the late 1890s and the years before World War I— the movements for the rights of workingmen and women, the immigrant, and the poor. During the Great Depression, women were actively involved in unionization, government welfare programs to alleviate the sufferings of the unemployed, and participated in radical politics just as they had done in the nineteenth century, and would do after the Second World War. Their experiences in these movements frequently showed them their own relegation to an inferior position. For example—and this is the most famous example of all for it led to the founding of the women's suffrage movement—leading abolitionists were refused seating at a World Anti-Slavery convention in London in 1840. Women in the civil rights and antiwar movements complained that men were interested in them as bed partners, domestic servants, mother-surrogates, and economic producers, but not as policy makers.[13]

Experiences during wartime also led women to reassess themselves. Sexuality, political power, and economic capabilities all become salient issues when women are expected to forego a sex life, and at the same time, expected to assume political and economic responsibilities, which have been the usual province of men. At such times, women are needed as a labor force—pulled into the factory and office during wartime, and pushed out when men can replace them. By these labor force activities, women learn they are capable of doing "man's work." It was during the Civil War, for example, that women became nurses, seamstresses, teachers, clerks in government offices, and farm laborers; they also developed political skills when they worked for the 13th amendment. After the Civil War, many women remained in the labor force, particularly as teachers and clerical workers. Middle-class women fought for admission to colleges and universities, and tried to enter the professions. Working-

---

[12] According to rabbinical literature, Lilith is the first wife of Adam, who refuses to submit to him and flies away to become a demon. God creates a second woman, Eve, who is more pliant and appropriately submissive than his first error. Ancient cultures list no fewer than 17 versions of this legend. See *Hebrew Myths: The Book of Genesis* (New York: McGraw-Hill, 1966).

[13] See, for example, Marge Piercy, "The Grand Coolie Damn," in Robin Morgan (ed.), *Sisterhood is Powerful* (New York: Vintage, 1970), 421–438.

class women tried to unionize, or at least, to improve working conditions. But, while women had shown some political successes during the war, they experienced a bitter defeat afterwards when the issue of the vote for women was dropped from the fight to enfranchise the newly emancipated black man. The denial of the vote to women led to a split in the women's rights movements. One faction began a state-by-state fight for suffrage over the next forty years that included 480 campaigns in 33 states—just to get the issue on the ballot seventeen times, and to gain suffrage for women in *two* states! The other faction argued, much more in accord with the contemporary women's movements, that women were social outcasts along with others in the society and that broad social changes—along with the vote—were necessary for any fundamental change in woman's position. Over fifty years later, in the aftermath of the liberalism which followed World War I, the suffrage movement gained the right to vote for women. This was the last major organized effort to expand women's rights for—dismally—nearly half a century.[14]

World War I had other effects on women than enfranchisement. Participation in the work force, as substitutes for absent men, gave them further confidence in their productive abilities; in the context of a newly developing recognition of the sexual needs of women, the absence of men during the war made middle-class women in particular aware of the frustration of their own needs while an improvement in contraceptive devices allowed them the freedom of extramarital sex. There was an increase in the proportion of women college graduates, an increase in the proportion of married women in the labor force, and an increase in the sexual freedom demanded by and granted to women. But, the "New Woman" was quickly submerged in the hardships of the Great Depression. Women became acutely aware that formal political equality—the vote—did not mean actual political or economic equality: they were excluded from participation in "the inner circles of the most important men's civic and political clubs, which are the real centers of power in modern political life,"[15] and virtually excluded from political office and government policy-making. Once again, hundreds of thousands of women were left unemployed only to find that government relief and public works projects almost always gave jobs to men. (This experience emphasizes, too, the vital importance to women of full employment; for full employment means women can easily enter and stay in the work force.)

One remnant of the pre-Depression "New Woman" remained. Severe

---

[14] Eleanor Flexner, *A Century of Struggle* (Cambridge, Massachusetts: The Belknap Press, 1959), 142–155.

[15] Elizabeth K. Nottingham, "Toward an Analysis of the Effects of Two World Wars on the Role and Status of Middle Class Women," *American Sociological Review* (December 1947, 12), 666–675.

economic conditions meant the postponement of marriage, but not the postponement of sexual intercourse for the idea of sexual freedom, made possible by new birth control techniques, and supported by Freudian theory, continued. The postponement of marriage and the possibility of never marrying made sexual relations outside of marriage an attractive alternative to abstinence, with considerably less social disapproval than earlier.

Women were again pulled into the work force during the Second World War, and again pushed out when the veterans returned to the labor force. Immediately after the war, both young women and men became more family conscious, and the births rose to pre-1930 levels. The feminine mystique, so beautifully documented by Betty Friedan,[16] dominated novels, movies, plays, and social science analysis. The "New Woman"—except for some of her sexual freedoms—now became submerged in the latest version of "Kuche, Kirch, Kinder" in the period of political quietism and "love America" that followed the end of the war.

Technological improvements, too, continued to be important in giving women the time and energy to develop an active interest in their position in society.[17] By the second half of the nineteenth century, tremendous technical improvements and the influx of immigrant girls decreased the amount of time and energy women—especially among the middle class—had to give to housework. Such improvement continued to gradually decrease the burden of housework. Rapidly accelerated changes after World War II, in the technology of work in the marketplace and in the household, created a situation somewhat similar to the beginning of the industrial revolution. The jobs of men seemed threatened by automation and increasing bureaucratization; the work of the housewife was threatened as market goods further replaced home-produced goods, and both private and public social services further supplanted the wife in the performance of such duties as care for the elderly, the poor, and the sick. In spite of the apparent danger to men of technological unemployment, the expansion of the economy made both part-time and full-time jobs available to women—especially in industry in the decade of the '60s. Women (even those with preschool age children) began entering the labor force in large numbers.

Technical control over childbearing released women from their most dangerous burden—frequent, physically debilitating pregnancies and the threat of death from childbirth. Maternal deaths dropped from an estimated 60.1 per 10,000 live births in 1915, to 2.9 by 1956. Contraceptive

---

[16] Betty Friedan, *The Feminine Mystique* (New York: Norton, 1963).
[17] Flexner, *A Century of Struggle*, p. 178.

techniques so improved by the 1960s that women now have almost complete control over reproduction. Women are kept from having complete control, at least formally, only because the federal government and most of the states oblige women to complete nearly all pregnancies. Today, women have more years without the responsibilities of childbearing and child care than with them. Women marry earlier, have fewer children, are more likely to marry and never have children, and to complete the years of childbearing earlier than ever before. While these activities have become less consuming, women have increased their time simply by an increase in life expectancy from 40 in 1850 to over 70 years by 1950.

The thinking of Sigmund Freud and modern contraception have freed women from a restricted sexuality though not without creating other problems for her. Freud expounded a view that recognizes women as sexual beings but portrays them as practically inevitably crippled by the hurdles of psychosexual development. Moreover, he presented a theory of psychophysiological development (discussed in detail in Part 2 of this book) that was actually physically impossible for women to attain. The concept of women in American culture as sex objects further complicates the problem of women's sexual identity and personal identity.

This brief examination of the impact of the economy, technology, ideology, and social crises on women's position shows initial losses, and later, gains. However, women's social position shows no simple relation in industrial societies to any ideology or economic system. Women are second-class citizens in the mixed economies[18] of the United States and Great Britain, in the welfare economies of Sweden and Denmark, and in the socialist economies of the Soviet Union and East Germany. While women in the latter two systems have broad job opportunities and earn as much as men in comparable positions—unlike the United States and Great Britain—they still carry the double burden of housewife and worker just as their sisters in the two English-speaking countries do. Some greater accommodations (such as day-care centers, and maternity leaves) are made to the childbearing and child-care responsibilities of women under the welfare and socialist systems. As in the United States and Great Britain, it is simply taken for granted that these are women's responsibilities. Socialism has not automatically brought sexual equality, though it may be a necessary condition for the liberation of women.

Readings. The first four articles in this section are concerned with documenting the historical changes in the position of women. Bernhard J. Stern presents an overview of the social position of women in the West

---

[18] *Mixed economy* means an economy with a significantly large public sector; the government provides job, invests, builds, et cetera, and government policy regulates the rate of activity in the private sector.

from the fourteenth century to the Great Depression. William J. Goode summarizes the changing legal and customary rights of individual family members, and speculates about the relation of family authority patterns to society-wide political systems. Ivy Pinchbeck, in the next reading, assesses the impact of the industrial revolution on the status of women. Finally, Elizabeth Waldman discusses the changing characteristics of the labor market and women who have entered the labor force from 1920 to the present.

INTEGRATIVE THEORIES OF WOMEN'S SOCIAL STATUS

In this second section of part one, two attempts to integrate theory and data from a variety of disciplines are presented. When social scientists attempt to build theories to explain woman's behavior as well as to account for her subordinate position in society, they usually use either data from one discipline, or concentrate on one specific aspect of women. Many of the readings in this book use that approach. Jacob Mincer, for example, uses data from economics to explain why married women enter the job market, while Mary Jane Sherfey weaves together data from developmental biology and psychiatry to clarify female sexuality.

While few researchers have attempted the more difficult task of building a theory which integrates a variety of lesser theories, or which integrates data from sociology, economics, anthropology, psychology and other disciplines, Helen Mayer Hacker and Juliet Mitchell are two women who do make the attempt.

Hacker applies parts of minority group theory to the condition of women in the United States. A minority group is not a proportion, but a condition: it is composed of people who are considered inferior because of their membership in a social category so that they are denied rights accorded to others, are held in low esteem, and so on. A minority group may be any proportion of a population—five percent as the Jews are in the United States, or 70 percent as the Bantus are in the Union of South Africa. Essentially, Hacker contrasts *sexism* (though that term antedates her essay) with *racism* to clarify the meaning of the treatment of women, and the social, psychological, and economic experiences they have. She is particularly careful to consider the husband-wife relationship, whose social intimacy might, at first glance, contradict the usual taboo against familial intimacy between minority and majority group persons. Her application of the theory to women explains some apparent contradictions in the behaviors of women and men as well as accounting for woman's inability to use her "opportunities," her position in the economy and her low earnings, her lack of self-esteem and her apparent lack of resentment against men for her social condition, whether she remains in "woman's place" or passes over into a "man's world."

The application of minority group theories to women suggests other questions which might be asked. Many characteristics of the current rights movements and society's reactions could also be usefully analyzed by using other theories of minority group relations. In addition, the question of what might be expected to happen to the women's rights movement if, for example, the United States experiences a severe economic depression, or political repression, or a war, might be suggested by studying similar problems encountered by minority groups, including minorities other than blacks.

The other reading which develops an integrated theory is the brief excerpt from a much longer and detailed analysis by Juliet Mitchell. Mitchell criticizes socialist theory for its failure to analyze women apart from other oppressed peoples; the theory has been limited by its consideration of the problems of women within a social class framework. The position of women is considered a derivative of the existing economic system and automatically is presumed to cease being a problem with the eventual and inevitable establishment of socialism: specifically, women's social condition is analyzed as if the economy and the family are the only two structures in which women are located. Mitchell proposes a more complex differentiation of structures into production, reproduction, sexuality, and socialization. Her argument has several special merits. First, she discards the usually unexamined assumption that the family is a *natural* unit, and moreover, the only natural unit in which women must be analyzed, and replaces it with a direct analysis of the functions of women. (Analytically, it would be as if slavery, as a natural context for the analysis of pre-Civil War blacks, were discarded and replaced by a consideration of immediate structures—such as production, politics—in which blacks were located at that point in history.) Second, by freeing the interpretation of the condition of women from a simple economic determinism, she is able, without any difficulty, to incorporate some of the many recent findings of psychology, child development and anthropology into her analysis. Finally, her views of these four interrelated structures suggest that many further studies, cross-cultural and interdisciplinary, should be conducted within nonfamilial as well as familial settings. Studies are needed of women outside of marriage, in women's communes, in mixed sex communes, in group marriages, and of women who live apart from any of these. Studies of varieties of sexuality, and the sexuality of men as well as women, of children as well as adults are needed. The use of a theoretical framework which does not view the conjugal family system as a necessary basic social unit might encourage investigations of existing life-styles within American society, and in other countries. Such studies might find that some social innovations could be considered *bona fide* alternative social systems, in the process of emerging, rather than aberrant offshoots incorporating those women—and men, too—who presumably have "failed" at marriage and family living. Such forms might also incorporate those women, who, given the excess of females in the society, would never have had a chance at conventional marriage.

THE FAMILY AND CULTURAL CHANGE

BERNHARD J. STERN

From the beginnings of culture there has been an intimate web of inter-relationships between the family and other institutions because the persons who make up the family are also participants in the economic, religious, and other social activities of a community.

One effective method of studying the impact of culture on the family is through an analysis of how cultural change affects the status and role of woman as wife and mother and, consequently, how it affects family form and function. Woman, by her ability to bear and nurture children and by definition in our culture, is the nucleus of family life. Historically, cultural changes, and in particular, economic changes have had decisive effects upon women's place in society and in the family. Women's rights have been inextricably bound up with the broader problem of human rights, and improvements in the status of the masses, through changes in productive relations, have had repercussions on the status of women. When the dominant ideology of an era has been humanitarian and rationalistic and geared to the enlargement of freedom and the release of human potentialities woman's status has advanced, if not always formally through legislation, nonetheless in practice. On the other hand, in periods of cultural retrogression, as under fascism, when human rights are curtailed, the earlier institutionalized restrictions which sanctioned and enforced the subordinate status of women are revived and intensified. . . .

In western society, the patriarchal social organization prevailed for centuries. Although there had been permutations in degrees of dominance, women unquestionably had been subordinate to men within the family throughout the ancient and medieval world. When in early modern times the bourgeoisie began to develop its attitudes, the subjection of women was accepted by both the Church and aristocracy. The exalted formalism and passionate eroticism of romantic chivalry were merely veneer that did not interfere with the application of corporal punishment

Excerpts reprinted from Bernhard J. Stern, "The Family and Cultural Change," *American Sociological Review*, 4, 1934, 199–208.

to wives as permitted by canon law. It was a manifestation of woman's changing relations when, beginning with the thirteenth century, the bourgeoisie began to exhibit in some respects more regard for the personality of the woman than did either the aristocracy or the Church. The wives of the bourgeoisie had entered into trade, both independently and as shopmanagers and assistants, and also the wives of artisans were admitted to some guilds on an equal footing with men. As a result, borough regulations permitted them to go to law and provided that their husbands were not to be held responsible for their debts. The middle class and artisan husband was, moreover, dependent upon his wife's assistance in these days of family and domestic industry. Neither husband nor wife could prosper without each other's help and it was to his interest that she be trained in some skill which would make her economically proficient. Traditional attitudes were tenacious but by the sixteenth century the cloistered life of woman of feudal days had begun to disappear.

These changes in outlook toward women cannot be ascribed to the reformation, although it liberalized the canonical view of divorce. Luther still regarded marriage as "a physic against incontinence" and declared that women "should remain at home, sit still, keep house, and bear and bring up children. . . ."

The improved position of women in the family that came with the rise of the middle class resulted in a large part from the desire of the thrifty citizen to make his life a success according to mercantile ideals. . . . There arose a vast literature of handbooks and printed guides which gave advice to the middle class on family happiness and crystallized attitudes independent of the tradition of the aristocracy. In these manuals, a gradual improvement in women's position is discernible. They repeatedly insist that the woman must be treated as the lieutenant of her husband, sharing his confidence and trust, and not as his chattel and slave. The husband retained his powers of discipline and his authority, but there was an increased emphasis on woman's rights. Family industry and domestic economy, however, by its very nature offered a limited horizon to women and perpetuated men's dominance in all essential respects.

With the introduction in England of industrial capitalism which broke away from the family system and dealt directly with individuals, husbands were freed to some extent from whatever economic dependence they had had on their wives. . . . Women no longer were given specialized training with the result that one of the first fruits of capitalist individualism was their exclusion from the journeymen's associations. Excluded from the skilled trades, the wives of the men who became capitalists withdrew from productive activity and became economically dependent and to a large degree parasitic. The wives of journeymen either were obliged to confine themselves to domestic work, or to enter the labor market as individuals in competition with their male relations. The competition which had previously existed only between families in which labor and capital had been united within the family group, was now introduced into the capitalist labor market where men and women struggled with each other to secure work and wages.... Educational, scientific, economic, and political associations formed for public purposes did not include women as members, which underscored their postulated inferiority and made their functioning in the larger community difficult.

It is erroneous to overestimate the rapidity with which domestic industry and the family life which centered around it disintegrated. As late as the mid-eighteenth century, the population of England remained mainly rural and women continued to be engaged in productive work in their homes and in some form of domestic industry, but from that time forward, agrarian and industrial changes deprived them of their employment.... As urbanization was accelerated concomitant with the introduction of power-driven machinery of the industrial revolution, women came to the cities in increasing number to sell their labor power as factory workers....

It is to the credit of Marx and Engels that they anticipated the advances in family life that these technological changes implied, identifying the distress occasioned by factory employment to the exploitive nature of capitalism rather than to the use of machines.

Development of the family in the United States paralleled in many respects that of the Old World. With the culture of colonial New England dominated by the Puritan clergy, the patriarchal regime of Biblical tradition prevailed.... For nearly 150 years after the landing of the Pilgrims there were practically no women wage earners in New England outside of domestic service. Later, however, theory and practice did not always coincide, for some women of the poor classes went outside of the home to work and others of the middle class engaged in independent enterprise....

Whatever distinctive characteristics the American family assumed were derived from the fact that the frontier areas of the United States were settled by individual families rather than by groups as in the agricultural villages of Europe. Their relative isolation tended to develop, therefore, a pronounced functional ingrown economic and affectional pattern. In the United States, moreover, diverse family forms were constantly being brought to these shores by different immigrant groups. These persisted as long as ethnic communities retained their strength but gave way, as their communities gave way, to the standardizing effects of industrial society.

The ferment created by the discussion of human rights that accompanied the American revolution penetrated into the home.... There was recognition of the fact that the problem of women's rights was but a part of the larger problem of minority rights. . . . It is significant that the organized women's rights movement in the 1840s was associated with the antislavery movement, which was women's recognition of the fact that their own inferior status had sociological implications comparable to the oppression of the Negro people. The campaign for the removal of woman's disabilities in the home as well as in the state became a part of a broader program for the extension of democratic rights.

The reinterpretations of family roles which recent social changes have produced may perhaps best be illustrated by comparing . . . contemporary guides to successful marriage for the middle classes of today, with their Elizabethan counterparts discussed earlier in this paper. There have been marked realignments of authority between the sexes to the advantage of wives, and a pronounced less doleful stress on duties of parents and children. Reciprocal responsibilities receive important attention, but the family is conceived as existing for the welfare of its members rather than they for the family. The family is not sacrificed to a strident individualism, but its very important function is as a training ground for personalities capable of adjustment to society. It soon becomes apparent that in the redefined family few of its earlier functions have been completely relinquished. The modern urban family is clearly no longer a productive unit, but that it has an economic function as a property sharing agency has been decisively underscored by the manner with which family members assumed mutual responsibilities during the [1929 depression] even when not obliged to do so by law. Although a child's formal education is as a rule acquired through public schools, the participation of the family in the educational process in conjunction with the school is decisive in the formation of personality and in the building of social attitudes. Recreational activities outside of the home have supplemented rather than replaced family gatherings, especially since the radio has brought the world into the home. The emphasis on the individuality and personality of the constituent members of the family has enhanced rather than minimized the difficult family function of giving emotional security and a sense of adequacy, through reciprocal affection, in order that the maturing child will be able to cope with the impact of a competitive society with its inevitable insecurities.

For all of its limitations, this form of the modern family which few families as yet share, has undeniably superior values as compared to earlier forms. To the degree that it prevails, it has been made possible by the improvement in living standards and by the advances in the status of women. Its survival and extension is contingent upon these conditions, and whatever social and political conditions affect them affect the family.

FAMILY PATTERNS AND HUMAN RIGHTS

WILLIAM J. GOODE

The fight for human rights is fraught with perils, not the least of which is that those to whom we wish to grant these freedoms may reject the gift, since they enjoy their chains.

The central sociological problem is to ascertain empirically just what are the social systems or social patterns which will maximize the protection of human rights. This is an almost completely neglected area of research, so that the question cannot really be answered from the data now available.

It cannot be a surprise to the sociological theorist, . . . that so much of this revolutionary wave has attempted to change family patterns. From at least the time of Plato two and a half millenniums ago, wise men have suggested that if human rights are to be guaranteed, if each human being is to be granted an adequate opportunity for the full development of his talents, the family system must be altered.

Every rigid stratification system, erecting barriers against the able poor, has relied on a highly controlled family system as its base, whether we look in the past at Tokugawa, Japan, or in the present at India. The family system is the keystone of every stratification system. Very likely, every utopia conceived by man has in imagination changed the existing family system. Every wise man has also said that to transform a society it is necessary to rear the children differently, to socialize them for a new set of role obligations. . . .

Since those who are concerned with human rights are not likely to be in positions of power, and therefore are more likely to view with alarm than to point with pride to accomplishments, it is perhaps useful to assert that at least in this one crucial area of human rights a considerable revolution is taking place.

Let me simply list the main points of change here.

MATE CHOICE. Prior to the Chinese Revolution of 1911, it is safe to

Excerpts reprinted from William J. Goode, "Family Patterns and Human Rights," *International Social Science Journal*, 18, 1966, n. 1, 41–54.

say, most marriages in the world were arranged by the parents of the couple. A high but unknown proportion of the girls who married were given little or no choice because they were married in their early teens. Since that time, and at an increasing tempo since the Second World War, young people in every major area of the world have gradually come to have a voice in this important decision.

BRIDE PRICE OR DOWRY. Linked with parental arrangement of marriages in most societies was some type of dowry or bride price. These were not typically purchases, of course, but merely reflected the economic stake of the elders in the alliance between families.

INTERCASTE AND INTERCLASS MARRIAGE. Barriers to intercaste and interclass marriages have been rooted in custom as well as law. In almost all parts of the world the legal barriers have been eliminated, and custom has been eroded, too, under the impact of the freedom of choice given to young people. That most marriages will continue to be intracaste and intraclass goes without saying, but the individual has a wider range of alternatives than a half century ago.

CONTROL BY ELDERS AND OTHER KIN. Most social systems, including those of great nations such as China, India, Japan and the Arab countries, permitted by law and custom a rather wide control by elders over the young. These areas included geographical mobility, occupational choice, the level of education to be achieved, the allocation of income, and the participation in religious rituals, not to mention more trivial matters. Of course, even in the most industrialized of nations the network of kin plays an important role in the lives of married couples, but in most countries the adult now has a greater freedom in choosing which relatives he will support or listen to.

INHERITANCE. Although it may be asserted that any inheritance system which permits much property to pass from one generation to the next within the same family gives an advantage to one set of people and thereby restricts the freedom of another set, some steps toward freedom in this area may be noted. In traditional societies, there is little testamentary freedom, since the direction of inheritance is clear and fixed.

In addition, most of these great societies omitted the female almost altogether. Islam did not, of course, but the girl received a half-share. The newer civil codes have moved steadily toward granting equal inheritance to all children, and widows have come to be recognized even in societies that were once only patrilineal.

CONTRACEPTION. The right to choose whether [or not] one will bear children, or how many, has until recently been granted to only a minority of the world's population.

It is also worth mentioning here that this is especially an area in which women have not been permitted any choice, although the burden of children was theirs. Numerous studies have shown that even in areas of high birth rates most women are generally willing, and more than men are, to limit their families.

ABORTION. Most countries continue to deny the right of the woman, in the event of an unwanted pregnancy, to end it. This freedom has been most widely granted in the Communist countries and in Japan, with somewhat less tolerance in the Scandinavian nations. . . .

DIVORCE. It is surely a denial of choice if individuals are forced to remain in a marriage they dislike, and at the present time almost all of the world's population is permitted by law to divorce. In India, Brahmins were not permitted to divorce, though some divorce did occur, and lower castes did have that permission. Of course, in India as in other nations permitting no divorce the husband typically had or has other alternatives open to him, such as concubines, second wives, and so on. The Westerner should keep in mind, however, that some nations and cultures did permit divorce before the modern era. Islam traditionally gave the husband great freedom to divorce, and divorce rates were very high among the farmers in Tokugawa and Meiji, Japan. Both of these were patrilineal societies. Matrilineal societies have ordinarily been relatively permissive regarding divorce.

EGALITARIANISM WITHIN THE FAMILY. Although there is little quantitative evidence on this point, almost all observers seem to agree that in almost all nations the woman has been given greater authority, respect and freedom within the family, and this relaxing of a patriarchal tradition has also improved the position of children.

One of the most striking consequences of this change has been that women have come to be permitted to occupy responsible positions outside the family. Again it is difficult to quantify such matters, but it seems likely that egalitarianism in the occupational sphere has spread most rapidly in the Socialist countries. It must be emphasized that I am not referring to 'women in the labour force.' After all, women have borne heavy burdens in all epochs and countries. Rather, I am pointing to a radically different phenomenon, the right of a woman to obtain a job (and the training necessary for it) and to be promoted within it, on the basis of her own merits without the permission of her husband or father. Needless to say, this factor supports egalitarianism within the family, since it reduces the dependence of women on the males, but it also creates a new respect for the woman as an individual.

Of course, with reference to all of these, the new civil codes are more advanced than the actual behaviour and attitudes of the populations concerned.

I doubt, . . . that any society will in our lifetime be able to create genuine egalitarian relations between men and women.

The trends noted are steps toward the securing of human rights. Granted, they do not at first glance seem to be so dramatic or spectacular as the freeing of slaves or the abolition of a feudal system. On the other hand, those liberations may in fact have consequences similar to those of such grander political acts. If one could construct a numerical index, I would predict that the extensions of human rights to women and children in their domestic and occupational roles would loom as large as any other single step in the contemporary fight for human rights—certainly, far more real progress than has occurred in the areas of freedom of speech, religion, and publication, or the right of free elections or assembly. That step added as much or more to the economic production of the nations in which it has taken place and, very likely, at levels which we cannot easily explore here, helped to lay a firmer foundation for human rights in still other areas.

The ideology of the conjugal family, as it is expressed in debates about family trends over much of the world, asserts the worth of the individual against the claims of caste, clan, or social stratum. It proclaims egalitarianism and the right to take part in important decisions.

In the West, its roots lie in the philosophic tradition that accompanied and interpreted the ascetic segment of the Protestant Revolution, and that runs counter to central philosophic elements of the Lutheran sects. Its fundamental human roots are still more universal, in that it radically asserts the rights of all to enjoy human freedom, that is, choices among real alternatives. That no society and no family system wholly lives up to these principles goes without saying, but the contemporary pressures toward those goals are hardly to be denied.

Even if most family systems of the world are moving toward granting more human rights to their members, can we assert that any particular kinds of family patterns or relations will produce a higher percentage of adults who will support the claims of their fellow citizens to the full enjoyment of human rights in the broader civic realm? Or, in a less cautious formulation, is it likely that the early experiences of the child in the family have *no* relationship with the willingness of the later adult to grant tolerance, freedom, and protection to others? Or, in a more utopian query, what type of family pattern would be most likely to produce adults who could live up to the really difficult role obligations that are demanded by the full extension of human rights to all?

The difficult task of socialization is not the inculcation of a love for one's personal freedom, which may be an easy goal: after all, any animal prefers at the outset to be free. But training children to support others' freedom and rights requires a more complex psychological and social pattern. Does any type of family pattern do that? Perhaps we might begin by taking note of a speculation often made by social philosophers and sociologists, essentially that extreme familism denies human rights to others. That is, when individuals are reared largely within the family and derive almost all of their satisfactions there, they are likely to overvalue the ingroup—the ethnic group, the tribe, the region. Consequently, they feel free to treat outsiders as of little value, not deserving of any protection.

This suggestion . . . also receives some slight support from the finding that children are more likely to be democratic in their social behaviour if they spend more of their time with peers (who have roughly equal power) than with parents, who have superior power (we shall, however, consider this point).

However, the renunciation of extreme familism is hardly sufficient as a directive for rearing children who will support human rights. Speculatively, one would suppose that a high degree of permissiveness and egalitarianism within the family would be more likely to produce individuals who could not adjust easily to a repressive political system, or who would not create such a system. What kinds of socialization experiences create the type of personality that is most prone to deny human rights to Jews, Negroes and other ethnic groups? However, the answers suggest parallel hypotheses about the denial of human rights generally.

Authoritarian control of the family by the father is correlated with such traits as these: deification of the parent, high evaluation of the father role, the child's passive adjustment to the present situation, the suppression of the child's aggression, suppression of sexual impulses in the child, and the fostering of dependency in the child. Democratic attitudes of fathers correlate with egalitarian treatment of children, encouragement of their independence, and affection as a means of control.

Adults who exhibit intolerance of others' rights are more likely than other adults to have grown up under authoritarian parental control and, of course, to continue that tradition with their own children. The stereotyping that is so characteristic of those who consider people who differ from themselves as having few redeeming traits is emphasized by parental efforts to ascribe fixed, clearly distinct, traits to the two sexes; indeed, the more authoritarian the mother's attitudes, the greater the children's imitation of the like-sex parent.

Perhaps central is the necessity of family interaction based on security and love, rather than threat, and that concedes the right of individuals to have pleasure without guilt. Under a régime of threat, the child—and later, the adult—feels the need to have precise instructions, for fear of making errors and being punished for it. There is, then, an intolerance of ambiguity, whereas in a society that guarantees human rights the individual must be able to interact with others without at all knowing exactly what they will do in turn. Similarly, in such families, individuals are conceded to have their own unique traits, and not to be forced rigidly into the categories of male and female—for example, chores might be shared on the basis of need and capacity, rather than sex.

One of the likely consequences of the collaborative style, in which parents and children cooperate to solve problems, is the development of faith or trust in other people. This, in turn, as most readers know, is negatively correlated with authoritarianism.

A complex relationship exists between these factors and love. The manipulation of love is one of the most effective techniques for developing a strong superego, but there is some evidence that the threat of love withdrawal creates many psychological problems. Among these is a distrust of others. If love is dependent, for example, on performance, performance may be high but regression is also a possible outcome. It seems likely that the security of parental love must be great enough to permit the child to face aggression by parent or outsider without great anxiety. The ability to face hostility without any inner compulsion to aggress against those who oppose; or without any inner compulsion to bow to that opposition when it is powerful (seeking love by compliance) can be most effectively based on security in parental love.

This security would appear to be based, in turn, on conveying to the child that he is loved as a unique person, not because of his status as elder or younger, male or female. The recognition that each member of the family is unique, with his or her own needs and demands, rather than merely a set of ascribed statuses, should contribute to the generalized feeling that other individuals are also unique: they need not be manipulated to serve one's own needs, or rejected as outcasts.

It is easier to push a highway through a jungle, or to purify a water supply, than to alter the details of family relations, as we know already from the repeated failures of birth control campaigns. Traditional parents are not more willing to share their authority with their children than are husbands to yield control over their wives. It is likely that the contemporary transformations in the political, economic, and social macrostructures of most nations will ultimately have more impact on the microstructure of the family than will any particular program aimed at changing those internal relations of the family.

WOMEN WORKERS AND THE INDUSTRIAL REVOLUTION

IVY PINCHBECK

The progress of the Industrial Revolution was marked by far-reaching changes. . . . [What were] their effect and the importance of the social and economic developments of the period on the position of women generally?

In the mid-eighteenth century the population of England was mainly rural, and women were largely engaged in productive work in their homes and in some form of domestic industry. In the towns the industrial woman wage earner was not unknown and a large number of women were engaged in some form of trade; but here again, women more often shared the activities of their husbands and acted as partners in the industrial, as in the agricultural sphere. As a result of the changes which took place in the latter half of the eighteenth century, this state of affairs became no longer possible. . . . Women's opportunities for productive work at home were gradually lessened as the agrarian revolution proceeded, while at the same time industrial changes deprived them of employment in the older domestic industries.

At the turn of the century, in the transition period before women were reabsorbed, or had found their place in the new order of things, there was a great deal of distress and unemployment among women. . . . At the same time the adoption of new methods and cultures and the desire of agriculturalists to keep down rates and wages by providing employment for women on the land, resulted in the development of a new class of women day laborers in agriculture. A large proportion of those who remained in rural areas was absorbed by this new and growing demand for cheap occasional labor, and the exploitation of women and children at its worst was seen in the Gang System. Meanwhile, the town population was rapidly increasing and here the factory system, especially after the adop-

Excerpts reprinted from I. Pinchbeck, *Women Workers and the Industrial Revolution, 1750–1850* (London: George Routledge and Sons, Ltd., 1930), pp. 306–316, with permission from Frank Cass and Co., Ltd., and the author. Republished by Frank Cass and Co., Ltd., 1968.

tion of steam power in the early nineteenth century, provided an ever widening field of employment for women.

These changes radically affected the lives of the women concerned. It has been generally admitted that women gained greatly by the transference of manufacture from the home to the factory. As Commissioner Hickson stated in his Report in 1840, "domestic happiness is not promoted, but impaired by all members of the family muddling together and jostling each other constantly in the same room." Moreover, dust and oil and offensive smells were often the necessary accompaniments of domestic industry; hence, however the industrial revolution may have affected the married woman's economic position in the home, it cannot be denied that it immensely improved her domestic conditions. Now that the home was no longer a workshop, many women were able, for the first time in the history of the industrial classes, to devote their energies to the business of homemaking and the care of their children, who stood to benefit greatly by the changed home conditions.

The women who found employment in the factory under the new industrial regime undoubtedly encountered difficulties and disadvantages in the early stages. As regards long hours and unhealthy conditions, there was at first little to choose between the old system and the new, but in addition, power driven machinery introduced a new element of compulsion. In the factory, human labor was "yoked with iron and steam," and the workers were subjected to a regularity and discipline which in their newness proved irksome and intolerable to those accustomed to the independence and irregular hours permitted by the domestic system. On the other hand, labor which was often heavy and unpleasant was exchanged for the lighter work of machine attendance, and although the latter has met with much adverse criticism on the score of monotony, it must be remembered that many of women's occupations in the domestic industries were equally monotonous and dull. And when, ultimately, the State regulated the hours and conditions of factory workers, the new system began to advance on lines which proved it to be immeasurably superior to the old domestic system, in its provisions for the health and well-being of the workers. Again, women undoubtedly benefited by the wider experience and more varied interests they gained by working together in a community. The women of the industrial areas in the North were by the 'forties already remarkable for their greater intelligence and acuteness as compared with women of the same class elsewhere. ... As scattered domestic workers women had had few opportunities for any interchange of ideas among themselves, and still less for any form of cooperation in their common interests. It was partly for this reason that women's work in the past had been so badly paid, and although the old tradition persisted and women's wages were still comparatively low, and the progress of cooperation was slow among women throughout the nineteenth century, yet it is interesting to note that there were signs of the beginnings of this new spirit among almost the first generation of factory workers.

In the same way the charges made against the factory system—that it resulted in the breaking up of home life, the lowering of the standard of domestic comfort and the debasement of life for the workers—must be examined in light of previous standards and those prevailing among the working class generally at this period. . . . In the entire factory population the proportion of married women who worked, to those who remained at home . . . [was] far too small to justify the statement that the factory system destroyed the home life of the workers generally.

The women of the working classes in the eighteenth century were busily engaged in earning their living in either agriculture or industry, but their facilities for acquiring any measure of skill in domestic management were exceedingly limited. Cottage accommodation was often of the meanest; food in many homes was limited to oatmeal porridge, milk, bread, cheese and potatoes, with meat as a rare luxury; cooking utensils were few and turf and furze were the common fuels used by a great proportion of the population . . . In these circumstances it is inconceivable that the standard of culinary skill could ever have been high, or that the training of children in domestic affairs could have been much superior to that of children who spent their early lives in the factory. . . . Not only factory women, but all women of the working classes were handicapped by ignorance and the lack of any proper system of instruction, and until some measure of education and training was placed within their reach, it was unreasonable to expect any raising of the general standard of domestic skill or intelligent use of their resources.

In the same way the moral degradation so often spoken of by opponents of the factory system was due less to a "debasement" of life through the system, as they believed, than to the standards prevailing among the working classes generally. "In regard to morals," states the Report of the Factory Commission in 1833, "we find that though the statements and depositions of the different witnesses that have been examined are to a considerable degree conflicting, yet there is no evidence to show that vice and immorality are more prevalent among these people, considered as a class, than amongst any other portion of the community in the same station, and with the same limited means of information." . . . Low standards were due not so much to congregating together in their work, as to the lack of education, the want of decency in their homes and bad conditions all round. . . . That prostitution was prevalent during periods of unemployment was also very probable, but this was equally true among dressmakers and milliners and all workers in seasonal trades. Here the moral standard which prevailed was the result in great measure of low wages, the lack of reserves for times of unemployment, the limited openings available for women and the general economic conditions which ruled in women's employment.

Although the workers did not participate to the extent they might have done in the advantages arising from the use of machinery, yet even so, for the majority of workers the factory meant higher wages, better food and clothing and an improved standard of living. This was especially so in the case of women, who in the first instance, were drawn from badly paid unskilled work in various trades, from agricultural labor and domestic service. . . . The rise in the standard of living was shown by the increased consumption of fresh meat—still a rarity among the agricultural classes, who at this time subsisted mainly on a bread and potato diet— and by the greatly improved clothing of all but thriftless workers. For the first time working women had the means to gratify a taste for dress, although expenditure under this head was a matter for much adverse criticism.

Economically, women were vitally affected by the industrial revolution. In the past, marriage for many women had been some sort of business partnership in agriculture, trade or domestic industry, but in the reorganization which accompanied the industrial revolution, the majority of married women lost their economic independence. Unless they became wage earners outside the home they ceased to contribute to the family resources and themselves became financially dependent upon their husbands. Married women had never possessed a legal right to their own earnings, or their share of the family wage, nevertheless, in the new situation their financial subjection was greater than in the days when they contributed their share to the family income. While from the individual standpoint this might appear to be a retrogressive tendency, yet, among the working classes, it was not always a sound economic proposition for the married woman to be a wage earner. Her earnings rarely balanced the loss to the family from the nonperformance of more important domestic duties; her own labor was often exploited and in many instances women's earnings only served to keep their husbands' wages at the level of individual subsistence. In this sense the industrial revolution marked a real advance, since it led to the assumption that men's wages should be paid on a family basis, and prepared the way for the more modern conception that in the rearing of children and in homemaking, the married woman makes an adequate economic contribution.

In the case of the single working woman, the most striking effect of the industrial revolution was her distinct gain in social and economic independence. In industries in which a family wage prevailed, women scarcely knew the extent of, or had any opportunity of handling, their own earnings, and among women who earned an individual wage, few earned sufficient to give them any real sense of independence. Under the new regime every woman received her own earnings as a matter of course. The significance of this change was at once seen in the new sense of freedom which prompted so many young women to retain control of their wages, and even to leave home at an early age in order to "become their own mistresses." Though the individual wage was at first bitterly resented by the heads of families, it led ultimately to a new attitude towards the whole question of economic independence for women.

It remains to sum up ... the effects of the industrial revolution on women's employment and economic status by a brief statement as to the position generally at the end of our period in the midnineteenth century. By that time the position of women in industry and their suitability for wage earning occupations outside the home, had become subjects for public discussion. Victorian reformers and philanthropists, led by Lord Shaftesbury, having first directed their attention to children, now laid a new emphasis on the social value of women and the importance of their influence on the national welfare. The facts revealed by various Parliamentary Commissions of inquiry supported their arguments for some measure of state protection, and national responsibility for women workers.

This new interest, and the conviction that certain forms of labor ... were unsuitable for women, was so far good. But Victorian sentiment and prejudice would have gone further and would have withdrawn women gradually from all forms of factory labor also. Too close themselves to the industrial revolution to grasp the full significance of its changes and their economic importance for women, and unmindful of the part played by women in the past, the Victorians were shocked and horrified by the appearance of a new class of women workers in industrial centers, and could only reiterate that women's place was in the home. It was fortunate for women as a class that the extremists did not win the day, and that the more moderate section of reformers concentrated on securing measures of protection which should make industrial employment a fitting occupation for women. As a result of their efforts, by the mid-nineteenth century, factory women were in the van of all other workers. Legislative protection had secured them a recognized place in productive industry, and the emancipation of working women had definitely begun.

The importance of this, at a time when factory work was the only expanding field of employment for women, can hardly be overestimated. The industrial revolution had enormously increased the amount of employment for men by new developments in mining, engineering and transport and the expansion of other industries, but there was no corresponding increase for women except in this sphere; in other directions their opportunities had actually declined. The Population Returns of 1841 were, for the first time in the case of women, made on an occupational basis, and although the information is not altogether accurate, the statistics at least give a rough idea of the distribution of women workers. At first sight, the great variety of women's occupations appears little short of amazing; but a closer examination soon reveals the fact that the great majority of women were working under five heads, as domestic servants, factory operatives, needlewomen, agricultural workers and those employed in domestic industries. Of all these, factory women were by far the best off, working the shortest hours and receiving the same rate of wages as men where they were employed in the same kinds of work. In other occupations low wages and bad conditions were the rule —the inevitable results of an overstocked labor market. Here lay the explanation for most of the drudgery of domestic service, and the sweated slavery of the needle workers, whose wages were kept down by a constant stream of women compelled by adverse fortunes to enter the labor market, and for whom there was no alternative but the needle. Middle class women were in an even worse position. Victorian ideas of "refinement" prescribed a life of idleness for women, unless stern necessity ruled otherwise. Even then they were limited to the genteel but overcrowded trades of dressmakers and milliners, or to what Charlotte Brontë described as "governessing slavery."

By this time the effects of increased wealth and the exclusion of upper class women from industry and trade were easily discernible. "A lady, to be such, must be a mere lady, and nothing else," wrote Margaretta Greg in her diary in 1853. "She must not work for profit, or engage in any occupation that money can command, lest she invade the rights of the working classes, who live by their labor. Men in want of employment have pressed their way into nearly all the shopping and retail businesses that in my early years were managed in whole, or in part, by women. The conventional barrier that pronounces it ungenteel to be behind a counter, or serving the public in any mercantile capacity, is greatly extended. The same in household economy. Servants must be up to their offices, which is very well; but ladies, dismissed from the dairy, the confectionery, the store room, the still room, the poultry yard, the kitchen garden, and the orchard, have hardly yet found themselves a sphere equally useful and important in the pursuits of trade and art to which to apply their too abundant leisure."

It is only necessary to contrast the vigorous life of the eighteenth-century business woman, travelling about the country in her own interests, with the sheltered existence of the Victorian woman, to realise how much the latter had lost in initiative and independence by being protected from all real contact with life. To contemporaries, however, the new independence of working women was an even more striking contrast. Individual women among the middle classes were awakening to a consciousness of their position, and the importance of the economic emancipation of working women was at once manifested in its influence on better-class women and their demands for a wider sphere and the right to individual independence.

With the desire on their part for social and economic freedom came first, in the mid-nineteenth century, the demand for higher education and training, and secondly, the agitation for the readmission of women to industry and the professions. How far these demands have been successful is a matter of contemporary history. Women's work in these spheres as has been shown, is not an altogether new thing; but it is new in the sense that it is now definitely based on education and training which are enabling women to take their proper place in the affairs of the world, and that it is accompanied by new ideals of economic independence. In these respects the position of women today marks a very real advance—the possibilities of which we are as yet scarcely able to determine. Herein lies the ultimate importance of the industrial revolution for women.

CHANGES IN THE LABOR FORCE ACTIVITY OF WOMEN

ELIZABETH WALDMAN

One of the most pronounced differences between the life patterns of women today and those of their grandmothers is the number and proportion of women who are in paid employment outside of their homes. Nearly 31 million or 42 percent of American women 16 years old and over were working or looking for work in January 1970. Roughly one-fourth that number (8.2 million, or 23 percent of working-age women) were in the labor force in January 1920, the same year that women gained the right to vote and the Women's Bureau was established in the U.S. Department of Labor "to formulate standards and policies which shall promote the welfare of wage-earning women, improve their working conditions, increase their efficiency, and advance their opportunities for profitable employment." This article reviews the role of women in today's labor force and supplies some background information about their status in the past.

CHANGES, 1920–70

A rich body of literature describes the advance of women in the American labor force from the "working class" women of colonial and pioneering days, who worked on farms, in cottage industries, and menial domestic work; to the factory women of the industrial revolution; and to the predominantly white-collar and professional women of today. World War I drew more women from the middle and upper social classes out of their homes and into nursing, teaching, and food services, in addition to volunteer work.

Each decade since 1920 has seen the proportion of working women

Excerpted from Elizabeth Waldman, "Changes in the Labor Force Activity of Women," *Monthly Labor Review* (Washington: U.S. Department of Labor, Bureau of Labor Statistics, June 1970), 10–18.

increase in a variety of economic settings and amid many social and technological changes, frequently kaleidoscopic in nature.

If the door to more paid job opportunities for all classes of women opened slightly in the 1920s, World War II in the forties and the shift in employment concentration from goods production industries to the services in the fifties pushed the door open much wider. In 1956, white-collar jobs became more prevalent than blue-collar jobs and throughout this period, the movement from farm to city brought women to where job opportunities were developing. With the swelling demand for labor in the late 1960s, larger proportions of women, even those with young children, were drawn into the labor force, particularly into white-collar work. Plentiful job opportunities for women undoubtedly were a factor in the decisions of many young couples to postpone having their first child. By early 1970, working women represented 42 percent of all women 16 years old and over in the population, close to double the proportion for 1920.

Today, nearly 2 out of every 5 American workers are women. Most of these women are married, and half are over 39 years old. If asked why they work, there is a good chance they would say that they are supplementing family income to provide their children with a college education, or to help buy or furnish a new home, or to pay for an additional car.

In 1920, the typical working woman was single, about 28 years old, and from the working class. Esther Peterson has described her situation: "The young woman who entered the work force seldom had any intention of remaining long. As soon as 'Mr. Right' came along she handed in her resignation, put the finishing touches on her hope chest, and made plans for the wedding. After the honeymoon she settled down to devote her life to the physical, intellectual, and spiritual needs of her family. Only the tragedy of penniless widowhood or a broken marriage could drive her back into the labor market. The woman who did not marry was apt to be an object of pity."

Nowadays a substantial proportion of total labor force growth is due to the continuous influx of married women. Since 1960, nearly half of the increase in the labor force was accounted for by married women. In early 1970, over 18 million married women were working or looking for work, representing about 60 percent of the female labor force. In 1940, these figures were only about 4.2 million, and 30 percent. The 30-year increase of about 320 percent in the number of working wives far outstrips the 50-percent increase in the size of their population.

Single women predominated among women workers in 1940, reflecting the high labor force participation rate for teens just out of high school (43 percent), and the peak rate of 48 percent for the mostly single 20-

to 24-year-olds. The rate for each older group successively declined since the older, mostly married women were predominantly homemakers. In 1950, peak rates still obtained for women just out of school, but the rates for older women [shifted upward] . . . partly because many women either continued to work after World War II or returned to work after leaving wartime jobs. By 1960 . . . the labor force participation rates among women 35 to 54 years old had shifted markedly upward so that they exceeded those for women 18 to 24 years old. These rates reflected mostly mothers returning to the work force when their children were older and homemaking responsibilities had lessened. In 1970, peak participation shifted back to young 20- to 24-year-old women, but the 45- to 54-year-olds took a close second place, with rates slightly higher than for girls 18 and 19.

There are several reasons for these recent changes in rates among young women. First, the proportion of women 20 to 24 years old who are married has shown a small but perceptible decline in the last few years, partly because of the larger number of young men in the Armed Forces since the Viet Nam War started, and the so-called "marriage squeeze," the imbalance resulting from a larger number of women than of men in the prime marriage ages. Second, since the birth rate has fallen, a somewhat smaller proportion of married women in these ages have young children to care for.

Single women no longer predominate in the work force and the percentage of widows, divorcees, and separated working women is also comparatively small. Table 1 shows that married women whose husbands are present far outnumber all other groups of working women. Yet only 40 percent of all married women worked, clearly a significantly lower labor force participation rate than that for all other women except widows, who are generally in a considerably older age group. Despite the enormous increases of the late 1960s, most wives and mothers do not work outside the home, especially if they have preschool age children, as shown in the following tabulation:

	Labor force participation rate, March 1969		
	Total	Under 35 years	35 years and over
Total wives	39.6	40.1	39.3
With no children under 18	41.0	66.8	35.7
With children 6 to 17 only	48.6	50.7	48.1
With children under 6	28.5	28.9	27.1

Historically, Negro wives have had a higher labor force participation rate than white wives. However, the current difference in rates is considerably smaller than in past decades when the Negro rate was as much as 20 percentage points higher. Through the 1960s, the gap declined at a slow, steady yearly pace. In March 1969, the labor force participation rate of 51 percent for Negro wives was 12 percentage points higher than that of white wives.

Negro wives are younger than white wives, a factor contributing to the different patterns of labor force participation. Whatever their age, the ages of their children, the ages of their husbands, or the income of their husbands, Negro wives are more likely to be in the labor force than white wives. For example, among families with preschool age children, 44 percent of Negro wives but only 27 percent of the white wives were in the work force in March 1969. Among families where the husband's yearly income was $10,000 or more, about half of the Negro wives compared with a third of the white wives were working or looking for work.

EMPLOYMENT

Three-quarters of all employed women hold full-time jobs, a proportion that has changed little over the years. Divorced and separated women are even more likely to hold full-time jobs. Historical changes in the occupational distributions of women are not nearly so striking as changes in the number of women working. Although women now work in virtually every job listed by the Bureau of the Census, the great majority of them are concentrated in occupations in which women employees predominate over men—domestic service, teaching, clerical work, nursing, and retail sales. One of the largest single occupational groups among women today is still the clerical one—stenographers, typists, secretaries— a category that first gained prominence in the occupational distribution of women over a half century ago. Thus, despite the increased reliance of the American economy on women in the labor force, many jobs in new occupational fields have not opened to them. The broad category of professional jobs is a notorious example of a field divided along sexual lines. Here, about two-thirds of all women are employed as either nurses or teachers, and even as teachers, most women teach in the primary grades while most men teach in high school.

A further illustration of the concentration of women in certain types of employment is the fact that if the industrial–occupational composition of an area is known, it is possible to predict the relative labor force participation rate of women in that area. Several studies have shown that women's labor force participation rates are higher in areas where there is a relatively heavy concentration on nondurable goods manufacturing and service industries that require large proportions of operatives and white-collar and service workers.

Table 1 shows that white-collar occupations predominate among women employed full time and, to a lesser extent, among married and single women with part-time jobs. Much larger proportions of part-time women workers, regardless of marital status, are employed in service jobs, including private household.

The proportion of Negro women in white-collar work in each marital category lags far behind that of white women. In recent years, a small shift toward more white-collar work has occurred among Negro women, while the occupational distribution among white women remained about the same. In March 1969, 63 percent of employed white women held white-collar jobs, compared with 34 percent of employed Negro women. A few years earlier, the proportions were 62 percent of white and only 26 percent of Negro women. However, the shifts were not strong enough to significantly bring closer together the general occupational patterns of white and Negro women.

Major differences in occupational distributions of Negro and white women persist, and relatively more Negro women in each marital category still work in jobs that generally pay lower wages and are the least secure in job tenure.

Regardless of marital status, younger Negro women had a better occupational profile at the close of the 1960s—in part because of their stronger educational background—than older, less educated Negro women. Median years of school completed by women 18 to 34 years old in March 1969 were 12.5, white and 12.2, Negro; for women 35 years old and over they were 12.1 and only 8.8, respectively. The current occupational distribution of younger Negro women reflects the changed economic and social climate of recent years, which not only enabled them to obtain more educational and vocational training, but also helped them to get jobs at which they could utilize their skills.

EDUCATION

The more education women have, the more likely they are to be in the labor force. The more education they bring to their jobs, the higher their earnings. Among women who were high school graduates, 49 percent were in the labor force in 1969, compared with 30 percent for those who completed grade school only. This low rate reflects in part the higher proportion of the latter women in the older age groups. The labor force participation rate increased to 54 percent for college graduates and to 69 percent for those who had completed 5 years or more of college. Among the latter well-educated women, 83 percent are workers at ages 45 to 54. This high labor force participation rate indicates a very strong commit-

TABLE 1. SELECTED CHARACTERISTICS OF WOMEN IN THE LABOR FORCE, BY COLOR, MARCH 1969

[Number of women 16 years and over, in thousands]

Characteristics	All women							Negro and other races						
	Total	Never married	Married, husband present	Other marital status Total	Widowed	Divorced	Husband absent	Total	Never married	Married, husband present	Other marital status Total	Widowed	Divorced	Husband absent
Population	71,919	12,689	44,440	14,790	9,500	2,505	2,785	7,880	1,789	3,631	2,460	1,145	341	974
In labor force	29,898	6,501	17,595	5,802	2,504	1,793	1,505	3,797	817	1,853	1,127	345	227	555
As percent of population	41.6	51.2	39.6	39.2	26.4	71.6	54.0	48.2	45.7	51.0	45.8	30.1	66.6	57.0
Median age	40	22	41	50	59	44	37	41	23	39	45	56	41	39
Employed	28,613	6,093	16,947	5,573	2,427	1,734	1,412	3,517	701	1,747	1,069	334	214	521
Median age	39	22	41	50	59	43	37	41	23	39	45	55	40	39
Unemployed	1,285	408	648	229	77	59	93	280	116	106	58	11	13	34
As percent of labor force	4.3	6.3	3.7	3.9	3.1	3.3	6.2	7.4	14.2	5.7	5.1	3.2	5.7	6.1
Mean duration (in weeks)	8.0	8.1	8.2	3.0		{3.2}	2.6	8.7	9.1	7.9	(²)	(²)	(²)	(²)
Median age	26	19	32	41		{55}	27	23	20	29	(²)	(²)	(²)	(²)
AGE	**Labor force participation rate**													
16 to 19 years	37.2	37.1	35.4	51.8	(¹)	(²)	50.6	30.4	29.3	36.2	(²)	(¹)	(²)	(²)
20 to 24 years	56.6	69.4	47.9	62.9	(²)	73.6	60.1	58.2	64.0	51.7	58.7	(²)	(²)	56.4
25 to 34 years	43.4	80.9	36.9	63.5	46.7	81.9	53.2	56.7	62.8	53.7	60.6	(²)	77.4	55.7
35 to 44 years	49.3	72.3	45.4	66.4	54.7	79.7	59.9	57.5	57.4	57.9	56.8	49.5	61.9	58.0
45 to 54 years	52.9	72.8	48.2	68.5	67.1	78.3	58.7	57.5	(²)	55.2	60.4	52.2	(²)	63.2
55 to 64 years	42.7	62.8	35.4	55.0	51.3	70.7	56.4	47.7	(²)	41.2	54.9	46.4	(²)	72.6
65 years and over	10.0	18.4	7.6	10.2	9.7	18.4	16.0	12.8	(²)	15.4	11.9	10.8	(²)	(²)
	Percent distribution													
Employed: Total	100.0	100.0	100.0	100.0	100.0	100.0	100.0	100.0	100.0	100.0	100.0	100.0	100.0	100.0
Full time[3]	74.0	68.8	73.7	80.3	71.6	90.7	82.6	74.5	72.1	74.4	76.0	61.9	88.8	79.8
Part time[3]	26.0	31.2	26.3	19.7	28.4	9.3	17.4	25.5	27.9	25.6	24.0	38.1	11.2	20.2
Full time, total	100.0	100.0	100.0	100.0	100.0	100.0	100.0	100.0	100.0	100.0	100.0	100.0	100.0	100.0
White-collar	61.5	73.2	61.1	51.8	50.1	61.3	41.4	37.7	47.1	42.1	24.7	17.5	37.9	22.2
Blue-collar	20.0	12.8	21.9	21.6	21.1	17.9	27.4	23.5	21.5	23.3	25.2	20.4	25.2	31.3
Service	17.4	13.8	15.5	26.0	27.8	20.5	30.9	38.1	30.4	34.1	49.5	60.2	45.2	46.3
Private household	3.0	3.0	1.9	6.1	8.4	3.6	6.0	11.2	9.7	8.4	16.6	27.2	16.9	11.6
Other	14.4	10.8	13.6	19.9	19.4	16.9	24.9	26.9	20.7	25.7	32.9	33.0	28.9	34.7
Farm	1.1	.3	1.5	.6	1.2	.3	.3	.6	1.0	.5	.6	1.9	(¹)	.2
Part time, total	100.0	100.0	100.0	100.0	100.0	100.0	100.0	100.0	100.0	100.0	100.0	100.0	(²)	100.0
White-collar	53.3	54.8	57.2	34.9	34.8	46.3	27.8	23.2	46.7	21.1	9.0	6.3	......	9.5
Blue-collar	7.0	3.4	7.9	9.2	10.0	10.5	6.1	6.0	3.1	7.6	5.5	5.5	......	5.7
Service	37.0	40.8	31.2	54.3	53.0	43.2	65.3	69.3	49.2	69.7	83.6	85.8	......	82.9
Private household	13.8	17.1	8.6	28.9	28.9	19.1	36.7	46.2	24.1	43.5	67.6	74.8	......	61.9
Other	23.2	23.7	22.6	25.1	24.1	24.1	28.6	23.1	25.1	26.2	16.0	11.0	......	21.0
Farm	2.7	1.0	3.7	1.6	2.2	(¹)	.8	1.6	1.0	1.6	2.0	2.4	......	1.9

¹ Less than 0.05 percent.
² Figures not shown where base is less than 75,000.
³ Full-time workers are those who during the survey week worked 35 hours or more and those who usually work full time but worked 1 to 34 hours. Part-time workers are persons who usually work 1 to 34 hours and worked 1 to 34 hours during the survey week. Persons with a job but not at work during the survey week are classified according to whether they usually work full or part time.
NOTE: Sums of individual items may not add to totals due to rounding.

ment to both marriage and a career, a far stronger one than prevailed among high school graduates the same ages (57 percent).

UNEMPLOYMENT

For every 20 women with a job in 1969, another woman was a jobseeker. Unemployed women numbered 1.4 million and accounted for half of all unemployed persons in the nation. Their unemployment rate was 4.7 percent, substantially higher than the 2.8 percent for men. Generally the gap between men's and women's rates widens when business activity is buoyant and narrows during more sluggish periods. To illustrate, when the adult unemployment rate was 3 percent or less from 1967 to 1969, the rate for women was at least 1.6 percentage points higher than that for men. During 1959–61, when the adult unemployment rates were about 5 to 6 percent, the women's rate was about half a percentage point higher than that for men.

One reason the women's unemployment rate is usually much higher than that for men when economic conditions are good is that a greater proportion of women than of men enter or reenter the labor force. In 1969, 45 percent of the jobseeking women 20 years old and over had reentered the labor force, a proportion double that of men. At the same time, only 33 percent of the unemployed women compared with 58 percent of the jobless men were job losers, those whose employment had ended involuntarily and who immediately began looking for work, or those on layoff. Almost 60 percent of the unemployed adult women were looking for work for a month or less, a somewhat higher proportion than for adult men.

By marital status, single and separated women have the highest unemployment rates. Age is the overriding element in unemployment among single women, since two-thirds of those unemployed (in March 1969) were teenagers, many looking for their first jobs. A combination of factors may tend to produce a higher unemployment rate among separated women than among wives and divorcees. Because they are somewhat younger than wives and divorcees, and their children tend to be younger than those of other women, their conditions for taking a job may be more restrictive and difficult for employers to meet.

A YEAR'S WORK EXPERIENCE

Data on work experience over a calendar year provide one of the best measures of the strength of women's attachment to the labor force, because a larger number of them work at some time during a year than in any one month of the year. The 12-month record accounts for *all* women who were in the labor force at *any* time during the year by how many weeks they worked or looked for work and many other characteristics. For example, out of the 72 million women in the civilian population 16 years old and over in March 1969, 30 million, or 42 percent, were in the labor force in March, but 37 million (52 percent) had worked at one time or another in 1968. About 15 million women had worked year round at full-time jobs. The extent of women's work experience in 1968 is shown as follows:

	Total, 16 years and over	Single	Married, husband present	Other marital status
Percent with work experience	52.0	68.0	49.7	45.7
Distribution of women with work experience in 1968 (percent):				
Total	100.0	100.0	100.0	100.0
Full-time jobs:				
50 to 52 weeks	41.4	36.2	40.2	52.3
27 to 49 weeks	13.6	9.8	14.5	15.2
1 to 26 weeks	15.4	19.3	15.2	10.8
Part-time jobs	29.7	34.7	30.1	21.7

The figures for single women are affected by the heavy weighting of teenagers and college-age women among them. Relatively more of the single women held a job during the year than other women, but greater proportions worked part time or for less than a half year at full-time jobs. Of 44.4 million wives in the population, half had worked in 1968 and 4 out of every 10 who worked did so full time year round.

The difference between the proportion of wives working at some time during the year and in any selected month is far higher for mothers of young children than for other women:

		Percent of population	
	Population (In thousands)	In labor force, March 1969	With work experience of 1 week or more in 1968
Total, 16 years old and over	44,440	39.6	50.3
With no children under 18 years	19,173	41.0	49.2
With children under 18 years	25,267	38.6	51.1
With children 6 to 17 years	12,650	48.6	58.2
With some children under 6, none under 3 years	5,137	34.7	46.5
With some children under 3 years	7,480	24.2	41.9

For wives with children under 3, the differences represent to some extent their leaving the work force at the birth of a child. But for wives with children of nursery school age, 3 to 5 years, this might be some indication of the reserve of young wives who can step into the American labor force. Because of their older age composition—half were at least 55 years old—

the labor force rate among wives with no children under 18 was lower than that of wives with school-age children.

PATTERNS

This article has reviewed some major elements affecting the work patterns of women such as marital status, presence and age of children, family income, race, education, and job opportunities. From the data, it is clear that women continue to respond to labor market needs for additional workers, and that they work for a variety of reasons, with economic necessity the most frequently cited. A recent analysis of the lifetime work expectancy of women shows that they typically take a job in their late teens or early 20's, leave the labor force after marriage, resume work when their child rearing responsibilities decrease, and retire from the job world in their late 50's or early 60's. This information on work life expectancy, based on 1960 labor force patterns, shows that at 20 years old, working women who never marry can expect to work about 45 years. Working wives, 20 years old, who will never have children may expect a work life of 35 years. The work-life expectancies of wives with children are more mixed because of variability in the number of children they have and when they have them. For example, women who marry at age 20 and will have only one child have a work life expectancy of 25 years; with 2 children, 22 years, with 3 children, 20 years, and with 4 or more children, 17 years.

Since 1960, considerable changes have taken place. Labor force data discussed earlier indicate that younger adult wives are staying in the labor force longer before starting their families. Patterns in the spacing of child births appear to be changing. These are among the more influential elements that have an impact on work life expectancy and labor force participation, *and* as such, they bear close watching in the 1970s.

WOMEN AS A MINORITY GROUP

HELEN MAYER HACKER
ADELPHI UNIVERSITY

The purpose of this paper is to apply to women some portion of that body of sociological theory and methodology customarily used for investigating such minority groups as Negroes, Jews, immigrants, et cetera.

... In defining the term "minority group," the presence of discrimination is the identifying factor. According to Louis Wirth:

> A minority group is any group of people who because of their physical or cultural characteristics, are singled out from the others in the society in which they live for differential and unequal treatment, and who therefore regard themselves as objects of collective discrimination.

It is apparent that this definition includes both objective and subjective characteristics of a minority group: the fact of discrimination and the awareness of discrimination, with attendant reactions to that awareness. A person who on the basis of his group affiliation is denied full participation in those opportunities which the value system of his culture extends to all members of the society satisfies the objective criterion, but there are various circumstances which may prevent him from fulfilling the subjective criterion.

In the first place, a person may be unaware of the extent to which his group membership influences the way others treat him.

... It is frequently the case that a person knows that because of his group affiliation he receives differential treatment, but feels that this treatment is warranted by the distinctive characteristics of his group.

... Women often manifest many of the psychological characteristics which have been imputed to self-conscious minority groups. Kurt Lewin has pointed to group self-hatred as a frequent reaction of the minority group member to his group affiliation. This feeling is exhibited in the person's tendency to denigrate other members of the group, to accept

---

Excerpts reprinted from Helen Mayer Hacker, "Women as a Minority Group," *Social Forces*, 30, 1951, 60–69.

the dominant group's stereotyped conception of them, and to indulge in "mea culpa" breast-beating.

... Like those minority groups whose self-castigation outdoes dominant group derision of them, women frequently exceed men in the violence of their vituperations of their sex. They are more severe in moral judgments, especially in sexual matters. ... Women express themselves as disliking other women, as preferring to work under men, and as finding exclusively female gatherings repugnant.

... Militating against a feeling of group identification on the part of women is a differential factor in their socialization. Members of a minority group are frequently socialized within their own group. ... But only rarely does a woman experience this type of group belongingness. Her interactions with members of the opposite sex may be as frequent as her relationships with members of her own sex. Women's conceptions of themselves, therefore, spring as much from their intimate relationships with men as with women.

... Women [like] racial and ethnic minorities ... tend to develop a separate subculture. Women have their own language, comparable to the argot of the underworld and professional groups. ... In contrast to men's interest in physical health, safety, money, and sex, women attach greater importance to attractiveness, personality, home, family, and other people. How much of the "woman's world" is predicated on their relationship to men is too difficult a question to discuss here.

... We must return now to the original question of the aptness of the designation of minority group for women.

... Formal discriminations against women are too well-known for any but the most summary description. In general they take the form of being barred from certain activities or, if admitted, being treated unequally.

As female, in the economic sphere, women are largely confined to sedentary, monotonous work under the supervision of men, and are treated unequally with regard to pay, promotion, and responsibility. ... Women's colleges are frequently inferior to men's. In coeducational schools women's participation in campus activities is limited. ... Socially, women have less freedom of movement, and are permitted fewer deviations in the properties of dress, speech, manners. In social intercourse they are confined to a narrower range of personality expression.

[Except as affected by the Civil Rights Act of 1964] in the specially ascribed status of wife, a woman—in several states—has no exclusive right to her earnings, is discriminated against in employment, must take the domicile of her husband, and in general must meet the social expectation of subordination to her husband's interests. As a mother, she may not have the guardianship of her children, bears the chief stigma in the case of an illegitimate child, is rarely given leave of absence for pregnancy.

As a sister, she frequently suffers unequal distribution of domestic duties between herself and her brother, must yield preference to him in obtaining an education, and in such other psychic and material gratifications as cars, trips, and living away from home.

If it is conceded that women have a minority group status, what may be learned from applying to women various theoretical constructs in the field of intergroup relations?

SOCIAL DISTANCE BETWEEN MEN AND WOMEN

One instrument of diagnostic value is the measurement of social distance between dominant and minority group.... One extreme would represent a complete "ghetto" status, the women whose contacts with men were of the most secondary kind. At the other extreme ... we put the woman who has prolonged and repeated associations with men, but only in those situations in which sex-awareness plays a prominent role or the woman who enters into a variety of relationships with men in which her sex identity is to a large extent irrelevant.

... Social distance may be measured from the standpoint of the minority group or the dominant group.... On all scales marriage represents the minimum social distance, and implies willingness for associations of all levels of lesser intimacy. May the customary scale be applied to men and women?

... In our culture, however, men who wish to marry must perforce marry women, and even if they accept this relationship, they may still wish to limit their association with women in other situations. The male physician may not care for the addition of female physicians to his hospital staff. The male poker player may be thrown off his game if women participate. A damper may be put upon the hunting expedition if women come along. The average man may not wish to consult a woman lawyer. And so on.

... The question may be raised as to whether marriage in fact represents the point of minimum social distance. It may not imply anything but physical intimacy and work accommodation, as was frequently true....

... Part of the explanation may be found in the subordination of wives to husbands in our culture, which is expressed in the separate spheres of activity for men and women.

... The presence of love does not in itself argue for either equality of status nor fullness of communication. We may love those who are either inferior or superior to us, and we may love persons whom we do not understand.

... Since inequalities of status are preserved in marriage, a dominant group member may be willing to marry a member of a group which, in general, he would not wish admitted to his club. The social distance scale which uses marriage as a sign of an extreme degree of acceptance is inadequate for appreciating the position of women, and perhaps for other minority groups as well. The relationships among similarity of status, communication as a measure of intimacy, and love must be clarified before social distance tests can be applied usefully to attitudes between men and women.

Is the separation between males and females in our society a caste line? ... The relation between women and Negroes is historical, as well as [analogous]. ... Obvious similarities in the status of women and Negroes are indicated in Chart 1.

While these similarities in the situation of women and Negroes may lead to increased understanding of their social roles, account must also be taken of differences which impose qualifications on the comparison of the two groups. Most importantly, the influence of marriage as a social

CHART 1. CASTELIKE STATUS OF WOMEN AND NEGROES

Negroes	Women
1. High Social Visibility	
a. Skin color, other "racial" characteristics.	a. Secondary sex characteristics.
b. (Sometimes) distinctive dress—bandana, flashy clothes.	b. Distinctive dress, skirts, et cetera.
2. Ascribed Attributes	
a. Inferior intelligence, smaller brain, less convoluted, scarity of geniuses.	a. ditto.
b. More free in instinctual gratifications. More emotional, "primitive" and childlike. Imagined sexual prowess envied.	b. Irresponsible, inconsistent, emotionally unstable. Lack strong super-ego. Women as "temptresses."
c. Common stereotype "inferior."	c. "Weaker."
3. Rationalizations of Status	
a. Thought all right in his place.	a. Woman's place is in the home.
b. Myth of contented Negro.	b. Myth of contented woman—"feminine" woman is happy in subordinate role.
4. Accommodation Attitudes	
a. Supplicatory whining intonation of voice.	a. Rising inflection, smiles, laughs, downward glances.
b. Deferential manner.	b. Flattering manner.
c. Concealment of real feelings.	c. "Feminine wiles."
d. Outwit "white folks."	d. Outwit "menfolk."
e. Careful study of points at which dominant group is susceptible to influence.	e. ditto.
f. Fake appeals for directives; show of ignorance.	f. Appearance of helplessness.
5. Discriminations	
a. Limitations on education—should fit "place" in society.	a. ditto.
b. Confined to traditional jobs—barred from supervisory positions.	b. ditto.
c. Their competition feared, no family precedents for new aspirations. Deprived of political importance.	c. ditto.
d. Social and professional segregation.	d. ditto.
e. More vulnerable to criticism.	e. For example, conduct in bars.
6. Similar Problems	
a. Roles not clearly defined, but in flux as result of social change. Conflict between achieved status and ascribed status.	

elevator for women, but not for Negroes, must be considered. Obvious, too, is the greater importance of women to the dominant group, despite the economic, sexual, and prestige gains which Negroes afford the white South. Ambivalence is probably more marked in the attitude of white males toward women than toward Negroes. The "war of the sexes" is only an expression of men's and women's vital need of each other.

. . . Women's privileges exceed those of Negroes. Protective attitudes toward Negroes have faded into abeyance, even in the South, but most boys are still taught to take care of girls, and many evidences of male chivalry remain.

. . . Exemplary of the possible usefulness of applying the caste principle to women is viewing some of the confusion surrounding women's roles as reflecting a conflict between class and caste status. Such a conflict is present in the thinking and feeling of both dominant and minority groups toward upper class Negroes and educated women. Should a woman judge be treated with the respect due a judge or the gallantry accorded a woman?

. . . Role segmentation as a mode of adjustment is illustrated by Negroes who indulge in occasional passing and women who vary their behavior according to their definition of the situation.

. . . A third type of reaction is to fight for recognition of class status. Negro race leaders seek greater prerogatives for Negroes. Feminist women, acting either through organizations or as individuals, push for public disavowal of any differential treatment of men and women.

The "race relations cycle," as defined by Robert E. Park, describes the social processes of reeducation in the relations between two or more groups who are living in a common territory under a single political or economic system. The sequence of competition, conflict, accommodation, and assimilation may also occur when social change introduces dissociative forces into an assimilated group or causes accommodated groups to seek new definitions of the situation.

. . . The sex relations cycle bears important similarities to the race relations cycle. In the wake of the Industrial Revolution, as women acquired industrial, business, and professional skills, they increasingly sought employment in competition with men. Men were quick to perceive them as a rival group and made use of economic, legal, and ideological weapons to eliminate or reduce their competition. They excluded women from the trade unions, made contracts with employers to prevent their hiring women, passed laws restricting the employment of married women, caricatured the working woman, and carried on ceaseless propaganda to return women to the home or keep them there. Since the days of the suffragettes there has been no overt conflict between men and women on a group basis. Rather than conflict, the dissociative process between the sexes is that of contravention, a type of opposition intermediate between competition and conflict. According to Wiese and Becker, it includes rebuffing, repulsing, working against, hindering, protesting, obstructing, restraining, and upsetting another's plans.

The present contravention of the sexes, arising from women's competition with men, is manifested in the discriminations against women, as well as in the doubts and uncertainties expressed concerning women's character, abilities, motives. The processes of competition and contravention are continually giving way to accommodation in the relationships between men and women. Like other minority groups, women have sought a protected position, a niche in the economy which they could occupy, and, like other minority groups, they have found these positions in new occupations in which dominant group members had not yet established themselves and in old occupations which they no longer wanted.

... What would assimilation of men and women mean? ... If men and women were truly assimilated, we would find no cleavages of interest along sex lines. The special provinces of men and women would be abolished. Women's pages would disappear from the newspaper and women's magazines from the stands. ... Women's talk would be no different from men's talk, and frank and full communication would obtain between the sexes.

THE MARGINAL WOMAN

Group relationships are reflected in personal adjustments. Arising out of the present contravention of the sexes is the marginal woman, torn between rejection and acceptance of traditional roles and attributes. Uncertain of the ground on which she stands, subjected to conflicting cultural expectations, the marginal woman suffers the psychological ravages of instability, conflict, self-hate, anxiety, and resentment.

WOMEN: THE LONGEST REVOLUTION

JULIET MITCHELL

The situation of women is different from that of any other social group. This is because they are not one of a number of isolable units, but half a totality: the human species. Women are essential and irreplaceable; they cannot therefore be exploited in the same way as other social groups can. They are fundamental to the human condition, yet in their economic, social and political roles, they are marginal. It is precisely this combination—fundamental and marginal at one and the same time—that has been fatal to them. Within the world of men their position is comparable to that of an oppressed minority: but they also exist outside the world of men. . . .

. . . Until there is a revolution in production, the labor situation will prescribe women's situation within the world of men. But women are offered a universe of their own: the family. Like woman herself, the family appears as a natural object, but it is actually a cultural creation. There is nothing inevitable about the form or role of the family any more than there is about the character or role of women. It is the function of ideology to present these given social types as aspects of Nature itself. . . .

. . . The apparently natural condition can be made to appear more attractive than the arduous advance of human beings towards culture. But what Marx wrote about the bourgeois myths of the Golden Ancient World describes precisely women's realm:

> . . . in one way the child-like world of the ancients appears to be superior, and this is so, insofar as we seek for closed shape, form and established limitation. The ancients provide a narrow satisfaction, whereas the modern world leaves us unsatisfied or where it appears to be satisfied with itself, is vulgar and mean. . . .

The lesson of [my] . . . reflections is that the liberation of women can only be achieved if *all four* structures[1] in which they are integrated are

---

Excerpted from Juliet Mitchell, "Women: The Longest Revolution," *New Left Review,* December, 1966, 11–37.

[1] The four structures are (1) Production; (2) Reproduction; (3) Socialization; and (4) Sexuality.

transformed. A modification of any one of them can be offset by a reinforcement of another, so that mere permutation of the form of exploitation is achieved. The history of the last 60 years provides ample evidence of this. In the early 20th century, militant feminism in England or the USA surpassed the labor movement in the violence of its assault on bourgeois society, in pursuit of suffrage. This political right was eventually won. Nonetheless, though a simple completion of the formal legal equality of bourgeois society, it left the socioeconomic situation of women virtually unchanged.

The Russian Revolution produced a quite different experience. In the Soviet Union in the 1920s, advanced social legislation aimed at liberating women above all in the field of sexuality: divorce was made free and automatic for either partner, thus effectively liquidating marriage; illegitimacy was abolished, abortion was free, et cetera. The social and demographic effects of these laws in a backward, semiliterate society bent on rapid industrialization (needing, therefore, a high birthrate) were—predictably—catastrophic. Stalinism soon produced a restoration of iron traditional norms. Inheritance was reinstated, divorce inaccessible, abortion illegal, et cetera.

Women still retained the right and obligation to work, but because these gains had not been integrated into the earlier attempts to abolish the family and free sexuality no general liberation has occurred. In China, still another experience is being played out today. At a comparable stage of the revolution, all the emphasis is being placed on liberating women in *production.* This has produced an impressive social promotion of women. But it has been accompanied by a tremendous repression of sexuality and a rigorous puritanism (currently rampant in civic life). This corresponds not only to the need to mobilize women massively in economic life, but to a deep cultural reaction against the corruption and prostitution prevalent in Imperial and Kuo Ming Tang China (a phenomenon unlike anything in Czarist Russia). Because the exploitation of women was so great in the *ancien régime* women's participation at village level in the Chinese Revolution was uniquely high. As for reproduction, the Russian cult of maternity in the 1930s and 1940s has not been repeated for demographic reasons: indeed, China may be one of the first countries in the world to provide free State authorized contraception on a universal scale to the population. Again, however, given the low level of industrialization and fear produced by imperialist encirclement, no all-round advance could be expected.

It is only in the highly developed societies of the West that an authentic liberation of women can be envisaged today. But for this to occur, there must be a transformation of all the structures into which they are integrated, and an *'unité de rupture.'* A revolutionary movement must base its analysis on the uneven development of each, and attack the weakest link in the combination. This may then become the point of departure for a general transformation. What is the situation of the different structures today?

Production. The long-term development of the forces of production must command any socialist perspective. The hopes which the advent of machine technology raised as early as the 19th century have . . . proved illusory. Today, automation promises the *technical* possibility of abolishing completely the physical differential between man and woman in production, but under capitalist relations of production, the *social* possibility of this abolition is permanently threatened, and can easily be turned into its opposite, the actual diminution of woman's role in production as the labor force contracts. . . . woman's role in production is virtually stationary, and has been so for a long time now. In England in 1911, 30 percent of the work-force were women; in the 1960s, 34 percent. The composition of these jobs has not changed decisively either. The jobs are very rarely careers. When they are not in the lowest positions on the factory-floor they are normally white-collar auxiliary positions (such as secretaries)— supportive to masculine roles. They are often jobs with a high expressive content, such as service tasks. Parsons says bluntly: "Within the occupational organization they are analogous to the wife-mother role in the family." The educational system underpins this role-structure. 75 percent of 18-year-old girls in England are receiving neither training nor education today. The pattern of 'instrumental' father and 'expressive' mother is not substantially changed when the woman is gainfully employed, as her job tends to be inferior to that of the man's, to which the family then adapts.

Reproduction. Scientific advance in contraception could . . . make involuntary reproduction—which accounts for the vast majority of births in the world today, and for a major proportion even in the West—a phenomenon of the past. But oral contraception—which has so far been developed in a form which exactly repeats the sexual inequality of Western society—is only at its beginnings. It is inadequately distributed across classes and countries and awaits further technical improvements. Its main initial impact is, in the advanced countries, likely to be psychological— it will certainly free women's sexual experience from many of the anxieties and inhibitions which have always afflicted it.

The demographic pattern of reproduction in the West may or may not be widely affected by oral contraception. One of the most striking phenomena of very recent years in the United States has been the sudden increase in the birth-rate. . . . In fact, this reflects simply the lesser economic burden of a large family in conditions of economic boom in the richest country in the world. But it also reflects the magnification of familial ideology as a social force. This leads to the next structure.

Socialization. The changes in the composition of the work-force, the size of the family, the structure of education, et cetera—however limited from an ideal standpoint—have undoubtedly diminished the societal function and importance of the family. As an organization it is not a significant unit in the political power system, it plays little part in economic production and it is rarely the sole agency of integration into the larger society; thus at the macroscopic level it serves very little purpose.

The result has been a major displacement of emphasis on to the family's psychosocial function, for the infant and for the couple. Parsons writes: "...the society is dependent *more* exclusively on it for the performance of *certain* of its vital functions." The vital nucleus of truth in the emphasis on socialization of the child has been discussed [elsewhere]. ...It is essential that socialists should acknowledge it and integrate it entirely into any program for the liberation of women.

... There is no doubt that the need for permanent, intelligent care of children in the initial three or four years of their lives can (and has been) exploited ideologically to perpetuate the family as a total unit, when its other functions have been visibly declining. Indeed, the attempt to focus women's existence exclusively on bringing up children is manifestly harmful to children.

An increased awareness of the critical importance of socialization, far from leading to a restitution of classical maternal roles, should lead to a reconsideration of them—of what makes a good socializing agent, who can genuinely provide security and stability for the child.

The beliefs that the family provides an impregnable enclave of intimacy and security in an atomized and chaotic cosmos assumes the absurd —that the family can be isolated from the community, and that its internal relationships will not reproduce in their own terms the external relationships which dominate the society. The family as refuge in a bourgeois society inevitably becomes a reflection of it.

Sexuality. It is difficult not to conclude that the major structure which at present is in rapid evolution is sexuality.

... the dominant sexual ideology is proving less and less successful in regulating spontaneous behavior. Marriage in its classical form is increasingly threatened by the liberalization of relationships before and after [marriage], which affects all classes today. In this sense, it is evidently the weak link in the chain—the particular structure that is the site of the most contradictions.

In a context of juridical equality, the liberation of sexual experience from relations which are extraneous to it—whether procreation or property—could lead to true intersexual freedom. But it could also lead simply to new forms of neocapitalist ideology and practice. For one of the forces behind the current acceleration of sexual freedom has undoubtedly been the conversion of contemporary capitalism from a production-and-work ethos to a consumption-and-fun ethos.

The gist of [David] Riesman's argument is that in a society bored by work, sex is the only activity, the only reminder of one's energies, the only competitive act; the last defense against *vis inertiae*. This same insight can be found, with greater theoretical depth, in Marcuse's notion of repressive de-sublimation—the freeing of sexuality for its own frustration in the service of a totally coordinated and drugged social machine. Bourgeois society at present can well afford a play area of premarital *non*procreative sexuality. Even marriage can save itself by increasing divorce and remarriage rates, signifying the importance of the institution itself. These considerations make it clear that sexuality, while it presently may contain the greatest potential for liberation—can equally well be organized against any increase of its human possibilities.

This is a reminder that while one structure may be the *weak link* in a unity like that of woman's condition, there can never be a solution through it alone. The utopianism of Fourier or Reich was precisely to think that sexuality could inaugurate such a general solution. Lenin's remark to Clara Zetkin is a salutary if overstated corrective: However wild and revolutionary (sexual freedom) may be, it is still really quite bourgeois. It is mainly a hobby of the intellectuals and of the sections nearest them. . . .

For a general solution can only be found in a strategy which affects *all* the structures of women's exploitation. This means a rejection of two beliefs prevalent on the left:

REFORMISM. This now takes the form of limited ameliorative demands: equal pay for women, more nursery schools, better retraining facilities, et cetera. In its contemporary version it is wholly divorced from any fundamental critique of women's condition or any vision of their real liberation (it was not always so).

VOLUNTARISM. This takes the form of maximalist demands—the abolition of the family, abrogation of all sexual restrictions, forceful separation of parents from children—which have no chance of winning any wide support at present, and which merely serve as a substitute for the job of theoretical analysis or practical persuasion. By pitching the whole subject in totally intransigent terms, voluntarism objectively helps to maintain it outside the framework of normal political discussion.

What, then, is the responsible revolutionary attitude? It must include both immediate and fundamental demands, in a single critique of the *whole* of women's situation, that does not fetishize any dimension of it.

Modern industrial development, as has been seen, tends towards the separating out of the originally unified functions of the family—procreation, socialization, sexuality, economic subsistence, et cetera—even if this structural differentiation (to use a term of Parsons') has been checked and disguised by the maintenance of a powerful family ideology. This differentiation provides the real historical basis for the ideal demands which should be posed: structural differentiation is precisely what distinguishes an advanced from a primitive society (in which all social functions are fused *en bloc*).

In practical terms this means a coherent system of demands. The four elements of women's condition cannot merely be considered each in isolation; they form a structure of specific interrelations. The contemporary bourgeois family can be seen as a triptych of sexual, reproductive and socializatory functions (the woman's world) embraced by production (the man's world)—precisely a structure which in the final instance is determined by the economy. The exclusion of women from production —social human activity—and their confinement to a monolithic condensation of functions in a unity—the family—which is precisely unified in the *natural part* of each function, is the root cause of the contemporary *social* definition of women as *natural* beings. Hence the main thrust of any emancipation movement must still concentrate on the economic element —the entry of women fully into public industry.

. . . accompanied by coherent policies for the other three elements, policies which at particular junctures may take over the primary role in immediate action.

Economically, the most elementary demand is not the right to work or receive equal pay for work—the two traditional reformist demands—but *the right to equal work itself*. At present, women perform unskilled, uncreative service jobs that can be regarded as extensions of their expressive familial role. . . . But only two in a hundred women are in administrative or managerial jobs, and less than five in a thousand are in the professions. Women are poorly unionized (25 percent) and receive less money than men for the manual work they do perform: in 1961 the average industrial wage for women was less than half that for men, which, even setting off part-time work, represents a massive increment of exploitation for the employer.

EDUCATION

The whole pyramid of discrimination rests on a solid extra-economic foundation—education. The demand for equal work, in Britain, should above all take the form of a demand for an *equal educational system,* since this is at present the main single filter selecting women for inferior work-roles. . . .

Until these injustices are ended, there is no chance of equal work for women. It goes without saying that the content of the educational system, which actually instills limitation of aspiration in girls needs to be changed as much as methods of selection. Education is probably the key area for immediate economic advance at present.

. . . Reproduction, sexuality, and socialization also need to be free from coercive forms of unification. Traditionally, the socialist movement has called for the "abolition of the bourgeois family." This slogan must be rejected as incorrect today. It is maximalist in the bad sense, posing a demand which is merely a negation without any coherent construction subsequent to it.

The reasons for the historic weakness of the [socialist] notion is that the family was never analyzed structurally—in terms of its different functions. It was a hypostasized entity; the abstraction of its abolition corresponds to the abstraction of its conception. The strategic concern for socialists should be for the equality of the sexes, not the abolition of the family. . . .

The family as it exists at present is, in fact, incompatible with the equality of the sexes. But this equality will not come from its administrative abolition, but from the historical differentiation of its functions. The revolutionary demand should be for the liberation of these functions from a monolithic fusion which oppresses each. Thus dissociation of reproduction from sexuality frees sexuality from alienation in unwanted reproduction (and fear of it), and reproduction from subjugation to chance and uncontrollable causality. It is thus an elementary demand to press for free State provision of oral contraception. The legalization of homosexuality—which is one of the forms of nonreproductive sexuality—should be supported for just the same reason, and regressive campaigns against it in Cuba or elsewhere should be unhesitatingly criticized. The straightforward abolition of illegitimacy as a legal notion as in Sweden and Russia has a similar implication; it would separate marriage civically from parenthood.

FROM NATURE TO CULTURE

The problem of socialization poses more difficult questions, as has been seen. But the need for intensive maternal care in the early years of a child's life does not mean that the present single sanctioned form of socialization—marriage and family—is inevitable. Far from it. The fundamental characteristic of the present system of marriage and family is in our society its *monolithism:* there is only one institutionalized form of intersexual or intergenerational relationship possible.

... all human experience shows that intersexual and intergenerational relationships are infinitely various—indeed, much of our creative literature is a celebration of the fact—while the institutionalized expression of them in our capitalist society is utterly simple and rigid.

Socialism should properly mean not the abolition of the family, but the diversification of the socially acknowledged relationships which are today forcibly and rigidly compressed into it. This would mean a plural range of institutions—where the family is only one, and its abolition implies none. Couples living together or not living together, long-term unions with children, single parents bringing up children, children socialized by conventional rather than biological parents, extended kin groups, et cetera—all these could be encompassed in a range of institutions which match the free invention and variety of men and women. Socialism will be a process of change, of becoming. A fixed image of the future is in the worst sense ahistorical; the form that socialism takes will depend on the prior type of capitalism and the nature of its collapse.

The liberation of women under socialism will not be 'rational' but a human achievement, in the long passage from Nature to Culture which is the definition of history and society.

"Why can't a woman be more like a man...?"
Professor Henry Higgins

Even women and men who think that *man* is not the appropriate model for *woman* seriously ask: "Why are women and men so different?" The differences between the lives of each sex seem obvious and numerous. Cliches about the differences abound. Women are passive and dependent, while men are assertive and independent. Women stay home to do husbandcare, childcare, and housecare, while men leave the household to earn income. Women's activities outside the home are in "cultural," and therefore, relatively less important activities, while men attend to the "serious" activities of running the society. Men become great poets, painters, writers, statesmen, inventors, and warriors, but few women are among the "greats" though recently history has begun to recognize more women of excellence. Men are considered attractive and interesting late into life so a man with a much younger wife is admired and envied. Women as they grow older are considered decreasingly attractive and less interesting as companions and sexual partners.

Much of the serious discussion of the differences between women and men has revolved around questions about (1) *the psychobiological nature of humans;* (2) *early childhood development;* (3) *the Marxian interpretation of the economic condition of women.* The readings in this part deal with some of the answers that have attracted considerable following in the scientific world; they have also served as guides in such diverse social activities as education, marital counseling, and revolutions.

Three topics are considered: (1) the psychobiological nature of women; (2) varieties of interpretations of socialization; and (3) the relationship between the type of economy and women's position in the family and society.

PSYCHOBIOLOGICAL DIFFERENCES

The first set of readings focuses specifically on the contribution of Sigmund Freud to the understanding of human sexuality and development. In the first reading, Sigmund Freud discusses his theory of female sexuality. The theory has been widely read and accepted in the United States from shortly after World War I to the present. Although many subsequent psychiatric theories have gained equal acceptance, even some of these suggest old wine in new bottles (for example, the theories of Erik Erikson).[1] Psychoanalysts, social scientists, educators, clinical psychologists, and child-guidance workers as well as novelists, poets, playwrights, and essayists are among those strongly influenced by his work.

The Judeo-Christian doctrine that women were subordinated to men by God and the 19th century repression of women found new support in the Freudian contention that women were biologically (that is, genitally) inferior to men and therefore, inferior to men in their potential for developing moral sensitivity. His theory may be considered an end product of religious doctrine, the disappearance of the family as an economically productive unit, and the ideology of the leisure class. Indeed, the rationale developed for keeping women in a subordinate social role and in the home shows an interesting progression to the present. Freud argued that it is the nature of *women* to bear children and to devote themselves to husband and children. Later, child psychologists argued that it is the nature of *children* that demands a full-time mother. When this latter was modified by research to recognize a demand for full-time mothering only during the child's first few years, sociologists developed a new supporting argument for a woman's place being in the home: the *husband-wife* relationship depends for its happiness and stability on an unequal balance of power and prestige as well as on complementary rather than competitive interests. (See Part 3, The Marriage Relationship.) Talcott Parsons even suggests that the clear and unequivocal dependence of the family on the man's occupation for prestige and social class placement helps the psychological health of the family.

---

[1] See Erik H. Erikson, "Inner and Outer Space: Reflections on Womanhood," *Daedalus* (Spring 1964), 582–606.

Following the selection by Freud, Mary Jane Sherfey discusses the development and physiology of the human embryo and of female orgasm. Her discussion raises several serious objections to Freud's assumptions about women's biology, from which he derives his theory of female sexuality.

SOCIALIZATION

In the second section, socialization is considered from three theoretical perspectives—cognitive development, social learning, and identification. Socialization is the process by which women and men learn the attitudes and goals of their own groups. The problem is *how* do women and men become socialized, and what, if any, are the differences between the sexes in the outcome. Karen Horney's essay, though it originally appeared many years ago, is still historically interesting, and presently pertinent. Horney and Freud both attempted to explain some of the same biological facts and processes of human cognition, but Horney's writings—from a woman's perspective—were sometimes overlooked. What she does in the essay reprinted here is to turn Freud's argument about female sexuality around, and to suggest an alternative which practicing psychiatrists only now admit to seeing among their male patients: "womb envy."

In the next reading, Mabel Blake Cohen uses a social learning perspective to explore the relationship between the development of an adequate sense of personal identity and sexual identity. Those who believe that the lack of a clear *sex* identity is the contemporary woman's problem are challenged by an alternative: the content rather than the clearness of the sex role causes problems, for women and men. The culture demands sex roles from both sexes that are incompatible with a meaningful personal identity.

In the course of the development of a sex identity, Freud says that the girl is at a disadvantage compared to the boy because she has two difficult tasks. First, to attain maturity, she has to change from her initial love object of the same sex—her mother—to that of the opposite sex while the boy begins and ends by loving a person of the opposite sex. Second, the girl has the problem of transferring her genital sexual interest from the clitoris of childhood to the vagina of adulthood while the boy has a constant genital focus on his penis. David B. Lynn, in the next article, surveys the literature on sexual identification to conclude that girls rather than boys have the advantage in the development of sexual identity. Later in life, though, he writes, the woman is at a disadvantage because of limitations placed on her by society, not by her psychobiological nature.

One implication of Lynn's analysis is this: according to Freud, the relatively more arduous task of the girl's attaining mature womanhood compared to the boy's attainment of manhood is that the girl is left depleted of the necessary energy for the development of a sound sense of justice. Hence, it makes sense that men fill the important positions in society—in government and in the economy. If Lynn is correct, then there is a substantive answer to the assertions that women do not belong in important positions because of their tendency towards what in modern terms would be called "playing favorites," rather than applying general rules of law.

In the final selection on socialization, Erving Goffman analyzes the process of social interaction relating to bearing a stigma—"the situation of the individual who is disqualified from full social acceptance" because of some characteristic such as membership in a race, or a physical disability. Women are not analyzed in any detail by Goffman, though their sex is mentioned as a stigma. The application of his analysis of stigma to women can be a useful indication of the status of women in a group; it may clarify the behaviors between women and men, and those among women which stabilize the position of women. These processes may discourage women from engaging in certain activities, entering certain social groups, or remaining involved in either. Language use, as in the labeling of a position occupied by women, may convey the stigma: "lady novelist" uses the adjective for the profession to mean it is usually reserved for men. In the process of social interaction statements such as "You drive pretty well for a girl," are a way by which men recognize the stigma. Women recognize the stigma when they are tempted to use the initial of their first name when applying for credit; women indicate that they accept the stigma when they (as well as men) say they prefer a man to a woman as a teacher, and choose to become a nurse rather than a doctor.

PRODUCTION

The final section is concerned with evaluating and expanding the Marxian analysis of the social position of women. No social theory about the origins of women's subordination to men has been as influential as the work of Friedrich Engels. His theory serves as a base both for many contemporary analyses, and for demands for social changes. The excerpts by Engels with which this section begins consider the relationship between the development of private property, changes in the structure of the family, and the social position of women. He develops a structural and materialist interpretation to explain the condition of women, in contrast to the ideas of his day that explained her subordination as a natural phenomenon (she *was* inferior), or as the will of God, or as one part of an evolutionary process which placed the bourgeois family at the pinnacle. To Engels, the final stage of evolution—for he, like many of his contemporaries, was an evolutionist—is the establishment of socialism with its subsequent disappearance of the family, and the consequential freeing of women. Obviously, his conclusions about the future have not been widely supported, for the disappearance of private ownership of the means of production in certain societies has not eliminated the subordination of women; however, it indeed alleviates many aspects of their condition, and narrows some of the gaps between the general social conditions of women and men.

Engels' influence makes it important to assess the accuracy of his analysis, especially in relation to the findings and theories of contemporary anthropology. In the next reading, Kathleen Gough presents a detailed critique of Engels on the evolution of the family. Gough is critical of many of Engels' conclusions and indicates some of the limitations of his data, as well as areas of importance which he neglects in his study. Nevertheless, she concludes that the general trend of his argument is correct, and she stresses that economic changes appear to be critical to any improvement in the status of women.

Marx's social analysis is a theory of classes in which the moving force is a struggle between the classes; therefore, applying Marxian theory directly to an analysis of woman's position is impossible because women are in all social classes. In the final reading, Margaret Benston attempts to extend Marx's analysis to an explanation of the oppression of women. First, she distinguishes women from men by their relation to the productive process—a woman produces goods in the household with use-value but no exchange-value, whereas a man produces goods in the market economy with both use-value and exchange-value. This lack of exchange-value of a woman's household production leaves her outside the main area of economic activity, the market economy, and thus, makes her production seem valueless. This is the economic foundation of women's inferior status. In conclusion, Benston further extends Marxian analysis, asserting that socialism alone is not a sufficient precondition for the liberation of women: the additional necessity is the transformation of household production through industrialization into market production (which she calls public economy).

THE PSYCHOLOGY OF WOMEN: BIOLOGY AS DESTINY

SIGMUND FREUD

The anatomical distinction between the sexes must, after all, leave its mark in mental life. . . . In the boy the castration-complex is formed after he has learnt from the sight of the female genitals that the sexual organ which he prizes so highly is not a necessary part of every human body. The castration-complex in the girl, as well, is started by the sight of the genital organs of the other sex. . . . She immediately notices the difference, and—it must be admitted—its significance. She feels herself at a great disadvantage, and often declares that she would "like to have something like that too," and falls a victim to *penis-envy*, which leaves ineradicable traces on her development and character-formation, and, even in the most favorable instances, is not overcome without a great expenditure of mental energy.

One cannot very well doubt the importance of penis-envy. Perhaps you will regard the hypothesis that envy and jealousy play a greater part in the mental life of women than they do in that of men as an example of male unfairness. . . . The discovery of her castration is a turning-point in the life of the girl. Three lines of development diverge from it; one leads to sexual inhibition or to neurosis, the second to a modification of character in the sense of masculinity complex, and the third to normal femininity. . . . The fundamental content of the first is that the little girl, who has hitherto lived a masculine life, and has been able to obtain pleasure through the excitation of her clitoris, and has connected this behavior with the sexual wishes (often of an active character) which she has directed towards her mother, finds her enjoyment of phallic sexuality spoilt by the influence of penis-envy. She is wounded in her self-love by the unfavorable comparison with boy, who is so much better equipped, and therefore gives up the masturbatory satisfaction which she obtained from her clitoris, repudiates her love towards her mother, and at the same time often represses a good deal of her sexual impulses in general. . . .

Excerpts reprinted from Sigmund Freud, *New Introductory Lectures on Psychoanalysis* (New York: W. W. Norton and Company, Inc., 1933), 170–185.

With the discovery that the mother is castrated it becomes possible to drop her as a love-object, so that the incentives to hostility which have been so long accumulating, get the upper hand. This means, therefore, that as a result of the discovery of the absence of a penis, women are as much depreciated in the eyes of the girl as in the eyes of the boy, and later, perhaps, of the man.

... The wish with which the girl turns to her father is, no doubt, ultimately the wish for the penis, which her mother has refused her and which she now expects from her father. The feminine situation is, however, only established when the wish for the penis is replaced by the wish for a child—the child taking the place of the penis, in accordance with the old symbolic equation. It does not escape us that at an earlier stage the girl has already desired a child, before the phallic phase was interfered with; that was the meaning of her playing with dolls. But this play was not really an expression of her femininity, it served, in identifying her with her mother, the purpose of substituting activity for passivity. She was the mother, and the doll was herself; now she could do everything to the doll that her mother used to do with her. Only with the onset of the desire for a penis does the doll-child become a child by the father, and thenceforward, the strongest feminine wish. Her happiness is great indeed when this desire for child one day finds a real fulfillment; but especially is this so if the child is a little boy, who brings the longed-for penis with him.

... The girl remains in the Oedipus situation for an idefinite period, she only abandons it late in life, and then incompletely. The formation of the superego must suffer in these circumstances; it cannot attain the strength and independence which give it its cultural importance, and feminists are not pleased if one points to the way in which this factor affects the development of the average feminine character. ... We have mentioned, as the second possible reaction after the discovery of female castration, the development of a strong masculinity complex. What is meant by this is that the girl refuses, as it were, to accept the unpalatable fact, and, in an outburst of defiance, exaggerates still further the masculinity which she has displayed hitherto. She clings to her clitoritic activities, and takes refuge in an identification either with the phallic mother, or with the father. What is the determinant which leads to this state of affairs? We can picture it as nothing other than a constitutional factor: the possession of a greater degree of activity, such as is usually characteristic of the male. The essential thing about the process is, after all, that at this point of development the onset of passivity, which makes possible the change over to femininity, is avoided. The most extreme achievement of this masculinity complex seems to occur when it influences the girl's object-choice in the direction of manifest homosexuality. Analytic experience teaches us, it is true, that female homosexuality is seldom or never a direct continuation of infantile masculinity. It seems to be characteristic of female homosexuals that they too take the father as love-object for a while, and thus become implicated in the Oedipus situation. Then, however, they are driven by the inevitable disappointments which they experience from the father into a regression to their early masculinity complex. One must not overestimate the importance of these disappointments; girls who eventually achieve femininity also experience them without the same results. . . .

I have promised to put before you a few more of the mental characteristics of mature femininity, as we find them in our analytical observation. . . . We do not claim for these assertions more than that they are true on the whole; and it is not always easy to distinguish between what is due to the influence of the sexual function and what to social training. . . . We attribute to women a greater amount of narcissism (and this influences their object-choice) so that for them to be loved is a stronger need than to love. Their vanity is partly a further effect of penis-envy, for they are driven to rate their physical charms more highly as a belated compensation for their original sexual inferiority. Modesty, . . . was, in our opinion, originally designed to hide the deficiency in her genitals. . . . People say that women contributed but little to the discoveries and inventions of civilization, but perhaps after all they did discover one technical process, that of plaiting and weaving. If this is so, one is tempted to guess at the unconscious motive at the back of this achievement. . . .

It must be admitted that women have but little sense of justice, and this is no doubt connected with the preponderance of envy in their mental life; for the demands of justice are a modification of envy; they lay down the conditions under which one is willing to part with it. We say also of women that their social interests are weaker than those of men, and that their capacity for the sublimation of their instincts is less. The former is no doubt derived from the unsocial character which undoubtedly attaches to all sexual relationships. Lovers find complete satisfaction in each other, and even the family resists absorption into wider organizations. . . . I cannot refrain from mentioning an impression which one receives over and over again in analytic work. A man of about thirty seems a youthful, and, in a sense, an incompletely developed individual, of whom we expect that he will be able to make good use of the possibilities of development, which analysis lays open to him. But a woman of about the same age frequently staggers us by her psychological rigidity and unchangeability. . . . The difficult development which leads to femininity had exhausted all the possibilities of the individual.

That is all I had to say to you about the psychology of women. It is admittedly incomplete and fragmentary, and sometimes it does not sound altogether flattering. You must not forget, however, that we have only described women in so far as their natures are determined by their sexual function. The influence of this factor is, of course, very far-reaching, but we must remember that an individual woman may be a human being apart from this. If you want to know more about femininity, you must interrogate your own experience, or turn to the poets, or else wait until Science can give you more profound and more coherent information.

FEMALE SEXUALITY AND PSYCHOANALYTIC THEORY

MARY JANE SHERFEY

... For Freud, the woman's entire personality is colored and complicated by the dual nature of her sexuality with its fundamental struggle in childhood and early adolescence to relinquish the active, aggressive, masculine sexual pleasure emanating from infantile clitoral activity, which in turn is the result of the innately bisexual nature of the embryo, that is, clitoral erotism is the remaining functional, masculine component after differentiation of the female has occurred and must undergo still further regression to practically a vestigial state before the fullest maturity can be reached.

The biological aspects of Freud's thinking have been expanded by other analysts in two directions. One stresses the erroneous embryological concept that the penile-clitoral tubercle of the early embryo develops from the urogenital sinus which provides the urethra to the penile shaft; hence "phallic" qualities can be attributed to all the structures in the female derived from both the tubercle and the urogenital sinus (clitoris, labia minora, vestibule, Bartholin's glands, and the lower portion of the vagina). This tendency is exemplified by Lorand, who termed the lower third of the vagina "anatomically vestibular and pleasure-physiologically phallic."

From here, it is hardly another step to regard all the female external genitalia as more or less miniature structures derived from male Anlagen. (That the reverse could be true, that is, the penis is an exaggerated clitoris, the phallus is "pleasure-physiologically clitoral," the scrotum is derived from the Anlage of the labia majora, etc., has certainly never been given the least consideration.) Bonaparte carried this line of thinking to its logical conclusion, postulating that since the female retains a rudimentary masculine clitoris, relinquished with such difficulty, the basic libido of the external genitalia is innately masculine. All women are burdened with the extremely difficult task of shifting not only from

Excerpted from Mary Jane Sherfey, *The Nature and Evolution of Female Sexuality*, © 1966 by American Psychoanalytic Association. Reprinted by permission of Random House, Inc.

the clitoris to the vagina, but also from an innately masculine sexual drive to an acquired passive, and in many ways, masochistic feminine sexual drive. This whole line of thought essentially states that normal feminine sexuality is derived from an innately masculine sexuality. Thus it is that psychoanalytic theory has led us through a series of perfectly logical steps to a position which is, in essence, anachronistic: a scientific restatement of the Eve-out-of-Adam myth.

The original Freudian transfer theory has now become almost a statement of female psychosexual development as an evolutionary ideal toward which most women must still strive. Only a few superior women have the highly evolved or trained cortex necessary to produce the vaginal orgasm. Therefore vaginal orgastic competency becomes a function of the higher centers and the intellect. Again we are led by clear logic to the very uncomfortable position stating that the majority of women remain biologically inferior, retarded in their psychosexual evolution compared to men, not sufficiently evolved emotionally and intellectually to achieve the vaginal orgasm—albeit all possibilities are open for them to catch up in the near evolutionary future—but they are still more highly evolved than the animals. (Just why all men and all male animals, even those with a bare cortical minimum, should have an orgasm so easily is not clarified; nor is the ease of the male animal's performance correlated with the related concept that the human male has evolved the highest degree of cortical control of sexuality.)

THE INDUCTOR THEORY OF PRIMARY SEXUAL DIFFERENTIATION

The most important contribution from modern comparative embryology to psychiatry is the elucidation of the process of primary sexual differentiation and its relationship to the evolution of viviparity. While many psychiatrists may be familiar with this theory, others no doubt are not; and its fundamental facts have not been integrated into psychiatric theory. To begin this integration, the inductor theory is now presented in sufficient detail to support its conclusions and certain theoretical possibilities related to psychosexual development to be advanced.

Strictly speaking, we can no longer refer to the "undifferentiated" or "bisexual" phase of initial embryonic existence. The early embryo is not undifferentiated: "it" is a female. In the beginning, we were all created females; and if this were not so, we would not be here at all.

Genetic sex is established at fertilization; but the influence of the sex genes is not brought to bear until the fifth to sixth week of fetal life (in humans). During those first weeks, all embryos are morphologically females. If the fetal gonads are removed before differentiation occurs the embryo will develop into a normal female, lacking only ovaries, regardless of the genetic sex.

If the genetic sex is male, the primordial germ cells arising in the endoderm of the yolk sac and hindgut migrate to the gonadal medulla (future testes) during the fifth week of embryonic life. Once there, they stimulate the production of a "testicular inductor substance" which stimulates medullary growth and the elaboration of fetal androgen which suppresses the growth of the Mullerian ducts (oviducts) and the gonadal cortex (ovaries); subsequently fetal androgen induces the rest of the internal and external genital tract into the male growth pattern. Externally this becomes barely evident by the seventh week or a little later. From the seventh to the twelfth week, the full transformation of the male structures is slowly accomplished. After the twelfth week, the masculine nature of the reproductive tract is fully established; sex reversals of these tissues are then no longer possible. (Suppression of growth and function can take place, of course, throughout life.) The time limits during which reversals can occur vary considerably in the different species relative to the life spans. Within each species, the critical period of sexual differentiation is remarkably constant in its time limits and remarkably sensitive to the exact quantity of the heterologous hormone required to effect reversal.

If the genetic sex is female, the germ cells arrive at the gonadal cortex (ovaries) and eventually stimulate the production of the primordial follicles and fetal estrogens. However, these estrogens are not necessary for the continued feminization of the reproductive tract. If the gonads are removed before the seventh week so that no estrogen is produced, the embryo will still develop normal female anatomy. No ovarian inductor substance or estrogens are elaborated because none are needed. Female differentiation results from the innate, genetically determined female morphology of all mammalian embryos.

That the circulating maternal estrogens do not cause female differentiation has been demonstrated by ingenious experiments in which embryonic reproductive tracts are entirely removed and kept alive *in vitro* sufficiently long for the critical period to be completed. The growth pattern in all embryos remains female. However, just as androgen is needed for the fullest elaboration of the male pattern, so estrogens are required for the full development of the female pattern. It is not known to what extent the circulating maternal estrogens are involved in this task of secondarily "exploiting" the female pattern. Fetal ovaries could well play an insignificant role, and maternal estrogens, an important one, at least for some organs. For example, both male and female human neonates have enlarged breasts which subside to the infantile level by the second postnatal week—in both sexes, the breasts may even secrete a few drops of milk, that is, "witch's milk." It would seem that the maternal estrogens strongly affect male and female embryos to fairly equal degrees.

Therefore only the male embryo is required to undergo a differentiating transformation of the sexual anatomy; and only one hormone, androgen, is necessary for the masculinization of the originally female genital tract. Female development is autonomous.

Theoretical Perspectives. The concept of innate embryonic bisexuality must be amended. Female development pursues a straight course with the reproductive organs not subjected to any hormonal differentiating transformation. Fetal and maternal estrogens merely enhance, and this later, slowly, and to a relatively moderate degree, the already unfolding female morphology. On the other hand, strong activity from fetal androgen is necessary to change the female morphology into the masculine pattern; hence male development "can be considered as a deviation from the basic female pattern."

The male may be said to go through a "bisexual" or "hermaphroditic" hormonal stage, I suppose, as the increasing production of androgen gradually overcomes the innate female anatomy and the maternal estrogens, veering the female structures into the male growth direction.

Therefore the primacy of the embryonic female morphology forces us to reverse long-held concepts on the nature of sexual differentiation. Embryologically speaking, it *is* correct to say that the penis is an exaggerated clitoris, the scrotum is derived from the labia majora, the original libido is feminine, etc. The reverse is true only for the birds and reptiles. For all mammals, modern embryology calls for an Adam-out-of-Eve myth!

With this understanding of evolutionary and embryological development, one conclusion must force itself upon psychiatric theory: *to reduce clitoral erotism to the level of psychopathology because the clitoris is an innately masculine organ or the original libido is masculine in nature must now be considered a travesty of the facts.*

The implications of this biology for psychoanalytic theory become clear. In a very important sense, Freud was right. He had perceived a basic truth but could not develop it accurately with the biological knowledge at his disposal. Females *do* possess a fundamental "masculinelike" sexual drive based on a highly effective clitoral erotism. However, this drive is powered by both androgens and estrogens and is a universal characteristic of all women.

In order to substantiate these concepts on the evolution and nature of the human female's sexual drive, it is necessary to know the precise anatomy and physiology of women's sexual system with all the detail and accuracy which we so diligently demand for every other system of the body. Fortunately, the Masters and Johnson research program has provided us, I believe, with the most accurate and complete information on the sexual responses of women thus far produced.

Masters and Johnson have shown that repeated relaxations and retractions of the [clitoral] shaft take place, equal in number to the number of thrusting movements [of the penis]. Consequently the more the thrusting, the more the erotic arousal in the woman.

It is now clear why so few women (or primates) employ digital stimulation of the lower vagina during masturbation or prefer it during foreplay as a primary source of arousal. The glans has a much higher erotogenic potential than the mucosa of the lower third, moreover, considerable distension of the vaginal orifice must occur before traction on the labia can be effective.

The data thus far permit two important conclusions: The mucosa lining the lower third of the vagina is an erotogenic zone during the thrusting action in coitus, with an unknown degree of sensitivity. . . . However, *no part of the vagina itself produces the orgasmic contractions.* The muscular contractions engendering the actual sensation of orgasm are produced by the extravaginal muscles contracting, not against the vaginal wall directly, but against the circumvaginal venous chambers. The lower vaginal wall is passively pushed in and out by these contractions.

Therefore there is no such thing as an orgasm of the vagina. What exists is an orgasm of the circumvaginal venous chambers. The actual apparatus for orgasmic production is the same in the female as in the male: contractions of the responding muscles against the erectile chambers in men produce expulsion of blood and, indirectly, of semen by compressing the urethra; in the female, contractions produce expulsion of blood and, indirectly, contractions of the lower vagina.

Multiple Orgasms. An observation by Masters and Johnson which has received, surprisingly, not the least attention in the psychoanalytic or any psychiatric literature, I believe, is the normal and regular occurrence of multiple orgasms in women. The authors state:

> If a female who is capable of having regular orgasms is properly stimulated within a short period after her first climax, she will *in most instances* be capable of having a second, third, fourth, and even a fifth and sixth orgasm before she is fully satiated. As contrasted with the male's usual inability to have more than one orgasm in a short period, many females, *especially when clitorally stimulated,* can regularly have five or six full orgasms within a matter of minutes [italics added].

Multiple orgasms in women are well explained by the physiodynamics of the sexual cycle.

COMMENTS. The common idea that clitorally induced orgasms are confined to the clitoris and are necessarily less satisfying *physically* than vaginally induced orgasms is manifestly erroneous. In addition, the popular idea that a woman should have one intense orgasm which should bring "full satisfaction," act as a strong sedative, and alleviate sexual tension for several days to come is simply fallacious. It should be stressed that the intensities of the multiple orgasms do not abate until fatigue of the responding muscles has set in. Each orgasm is followed promptly by refilling of the venous erectile chambers, distension creates engorgement and edema, which create more tissue tension, etc. The supply of blood and edema fluid to the pelvis is inexhaustible.

Consequently, the more orgasms a woman has, the stronger they become; the more orgasms she has, the more she *can* have. To all intents and purposes, *the human female is sexually insatiable in the presence of the highest degrees of sexual satiation.*

The nearly universal sentiment, still very prevalent in our Hebrew-Christian culture, that the female of the species does not, need not, or should not require orgasmic release can now be said to be biologically unthinkable. The selective advantage for reproductive success of the orgasm in males is unquestionably accepted. The fact that the human female can be impregnated without an orgasm is hardly proof that such is biologically normal. That the female could have the same orgasmic anatomy (all of which is female to begin with) and not be expected to use it simply defies the very nature of the biological properties of evolutionary and morphogenetic processes. With the mammalian female carrying the bigger burden for the perpetuation of the species, in reproduction and care of the young, there is no logic in the idea that selection pressure, selecting for the reproductive advantage of the orgasmic capacity of the male, should find this same capacity disadvantageous and unrewarding for the female. And from all the foregoing, it is clear that the entire evolution of the sexual edema, the bulbs and circumvaginal plexi, the preputial-glandar mechanism, and the responding muscles in the primate line, culminating in the human female, is evidence of the high breeding premium which is awarded the female's erotogenic *and* orgasmic competency.

Our myth of the female's relative asexuality is a biological absurdity.

CHANGING PATTERNS OF FEMININITY AND MASCULINITY

There is probably no area in Freud's writings more fraught with theoretical and clinical contradictions than his pronouncements concerning feminine psychophysiology. In what follows, I shall examine these pronouncements in the light of certain developments and changes in the behavioral patterns of twentieth-century women, with some consideration to the impact of these changes on the institution of Western marriage.

THE EMANCIPATION OF MODERN WOMAN

What concerns us . . . here is that in American and European history, up to the end of the eighteenth century, woman's position, for the most part, was distinctly subordinate to that of man. She was totally dependent upon him economically, had no vote and relatively few legal rights, and was denied access to formal education. Early in the nineteenth century, however, in the wake of the egalitarian spirit set into motion by the American and French revolutions and of the sociological changes engendered by the Industrial Revolution, women in England and America began, for the first time in modern history, to assert their prerogatives in relationship to men. Nevertheless, it was almost a hundred years before they obtained the right to vote and began to move toward fuller equality before the law. . . . even within our lifetime there has been a discernible ebb and flow to this pattern. The "feminine revolt" that was so manifest in the twenties through the forties seems to have given way to the "feminine mystique" of the fifties. Where after World War I women were struggling to get out of the home, the current trend seems to be back to the home. A smaller percentage of college graduates today are women

Excerpted from Chapter 3, "Changing Patterns of Femininity: Psychanalytic Implications" by Judd Marmor, in *The Marriage Relationship* edited by Salo Rosenbaum and Ian Alger, © 1968 by Society of Medical Psychoanalysts, Basic Books, Inc., Publishers, New York.

than were thirty years ago, and American women constitute a smaller proportion of the professional world today than they did then. . . .

The reasons for this apparent recession in the revolutionary upsurge of women in America are complex. Some classical Freudians would argue that the entire feminine revolution was essentially a neurotic outbreak of "penis envy" and that what we are now witnessing is a healthy return to "normal" patterns of femininity. . . .

Certain broad socioeconomic factors have been involved, notably the gradual increase of automation and the pressure from men to push women out of the shrinking labor market except in those areas traditionally reserved for them (domestic work, secretarial and teaching positions, retail selling, and so forth). Friedan suggests that an additional factor may have been the increased awareness of American business and merchandising executives that "women will buy more things if they are kept in the under-used, nameless-yearning, energy-to-get-rid-of state of being housewives." . . .

CHANGING MALE-FEMALE RELATIONSHIPS

What are some of the changes that have taken place? By and large there has been a considerable relaxation of the social and sexual restrictions placed upon female children born after World War I. Little girls are now allowed to play more vigorously and competitively, with resultant greater muscular strength and athletic capability. During the preadolescent and adolescent years, contacts between the sexes have become freer, and adolescent as well as preadolescent petting occurs with much greater frequency than in previous decades. Post-World War I mores have also accorded women greater freedom in taking the initiative in reaching out to men both socially and sexually, and as a result much feminine assertiveness that would have been dampened or totally inhibited by the convention of earlier eras has been enabled to flourish.

These changing conventions have been reflected in current patterns of marital relationships also. Women have tended to become more dominant in the home, in an interpersonal sense. Discipline, once the exclusive domain of the father, has been increasingly delegated to the mother.

Another important indication of this shift in marital equilibrium has been the increasing emphasis upon female orgasm. In the Victorian era, "it was considered unfeminine for a woman to acknowledge or display sexual feelings of any kind, even in the conjugal relationship." Now a significant proportion of women express their sexual desires quite openly and engage in the sexual act not as passive recipients but as active participants, indeed often taking the initiative in arousing the man. Sexual intercourse now is expected to culminate in orgasm for the woman no less than for the man, and failure to achieve orgasm is generally as disappointing to the woman as it would be to the man.

American women are assuming an increasingly important economic role in the family, not merely as the primary spenders of the family income, but also as wage earners. An additional factor in this growing economic importance is the fact that many women outlive their husbands and end up controlling their estates.

PSYCHOANALYTIC IMPLICATIONS

The classical psychoanalytic position on women as outlined by Freud can be outlined briefly as follows:

1. ANATOMY IS FATE. The basic nature of woman is determined by her anatomy; most importantly by her discovery that she does not possess a penis.

2. PENIS ENVY. All female children naturally envy males for having penises, and the desire for a penis is a universal fact of normal feminine psychology, only partially compensated for by giving birth to a male child. Helene Deutsch asserts that penis envy is a natural consequence of the fact that the clitoris actually is "an inferior organ" in terms of its capacity to provide libidinal gratification, as well as for its lack of "the forward thrusting, penetrating qualities of the penis."

3. MASOCHISM AND PASSIVITY. These are outgrowths of normal feminine development and are natural and essential components of healthy femininity.

4. FAULTY SUPEREGO DEVELOPMENT. Due to the fact that the feminine castration-complex (precipitated by the little girl's discovery that she has no penis) pushes the little girl *away* from her mother *into* an Oedipal attachment for her father, the little girl has greater difficulty than the boy in resolving the Oedipal complex. Consequently, she tends to develop a defective superego (because the latter presumably comes into being only as the "heir" of the repressed Oedipal complex). The result in women, according to Freud, is an inadequate sense of justice, a predisposition to envy, weaker social interests, and a lesser capacity for sublimation.

Let us now consider these formulations in the light of contemporary knowledge.

"ANATOMY IS FATE." That the anatomical differences between the sexes must inevitably be reflected in some personality differences, regardless of variations in cultural patterns, would seem to be almost axiomatic. Differences in body image, in the experience of menstruation at puberty, in the subsequent monthly cyclical variations of endocrine function, and in the experiences of sexual intercourse, pregnancy, childbirth, and menopause are all aspects of bodily sensation and function that are uniquely different for the woman as compared to the man; and in the biological-environmental interaction that leads to personality formation, these *must* result in significant personality variances between the sexes. . . . The fact is that only by taking into consideration *both* the biological differences between the sexes *and* the variations in cultural reactions to these differences—that is, the *field situation*—can the personality similarities and dissimilarities between men and women, at any given time and place, be fully understood.

Even as sophisticated an observer as Erik Erikson tends to fall into the error of trying to derive some of woman's psychological characteristics *solely* from her anatomical structure. In his recent, beautifully written "Inner and Outer Space: Reflections on Womanhood," he advances the thesis that women are prone to be more concerned with "inner-space" as compared to men's greater preoccupation with "outer-space," and that this is somehow due to "the existence of a *productive inner-bodily space* safely set in the center of female form and carriage." He presents as evidence for this conclusion the fact that in a study of 150 boys and 150 girls, aged ten to twelve, in which they were asked to construct a "scene" with toys on a table, two-thirds of the girls constructed *peaceful interior* scenes, while two-thirds of the boys constructed *aggressive exterior* scenes, or else structures with protruding walls. One need not question the accuracy of Erikson's observations to raise serious doubts concerning his conclusions that these differences derive somehow only from the anatomical differences between the sexes. What about the enormous multitude of acculturation factors—the toys, the games, the adult expectations, and so forth—that have played a part in shaping the fantasies, the perceptions, and the activities of these ten- to twelve-year-old children. . . .

The point, simply, is that to attempt to derive such differences solely from anatomical or physiological considerations inevitably results in oversimplifications. One must always take into consideration the interaction between these factors and the experiences they encounter in the environment—in time, place, family, and culture.

"PENIS ENVY." It is, for example, a massive oversimplification to assume, as Freud did, that the lack of a penis must inevitably be considered as a defect by the female child, in all times and cultures. Clara Thompson and others have quite correctly pointed out that the phenomenon of "penis envy" that Freud observed and described in his women patients was not a universal feminine occurrence but was related to the "culturally underprivileged" position that these women occupied. . . .

Meanwhile, another manifestation has begun to make its appearance with increasing frequency, a phenomenon in men which has been variously described as breast envy, womb envy, and woman envy, and which is derived from men's supposed jealousy of women's ability to bear and suckle children. In the past, when such a reaction was encountered in men, it was assumed to be deeply neurotic, but now it is beginning to be described as a more "universal" phenomenon. But how is it possible that a clinical genius like Freud would have failed to recognize such a common aspect of male psychology? The answer, of course, is that it was *not* a frequent occurrence in his time, and has become so only as a consequence of the shifting equilibrium between the sexes. . . .

When a society places greater value on the birth of a son than on that of a daughter, children in the family become aware of this in myriad subtle ways; the same is true when little boys are accorded greater freedom of movement and play, and when fathers are accorded greater respect and deference than mothers. In such a society little girls, and later women, will inevitably manifest many indications of penis envy, while indications of woman envy in men will be relatively rare. On the other hand, when these conditions no longer hold true, or become reversed (as has begun to happen in Western society in recent decades), *then we can expect to find that unconscious manifestations of penis envy will begin to diminish, and those of woman envy will begin to increase.* . . .

In this connection, Helene Deutsch's dismissal of the clitoris as "an inferior organ" in terms of its capability to provide libidinal gratification is a remarkable example of culturally influenced amblyopia, coming as it does from a woman. The actual fact, as Dickinson has pointed out, is that although "the female organ is minute compared with the male organ . . . the size of its nerves . . . and nerve endings . . . compare strikingly with the same provision for the male. Indeed . . . the glans of the clitoris is demonstrably richer in nerves than the male glans, for the two stems of the dorsalis clitoridis are relatively three to four times as large as the equivalent nerves of the penis. . . ." Little wonder that this "inferior organ" enables the orgastically potent female often to have multiple orgasms to every single orgasm of the male! Not only is clitoral stimulation capable of producing multiple orgasms to an extent unknown in men (as many as twenty to fifty consecutive orgasms have been recorded within the span of an hour!), but also the average orgastic response in women is generally more prolonged than that of men and just as intense in terms of their muscular capacities.

"MASOCHISM AND PASSIVITY." The assumption that normal men are naturally dominant and aggressive, while normal women are naturally submissive and masochistic, is another myth that the changing patterns of relationship between the sexes has begun to dispel. The effort to justify this myth on the basis of the differences in roles in sexual intercourse similarly fails to stand up under careful analysis. The common argument advanced here is that in the sexual act it is the male who must be the penetrator, while the woman is merely the recipient, and that the aggressivity of the male and the passivity of the female naturally follow from this. The error here lies in confusing a *behavioral* phenomenon with a *motivational* one. A male can be a passive and submissive penetrator, while a female can be an aggressive and dominant recipient in the sexual act. Indeed, recent researches indicate that the female genital apparatus during orgasm is extremely active. Receptivity and passivity are not synonymous. It is a striking commentary on the power of a cultural prejudice that both male and female classical Freudians have always assumed that the vagina, as a hollow organ, *had* to be a passive receptacle, although they came to no such conclusions about either the mouth or the anus. "Oral" and "anal" aggression were readily recognized, but the same theoreticians, caught in the meshes of an unconscious common prejudice, were unable to see that, under certain conditions, the vagina too could be an aggressively seeking, grasping, holding, or expulsive organ.

An additional refutation of the myth of "normal feminine masochism" is that women who are passive and submissive in relation to men are *less* apt to be orgastically potent than those who are more assertive, self-confident, and dominant. The little girl, relatively early in her life, under conflict-free circumstances, experiences the insertion of objects (or her finger) into her vagina as a pleasurable, not a painful, experience. Fantasies of being penetrated *may or may not* be associated with anxiety or masochistic implications. . . .

"FAULTY SUPEREGO DEVELOPMENT." Nowhere does the cultural bias inherent in Freud's views about the nature of women become more apparent than in his bland assumption that women have less adequate superegos than men. . . .

Certainly no objective mid-twentieth-century American behavioral scientist would seriously argue any longer that women inherently have a lesser sense of justice, a greater disposition to envy, weaker social interests, or a lesser capacity for sublimation than men. The record of women in England and America in the past four decades on behalf of social justice and human brotherhood compares more than favorably with that of men.

Indeed, the evidence is that since, culturally, little girls are expected to be better behaved than little boys, the pressure of this process is *greater* upon girls than upon boys. As a result, as might be anticipated, females in our culture, at least in their early years, are apt to show evidence of *better* superego development than do males—the very reverse of Freud's theoretical assumption.

KAREN HORNEY

And as thrilling with pleasure he wakes from his rest,
The waters are murmuring over his breast;
And a voice from the deep cries,
"With me thou must go, I charm the young shepherd,
I lure him below."
(Translation by THEODORE MARTIN)

Men have never tired of fashioning expressions for this experience: the violent force by which the man feels himself drawn to the woman, and, side by side with his longing, the dread lest through her he might die and be undone. . . .

Is it not really remarkable (we ask ourselves in amazement), when one considers the overwhelming mass of this transparent material, that so little recognition and attention are paid to the fact of men's secret dread of women? . . . The man on his side has in the first place very obvious strategic reasons for keeping his dread quiet. . . . We may conjecture that even his glorification of women has its source not only in the cravings of love, but also in his desire to give the lie to his dread. A similar relief is, however, also sought and found in the disparagement of women which men often display ostentatiously in all their attitudes. The attitude of love and adoration signifies: 'There is no need for me to dread a being so wonderful, so beautiful, nay, so saintly'; that of disparagement implies: 'It would be too ridiculous to dread a creature who, if you take her all round, is such a poor thing.' This last way of allaying his anxiety has a special advantage for the man: it helps to support his masculine self-respect. The latter seems to feel itself far worse threatened—far more threatened at its very core—by the admission of a dread of women than by the admission of dread of a man (the father). The reason why the self-feeling of men is so peculiarly sensitive just in relation to women can only be understood by reference to their early development, to which I shall return later. . . .

Excerpted from Karen Horney "The Dread of Woman," *International Journal of Psycho-Analysis*, XIII, Part III, (1932), 349–360.

A boy's castration-anxiety in relation to his father is not an adequate reason for his dread of a being [woman] whom this punishment has already overtaken. Besides the dread of the father there must be a further dread, the object of which is the woman or the female genital. Now this dread of the vagina itself appears unmistakably not only in homosexuals and perverts, but also in the dreams of every male analysand.

No doubt the dread of the vagina often conceals itself behind the dread of the father, which is also present; or, in the language of the unconscious, behind the dread of the penis in the woman's vagina. . . .

There are two reasons for this: in the first place . . . masculine self-regard suffers less in this way, and, secondly, the dread of the father is more actual and tangible, less uncanny in quality. We might compare the difference to that between the fear of a real enemy and of a ghost. . . .

Freud states that it is characteristic that the boy's interest is [during the 'phallic phase'] concentrated in a markedly narcissistic manner on his own penis: 'The driving force which this male portion of his body will generate later at puberty expresses itself in childhood essentially as an impulsion to inquire into things—as sexual curiosity.' A very important part is played by questions as to the existence and size of the phallus in other living beings.

But surely the essence of the phallic impulses proper, starting as they do from organ sensations, is a desire to *penetrate*. That these impulses do exist can hardly be doubted: they manifest themselves too plainly in children's games and in the analysis of little children. . . . On the one hand, of course, a boy will automatically conclude that everyone else is made like himself; but on the other hand his phallic impulses surely bid him instinctively to search for the appropriate opening in the female body—an opening, moreover, which he himself lacks, for the one sex always seeks in the other that which is complementary to it or of a nature different from its own. If we seriously accept Freud's dictum that the sexual theories formed by children are modelled on their own sexual constitution, it must surely mean in the present connection that the boy, urged on by his impulses to penetrate, pictures in phantasy a complementary female organ. And this is just what we should infer from all the material I quoted at the outset in connection with the masculine dread of the female genital. . . .

At puberty a normal boy has already acquired a conscious knowledge of the vagina, but what he fears in women is something uncanny, unfamiliar and mysterious. If the grown man continues to regard woman as the great mystery, in whom is a secret he cannot divine, this feeling of his can only relate ultimately to one thing in her: the mystery of motherhood. Everything else is merely the residue of his dread of this. . . .

What is the origin of this anxiety? What are its characteristics? And what are the factors which cloud the boy's early relations with his mother? . . .

The anatomical differences between the sexes lead to a totally different situation in girls and in boys, and really to understand both their anxiety and the diversity of their anxiety we must take into account first of all *the children's real situation* in the period of their early sexuality. The girl's nature as biologically conditioned gives her the desire to receive, to take into herself; she feels or knows that her genital is too small for her father's penis and this makes her react to her own genital wishes with direct anxiety: she dreads that if her wishes were fulfilled, she herself or her genital would be destroyed.

The boy, on the other hand, feels or instinctively judges that his penis is much too small for his mother's genital and reacts with the dread of his own inadequacy, of being rejected and derided. Thus he experiences anxiety which is located in quite a different quarter from the girl's: his original dread of women is not castration-anxiety at all, but a reaction to the menace to his self-respect. . . .

Because of this reaction on the part of the boy, he is affected in another way and more severely by his frustration at the hands of his mother than is the girl by her experience with her father. A blow is struck at the libidinal impulses in either case. But the girl has a certain consolation in her frustration: she preserves her physical integrity; whereas the boy is hit in a second sensitive spot—his sense of genital inadequacy, which has presumably accompanied his libidinal desires from the beginning. If we assume that the most general reason for violent anger is the foiling of impulses which at the moment are of vital importance, it follows that the boy's frustration by his mother must arouse a twofold fury in him: first through the thrusting back of his libido upon itself and, second, through the wounding of his masculine self-regard. . . .

Very often castration anxiety leaves a lasting mark on the man's attitude to women, as we learn from the examples already given at random from very different periods and races. But I do not think that it occurs regularly in all men in any considerable degree, and certainly it is not a *distinctive* characteristic of the man's relation to the other sex. Anxiety of this sort strongly resembles *mutatis mutandis*, anxiety which we meet with in women. When in analysis we find it occurring in any noteworthy intensity, the subject is invariably a man whose whole attitude towards women has a markedly neurotic twist.

On the other hand I think that the anxiety connected with his self-respect leaves more or less distinct traces in every man and gives to his general attitude to women a particular stamp which either does not exist in women's attitude to men or, if it does, is acquired secondarily.

According to my experience the dread of being rejected and derided is a typical ingredient in the analysis of every man, no matter what his mentality or the structure of his neurosis. The analytic situation and the constant reserve of the woman analyst bring out this anxiety and sensitiveness more clearly than they appear in ordinary life, which gives men plenty of opportunity to escape from these feelings either by avoiding situations calculated to evoke them or by a process of overcompensation. . . . The early wound to his self-regard is probably one of the factors liable to disgust the boy with his male rôle.

His typical reaction to that wound and to the dread of his mother which follows from it is obviously to withdraw his libido from her and to concentrate it on himself and his genital. From the economic point of view this process is doubly advantageous: it enables him to escape from the distressing or anxiety-fraught situation which has developed between himself and his mother, and it restores his masculine self-respect by reactively strengthening his phallic narcissism. The female genital no longer exists for him: the 'undiscovered' vagina is a denied vagina. . . .

His first reaction, then, is in the direction of a heightened phallic narcissism. The result is that to the wish to be a woman, which younger boys utter without embarrassment, he now reacts partly with renewed anxiety lest he should not be taken seriously and partly with castration-anxiety. Once we realize that masculine castration-anxiety is very largely the ego's response to the *wish to be a woman*, we shall not altogether share Freud's conviction that bisexuality manifests itself more clearly in the female than in the male. We shall prefer to leave it an open question. . . .

Now one of the exigencies of the biological differences between the sexes is this: that the man is actually obliged to go on proving his manhood to the woman. There is no analogous necessity for her: even if she is frigid, she can engage in sexual intercourse and conceive and bear a child. She performs her part by merely *being*, without any *doing*—a fact which has always filled men with admiration and resentment. The man on the other hand has to *do* something in order to fulfil himself. The ideal of 'efficiency' is a typical masculine ideal. . . .

In sexual life itself we see how the simple craving of love which drives men to women is very often overshadowed by their overwhelming inner compulsion to prove their manhood again and again to themselves and others. A man of this type in its more extreme form has therefore one interest only: to conquer. His aim is to have 'possessed' many women, and the most beautiful and most sought-after women.

Another way of averting the soreness of the narcissistic scar is by adopting the attitude described by Freud as the propensity to debase the love-object. If a man does not desire any woman who is his equal or even his superior—may it not be that he is protecting his threatened self-regard in accordance with that most useful principle of sour grapes? From the prostitute or the woman of easy virtue one need fear no rejection, and no demands in the sexual, ethical or intellectual sphere: one can feel oneself the superior. . . .

This brings us to a third way, the most important and the most ominous in its cultural consequences: that of diminishing the self-respect of the woman. I think that I have shown that men's disparagement of women is based upon a definite psychic trend towards disparaging them —a tendency rooted in the man's psychic reactions to certain given biological facts, as might be expected of a mental attitude so widespread and so obstinately maintained. The view that women are infantile and emotional creatures and, as such, incapable of responsibility and independence is the work of the masculine tendency to lower their self-respect. When men justify such an attitude by pointing out that a very large number of women really do correspond to this description, we must consider whether this type of woman has not been cultivated by a systematic selection on the part of men. The important point is not that individual minds of greater or lesser calibre, from Aristotle to Moebius, have expended an astonishing amount of energy and intellectual capacity in proving the superiority of the masculine principle. What really counts is the fact that the ever-precarious self-respect of the average man causes him over and over again to choose a feminine type which is infantile, nonmaternal and hysterical, and by so doing to expose each new generation to the influence of such women.

MABEL BLAKE COHEN

It sometimes seems to me that the roles of both male and female, as popularly defined in our culture, are impossible to play. There are a number of catchwords applied—for instance, courage, strength, activity, leadership to the male; or receptivity, passivity, nurturance, giving to the female. When one strives to contemplate the task of being always, or almost always, brave, one becomes rebellious and weary with its naïveté.

What, exactly, is meant by the term identity? . . . It could be thought of as the self as it is experienced and as it functions in life situations. It would, then, include conscious motivations and also the less conscious identifications, drives, and defenses which give it some of its individual coloring. It would be formed by the interaction of heredity, constitution, and experience, over time. This view gives a great deal of weight to learning experiences throughout the life cycle in influencing behavior and improving adaptation.

My thesis in this paper is that there is a considerable incompatibility between many people's sense of identity as persons and as sexual beings, or, to put it another way, between society's traditional definition of the person's sexual role and the optimal development of his assets as a person.

First, I should like to consider the contrasts between the traditional definitions of masculinity and femininity, on the one hand, and actual adult male or female functioning, on the other. Kagan and Moss, in their recent report of a longitudinal study of children's development[1] define the traditional masculine model as active sexually, athletic, independent, dominant, courageous, and competitive. His choice of career is not highly intellectual, but is more likely to be that of salesman, businessman, athletic coach, or the like. The feminine model is passive and dependent, showing

Adapted and excerpted from Mabel Blake Cohen, "Personal Identity and Sexual Identity," *Psychiatry*, 29, 1966, 1–14. Reprinted by special permission of the William Alanson White Psychiatric Foundation, Inc.

[1] Jerome Kagan and Howard A. Moss, *Birth to Maturity: A Study in Psychological Development* (New York: Wiley, 1962).

both sexual timidity and social anxiety, fearing and avoiding problem situations, and pursuing homemaking activities rather than career ones. The actuality of these concepts as models for development of many children in our culture is supported by a number of studies of children's attitudes toward the sexes. For instance, Bandura, Ross, and Ross noted in testing children's tendency to imitate adults that the boys normally regarded the male figure as the source of power and the female figure more as the distributor, regardless of the actual power structure of the experimental situation.[2] And Ruth Hartley's studies of children's concepts of male and female roles showed that the shifts in feminine behavior in our society in recent years have not yet affected these concepts.[3]

The traditional concepts of masculinity and femininity undergo many vicissitudes, of course. From the beginning there is constant pressure on the boy to be active, athletic, and competitive; however, in school, and especially in the high-school years, the pressures to develop intellectually, to go to college, and to prepare for a career become more insistent and tend to replace the high valuation of physical activity. But adolescence is also the courtship period, and in this area the older traditions continue to take first place. With the girl, there is considerable indulgence of tomboy behavior up until puberty. After that time, the pressures for traditional femininity, prettiness, ladylike behavior, and apparent passivity in courtship become very strong. Attitudes toward intellectual development in the girl are more ambivalent; in some families intellectual achievements are highly regarded, while in others they are either disapproved or regarded with neutrality. . . .

It is not until after marriage and the establishment of a family that the carrying out of male and female functions has a weighty impact on behavior. . . . It is only with the conception, gestation, and birth of the baby that a decisive division of labor must occur. Now the man becomes in reality the support of the family, and concomitant with this comes an increased feeling of responsibility. The woman, under the ordinary circumstances of raising her children herself, now must withdraw from her career activities, or at least relegate them to second place. She and her child have to become the supported, and hence she must assume a relatively passive and receptive position in relation to her husband in such important areas as money matters, career interests, and coming and going. She also needs to accept the giving or service role in the family, in such matters as baby-tending, meal-supplying, and so forth. Now the stereotypes of childhood and adolescence must give way before the

---

[2] Albert Bandura, Dorothea Ross, and Shella A. Ross, "A Comparative Test of the Status Envy, Social Power, and Secondary Reinforcement Theories of Identificatory Learning," *Journal of Abnormal and Social Psychology*, (1963) 67:527–534.

[3] Ruth Hartley, "Children's Concepts of Male and Female Roles," *Merrill-Palmer Quarterly* (1960) 6:88–91.

realities of everyday adult life, in which neither the masculine nor the feminine one has a chance of success. This brave, strong, dominant male is expected to get up at night with a colicky infant, and this passive, helpless, and dependent woman is expected to deal courageously and with common sense with all the accidents and upsets of life with a small baby. Neither compliance with the cultural stereotypes nor rebellion against them and insistence on differences will solve the problems of the adult marriage partners.

A good deal of new information on childhood development has recently become available from two sources: First, carefully controlled observations of the earliest days of infancy, and, second, longitudinal studies such as those from Berkeley and from the Fels Institute. . . .

The observations of early infancy point to some patterns of response present from birth which are related to subsequent development. . . . There appears to be a wide range, with two extreme types. One type of infant is characterized as a newborn by quiescent sleep and lean body build, and at a month's age by low waking arousal, lack of assertion of needs in the face of brief deprivation, and a strong positive response to maternal contact. At two and a half years, this type showed cautious, restless, shifting play and positive orientation toward contact with supportive adults. The other type manifested chubby body build, strong appetite, a high level of arousal during sleep in the newborn period, and a high level of responsiveness and arousal coupled with aversive response to maternal contact at the end of the first month. At two and a half years this type showed intense, fearless play with inanimate objects and low orientation toward adult supportive figures and peers.

. . . It would seem highly probable that the difference in the baby's response would in turn have considerable influence on what the mother offers. Both types of arousal pattern occur in each sex, although there is a greater proportion of the first, or cuddly, type among girls. . . .

Differential handling of boys and girls is apparent from birth on. Moss has observed that mothers tend to be more responsive to male infants, holding them proportionately more time and generally attending to them more than do mothers of female infants. Somewhat later, at seven months, both parents use more sugary and baby-talk terms to girl babies and work harder to get them to smile and vocalize. These differential ways of handling the two sexes were independent of the activity level of the infant.[4]

Longitudinal studies so far provide only partial information about influences on child development. . . .

The Berkeley study rated maternal behavior in two aspects—the degree

---

[4] Howard A. Moss, communicated at the Conference on Mental Health in Pregnancy, National Institute of Mental Health, Bethesda, Md., April, 1965.

of affection and the degree of control exercised by the mother. The investigators found the predictable better development in infancy and early childhood when the mother was affectionate and not too controlling, but surprisingly also found that with girls the positive correlation between good development and loving maternal behavior dropped out after the age of four. . . . Kagan and Moss in the Fels longitudinal study . . . observed that strong intellectual strivings in boys were correlated positively with maternal protection in the first six years, while strong intellectual strivings in girls were correlated positively with critical maternal attitudes in the same years. One gets the picture, for the girls, of a mother who is in opposition to the traditional feminine stereotype, and who urges and drives her daughter in the direction of intellectual development. . . . When the striving girls reached adulthood, they exhibited intellectual competitiveness and masculine-type interests. . . . The girls who were passive and maternally protected in childhood tended to become passive women, dependent on their families, withdrawing from problem situations, showing high social anxiety, and involved in traditional feminine pursuits.

Many of the active and competitive ones [girls] dropped these behaviors during adolescence and assumed more feminine interests. The girls also showed a rapid increase during early school years of withdrawal from challenging problem situations, and the I.Q. levels of the achieving girls did not increase through the years of school as did those of the boys.

The overall pattern which emerges from this study is that of cultural disparagement of passivity and dependency in the boys and a gradual diminution in the frequency and intensity of these characteristics. . . .

With the girls, aggression and activity were discouraged while dependency and passivity were rewarded, with a resulting alteration in these behaviors which was most conspicuous in preadolescence and adolescence when heterosexual interests begin to flower. However, even prior to that the girls began to show timidity and withdrawal from challenging tasks and also a tendency toward stability or stagnation of intellectual development.

If the greatest value is placed on successful development of so-called typical masculine and feminine types of behavior, then creativity and maximum intellectual development seem to suffer in both sexes.

To illustrate some of the results of these childhood developmental processes, I would like to turn now to some material from an exploratory and descriptive study of pregnant women and their husbands. . . .

We have quite full material on more than fifty subjects, which includes weekly interviews with the wives, beginning in the third or fourth month of pregnancy and continuing through the first three months of the postpartum period. This interview material, . . . was supplemented by psychological examinations, one in the sixth month of pregnancy and a second one at the end of the subject's participation. . . . We had two interviews with each husband, one before and one after the child was born. Our subjects came to us by referral from obstetricians in private practice and from local mental hygiene clinics. Women with problems were therefore in the majority, although there were also some well-adjusted ones who volunteered because they were interested in learning about themselves and their children. . . . Our subjects . . . were mainly middle-class Protestants with reasonable financial security and considerable freedom of choice about their family size. . . .

We . . . distinguished five principal groups: First, those who seemed mentally healthy and had no problems during pregnancy; a second small group who were emotionally well-adjusted but had other problems, such as physical illness; a third group who had obvious neurotic difficulties but were not worse during pregnancy; a fourth group of neurotic women who improved during pregnancy; and the fifth and largest group of those who showed signs of neurotic illness and felt and functioned worse during pregnancy.

In general, the more maladjusted subjects had had a history of greater tension and conflict in the childhood home and had more difficulties in their marriages. Most of our first group of problem-free women had come from harmonious childhood homes and were happily adjusted in their marriages, with feelings of affection and security on the part of both husband and wife. . . . These subjects all had had good relationships with their mothers, although in some cases the relationships with their fathers had been more conflicted. . . . These women were mature, competent, and quite free of conflicts about femininity. Whether they pursued careers or not, they and their husbands had established a relationship which was satisfying to both, not only sexually but also in their workaday living. In contrast, a high proportion of our fifth group, the most troubled ones, had come from unhappy, frustrated, conflictful childhood homes, and inevitably there were marital problems.

Group three, those who were not worse during pregnancy, is particularly interesting to contrast with group five. Despite serious childhood trauma, almost all of them had made successful marriages. In some, it seemed that the happy fortune of marrying a stable and supportive husband had had a curative effect on a woman who otherwise might have gone on toward increasing maladjustment.

Group four, those whose adjustment improved during pregnancy, also had a particular coloring. For these women the states of being pregnant and of being a mother were so intensely satisfying that other relationships and conflicts faded into the background.

We found the sharpest identity conflicts in the most problem-ridden group.... Issues around comfortable acceptance of the feminine role, adequacy of personal development, and satisfaction of dependent needs were intimately interwoven and were of prime importance in success or failure during pregnancy.... The husband's part was forcibly brought to our attention with our first cases.

... The issues which determined the adequacy of his collaboration were similar to those in his wife—namely, his feeling about himself as a man, his adequacy as a person, and his handling of his dependent needs *vis-à-vis* his wife.

We found the problem of dependency to be intimately related to questions of masculine and feminine identity. Dependency is a somewhat confused concept; as most often used, it describes a pathological state of childish demandingness. There is a tendency to overlook interdependency as a part of healthy human relations, both those of husband and wife and also those of people in general.... On the whole, we are more comfortable with the objective, material types of dependency, as when we depend on the fire department to put out our fires. The emotional type of dependency is more problematic. It involves needs for reassurance, support, proof of love or concern, approval, confirmation of our worth, and so on.... We do not clearly know what is an adequate and "normal" dose and what goes beyond that point.... One criterion of suitable degrees of dependency is that of the willingness of the other to be involved. One reacts against a patient's or friend's dependency needs if he seems to ask more than one is willing to give. Perhaps a bargain is inherent in the relationship between two adequate, self-sufficient, successfully dependent adults—namely, that the giving goes both ways.

Part of the mythology of the sexes is that the man is independent and the woman dependent, but this is only a myth.... The need to feel cared for is present in both and undoubtedly goes back to early experience with the mother. A central condition for satisfaction is that the caring-for, whatever it may be, must be freely given by the other, rather than extracted from him. For the more maladjusted, in whom there is a grave lack of trust in the self and the other, gratification of dependency needs is difficult if not impossible of attainment. On the one hand, the freedom of the giving is doubted, and on the other the needs are frequently not expressed. The person tends to rely ... on the hope that the other will guess his needs and supply them in such a way as to resolve his doubts, a hope which is forever being frustrated.

Another type of conflict regarding dependency occurs when such needs have to be denied, a situation frequent in those whose serious doubts of their own worth are covered up by compensatory strivings for strength and self-sufficiency. Such a defensive structure is seen most often in men, but it certainly occurs frequently in women too.

In any marriage, there are initially a good many illusions, both as to the perfection of the other and also as to the promise of fulfillment of all needs. Conflicts and disappointments are inevitable, but in fortunate instances a compromise eventually emerges. . . . In the so-called ideal, typical marriage the man carries more of the responsibility; he is the more active one, the initiator or, as current terminology puts it, the instrumental one. The woman tends to be more passive and is responsive rather than initiating; she is the expressive one. However, this balance may not suit the particular personalities involved and it is easy to see instances of a more equal balance, a sort of comradeship arrangement, and, on the other side of the scale, examples of relationships in which the woman exhibits the greater degree of initiative, energy, and decision-making, while the man is relatively passive. The active-passive balance between the two is not congruent with the dependency-need balance, since an active person's dependency needs are met when he receives confirmation and appreciation for his actions. In terms of dependency needs, the equilibrium must be flexible enough to allow for shifts in situations of stress, and there must be ways of communicating requests between the two.

Especially during pregnancy and the early postpartum period, there is an increase in the woman's dependency needs. In the early stages of the pregnancy, of course, the stresses are largely symbolic, stemming from fears of the pregnancy, of the ordeal of the delivery, and of the increased responsibility after the baby is born. Fear of loss of attractiveness, physical damage, pain, and death, as well as concern about the welfare of the fetus, all make the woman turn toward her husband with increased demands. Later on, in the third trimester and the postpartum period, there are realistic needs for more care and attention from the husband. Our subjects quite frequently asked for a kind of mothering care from their husbands, wanting sympathy, small favors, interest in the developing child, reassurance about their attractiveness, help with planning, and so forth. . . .

The women in our study showed a readiness to accept help from us and to change habitual patterns of behavior which was perhaps related to their increased vulnerability during pregnancy. . . . Where the husbands were able to offer a more sensitive response to their wives, and where the wives could become more open and realistic in their demands, the relationships improved in ways that promised well for the future. . . .

In our most troubled group, we found patterns of interaction between husband and wife which often represented extreme exaggerations of those in the more normal marriages. Like Jack Spratt and his wife, the two have formed a combination which has all-or-nothing qualities about it, and when the pregnancy demands flexibility and shifts in the various aspects of the relationship, the adjustment breaks down. There are three rather typical groups of maladjustment—those in which sexual identity problems are foremost, those in which personal identity issues predominate, and those in which immaturity in both respects is so abysmal that constructive mutuality is impossible. . . .

The first type of couple provides a sort of caricature of ideal, typical masculinity and femininity. The women are usually attractive, feminine in manner, and impeccably groomed. The men are active, energetic, ambitious, and closely follow the masculine model. The women are usually rather idle, with little to do except to run a small apartment and occasionally sew for themselves. The men are usually ambitious and overworked, often going to school at night as well as working hard at their jobs and their hobbies. The women show an increasing trend toward inadequacy, in the sense of leaving more and more up to their husbands; they are often demanding and irritable. The men are increasingly occupied with outside interests and activities and consequently are less and less committed to satisfaction in family life. Both partners accept the idea of the woman as dependent child and the man as active protector. Subjects in this group illustrate one of the imbalances between sexual development and personal development. Although the women are successfully feminine, as the culture defines it, they are limited if not infantile in their growth in the intellectual, social, and mastery aspects of living. The men are successful masculine types but are limited as human beings by rigidity, fear of and avoidance of emotion, and inability to participate in a comfortable intimate relationship. . . .

In some pairs who follow this pattern, the division between the two is even greater, for the husband is oblivious of his wife's emotional needs, acting as though achieving success in the material world and taking total responsibility for the mechanics of living were his only functions. Child-rearing is then left up to an exceedingly infantile wife with disastrous results. Quite commonly such pairs come to child-guidance clinics with problem children, and then it is the experience of the therapists that the husband resists getting involved in the treatment situation and cannot be convinced that he has anything to do with the problem.

The balance of dependency is seen in reverse in another group of subjects in which the wife is the active, efficient one and the husband is quiescent, passive, often openly dependent. . . . In these marriages there is more open strife between the two, because the wife, while acting quite independently, at the same time resents the husband's passivity. . . . The husband, too, while lethargic and inactive, shows signs of ambivalence. He resents his wife's managerial efforts and tends to blame or condemn her for them. He also resists her dependency demands, withholding himself from her. Quite frequently in this combination the husband's potency is impaired, adding yet another reason for resentment and frustration in the wife. . . .

There seems to be a constant dissatisfaction which presses both partners to struggle for a better solution. In part, I would presume that the pressure of discontent comes from the violation of cultural norms.

In these marriages there is more open combat, more neurotic symptomatology, and more rebellion against their lot in life. The woman may be primarily aggressive, demanding, complaining, or reproaching, or she may develop various phobias or depression. The man may show passive resistance, rigidity, moral condemnation, or withdrawal; he may sometimes be impotent and sometimes alcoholic. . . .

A third style of marital disharmony might be called the sibling-rivalry relationship. Here it seems that both people are intent on having their own needs met without regard to the other. Wife and husband are both immature, not only in their adolescent view of sexuality but also in their inability to assume responsibility, to control their impulses, and plan for the future. Sometimes they are in competition as to who will be the dependent one, receiving support, reassurance, and care from the other. There is more concern with competition than cooperation, more interest in outward appearances than inner experiences, and each is preoccupied with getting his own way and with his own grievances. . . .

Summarizing our study of pregnancy, I believe that we have shown the importance for the welfare of the family unit of, first, a sense of security on the part of both man and woman as to their worth as sexual beings and as to their development as persons, and, second, a balance or equilibrium between the two people as to their dependency needs, a balance which can take account of the varying intensity of such needs in various kinds of personalities, and which also can shift with the vicissitudes of living. . . .

I believe the evidence presented here shows the invalidity of either activity–passivity or independence–dependence as indices of masculine–feminine development. Unfortunately, these are embedded in the culture. They are passed on to children by mothers and fathers uncertain of their own feminine or masculine worth, reinforced by schooling, by storybooks, by TV programs, and by peer-group attitudes. Regrettably, they are also held by many professional workers in the behavioral sciences. Sometimes the assumption is made that such qualities are inborn, as sexually determined characteristics. The material from observations of children contradicts this. Others assume that these qualities are either taught or reinforced as part of the acculturation process. Again, the evidence from longitudinal studies indicates that such acculturation is far from successful. The constitutional tendencies toward activity and passivity do not reverse themselves under the pressures of socialization. Rather they linger on in one guise or another, and the anxieties which are aroused by social disapproval of passivity in boys or activity in girls can be seen in the multitudinous fears experienced by both sexes about not being thought appropriately masculine or feminine. Much of the castration anxiety in men and its counterpart, penis envy, in women seems to spring from fear of condemnation if one does not conform to the model.

... For the woman, emphasis on dependency, passivity, and even inadequacy interferes with her functioning as homemaker, wife, and mother just as severely as with her functioning in a career. The career of housewife ... requires competence, good judgment, and ability to take responsibility. Indeed, constructive use of the long hours alone, which are part of the experience of the housewife, requires a considerable degree of inner richness if retrogression and inertia are not to set in. For the man, the overemphasis on strength, courage, initiative, and leadership does violence to his appropriate needs for rest, receiving emotional support, and getting rid of the tensions of the marketplace. ...

I would not be thought to be an advocate of abolishing maleness and femaleness in favor of one uniform sex, as Simone de Beauvoir seems to do. Rather, my aim would be to encourage a more critical scrutiny of our assumptions about sex-typical behavior. ...

The idea that, as women become more secure, men become more insecure, and vice versa, makes one wonder. Is it really true that we are on a teeter-totter and that only one sex can be secure at a time? The evidence from our study contradicts this assumption, as does common sense. Forty years ago, in a letter to Romain Rolland, Freud wrote, "Given our drive dispositions and our environment, the love for fellow man must be considered just as indispensable for the survival of mankind as is technology." ... In a parallel fashion to man's other ills, our narrow conceptions of what is manly and hence not womanly, of what is womanly and hence not manly (conceptions which exclude large areas of thought and feeling which might appropriately be considered as human rather than narrowly sex-bound) can be seen to give rise to difficulties in our development and our relations with each other and with our children. They need to be modified by cultural expectations more flexibly in accord with individual needs as they are actually found in males and females.

SEX DIFFERENCES IN IDENTIFICATION DEVELOPMENT

DAVID B. LYNN

The purpose of this paper is to contribute to the theoretical formulation of sex differences in the development of identification, and to review data relevant to this formulation. The concept of identification has held a prominent position in the behavioral sciences. Identification has not only been used in relation to a given sex role or to a parental role, but it has also been used to indicate the feeling of belonging to a group, one's solidarity or involvement with the group, and one's incorporation of the group's values and attitudes. Since the term identification does carry varied meanings, let us define identification as it is used here by first differentiating it from other related concepts. Brown contrasted identification to *sex role preference*. Sex role preference refers to the desire to adopt the behavior associated with one sex or the perception of such behavior as preferable or more desirable. In a previous paper . . . this investigator suggested that identification can also be contrasted to *sex role adoption*. Sex role adoption refers to the actual adoption of behavior characteristics of one sex or the other, not simply the desire to adopt such behavior. The fact that a woman on appropriate occasions wears trousers or short hair does not necessarily mean that she is identified with the male role, even though she is adopting certain aspects characteristic of that role. *Sex role identification* is reserved to refer to the actual incorporation of the role of a given sex, and to the unconscious reactions characteristic of that role. The differentiation among these concepts is elaborated at greater length in this investigator's previous paper.

THEORETICAL FORMULATION

The present formulation differs from the classical Freudian position which postulates that the boy's anatomical advantage arouses intense re-

Excerpted from David B. Lynn, "Sex Differences in Identification Development," *Sociometry*, 24, 1961, 372–383.

sentment and envy in the girl, drives her in the direction of masculinity, and hence, makes the acceptance of femininity difficult. On the contrary, the position taken in this paper follows Mowrer, Parsons, and others in stressing that the early closeness of the girl to the same-sex parent (the mother) gives her an initial, if temporary, advantage in progressing toward appropriate identification. This initial advantage may be largely counterbalanced by later learning experiences in this masculine-oriented culture.

It is postulated that both male and female infants learn to identify with the mother (or the person playing the mother-role). Learning to identify with the mother is among the individual's earliest learning experiences. One of the basic learning principles states that early learning has "primacy" over later learning, that is, early learning is more easily reinforced, and weakens more slowly with time than later learning.

In the present formulation, one of the major sex differences in the development of sex role identification is postulated as follows: The boy must shift from his initial identification with the mother and achieve identification with the masculine role, whereas the girl need make no such shift. Since this early learned identification with the mother is accorded primacy over later learning, one would hypothesize that the shift from mother to masculine identification may be psychologically difficult for boys. Because of the difficulty in shifting identification for the boy, and the fact that the girl need make no such identification shift, it is predicted that a higher proportion of males than females will fail more or less completely to form a same-sex identification.

Although recognizing that not all homosexuals are inverted in identification, it is nevertheless assumed that the *relative* incidence of homosexuality for males and females reflects the *relative* incidence of individuals who more or less completely fail to form same-sex identification. Brown made the prediction that there would be a higher incidence of male than female inverts.

Brown used the Kinsey reports to suggest whether or not the relative incidence of inversion differs in males and females. The Kinsey studies show a greater frequency of homosexuality among males, consistent with the hypothesis that more males than females fail to achieve same-sex identification, but rather form an opposite-sex identification.

The literature contains seemingly contradictory findings, showing more adult males than females who state preference for being a member of their own sex and a higher proportion of adult males than females who draw the same-sex figure first, while on the other hand, the data referred to above indicate that there are more male than female homosexuals. If males prefer being male more than females prefer being female, and if males are better same-sex identified than females (assuming that drawing the same-sex figure first reflects appropriate identification), then why should there be more male than female homosexuals? In the present formulation, those males who fail in forming same-sex identification are, for whatever reasons, unable to overcome the primacy of the early learned identification with the mother and remain "fixated" at that level. If the boy fails to make progress in this initial shift from mother to masculine identification, he may be unable to profit by the elaborate system of reinforcements provided males by the culture in developing masculine identification.

Now to proceed with the formulation. Those boys who do manage the shift from mother to masculine identification discover that they do not belong to the same sex category to which the mother belongs, but rather to the sex category to which the father belongs. The young boy discovers that he is no longer almost completely in a woman's world characterized by the maternal care received during infancy, but is now increasingly in a man's world. The boy is under considerable pressure to adopt the masculine role, to be a "little man." These demands are made on him despite the fact that he has fewer men than women models for identification. Not only are his teachers typically women, but, because his father works all day, he is separated from his father more than from his mother. Despite the shortage of male models, a somewhat stereotyped and conventional masculine role is nonetheless spelled out for him. Sherriffs and Jarrett found that men and women share the same stereotypes about the two sexes.

The development of the appropriate sex-role identification for the girl, in this formulation, is quite different from that for the boy. In many ways her development is the converse of that for the boy. When the girl leaves infancy, she goes from a woman's (same-sex) world of mother care to a man's (opposite-sex) world. As Brown pointed out, "The superior position and privileged status of the male permeates nearly every aspect, minor and major, of our social life." In this connection Smith found results to suggest that children, as they grow older, increasingly learn to give males prestige; and Kitay found that women share with men the prejudice prevailing in our culture against their own sex.

The girl is affected by many cultural pressures despite the fact that she need not shift identification, and despite the physical presence of the mother during her development. In this formulation it is postulated that sex-role identification, being a learned phenomenon and following the laws of learning, will tend to become extinguished without adequate reinforcement. It is assumed that in our society there is a relative lack of rewards for being female, and it is predicted that the lack of rewards for being female tends slowly to extinguish the girl's early learned feminine identification. It is further predicted that the prestige and privileges offered males but not females, and the lack of punishment for adopting aspects of the masculine role, have a slow, corrosive, weakening effect on the girl's feminine identification.

Another factor which may contribute to the girl's weakening identification with the feminine role is the mother's ambivalence in her own feminine identification. The strength of the girl's identification with her own mother may, paradoxically, contribute to weakening the girl's feminine-role identification. As this formulation develops, the importance of clearly distinguishing between identification with one's specific parent and identification with a more general sex role will become apparent. The girl, in being closely identified with her mother, also identifies with her mother's ambivalent feminine identification.

Thus, for these various reasons, it is predicted that, with increasing age, the female becomes less firmly identified with the feminine role. Conversely, the prestige and privileges accorded the male, the rewards offered for adopting the masculine role, and the punishment for not doing so are predicted to have a gradual strengthening effect on the boy's masculine identification. [Previously], this investigator reviewed literature which suggests the validity of this hypothesis, assuming that sex role identification is reflected in the figure drawn first when the child is requested to draw a person. Brown and Tolor reviewed a number of studies on human figure drawings. The studies on figure drawings with children show that, with younger children, a higher proportion of girls than boys drew the same-sex figure first, and with older children this trend is reversed, and a larger proportion of boys than girls drew the same-sex figure first. It follows that a much higher proportion of boys than girls should develop psychological problems at a very early age, because young boys are postulated to be less firmly same-sex identified than young girls. It is predicted that males, with increasing age, develop psychological disturbances at a more slowly accelerating rate than females.

. . . The argument may be pursued as follows: To the extent that an individual is poorly identified with his own sex, he is what Brown calls a "psychosomatic misfit." To the extent that same-sex identification is replaced by opposite-sex identification, the individual has the bodily characteristics of one sex and the psychological characteristics of the other. One would expect conflicts stemming from the obvious realities of one's anatomical classification and one's tendencies toward opposite-sex identification. Conflicts might also arise from the expectations of society and one's inadequate same-sex identification and/or one's tendencies toward opposite-sex identification. Anxiety would be expected to accompany such conflicts. Various defense mechanisms would develop to cope with the anxiety.

... Mowrer goes so far as to postulate specific kinds of psychological disturbances as associated with various stages of identification. According to Mowrer, identification with the same-sex parent results in normal adult sex-role behavior; identification with the opposite-sex parent results in inverted adult sex-role behavior; and identification of a confused, ambivalent nature with both parents results in neurotic adult sex-role behavior.

Despite the theoretical rationale for the assumption that psychological disturbances should be associated with inadequate same-sex identification, the research in this area is meager, and the operational definitions of identification often differ, as do the criteria of psychological disturbance.

Several relevant studies considered perceived similarity between the subject and a parent as a measure of identification. Perceived similarity involves the subject's giving responses to one or another psychological scale in the usual way, and then responding to the same scale as he *thinks* his parent might. This criterion of parental identification does not satisfy the definition utilized in this paper, which would require the *actual* (not just perceived) similarity in reaction between a subject and his parent. Cowan utilized the semantic differential to obtain ratings by each subject of his actual self, ideal self, mother, and father. He found that normal eighth-grade public school males or females did not differ from emotionally disturbed ones in the degree of their perceived similarity with either parent. On the other hand, Sopchak, having subjects take the MMPI in the usual way, as their father would, and as their mother would, found that men with tendencies toward abnormality show greater lack of perceived similarity with fathers than with mothers, but they also fail to show perceived similarity with mothers. He also found that for both men and women, failure to "identify" with the father is more closely associated with trends toward abnormality than is failure to "identify" with the mother. Cava and Raush, in a study in which adolescent boys filled out the Strong Vocational Interest Blank in the usual way and as they thought their fathers would, found that those showing the least perceived similarity showed the most conflict in the Blacky Test, especially in the castration fear area. Schoeppe, Haggard, and Havighurst, who did not use perceived similarity as a measure of identification, but rather based their conclusions on a great volume of material obtained in an intensive interdisciplinary study of 16-year-old adolescents, found that for boys, but not for girls, success in achieving emotional independence and in performing sex-role tasks is associated with primary identification with the same-sex parent.

The research data, although inadequately testing the assumption, suggest a relationship between poor same-sex identification and psychological disturbance for males, but not for females. However, the data are inconclusive for both. More research concerning this crucial assumption, using more adequate criteria of identification, is badly needed.

. . . On the basis of the available research data, no relationship between same-sex identification and psychological disturbances can safely be assumed for the female. Therefore, the rate of psychological disturbances in the various age groups for females can serve as a standard against which to measure the changes with age in rate of disturbances for males.

If psychological disturbances are associated with inadequate same-sex identification for males, and if young boys are less firmly same-sex identified than young girls but become more firmly same-sex identified with increasing age, then it follows that *with increasing age, males develop psychological disturbances at a more slowly accelerating rate than females*. . . . It should be clearly recognized that . . . data do not adequately test the theoretical basis for this hypothesis, but, rather, are suggestive only.

If this hypothesis is valid, such a trend should be reflected in demographic data related to the frequency of psychological disturbances in the two sexes. This trend should be reflected in the data showing the relative frequency of referrals to child guidance clinics, and in admissions and residence in psychopathic hospitals and prolonged-care mental institutions. With increasing age males should use such facilities at a more slowly accelerating rate than females, the rate for females being considered a standard against which to measure age changes in males. This is precisely what the demographic data show. Gilbert did a survey of referral problems in metropolitan child guidance centers. Calculations on Gilbert's data show that at age six and below, 2.47 times as many boys as girls were referred to child guidance centers. At ages 14 through 17, only 2.16 times as many boys as girls were referred. However, the reader might raise the objection that this trend, assuming it is a stable one, can be accounted for by the fact that psychiatric referrals in early childhood are most likely to occur when there is a problem involving aggressive behavior. Since boys are more aggressive than girls, this would account for more boys than girls being referred to child guidance clinics in the very early years. However, psychological problems other than those involving aggressive behavior will sooner or later manifest themselves, and for that reason the boys, with increasing age, are brought to child guidance clinics at a more slowly accelerating rate than are girls.

If this objection is valid, then a recalculation of Gilbert's data, leaving out of the calculation those cases falling into the category "aggressive and anti-social behavior," should *fail* to show boys, as they grow older, using child guidance clinics at a more slowly accelerating rate than girls. This investigator did recalculate Gilbert's data, deleting from the calculation those cases falling in the "aggressive and anti-social" category. He found that, even without this category, at age six and below, 2.36 times as many boys as girls were referred to child guidance centers. At age 14 through 17, 2.10 times as many boys as girls were referred. Thus, the trend persists even when the category for aggressive and anti-social behavior is deleted. This suggests that this trend cannot be accounted for simply by the more aggressive nature of boys.

Data from U.S. Public Health publications show that this same trend persists into adulthood both in terms of first admissions and of patients in residence in public and private psychopathic hospitals and public prolonged-care institutions.... With increasing age, through age category 25 through 34, males almost uniformly use these facilities at a more slowly accelerating rate than do females.

Perhaps only psychotic or neurotic patients would better represent psychological disturbances which should relate to inadequate identification. ... This trend holds not only for the total patient population, but it holds also for the patients with psychotic disorders and those with psychoneurotic reactions alike.

Thus, the hypothesis that, with increasing age, males develop psychological disturbances at a more slowly accelerating rate than do females was almost uniformly supported by the available demographic data.

SUMMARY

Despite the fact that the girl need not shift her identification, and despite the physical presence of the mother during her development, the girl is still affected by many cultural pressures. The prestige and privileges offered males, but not females, and the lack of punishment for adopting aspects of the masculine role are predicted to have a gradual weakening effect on the girl's feminine identification. Conversely, the prestige and privileges accorded the male, and the punishment for not adopting the male role are predicted slowly to strengthen the boy's masculine identification.

From these considerations, the following hypotheses emerged:

1. More males than females fail more or less completely in achieving same-sex identification, but rather make an opposite-sex identification.

2. With increasing age, males develop psychological disturbances at a more slowly accelerating rate than females.

These hypotheses seemed to be generally supported by available data.

ERVING GOFFMAN

PRELIMINARY CONCEPTIONS

Society establishes the means of categorizing persons and the complement of attributes felt to be ordinary and natural for members of each of these categories. Social settings establish the categories of persons likely to be encountered there. The routines of social intercourse in established settings allow us to deal with anticipated others without special attention or thought. When a stranger comes into our presence, then, first appearances are likely to enable us to anticipate his category and attributes, his "social identity"—to use a term that is better than "social status" because personal attributes such as "honesty" are involved, as well as structural ones, like "occupation."

We lean on these anticipations that we have, transforming them into normative expectations, into righteously presented demands.

Typically, we do not become aware that we have made these demands or aware of what they are until an active question arises as to whether or not they will be fulfilled. It is then that we are likely to realize that all along we had been making certain assumptions as to what the individual before us ought to be. Thus, the demands we make might better be called demands made "in effect," and the character we impute to the individual might better be seen as an imputation made in potential retrospect—a characterization "in effect," a *virtual social identity*. The category and attributes he could in fact be proved to possess will be called his *actual social identity*.

The term stigma, then, will be used to refer to an attribute that is deeply discrediting, but it should be seen that a language of relationships, not attributes, is really needed. An attribute that stigmatizes one type of possessor can confirm the usualness of another, and therefore is neither creditable nor discreditable as a thing in itself. For example, some jobs in

Erving Goffman, *Stigma*, © 1963. Reprinted by permission of Prentice-Hall, Inc., Englewood Cliffs, New Jersey.

America cause holders without the expected college education to conceal this fact; other jobs, however, can lead the few of their holders who have a higher education to keep this a secret, lest they be marked as failures and outsiders.

Three grossly different types of stigma may be mentioned. First there are abominations of the body—the various physical deformities. Next there are blemishes of individual character perceived as weak will, domineering or unnatural passions, treacherous and rigid beliefs, and dishonesty, these being inferred from a known record of, for example, mental disorder, imprisonment, addiction, alcoholism, homosexuality, unemployment, suicidal attempts, and radical political behavior. Finally there are the tribal stigma of race, nation, and religion, these being stigma that can be transmitted through lineages and equally contaminate all members of a family. In all of these various instances of stigma, however, including those the Greeks had in mind, the same sociological features are found: an individual who might have been received easily in ordinary social intercourse possesses a trait that can obtrude itself upon attention and turn those of us whom he meets away from him, breaking the claim that his other attributes have on us. He possesses a stigma, an undesired differentness from what we had anticipated. We and those who do not depart negatively from the particular expectations at issue I shall call the *normals*.

The attitudes we normals have toward a person with a stigma, and the actions we take in regard to him, are well known, since these responses are what benevolent social action is designed to soften and ameliorate. By definition, of course, we believe the person with a stigma is not quite human. On this assumption we exercise varieties of discrimination, through which we effectively, if often unthinkingly, reduce his life chances. We construct a stigma-theory, an ideology to explain his inferiority and account for the danger he represents, sometimes rationalizing an animosity based on other differences, such as those of social class. We tend to impute a wide range of imperfections on the basis of the original one, and at the same time to impute some desirable but undesired attributes, often of a supernatural cast, such as "sixth sense," or "understanding." Further, we may perceive his defensive response to his situation as a direct expression of his defect, and then see both defect and response as just retribution for something he or his parents or his tribe did, and hence a justification of the way we treat him. The stigmatized individual tends to hold the same beliefs about identity that we do; this is a pivotal fact. His deepest feelings about what he is may be his sense of being a "normal person," a human being like anyone else, a person, therefore, who deserves a fair chance and a fair break.

The central feature of the stigmatized individual's situation in life can now be stated. It is a question of what is often, if vaguely, called "acceptance." Those who have dealings with him fail to accord him the respect and regard which the uncontaminated aspects of his social identity have led them to anticipate extending, and have led him to anticipate receiving; he echoes this denial by finding that some of his own attributes warrant it.

How does the stigmatized person respond to his situation? In some cases it will be possible for him to make a direct attempt to correct what he sees as the objective basis of his failing, as when a physically deformed person undergoes plastic surgery, a blind person eye treatment, an illiterate remedial education, a homosexual psychotherapy. (Where such repair is possible, what often results is not the acquisition of fully normal status, but a transformation of self from someone with a particular blemish into someone with a record of having corrected a particular blemish.)

The stigmatized individual can also attempt to correct his condition indirectly by devoting much private effort to the mastery of areas of activity ordinarily felt to be closed on incidental and physical grounds to one with his shortcoming. This is illustrated by the lame person who learns or relearns to swim, ride, play tennis, or fly an airplane. Finally, the person with a shameful differentness can break with what is called reality, and obstinately attempt to employ an unconventional interpretation of the character of his social identity.

The stigmatized individual is likely to use his stigma for "secondary gains," as an excuse for ill success that has come his way for other reasons: he may also see the trials he has suffered as a blessing in disguise, especially because of what it is felt that suffering can teach one about life and people. Our concern is ... with the issue of "mixed contacts"—the moments when stigmatized and normal are in the same "social situation," that is, in one another's immediate physical presence, whether in a conversation-like encounter or in the mere copresence of an unfocused gathering.

The very anticipation of such contacts can of course lead normals and the stigmatized to arrange life so as to avoid them. Lacking the salutary feed-back of daily social intercourse with others, the self-isolate can become suspicious, depressed, hostile, anxious, and bewildered.

When normals and stigmatized do in fact enter one another's immediate presence, especially when they there attempt to sustain a joint conversational encounter, there occurs one of the primal scenes of sociology; for, in many cases, these moments will be the ones when the causes and effects of stigma must be directly confronted by both sides.

The stigmatized individual may find that he feels unsure of how we normals will identify and receive him. In the stigmatized arises the sense of not knowing what the others present are "really" thinking about him.

Further, during mixed contacts, the stigmatized individual is likely to feel that he is "on," having to be self-conscious and calculating about the impression he is making, to a degree and in areas of conduct which he assumes others are not.

At the same time, minor failings or incidental impropriety may, he feels, be interpreted as a direct expression of his stigmatized directness. Ex-mental patients, for example, are sometimes afraid to engage in sharp in-terchanges with spouse or employer because of what a show of emotion might be taken as a sign of.

When the stigmatized person's failing can be perceived by our merely directing attention (typically, visual) to him—when, in short, he is a dis-credited, not discreditable, person—he is likely to feel that to be present among normals nakedly exposes him to invasions of privacy.

Given what the stigmatized individual may well face upon entering a mixed social situation, he may anticipatorily respond by defensive cowering.

Instead of cowering, the stigmatized individual may attempt to ap-proach mixed contacts with hostile bravado, but this can induce from others its own set of troublesome reciprocations. It may be added that the stigmatized person sometimes vacillates between cowering and bravado, racing from one to the other, thus demonstrating one central way in which ordinary face-to-face interaction can run wild.

I am suggesting, then, that the stigmatized individual—at least the "visibly" stigmatized one—will have special reasons for feeling that mixed social situations make for anxious unanchored interaction. But if this is so, then it is to be suspected that we normals will find these situations shaky too. We will feel that the stigmatized individual is either too aggressive or too shamefaced, and in either case too ready to read unintended meanings into our actions. We ourselves may feel that if we show direct sympathetic concern for his condition, we may be overstepping ourselves; and yet if we actually forget that he has a failing we are likely to make impossible demands of him or unthinkingly slight his fellow-sufferers. Each potential source of discomfort for him when we are with him can become something we sense he is aware of, aware that we are aware of, and even aware of our state of awareness about his awareness; the stage is then set for the infinite regress of mutual consideration that Meadian social psychology tells us how to begin but not how to terminate.

THE ORIGINS OF THE STATUS OF WOMEN

FRIEDRICH ENGELS

The development of the family . . . is founded on the continual contraction of the circle, originally comprising the whole tribe, within which marital intercourse between both sexes was general. By the continual exclusion, first of near, then of ever remoter relatives, including finally even those who were simply related legally, all group marriage becomes practically impossible. At last only one couple, temporarily and loosely united, remains; that molecule, the dissolution of which absolutely puts an end to marriage. Even from this we may infer how little the sexual love of the individual in the modern sense of the word had to do with the origin of monogamy. The practice of all nations of that stage still more proves this. While in the previous form of the family the men were never embarrassed for women, but rather had more than enough of them, women now became scarce and were sought after. With the pairing family, therefore, the abduction and barter of women began—widespread symptoms, and nothing but that, of a new and much more profound change.

The pairing family, being too weak and too unstable to make an independent household necessary or even desirable, in no way dissolves the traditional communistic way of housekeeping. But household communism implies supremacy of women in the house as surely as exclusive recognition of a natural mother and the consequent impossibility of identifying the natural father signify high esteem for women, that is, mothers. It is one of the most absurd notions derived from eighteenth century enlightenment, that in the beginning of society woman was the slave of man. Among all savages and barbarians of the lower and middle stages, sometimes even of the higher stage, women not only have freedom, but are held in high esteem. What they were even in the pairing family, let Arthur Wright, for many years a missionary among the Seneca Iroquois, testify: As to their families, at a time when they still lived in their old long houses (communistic households of several families) . . . a certain

---

Excerpted from Friedrich Engels, *The Origins of the Family, Private Property, and the States* (Chicago, Illinois: Charles H. Kerr and Company, 1902).

clan (gens) always reigned, so that the women choose their husbands from other clans (gentes).... The female part generally ruled the house; the provisions were held in common; but woe to the luckless husband or lover who was too indolent or too clumsy to contribute his share to the common stock. No matter how many children or how much private property he had in the house, he was liable at any moment to receive a hint to gather up his belongings and get out. And he could not dare to venture any resistance; the house was made too hot for him and he had no other choice, but to return to his own clan (gens) or, as was mostly the case, to look for another wife in some other clan. The women were the dominating power in the clans (gentes) and everywhere else. The communistic household, in which most or all the women belong to one and the same gens, while the husbands come from different gentes, is the cause and foundation of the general and widespread supremacy of women in primeval times.

... The division of labor between both sexes is caused by other reasons than the social condition of women. Nations where women have to work much harder than is proper for them in our opinion often respect women more highly than Europeans do.... Riches, once they had become the private property of certain families and augumented rapidly, gave a powerful impulse to society founded on the pairing family and the maternal gens. The pairing family had introduced a new element. By the side of the natural mother it had placed the authentic natural father. According to the division of labor in those times, the task of obtaining food and the tools necessary for this purpose fell to the share of the man; hence he owned the latter and kept them in case of a separation, as the women did the household goods. According to the social custom of that time, the man was also the owner of the new source of existence, the cattle, and later on of the new labor power, the slaves. But according to the same custom, his children could not inherit his property, for the following reasons: By maternal law, that is, while descent was traced only along the female line, and by the original custom of inheriting in the gens, the gentile relatives inherited the property of their deceased gentile relative. The wealth had to remain in the gens. In view of the insignificance of the objects, the property may have gone in practice to the closest gentile relatives, this is, the consanguine relatives on the mother's side. The children of the dead man, however, did not belong to his gens, but to that of their mother. They inherited first together with the other consanguine relatives of the mother, later on perhaps in preference to the others. But they could not inherit from their father, because they did not belong to his gens, where his property had to remain. Hence, after the death of a cattle owner, the cattle would fall to his brothers, sisters and the children of his sisters, or to the offspring of the sisters of his mother. His own children were disinherited.

In the measure of the increasing wealth man's position in the family became superior to that of woman, and the desire arose to use this fortified position for the purpose of overthrowing the traditional law of inheritance in favor of his children. But this was not feasible as long as maternal law was valid. The simple resolution was [the abolishment of] . . . the tracing of descent by female lineage and the maternal right of inheritance, and instituted descent by male lineage and the paternal right of inheritance. How and when this revolution was accomplished by the nations of the earth, we do not know. It belongs entirely to prehistoric times.

The downfall of maternal law was the historic defeat of the female sex. The men seized the reins also in the house, the women were stripped of their dignity, enslaved, tools of men's lust and mere machines for the generation of children. This degrading position of women, especially conspicuous among the Greeks of heroic and still more of classic times, was gradually glossed over and disguised or even clad in a milder form. But it is by no means obliterated.

The first effect of the established supremacy of men became now visible in the reappearance of the intermediate form of the patriarchal family. Its most significant feature is "the organization of a certain number of free and unfree persons into one family under the paternal authority of the head of the family. In the Semitic form this head of the family lives in polygamy, the unfree members have wife and children, and the purpose of the whole organization is the tending of herds in a limited territory." The essential points are the assimilation of the unfree element and the paternal authority. Hence the ideal type of this form of the family is the Roman family. The word familia did not originally signify the composite ideal of sentimentality and domestic strife in the present day philistine mind. Among the Romans it did not even apply in the beginning to the leading couple and its children, but to the slaves alone. Famulus means domestic slave, and familia is the aggregate number of slaves belonging to one man. At the time of Gajus, the familia, id est patrimonium (that is, paternal legacy), was still bequeathed by testament. The expression was invented by the Romans in order to designate a new social organism, the head of which had a wife, children and a number of slaves under his paternal authority and according to Roman law the right of life and death over all of them.

Marx adds: "The modern family contains the germ not only of slavery (servitus), but also of serfdom, because it has from the start a relation to agricultural service. It comprises in miniature all those contrasts that later on develop more broadly in society and the state." In order to secure the faithfulness of the wife, and hence the reliability of paternal lineage, the women are delivered absolutely into the power of the men; in killing his wife, the husband simply exercises his right.

Such was the origin of monogamy, as far as we may trace it in the most civilized and most highly developed nation of antiquity. It was by no means a fruit of individual sex-love and had nothing to do with the latter, for the marriages remained as conventional as ever. Monogamy was the first form of the family not founded on natural, but on economic conditions, . . . the victory of private property over primitive and natural collectivism. Supremacy of the man in the family and generation of children that could be his offspring alone and were destined to be the heirs of his wealth—these were openly avowed by the Greeks to be the sole objects of monogamy.

Monogamy, then, does by no means enter history as a reconciliation of man and wife and still less as the highest form of marriage. On the contrary, it enters as the subjugation of one sex by the other, as the proclamation of an antagonism between the sexes unknown in all preceding history. In an old unpublished manuscript written by Marx and myself in 1846, I find the following passage: "The first division of labor is that of man and wife in breeding children." And to-day I may add: The first class antagonism appearing in history coincides with the development of the antagonism of man and wife in monogamy, and the first class oppression with that of the female by the male sex. Monogamy was a great historical progress. But by the side of slavery and private property it marks at the same time that epoch which, reaching down to our days, takes with all progress also a step backwards, relatively speaking, and develops the welfare and advancement of one by the woe and submission of the other. It is the cellular form of civilized society which enables us to study the nature of its now fully developed contrasts and contradictions.

With the rise of different property relations, in the higher stage of barbarism, wage labor appears sporadically by the side of slavery, and at the same time its unavoidable companion, professional prostitution of free women by the side of the forced surrender of female slaves. It is the heirloom bequeathed by group marriage to civilization, a gift as ambiguous as everything else produced by ambiguous, double-faced, schismatic and contradictory civilization. Here monogamy, there hetaerism and its most extreme form, prostitution. Hetaerism is as much a social institution as all others. It continues the old sexual freedom—for the benefit of the men. In reality not only permitted, but also assiduously practiced by the ruling class, it is denounced only nominally. Still in practice this denunciation strikes by no means the men who indulge in it, but only the women. These are ostracized and cast out by society, in order to proclaim once more the fundamental law of unconditional male supremacy over the female sex.

However, a second contradiction is thereby developed within monogamy itself. By the side of the husband, who is making his life pleasant by hetaerism, stands the neglected wife. And you cannot have one side of the contradiction without the other, just as you cannot have the whole apple after eating half of it. Nevertheless this seems to have been the idea of the men, until their wives taught them a lesson. Monogamy introduces two permanent social characters that were formerly unknown: the standing lover of the wife and the cuckold. The men had gained the victory over the women, but the vanquished magnanimously provided the coronation. In addition to monogamy and hetaerism, adultery became an unavoidable social institution—denounced, severely punished, but irrepressible.

Thus we have in the monogamous family, at least in those cases that remain true to historical development and clearly express the conflict between man and wife created by the exclusive supremacy of men, a miniature picture of the contrasts and contradictions of society at large.

The monogamous family, by the way, did not everywhere and always appear in the classic severe form it had among the Greeks. Although monogamy was the only one of all known forms of the family in which modern sex love could develop, this does not imply that it developed exclusively or even principally as mutual love of man and wife. The very nature of strict monogamy under man's rule excluded this. Among all historically active, that is, ruling, classes matrimony remained what it had been since the days of the pairing family—a conventional matter arranged by the parents.

In those countries where a legitimate portion of the parental wealth is assured to children and where these cannot be disinherited—in Germany, in countries with French law, et cetera—the children are bound to secure the consent of their parents for marrying. In countries with English law, where the consent of the parents is by no means a legal qualification of marriage, the parents have full liberty to bequeath their wealth to anyone and may disinherit their children at will. Hence it is clear that among classes having any property to bequeath the freedom to marry is not a particle greater in England and America than in France and Germany.

The legal equality of man and woman in marriage is by no means better founded. Their legal inequality inherited from earlier stages of society is not the cause, but the effect of the economic oppression of women. In the ancient communistic household comprising many married couples and their children, the administration of the household entrusted to women was just as much a public function, a socially necessary industry, as the procuring of food by men. In the patriarchal and still more in the monogamous family this was changed. The administration of the household lost its public character. It was no longer a concern of society. It became a private service. The woman became the first servant of the house, excluded from participation in social production. Only by the great industries of our time the access to social production was again opened for women—for proletarian women alone, however. This is done in such a manner that they remain excluded from public production and cannot earn anything, if they fulfill their duties in the private service of the family; or that they are unable to attend to their family duties, if they wish to participate in public industries and earn a living independently. As in the factory, so women are situated in all business departments up to the medical and legal professions. The modern monogamous family is founded on the open or disguised domestic slavery of women, and modern society is a mass composed of molecules in the form of monogamous families. In the great majority of cases the man has to earn a living and to support his family, at least among the possessing classes. He thereby obtains a superior position that has no need of any legal special privilege. In the family, he is the bourgeois, the woman represents the proletariat.

We are now approaching a social revolution, in which the old economic foundations of monogamy will disappear just as surely as those of its complement, prostitution. Monogamy arose through the concentration of considerable wealth in one hand—a man's hand—and from the endeavor to bequeath this wealth to the children of this man to the exclusion of all others. This necessitated monogamy on the woman's, but not on the man's part. Hence this monogamy of women in no way hindered open or secret polygamy of men. Now, the impending social revolution will reduce this whole care of inheritance to a minimum by changing at least the overwhelming part of permanent and inheritable wealth—the means of production—into social property. Since monogamy was caused by economic conditions, will it disappear when these causes are abolished?

One might reply, not without reason: not only will it not disappear, but it will rather be perfectly realized. For with the transformation of the means of production into collective property, wage labor will also disappear, and with it the proletariat and the necessity for a certain, statistically ascertainable number of women to surrender for money. Prostitution disappears and monogamy, instead of going out of existence, at last becomes a reality—for men also.

With the transformation of the means of production into collective property the monogamous family ceases to be the economic unit of society. The private household changes to a social industry. The care and education of children becomes a public matter. Society cares equally well for all children, legal or illegal. This removes the care about the "consequences" which now forms the essential social factor—moral and economic—hindering a girl to surrender unconditionally to the beloved man. Will not this be sufficient cause for a gradual rise of a more unconventional intercourse of the sexes and a more lenient public opinion regarding virgin honor and female shame? And finally, did we not see that in the modern world monogamy and prostitution, though antitheses, are inseparable and poles of the same social condition? Can prostitution disappear without engulfing at the same time monogamy?

Hence the full freedom of marriage can become general only after all minor economic considerations that still exert such a powerful influence on the choice of a mate for life, have been removed by the abolition of capitalistic production and of the property relations created by it. Then no other motive will remain but mutual fondness. . . . Those peculiarities that were stamped upon the face of monogamy by its rise through property relations, will decidedly vanish, namely the supremacy of men and the indissolubility of marriage. The supremacy of man in marriage is simply the consequence of his economic superiority and will fall with the abolition of the latter.

The indissolubility of marriage is partly the consequence of economic conditions, under which monogamy arose, partly tradition from the time where the connection between this economic situation and monogamy, not yet clearly understood, was carried to extremes by religion. To-day, it has been perforated a thousand times. If marriage founded on love is alone moral, then it follows that marriage is moral only as long as love lasts.

What we may anticipate about the adjustment of sexual relations after the impending downfall of capitalist production is mainly of a negative nature and mostly confined to elements that will disappear. But what will be added? That will be decided after a new generation has come to maturity: a race of men who never in their lives have had any occasion for buying with money or other economic means of power the surrender of a woman; a race of women who have never had any occasion for surrendering to any man for any other reason but love, or for refusing to surrender to their lover from fear of economic consequences. Once such people are in the world, they will not give a moment's thought to what we today believe should be their course. They will follow their own practice and fashion their own public opinion about the individual practice of every person—only this and nothing more.

AN ANTHROPOLOGIST LOOKS AT ENGELS

KATHLEEN GOUGH

In *The Origin of the Family, Private Property and the State*, Engels, building on Lewis Henry Morgan's *Ancient Society,* tried to set forth the development of humanity with respect to economic, political and domestic life. As a whole, the attempt has not been surpassed by any subsequent writer. Several have recently outlined parts of the period of human evolution in the light of modern data. But these studies suffer from one of two drawbacks. Those of anthropologists familiar with recent prehistory and ethnography are almost entirely by upper and middle class men. They tend to assume universal male dominance both in power and creativity, and to ignore the changing conflicts of men and women, as well as of social classes. Those by women are chiefly the work of nonanthropologists whose data tend to be outmoded or inaccurate.[1]

SUMMARY

Engels, like Morgan, posits three main stages of cultural evolution, which Engels divides into nine sub-stages: Lower, Middle and Upper Savagery; Lower, Middle and Upper Barbarism; and Civilization, divided into centralized states characterized, in developmental order, by slavery, serfdom and wage labor.

According to Engels, in Lower Savagery humans, or perhaps prehumans, still lived partly in trees and subsisted on fruits, nuts and roots. Speech developed in this period. Members of the small local group had promiscuous sexual relations. Toward the end of the period, sex relations were banned between adjacent generations, but within each generation,

---

The editors are grateful to Kathleen Gough for kindly preparing the article especially for this anthology.
[1] Among the best of the works of male anthropologists are Leslie A. White, *The Evolution of Culture,* McGraw-Hill, 1959; Elman R. Service, *Primitive Social Organization,* Random House, 1962; and Morton H. Fried, *The Evolution of Political Society,* Random House, 1967. Those by women who are not anthropologists include Simone de Beauvoir's *The Second Sex,* Bantam Books, 1965, and Kate Millett's *Sexual Politics,* Doubleday, 1970.

brothers, sisters and cousins continued to mate indiscriminately and to form consanguine families.

In Middle Savagery, humans spread over the earth, developed fishing, fire-making and some hunting, and invented such weapons as clubs and spears. Engels puts the whole of the Paleolithic into Middle Savagery. Mating became outlawed within the local kin-group, but a group of sisters and female cousins in one band received and shared mates from other bands—often, the group of brothers and male cousins of an adjacent band. This kind of group marriage, which Morgan and Engels called punaluan, yielded a large matrilineal, matrilocal communistic household whose members continued to cooperate economically as well as in sex and in child care.

Upper Savagery saw the bow and arrow invented, hunting increased, and polished stone, basketry, timber houses, villages and dugout canoes come into use. The matrilineal communistic household persisted but toward the end of the period women effected a change from group marriage to pairing marriage—that is, serial monogamy, or occasional polygyny or polyandry, in which both spouses were free to divorce. Engels saw this happening partly because incest and marriage prohibitions became extended so widely that it was hard to continue with sororal or fraternal group marriage, and partly because feminine powers in the matrilocal household became strong enough to put an end to multiple sex unions, which the women found burdensome. The matrilocal communistic household, ruled largely by women, persisted into the era of Barbarism. As population increased, groups of related matrilineal households formed dispersed, out-marrying *gentes* (today more commonly called clans) within the larger tribe.

Pottery was invented in Lower Barbarism. Middle Barbarism began when plants were domesticated in the New World, and animals in the Old. Engels thought that cultivation came much later than the domestication of animals in the Old World, toward the end of Middle Barbarism. The period is represented by the Mexicans, Peruvians, Pueblo Indians and Central Americans in the New World and by the early Aryans and Semites in the Old. During this period in the Old World, private property—especially herds—began to be accumulated by men, who thus acquired new powers over women and were able to switch the descent rule from matriliny to patriliny. Matriarchy, or the rule of women in the domestic economy, was thus overthrown and patriarchy was instituted. Engels calls this the "world historic defeat of the female sex."

Patriarchy continued as the dominant mode through Upper Barbarism into Civilization, and persists in modified form in Western society. As men became supreme in the family as well as in society, they changed pairing marriage with its easy divorce and high status for women into monogamy, in which divorce was either prohibited entirely or permitted only to men. Engels, like Bachofen and others, thought that patriliny and patriarchy were made possible by the newly acquired knowledge of the male role in procreation and thus by the ability to determine physiological fatherhood with accuracy. This knowledge, plus the growth of heritable property in male hands, caused men to institute rules of legitimacy and chastity so that they could be sure that only their physiological sons inherited from them. Such rules, of course, greatly restricted the sexual and social freedom of women.

The position of women was further degraded in Middle Barbarism by slavery—a parallel to the subjugation of domesticated animals. Once slavery had arisen, class society was born, and men of the upper, property-owning class were able to exploit slave women both for their labor and as sexual rivals with their wives. From its beginnings therefore monogamy, far from being the culmination of equal sex love between men and women (as Victorian society portrayed it) in fact marked the oppression of women both as wives and as concubines, and the "double standard" in sexual morality. Women retaliated, however, by creating the cuckold and the paramour.

Along with monogamy, herding, and slavery came the patriarchal household, composed now not solely of relatives but of a nuclear family or group of patrilineal kinsfolk plus their bondservants. The head patriarch might share government of the group with a council of his adult male kinfolk or might have sole rights of life and death over the women, children and slaves.

The patriarchal family became consolidated in Upper Barbarism with the smelting of iron, the invention of the plow, wagon, chariot, et cetera, and the growth of large populations in fortified towns. The Homeric Greeks, the pre-Roman Italians, Tacitus' Germanic tribes, and the Viking Age Normans, exemplified Upper Barbarism.

Alphabetic writing ushered in the age of Civilization, and the state arose, as found in early Athens and Rome. Engels thought that these classical European powers plumbed the lowest depths in the degradation of women, Athens even more so than Rome. In some of the smaller or more peripheral states of early civilization, however, tribal vestiges remained, something similar to pairing marriage persisted, and women had a higher status. Among these were Sparta and—more significant—the Germans who overran the declining Roman empire. Engels erroneously thought that individual sex love arose among the German peoples because of their tendencies to pairing marriage, although he admits somewhat confusingly that it began as courtly or adulterous love, flourishing first in Provence, and only much later superseding the arranged marriages of the Germans.

In spite of the modern European tradition of romantic love and the transition from patriarchal to nuclear family households, marriage in the 1880s showed only a trifling improvement on that in the classical empires. Engels grimly satirizes the French arranged marriage, exhibiting "the fullest unfolding of the contradictions inherent in monogamy—flourishing hetaerism on the part of the husband, and flourishing adultery on the part of the wife." The Catholic church had abolished divorce because "it was convinced that for adultery, as for death, there is no cure whatsoever." Protestant "love" marriage was even worse: "Since the citizens of Protestant countries are mostly Philistines, Protestant monogamy leads merely . . . to a wedded life of leaden boredom, which is described as domestic bliss." In both types marriage was in fact determined by class position and the wife "differs from the ordinary courtesan only in that she does not hire out her body, like a wage worker, on piecework, but sells it into slavery once and for all."

Engels romanticized proletarian marriage, believing that women's work outside the home had removed "the last remnants of male domination in the home"—despite traces of "some of that brutality towards women which became firmly rooted with the establishment of monogamy." Among the propertied classes, however, the husband's position as bread-winner makes him the "bourgeois" within the family, while "the wife represents the proletariat" living in disguised domestic enslavement. Just as the sexual division of tasks in Savagery formed the foundation of all subsequent division of labor, and the subordination of women in Barbarism foreshadowed the birth of class society, so the modern bourgeois family contains within it the contradiction between bourgeoisie and proletariat. It can be resolved only by abolishing the sexual division of labor and instituting communal management of property, collective domestic work and child care, and the full entry of women into all forms of public work in a socialist society.

SOURCES

Engels' theories were limited by the knowledge of his time, and perhaps in part by his own predilections. To give salient examples, modern prehistory suggests that speech developed only long *after* prehumans descended to earth, evolved upright posture, separated the functions of hand and foot, and relied much on hunting.[2] Hunting as a male specialty, separate from female gathering and child care, may have been established

---

[2] See, for example, Charles F. Hockett and Robert Ascher, "The Human Revolution," in *Man in Adaptation: The Biosocial Background*, edited by Yehudi A. Cohen, Aldine, 1968.

up to two million years ago, and there is little evidence to date of its being preceded by an era of predominant fishing. The bow lacks the focal significance in hunting that Engels thought it possessed. All of this suggests a sexual division of labor between hunting and gathering coincident with, or even preceding, the development of language, which is the accepted criterion of the transition to humanness.[3]

Engels dismisses as dead-end side developments the societies of non-human primates as evidence of prehuman social life. Yet comparative primatology (greatly developed since Engels' time), combined with human paleontology and archeology, are the sole sources of real data for reconstructions and speculations about prehuman society. Similarly, accounts of the actual social lives of primitive hunters and gatherers in modern times, although imperfect, are better guides to those of early humans than are Morgan's and Engels' speculations about early family life on the basis of present day kinship terminologies or of classical mythology. The former do not in fact require group marriage to account for the "lumping" of relatives into categories reflective of clans, lineages or other types of kinship group.[4] The "evidence" on which Engels erects his theory of early group marriage is thus quite inadequate.

In the later periods, the domestication of plants in the Old World probably preceded or coincided with that of animals, rather than postdating it. Again, Engels apparently thought that ancient Greece was the first state to have arisen in history, whereas the Greek states were of course preceded by much earlier empires in Egypt, Mesopotamia, India and China. While he may not have known of the antiquity of Asian civilizations, Engels did know a great deal about their structure and about the types of production relations found in them, for he and Marx had earlier differentiated "Asiatic societies" both from slave states and from feudalism. Surprisingly, Engels makes almost no reference to Asian societies in this work, and leaves out the "Asiatic mode of production" as an alternative to slavery and to serfdom. This is unfortunate, for the position of women in the ancient Asian and Middle Eastern empires substantiates Engels' theory that women reached their lowest point of subordination and degradation after the rise of "civilization," the state and the alphabet.

---

[3] Speculations about the dating of speech vary greatly, however. Hockett (1968) puts it as early as the Australopithecenes, up to 1,750,000 years ago; Livingstone, as late as the Upper Paleolithic, some 70,000 to 50,000 years ago. (See Frank B. Livingstone, "Genetics, Ecology and the Origin of Incest and Exogamy," *Current Anthropology*, February 1969.) A more common view would see language, fire making, and some kind of family with incest prohibitions established sometime between the Pithecanthropines of 500,000 years ago and the Neanderthal people of about 100,000 years ago.

[4] For this and other criticisms of Morgan's and (by implication) Engels' theories of group marriage, see Robert H. Lowie, *The History of Ethnological Theory*, Rinehart and Co., 1937, p. 65.

Having mentioned some of the deficiencies of data, let us turn to the theories themselves. First, in spite of the modern increase in knowledge of early society, it must be frankly stated that the earliest forms of human sexual association, and the circumstances surrounding the origin of the family, are unknown. It is not even known whether some kind of family, with restrictions on mating, developed before or after we became human (that is, developed language).

Of mankind's nearer kinsfolk (the great apes), gibbons live in monogamous family groups of a female, her male partner, and her young children. Orangutans live in small clusters of one or two females plus young, with perhaps a nearby male, or in temporary male-female pairs, or in troops of young, unattached males. Gorillas have male-dominant polygynous families of an older male with several mates, sometimes accompanied by young males who may copulate occasionally with a female when the chief is tired or not looking. All of this suggests the possibility of a kind of prehuman family, although without any division of labor or cooperation between the sexes in food provision. (Each adult forages and nests independently; mothers share nests and food with their young.) There *may* have been prehuman restrictions on intercourse between parents and children. Gibbon parents drive off their young of opposite sex at puberty, although no such practice has been noted for orangutans or gorillas.[5]

On the other hand, chimpanzees—our closest primate relatives—do have promiscuous hordes varying in size from three or four to forty individuals. And of the modern great apes chimpanzees, as well as being genetically closest to man, inhabit ecological settings most similar to those from which early humans emerged. They live partly in trees but often on the ground, fleeing into trees from danger. Fruits, nuts, worms, grubs, or small or sick animals provide their food. Chimpanzees go mainly on all fours but sometimes on two feet, and can use and make simple tools. Males are dominant, but not very dominant, over females. Hierarchy among males is unstable, and males often move between groups. A mother attends her young until their puberty at about age ten, and the mother-child group is the only stable unit. That humans emerged—as Engels thought—from similar promiscuous bands seems a plausible, and to me the most likely, theory.

---

[5] Useful studies of primate social life include F. Clark Howell and Francois Bourliere (eds.): *African Ecology and Human Evolution,* 1963; Sherwood L. Washburn, ed.: *Social Life of Early Man and Classification and Human Evolution;* James N. Spuhler, ed.: *Genetic Diversity and Human Behavior,* all Viking Fund Publications in Anthropology; also John Buettner-Janusch: *Origins of Man,* John Wiley and Sons, Inc., 1966; Desmond Morris, ed.: *Primate Ethology,* Aldine, 1967; and as an introduction, Thomas W. McKern and Sharon McKern: *Human Origins: An Introduction to Physical Anthropology,* Prentice-Hall, Inc., 1969.

Assuming promiscuous prehuman or protohuman bands, through what stages did families develop? Here Engels is on shakier ground. There is no evidence whatever of actual, ongoing group marriage among modern hunters and gatherers, although, as Engels saw, there *is* a group quality to marriage in most hunting and gathering, and also in most horticultural and herding societies. Thus, individual marriages are arranged between groups, group members may substitute for dead spouses, and occasional group orgies may occur at festive seasons. But all of this is readily explicable in terms of existing group solidarity and group cooperation in production, distribution and defense; it cannot legitimately be attributed to prior group marriage. Similarly, the prevalence of premarital sex relations in hunting societies does not necessarily point to prior group marriage. It can be understood in that—given the sexual division between male hunting and female gathering—marriage and the family are economic necessities for both adults and children. But sex restrictions on women before marriage do not normally develop until male control of the state and of durable property make them the masters over women, imbued with notions of legitimacy and feminine chastity.

Again, the majority of hunting households are not "communistic" extended families at all but nuclear families of father, mother and children, with occasional polygyny. Still less commonly does the whole band constitute a common household, and when it does, the component nuclear families usually persist as separate residential, mating and commensal units. Although some fifty percent of hunting societies do contain some extended families or smaller stem-families,[6] large extended families as economic cooperative units are far more prevalent in cultivating and herding societies than among the more primitive hunters. And although sororal polygyny occurs in about 77 percent of known hunting societies, the rare institutions that are more suggestive of group marriage (combined polyandry and polygyny within one household, multiple visiting husbands, or what Engels aptly calls the "club" marriages of the Nayars) are found in a small number of specialized, relatively advanced cultivating societies— even in some states—rather than among hunters and gatherers.[7]

---

[6] For exact figures on types of household, marriage, sexual division of labor, band structure, incest and exogamic prohibitions, and other variables among hunters and gatherers compared with other kinds of societies, see G. P. Murdock, *World Ethnographic Sample*, American Anthropologist, 1957; Allan C. Coult, *Cross Tabulations of Murdock's World Ethnographic Sample*, University of Missouri, 1965; and G. P. Murdock, *Ethnographic Atlas*, University of Pittsburgh, 1967. In the last mentioned survey, out of 175 hunting societies, 47 percent had only nuclear families, 38 percent had stem-families, and 14 percent had extended families.

[7] Soviet anthropologists continued to believe in Morgan's and Engels' early "stages" longer than did anthropologists in the West, and some still think that a form of group marriage intervened between promiscuity and pairing marriage. Semyonov, for example,

Matrilocal residence and the germs of matrilineal descent, although found in some 16 percent of hunting societies today, are far less common than is partrilocal residence (63 percent) with incipient patrilineal descent. Statistically, matriliny and matrilocal residence are most closely related not with hunting but with preplow horticulture in the absence of large domesticated animals—that is, with types of economy that Engels would have placed in Lower Barbarism.[8] This does not mean that the very earliest human settlements, following the establishment of incest prohibitions, were definitely *not* matrilocal. In fact, they may have been, for male primates tend to wander between bands far more than do females, and many primate species exclude young bachelors from sex relations with females of their natal groups, driving them off or causing them to live on the periphery until they are old enough to oust their elders.

The earliest human incest prohibitions may, therefore, have involved the expulsion of pubertal males by their elders and their attachment to females of neighboring groups. We cannot, however, say that this was definitely so, and we must acknowledge that patrilocal residence must have occurred among a large proportion of hunting societies long before the domestication of plants and animals—and that it predominates among hunters today. It seems likely, in fact, that matrilineal descent and matrilocal residence never characterized a *general* evolutionary stage of cultural development, but only that they occurred as a common alternative among horticultural (but not predominantly herding) societies and even persisted in some few plow agricultural societies (for example, Nayar, Minangkabau), for some time after the rise of the state.

This leads us to two other points in connection with matriliny. One is that matriliny and patriliny are not related to ignorance or knowledge of physiological paternity, as Engels, Bachofen and others thought they were. All known matrilineal societies—indeed, all known societies—possess a social role of fatherhood, whether or not they understand the male role in procreation. *Social* fatherhood, found in the most primitive known

---

argues that in the stage of group marriage, mating was forbidden within the band but the men of one band had multiple visiting sex relations with the women of a paired, adjacent band. The difficulty is that most of the "survivals" from which Semyonov draws his evidence are found not among hunters but among horticulturalists. (See Y. I. Semyonov, "Group Marriage: Its Nature and Role in the Evolution of Marriage and Family Relations," Seventh International Congress of Anthropological and Ethnological Sciences, Volume IV, Moscow, 1967, pp. 26–31.)

[8] See David F. Aberle, "Matrilineal Descent in Cross Cultural Perspective," in Kathleen Gough and David M. Schneider, eds.: Matrilineal Kinship, University of California Press, 1961, pp. 655–730. The book as a whole is relevant to this discussion of matriliny and "matriarchy." See also Kathleen Gough, "The Origin of the Family," in *Up From Under*, New York, January, 1971.

societies, evidently springs not from physiological knowledge but from the sexual division of labor between men and women, especially in relation to the protection and maintenance of children. It is present in embryo among male apes, who protect females and young from predators, but it became crystallized with the human *economic* division of labor between the sexes, found to date in all known human societies.

The other point is that matriliny does not involve "matriarchy" or female dominance, either in the home or in society, as Engels tended to believe. Matriarchy, as the reverse of patriarchy, has in fact almost certainly never existed.[9] It is true that in most matrilineal societies women have greater personal freedom regarding movement, sexuality, divorce, property ownership and household management than in patrilineal societies of corresponding levels of productivity. These freedoms are perhaps most pronounced in matrilocal, horticultural tribes, where durable property is not yet extensive and husbands move to live with their wives. In particular, women in matrilineal societies experience relatively little control from their fathers and husbands, who belong to different kin groups from their own. Nevertheless, men predominate as heads of households, lineages and communities in matrilineal as in patrilineal societies, and women experience greater or less authority from their mothers' brothers, elder brothers, or even their grown sons. Some degree of male dominance has, in fact, been universal to date in human society, although matrilineal systems are usually kinder to women.

GENERAL APPROACHES

Like other nineteenth-century evolutionists, Engels placed uncritical reliance on what he thought were "survivals" of customs he wished to posit for the distant past. Temple prostitution, for example, is explicable as a product of class societies dominated by priesthoods, just as modern prostitution is explicable as a product of class societies dominated by private, secular ownership of property and by wage labor. Neither form offers evidence of earlier group marriage, or anything else.

With reference to general theory, also, Engels' analysis contains two major flaws. One is that although he purports to offer a "materialist" interpre-

---

[9] Morgan himself disproves the idea of female dominance among the Iroquois, one of the prime instances of "matriarchy" cited by Engels and by many later Marxists. Morgan refers to "the absence of equality between the sexes" and notes that women were subordinate to men, ate after men, and the women (but not men) were publicly whipped as punishment for adultery. War leaders, tribal chiefs, and *sachems* (heads of matrilineal lineages) were men. Women did, however, have a large say in the government of the long house or name of the matrilocal extended family, and women figured as tribal counsellors and religious officials, as well as arranging marriages (Lewis H. Morgan: *The League of the Ho-de-no-Sau-nee or Iroquois,* Human Relations Area Files, 1954).

tation of history—that is, one which traces laws and beliefs to their foundations in modes and relations of production—he does not in fact always do so. This is especially true with reference to group marriage, for Engels does not explain what changes in subsistence patterns underlay the transition from promiscuous to consanguine, consanguine to punaluan, or punaluan to pairing relations. If one considers how a promiscuous, chimpanzee-like group of partly arboreal, largely fructivorous prehunters might have descended to earth in a period of drought, developed a hunting and gathering way of life, and instituted a sexual division of labor and of child protection, it is in fact plausible to argue that they went straight from promiscuity to nuclear families of a kind similar to those among most hunters today. All that would be needed would be for particular male hunters to attach themselves to particular female gatherers and their young, instead of each individual's foraging alone. By such a simple union both sexes would be assured of adequate food, even though (as in most primate societies) they would continue to rely on the combined defense of several males for protection of the band and its young from predators. More durable attachments between male and female might then lead to the expulsion of pubertal males from the family by their mother's ongoing partner, as among gibbons, and perhaps also, of pubertal females by their mothers. This would mean that young males would be likely to mate with young females from other families or even from other bands. Partial "incest prohibitions" may thus have been instituted, which would become extended and regularized with the growth of language, wider economic cooperation, and moral precepts. Although it is not impossible that group marriage intervened between the eras of promiscuity and of family households, it is hard to see how this would come about on the basis of changing material relations, and Engels does not explain it.

The second objection is that when he does rest his argument on changes in material relations, Engels sometimes neglects the secondary impact of political institutions on family structures. Thus, while he traces—correctly, I think—the effect of the growth of private property in increasing male dominance, Engels does not directly refer to the rise of the state as *itself* a powerful factor further subordinating women of both ruling and subject classes. Yet it is clear that men—already the warriors and political leaders in prestate societies—occupied almost all the major governmental roles in early states. This allowed them to vest the male heads of households with previously unknown, despotic powers over women, children and slaves.

APPRAISAL

Despite these criticisms—and many more that could be made—the general trend of Engels' argument still appears to be sound. It is probable that our prehuman ancestors lived in promiscuous bands. It is improbable, but not disproven, that early humans passed through various types of group marriage before they instituted the forms of "pairing marriage," with occasional polygyny and polyandry, that characterize the hunting bands and the horticultural and fishing tribes of modern times. It is true that *gentes* or clans have developed almost universally out of smaller kin groups in "Upper Savagery" or in "Barbarism." It is true that although it is not group marriage in Engels' sense, marriage has a group character in many hunting bands and in most of the more complex tribal societies that have developed with the domestication of plants and animals. In such societies, each individual belongs to a household, a local kin group, a clan or a lineage, whose members are collectively responsible for one another and marry outside their group. Marriage thus entails the movement of either men or women between groups. It is arranged by group representatives; there may be occasional sexual sharing within the group; second spouses are commonly drawn from the same group as the first one; and a group may be obliged to substitute new spouses if former ones die or fail in their obligations. With the development of privately owned, heritable property, and especially with the rise of the state, this group character gradually disappears. Especially in the great agrarian and commercial empires, women become the personal wards of their fathers, their husbands, the male heads of the households in which they reside, or, in the case of bondservants, of their masters. In capitalist society the operative kin group becomes still further whittled away to the nuclear family, in which, in Engels' time, fathers and husbands retained virtually despotic *de facto* power over "their" womenfolk.

Although matriarchy is a fantasy, it is true that matrilineal descent and inheritance—arising historically out of matrilocal residence—is found in some hunting societies and is common, and may once have been very widespread, in horticultural tribes, chiefdoms, and even some small, simply organized states. It is true that women's status is usually higher in such societies than in patrilineal societies of comparable productivity. Engels does not do justice to the variety of kinship systems found in pre-state societies—the many forms of bilateral, nonunilineal, or even double-unilineal systems. It is true, however, that predominantly herding societies tend to be patrilineal and to encourage polygyny for men wealthy in herds. When such societies are not yet states, women are usually freer than they are in the patriarchal empires. They are often, for example, permitted relative freedom of divorce, remarriage, and even of having their children begotten by lovers, provided that such children are strictly allotted to the woman's legal husbands. Nevertheless, the emergence of male private property in herds does seem to have played a large role in the establishment of early patriarchal households and in the concept of legitimacy.

Again, monogamy is not as universal in "civilized" societies as Engels thought; the Islamic and many of the Far Eastern empires preserved optional polygyny, especially for the wealthy and powerful. But it is true that in the archaic states with their sharply divided ruling and subject classes and their reliance on permanent, often irrigated, landed estates and large-scale heritable property, the patriarchal family flowered almost universally, prostitution became endemic, and women of all classes were subjugated in the varying ways that Engels describes.

Engels' ironic picture of marriage in capitalist society largely applies today. The chief difference is that, as he foresaw, the *legal* rights of men and women have become progressively more equal, but (as in the case of racism) this only reveals more nakedly the social and economic discrimination applied to women in every sphere of public and domestic life. Engels is right, moreover, in asserting that only the abolition of privately owned productive property, the movement of women into public work *and* the socialization of domestic work and of child care can bring about equality between men and women. Modern socialist societies, whatever their problems, have gone a considerable distance in the first two respects but have tended to fail in the third. They have also failed to grant women control over their own bodily functions through free access to contraception and abortion and through the abolition of legitimacy. It may even yet be left to Western society to usher in the full emancipation of women, along with the abolition both of capitalism and of the state.

THE POLITICAL ECONOMY OF WOMEN'S LIBERATION

MARGARET BENSTON

The "woman question" is generally ignored in analyses of the class structure of society. This is so because, on the one hand, classes are generally defined by their relation to the means of production and, on the other hand, women are not supposed to have any unique relation to the means of production. The category seems instead to cut across all classes; one speaks of working-class women, middle-class women, et cetera. The status of women is clearly inferior to that of men, but analysis of this condition usually falls into discussing socialization, psychology, interpersonal relations, or the role of marriage as a social institution. Are these, however, the primary factors? In arguing that the roots of the secondary status of women are in fact economic, it can be shown that women as a group do indeed have a definite relation to the means of production and that this is different from that of men. The personal and psychological factors then follow from this special relation to production, and a change in the latter will be a necessary (but not sufficient) condition for changing the former. If this special relation of women to production is accepted, the analysis of the situation of women fits naturally into a class analysis of society.

The starting point for discussion of classes in a capitalist society is the distinction between those who own the means of production and those who sell their labor power for a wage. As Ernest Mandel says:

> The proletarian condition is, in a nutshell, the lack of access to the means of production or means of subsistence which, in a society of generalized commodity production, forces the proletarian to sell his labor power. In exchange for this labor power he receives a wage which then enables him to acquire the means of consumption necessary for satisfying his own needs and those of his family.
>
> This is the structural definition of wage earner, the proletarian. From it necessarily flows a certain relationship to his work, to the

---

Excerpted from Margaret Benston, "The Political Economy of Women's Liberation," *Monthly Review*, XXI (New York: Monthly Review, September, 1969), n. 4, 13–27.

products of his work, and to his overall situation in society, which can be summarized by the catchword alienation. But there does not follow from this structural definition any necessary conclusions as to the level of his consumption . . . the extent of his needs, or the degree to which he can satisfy them.[1]

We lack a corresponding structural definition of women. What is needed first is not a complete examination of the symptoms of the secondary status of women, but instead a statement of the material conditions in capitalist (and other) societies which define the group "women." Upon these conditions are built the specific superstructures which we know. An interesting passage from Mandel points the way to such a definition:

> The commodity . . . is a product created to be exchanged on the market, as opposed to one which has been made for direct consumption. *Every commodity must have both a use-value and an exchange-value.*
>
> It must have a use-value or else nobody would buy it. . . . A commodity without a use-value to anyone would consequently be unsalable, would constitute useless production, would have no exchange-value precisely because it had no use-value.
>
> On the other hand, every product which has use-value does not necessarily have exchange-value. It has an exchange-value only to the extent that the society itself, in which the commodity is produced, is founded on exchange, is a society where exchange is a common practice. . . .
>
> In capitalist society, commodity production, the production of exchange-values, has reached its greatest development. It is the first society in human history where the major part of production consists of commodities. It is not true, however, that all production under capitalism is commodity production. Two classes of products still remain simple use-value.
>
> The first group consists of all things produced by the peasantry for its own consumption, everything directly consumed on the farms where it is produced. . . .
>
> The second group of products in capitalist society which are not commodities but remain simple use-value consists of all things produced in the home. Despite the fact that considerable human labor goes into this type of household production, it still remains a production of use-values and not of commodities. Every time a soup is made or a button sewn on a garment, it constitutes production, but it is not production for the market.

---

[1] Ernest Mandel, "Workers Under Neocapitalism," paper delivered at Simon Fraser University. (Available through the Department of Political Science, Sociology and Anthropology, Simon Fraser University, Burnaby, B.C., Canada.)

> The appearance of commodity production and its subsequent
> regularization and generalization have radically transformed the
> way men labor and how they organize society.[2]

What Mandel may not have noticed is that his last paragraph is precisely correct. The appearance of commodity production has indeed transformed the way that *men* labor. As he points out, most household labor in capitalist society (and in the existing socialist societies, for that matter) remains in the premarket stage. This is the work which is reserved for women and it is in this fact that we can find the basis for a definition of women.

In sheer quantity, household labor, including child care, constitutes a huge amount of socially necessary production. Nevertheless, in a society based on commodity production, it is not usually considered "real work" since it is outside of trade and the marketplace. It is precapitalist in a very real sense. This assignment of household work as the function of a special category "women" means that this group *does* stand in a different relation to production than the group "men." We will tentatively define women, then, as that group of people who are responsible for the production of simple use-values in those activities associated with the home and family.

Since men carry no responsibility for such production, the difference between the two groups lies here. Notice that women are not excluded from commodity production. Their participation in wage labor occurs but, as a group, they have no structural responsibility in this area and such participation is ordinarily regarded as transient. Men, on the other hand, are responsible for commodity production; they are not, in principle, given any role in household labor. For example, when they do participate in household production, it is regarded as more than simply exceptional; it is demoralizing, emasculating, even harmful to health. (A story on the front page of the *Vancouver Sun* in January 1969 reported that men in Britain were having their health endangered because they had to do too much housework!)

The material basis for the inferior status of women is to be found in just this definition of women. In a society in which money determines value, women are a group who work outside the money economy. Their work is not worth money, is therefore valueless, is therefore not even real work. And women themselves, who do this valueless work, can hardly be expected to be worth as much as men, who work for money. In structural terms, the closest thing to the condition of women is the condition of

---

[2] Ernest Mandel, *An Introduction to Marxist Economic Theory* (New York: Merit Publishers, 1967), pp. 10–11.

others who are or were also outside of commodity production, that is, serfs and peasants.

In her recent paper on women, Juliet Mitchell introduces the subject as follows:

> In advanced industrial society, women's work is only marginal to the total economy. Yet it is through work that man changes natural conditions and thereby produces society. Until there is a revolution in production, the labor situation will prescribe women's situation within the world of men.[3]

The statement of the marginality of women's work is an unanalyzed recognition that the work women do is *different* from the work that men do. Such work is not marginal, however; it is just not wage labor and so is not counted. She even says later in the same article, "Domestic labor, even today, is enormous if quantified in terms of productive labor." She gives some figures to illustrate: in Sweden, 2,340 million hours a year are spent by women in housework compared with 1,290 million hours spent by women in industry. And the Chase Manhattan Bank estimates a woman's overall work week at 99.6 hours.

However, Mitchell gives little emphasis to the basic economic factors (in fact she condemns most Marxists for being "overly economist") and moves on hastily to superstructural factors, because she notices that "the advent of industrialization has not so far freed women." What she fails to see is that no society has thus far industrialized housework. Engels points out that the

> first premise for the emancipation of women is the reintroduction of the entire female sex into public industry. . . . And this has become possible not only as a result of modern large-scale industry, which not only permits the participation of women in production in large numbers, but actually calls for it and, moreover, strives to convert private domestic work also into a public industry.[4]

And later in the same passage:

> Here we see already that the emancipation of women and their equality with men are impossible and must remain so as long as

---

[3] Juliet Mitchell, "Women: The Longest Revolution," *New Left Review*, December 1966.

[4] Friedrich Engels, *Origin of the Family, Private Property and the State* (Moscow: Progress Publishers, 1968), Chapter IX, p. 158. The anthropological evidence known to Engels indicated primitive woman's dominance over man. Modern anthropology disputes this dominance but provides evidence for a more nearly equal position of women in the matrilineal societies used by Engels as examples. The arguments in this work of Engels do not require the former dominance of women but merely their former equality, and so the conclusions remain unchanged.

women are excluded from socially productive work and restricted to housework, which is private.

What Mitchell has not taken into account is that the problem is not simply one of getting women into *existing* industrial production but the more complex one of converting private production of household work into public production.

For most North Americans, domestic work as "public production" brings immediate images of Brave New World or of a vast institution—a cross between a home for orphans and an army barracks—where we would all be forced to live. For this reason, it is probably just as well to outline here, schematically and simplistically, the nature of industrialization.

A preindustrial production unit is one in which production is small-scale and reduplicative; that is, there is a great number of little units, each complete and just like all the others. Ordinarily such production units are in some way kin-based and they are multipurpose, fulfilling religious, recreational, educational, and sexual functions along with the economic function. In such a situation, desirable attributes of an individual, those which give prestige, are judged by more than purely economic criteria: for example, among approved character traits are proper behavior to kin or readiness to fulfill obligations.

Such production is originally not for exchange. But if exchange of commodities becomes important enough, then increased efficiency of production becomes necessary. Such efficiency is provided by the transition to industrialized production which involves the elimination of the kin-based production unit. A large-scale, nonreduplicative production unit is substituted which has only one function, the economic one, and where prestige or status is attained by economic skills. Production is rationalized, made vastly more efficient, and becomes more and more public—part of an integrated social network. An enormous expansion of man's productive potential takes place. Under capitalism such social productive forces are utilized almost exclusively for private profit. These can be thought of as *capitalized* forms of production.

If we apply the above to housework and child rearing, it is evident that each family, each household, constitutes an individual production unit, a preindustrial entity, in the same way that peasant farmers or cottage weavers constitute preindustrial production units. The main features are clear, with the reduplicative, kin-based, private nature of the work being the most important. (It is interesting to notice the other features: the multipurpose functions of the family, the fact that desirable attributes for women do not center on economic prowess, et cetera.) The rationalization of production effected by a transition to large-scale production has not taken place in this area.

Industrialization is, in itself, a great force for human good; exploitation and dehumanization go with capitalism and not necessarily with industrialization. To advocate the conversion of private domestic labor into a public industry under capitalism is quite a different thing from advocating such conversion in a socialist society. In the latter case the forces of production would operate for human welfare, not private profit, and the result should be liberation, not dehumanization. In this case we can speak of *socialized* forms of production.

These definitions are not meant to be technical but rather to differentiate between two important aspects of industrialization. Thus the fear of the barracks-like result of introducing housekeeping into the public economy is most realistic under capitalism. With socialized production and the removal of the profit motive and its attendant alienated labor, there is no reason why, *in an industrialized society*, industrialization of housework should not result in better production, that is, better food, more comfortable surroundings, more intelligent and loving child-care, et cetera, than in the present nuclear family.

The argument is often advanced that, under neocapitalism, the work in the home has been much reduced. Even if this is true, it is not structurally relevant. Except for the very rich, who can hire someone to do it, there is for most women, an irreducible minimum of necessary labor involved in caring for home, husband, and children. For a married woman without children this irreducible minimum of work probably takes fifteen to twenty hours a week; for a woman with small children the minimum is probably seventy or eighty hours a week. (There is some resistance to regarding child-rearing as a job. That labor is involved, that is, the production of use-value, can be clearly seen when exchange-value is also involved—when the work is done by babysitters, nurses, child-care centers, or teachers. An economist has already pointed out the paradox that if a man marries his housekeeper, he reduces the national income, since the money he gives her is no longer counted as wages.) The reduction of housework to the minimums given is also expensive; for low-income families more labor is required. In any case, household work remains structurally the same—a matter of private production.

One function of the family, the one taught to us in school and the one which is popularly accepted, is the satisfaction of emotional needs: the needs for closeness, community, and warm secure relationships. This society provides few other ways of satisfying such needs; for example, work relationships or friendships are not expected to be nearly as important as a man-woman-with-children relationship. Even other ties of kinship are increasingly secondary. This function of the family is important in stabilizing it so that it can fulfill the second, purely economic, function discussed above. The wage-earner, the husband-father, whose earnings support himself, also "pays for" the labor done by the mother-wife and supports the children. The wages of a man buy the labor of two people. The crucial importance of this second function of the family can be seen when the family unit breaks down in divorce. The continuation of the economic function is the major concern where children are involved; the man must continue to pay for the labor of the woman. His wage is very often insufficient to enable him to support a second family. In this case his emotional needs are sacrificed to the necessity to support his ex-wife and children. That is, when there is a conflict the economic function of the family very often takes precedence over the emotional one. And this in a society which teaches that the major function of the family is the satisfaction of emotional needs.

As an economic unit, the nuclear family is a valuable stabilizing force in capitalist society. Since the production which is done in the home is paid for by the husband-father's earnings, his ability to withhold his labor from the market is much reduced. Even his flexibility in changing jobs is limited. The woman, denied an active place in the market, has little control over the conditions that govern her life. Her economic dependence is reflected in emotional dependence, passivity, and other "typical" female personality traits. She is conservative, fearful, supportive of the status quo.

Furthermore, the structure of this family is such that it is an ideal consumption unit. But this fact, which is widely noted in Women's Liberation literature, should not be taken to mean that this is its primary function. If the above analysis is correct, the family should be seen primarily as a production unit for housework and child-rearing. *Everyone* in capitalist society is a consumer; the structure of the family simply means that it is particularly well suited to encourage consumption. Women in particular *are* good consumers; this follows naturally from their responsibility for matters in the home. Also, the inferior status of women, their general lack of a strong sense of worth and identity, make them more exploitable than men and hence better consumers.

The history of women in the industrialized sector of the economy has depended simply on the labor needs of that sector. Women function as a massive reserve army of labor. When labor is scarce (early industrialization, the two world wars, et cetera) then women form an important part of the labor force. When there is less demand for labor (as now under neocapitalism) women become a surplus labor force—but one for which their husbands and not society are economically responsible. The "cult of the home" makes its reappearance during times of labor surplus and is used to channel women out of the market economy. This is relatively easy since the pervading ideology ensures that no one, man or woman, takes women's participation in the labor force very seriously. Women's real work, we are taught, is in the home; this holds whether or not they are married, single, or the heads of households.

At all times household work is the responsibility of women. When they are working outside the home they must somehow manage to get both outside job and housework done (or they supervise a substitute for the housework). Women, particularly married women with children, who work outside the home simply do two jobs; their participation in the labor force is only allowed if they continue to fulfill their first responsibility in the home. This is particularly evident in countries like Russia and those in Eastern Europe where expanded opportunities for women in the labor force have not brought about a corresponding expansion in their liberty. Equal access to jobs outside the home, while one of the preconditions for women's liberation, will not in itself be sufficient to give equality for women; as long as work in the home remains a matter of private production and is the responsibility of women, they will simply carry a double work load.

A second prerequisite for women's liberation which follows from the above analysis is the conversion of the work now done in the home as private production into work to be done in the public economy. To be more specific, this means that child-rearing should no longer be the responsibility solely of the parents. Society must begin to take responsibility for children; the economic dependence of women and children on the husband-father must be ended. The other work that goes on in the home must also be changed—communal eating places and laundries for example. When such work is moved into the public sector, then the material basis for discrimination against women will be gone.

These are only preconditions. The idea of the inferior status of women is deeply rooted in the society and will take a great deal of effort to eradicate. But once the structures which produce and support that idea are changed then, and only then, can we hope to make progress. It is possible, for example, that a change to communal eating places would simply mean that women are moved from a home kitchen to a communal one. This *would* be an advance, to be sure, particularly in a socialist society where work would not have the inherently exploitative nature it does now. Once women are freed from private production in the home, it will probably be very difficult to maintain for any long period of time a rigid definition of jobs by sex. This illustrates the interrelation between the two preconditions given above: true equality in job opportunity is probably impossible without freedom from housework, and the industrialization of housework is unlikely unless women are leaving the home for jobs.

The changes in production necessary to get women out of the home might seem to be, in theory, possible under capitalism. One of the sources of women's liberation movements may be the fact that alternative capitalized forms of home production now exist. Day care is available, even if inadequate and perhaps expensive; convenience foods, home delivery of meals, and take-out meals are widespread; laundries and cleaners offer bulk rates. However, cost usually prohibits a complete dependence on such facilities, and they are not available everywhere, even in North America. These should probably then be regarded as embryonic forms rather than completed structures. However, they clearly stand as alternatives to the present system of getting such work done. Particularly in North America, where the growth of "service industries" is important in maintaining the growth of the economy, the contradictions between these alternatives and the need to keep women in the home will grow.

The need to keep women in the home arises from two major aspects of the present system. First, the amount of unpaid labor performed by women is very large and very profitable to those who own the means of production. To pay women for their work, even at minimum wage scales, would imply a massive redistribution of wealth. At present, the support of a family is a hidden tax on the wage earner—his wage buys the labor power of two people. And second, there is the problem of whether the economy can expand enough to put all women to work as a part of the normally employed labor force. The war economy has been adequate to draw women partially into the economy but not adequate to establish a need for all or most of them. If it is argued that the jobs created by the industrialization of housework will create this need, then one can counter by pointing to (1) the strong economic forces operating for the status quo and against capitalization discussed above, and (2) the fact that the present service industries, which somewhat counter these forces, have not been able to keep up with the growth of the labor force as presently constituted. The present trends in the service industries simply create "underemployment" in the home; they do not create new jobs for women. So long as this situation exists, women remain a very convenient and elastic part of the industrial reserve army. Their incorporation into the labor force on terms of equality—which would create pressure for capitalization of housework—is possible only with an economic expansion so far achieved by neocapitalism only under conditions of full-scale war mobilization.

In addition, such structural changes imply the complete breakdown of the present nuclear family. The stabilizing consuming functions of the family, plus the ability of the cult of the home to keep women out of the labor market, serve neocapitalism too well to be easily dispensed with. And, on a less fundamental level, even if these necessary changes in the nature of household production were achieved under capitalism it would have the unpleasant consequence of including *all* human relations in the cash nexus. The atomization and isolation of people in Western society is already sufficiently advanced to make it doubtful if such complete psychic isolation could be tolerated. It is likely in fact that one of the major negative emotional responses to women's liberation movements may be exactly such a fear. If this is the case, then possible alternatives—cooperatives, the kibbutz, et cetera—can be cited to show that psychic needs for community and warmth can in fact be better satisfied if other structures are substituted for the nuclear family.

At best the change to capitalization of housework would only give women the same limited freedom given most men in capitalist society. This does not mean, however, that women should wait to demand freedom from discrimination. There *is* a material basis for women's status; we are not merely discriminated against, we are exploited. At present, our unpaid labor in the home is necessary if the entire system is to function. Pressure created by women who challenge their role will reduce the effectiveness of this exploitation. In addition, such challenges will impede the functioning of the family and may make the channeling of women out of the labor force less effective. All of these will hopefully make quicker the transition to a society in which the necessary structural changes in production can actually be made. That such a transition will require a revolution I have no doubt; our task is to make sure that revolutionary changes in the society do in fact end women's oppression.

Who am I? What am I? Early socialization, in the family and in other primary groups, gives women such a deep sense of inferiority, reinforced later by further socialization and low-status roles, that they have not yet been able to develop a sustained interest in their social condition. Recent social movements for black civil rights and against the war in Viet Nam, and the expanding employment opportunities have, however, reawakened woman's concern about her customary low status. She has begun to probe her conflicting and ambiguous social roles. Women who have generally accepted their mixed feelings, frustrations, and lack of satisfaction with their lives as being due to some inner fault—a failure to be a good woman according to Biblical injunction, or Freudian precepts, or the latest findings of child psychologists—are now seeking new explanations.

The essentials of woman's problem in the United States can be reduced to this: *can I be both a successful woman and a successful person?* The dilemma has its contradictions in feelings and actions, in opportunities and rewards, and in rights and responsibilities. Every woman feels some of the effects of the ambiguous demands, of low prestige, of the lesser power of *woman* as compared to *person* (which in its usage often borders close to meaning "man"). Some effects are very evident: the desire for children and the inability to afford them—or conversely, unwanted children; the lack of daycare facilities for children, low pay, unequal job opportunities and training; the two jobs of the working wife. Others are more subtle, but no less important: the stigma attached to being an intellectual woman; the cult of youthfulness and of woman as sex object; her vague feelings of worthlessness if she accepts only the traditional roles of wife and mother, and her feelings of being unfeminine if she does not; her frequent lack of self-confidence; and her self-contempt which makes her prefer the company of men to that of women, perpetuating the myth of feminine duplicity.

WHAT IS THE SIGN OF A SUCCESSFUL WOMAN? Marriage. This is the cultural definition of the setting within which a woman is supposed to make a success of her life so that failure to marry, or failure in marriage is total failure for many women while for men, it is only a partial failure. Marriage defines a woman's responsibilities and her appropriate social character. She is a homemaker, and cares for her children while her husband leaves home to earn a living for the family. In her role as wife, she is expected to be dependent, and acquiescent; in her role as mother, she is expected to be independent and assertive. She must be more concerned with meeting the emotional needs of her husband and her children than with growing through an understanding of her own needs; this proves she has the so-called "giving ability" of the mature woman. She must be able to cope with a technical, bureaucratic society without having been encouraged, usually, to develop the necessary logic and assertiveness. Furthermore, she must somehow manage through all of this to remain an interesting person in her own right, sexually and emotionally attractive to her husband and to other men (though disinterested in other men!).

WHAT IS THE SIGN OF A SUCCESSFUL PERSON? Occupational achievement. A person's worth in American society is generally thought to be indicated by occupation (which is closely related to income) so that physicians, architects, businessmen, and college professors are considered of greater worth than upholsterers, taxi drivers, or salesmen. Men are usually expected to demonstrate their manhood by the ability to provide an income for their families. Physical attractiveness, the ability to attract and hold the affection of a member of the opposite sex, and performance as a spouse and parent are nearly the sole criteria by which women are usually judged. None of these come anywhere near to being as important in judging a man. To a minority of men, the argument that child-rearing and homemaking are very creative may carry a good deal of weight. Even to them, however, it is probably likely that homemaker and mother are not considered genuine equivalents of activities men do outside the home.

The primary occupation of most married women is that of housewife (known as "just-a-housewife" to television interviewers of many American women). She is treated as an unanalyzed, residual statistical unit in many social science analyses. Housewives are lumped together in most studies, or at most, categorized in terms of the occupation of the husband. The work women do in the household is considered less valuable than that performed in the marketplace. Thus, cooking, cleaning, sewing, home decorating, child care, and home entertaining carry relatively little prestige while large-scale food preparation, industrial cleaning, tailoring, interior decorating, teaching, and catering services are respected market activities. This low evaluation is partly perpetuated by the exclusion of household work from the calculation of Gross National Product—the most important measure of a nation's wealth.

There are occupations which are considered to be compatible with being an ideal woman; nursing, secretarial work, public school teaching, writing, and painting, for example, are acceptable. Women frequently find it difficult to get the necessary training for "less womanly" work. If she has the training, she may face other problems: she frequently finds it difficult to get a job, to be promoted, and to be paid the same as a comparably capable man. On the job, she may find herself excluded from colleague-ship and sponsorship—each of which is important in the furthering of careers. Moreover, a woman's full-time commitment to a job or a career is considered a stumbling block in the fulfillment of her duties as a woman; if she pursues a career, she supposedly lessens her likelihood of marrying, while if she does marry, the career woman presumably will neglect her husband and children. (When it seems convenient, the norms can be changed. Then, low-income mothers may be urged to leave their children while they enter the labor force to increase their self-respect.)

In contrast, a man's commitment to a career or to community activity is not considered to reduce his willingness to marry nor is it considered to interfere seriously with his duties to his wife and children; in fact, it enhances his worth in the eyes of both society, and his marriageable women friends.

Being a woman and a person is further complicated for the working wife. While working wives make an important contribution to family in-come—40 percent worked full-time by 1969—they continue to retain the major responsibility for homemaking and child care. A wife's job may even be seen by her husband as a threat to his own sense of success; it may even be a major source of tension between them, although this may exist more as a potential in the view of nonworking wives and their spouses than it does among couples where the wife works.

The problems outlined in this discussion will now be considered in more detail with respect to (1) sex-role differentiation, (2) the marriage rela-tionship, (3) the economic contribution of married women to the family, and (4) the job market for women.

SEX-ROLE DIFFERENTIATION

In American society, as in all others, some tasks are considered to be ap-propriately performed by women, others to be appropriately performed by men, and some are appropriately performed by either sex. There seems to be little relationship between the task which is assigned and the biological capabilities of the two sexes. In Western societies, as far as the day-by-day work tasks are concerned, the woman traditionally carries out home duties, while practically everything else is man's work; within the institutions outside the family, there is a similar division of labor by sex. Charlotte Perkins Gilman, a leading feminist, summarized the distribution of social roles, which still pertains today in spite of many changes, when she wrote in 1914:

> From her first faint struggles toward freedom and justice, to her present valiant efforts toward full economic and political equality, each step has been termed 'unfeminine,' and resented as an intrusion upon man's place and power. Woman's natural work as a female is that of the mother; man's natural work as a male is that of the father—but human work covers all our life outside of these specialities. That one sex should have monopolized all human activities, called them 'man's work,' and managed them as such, is what is meant by the phrase 'Androcentric Culture.'

What accounts for a continuing division of labor by sex? The answer may appear clear about societies which are not concerned with sexual equality; men, and frequently women, too, do not want, and will not allow changes to occur which would eliminate sex-roles in work, politics, home, and the like. It is more difficult to understand what happens in societies in which the avowed intention is to redistribute sex roles so that "man's work" and "woman's work" disappear.

In the first reading, Yonina Talmon examines the relationship of an egalitarian ideology, the life cycle, and affluence to sex-role differentiation in the kibbutz. She is only partly successful in her attempt to find the sociocultural variables that lead to a drift from undifferentiated sex roles back to the traditional roles. For example, she has not seriously considered the effects of the surrounding Israeli society, which is characterized by ideologies and social structures which may be more antagonistic than supportive of sex equality, nor has she seriously considered the effects of monogamous marriage on sex-role differentiation. Many assumptions about appropriate roles in the family are considered in more detail in the section on the marriage relationship which appears later in Part Three.

In the second reading, George Levinger considers the sex-role differentiation that occurs within the family starting from Talcott Parsons' theory that there must be a division of labor between husband and wife, where the former concentrates on instrumental tasks and the latter on socioemotional tasks. Thus, the husband manages the family's relation to the environment outside the home and brings income to the family; the wife carries out the socioemotional tasks which social scientists have asserted are related to the new needs which the family meets. Support for this division of labor, between instrumental and socioemotional tasks comes from studies of small groups. Levinger's study suggests, however, that while this division of labor may hold in multiple-person small groups, it does not seem to describe the two-person group. While Levinger's study cannot be taken as definitive—it is only one study, on a small sample of middle-class families—his findings suggest a lack of inevitability in this particular kind of sex-role differentiation.

THE MARRIAGE RELATIONSHIP

As the American family has gradually lost most of its traditional activities, social scientists have looked for new activities to explain why people persist in marrying and remarrying. In fact, in spite of a rising divorce rate, an increasing proportion of the population since 1900 has actually married. Supposedly, the activities which explained the existence of the family were those of providing a socially approved setting for production of goods and services, sexual relations, reproduction, and the socialization of children. Now, however, production occurs away from the home in the marketplace; extramarital sexual partners as well as pre- and postmarital partners are more easily available; birth control techniques and the preference for small families have limited reproductive activities; even childbearing outside of marriage is increasingly tolerated. The socialization of young children remains one of the few activities which is still carried on mainly by the family. Aside from socialization, there is one new activity which social scientists consider critical in explaining the persistence of the family. That activity is providing emotional support for family members, important for all members, but asserted to be the very basis of the husband-wife relationship.

While the conjugal family system is being given new importance by social scientists, it is currently subject by young people to the most severe criticism it has experienced since the Russians temporarily abolished obligatory marriage in 1926. For many young people do not agree with social scientists that the family is a natural and inevitable system, but rather they see it as a historically developed system. In America and Europe, young women and men are trying a variety of living arrangements inside and outside of marriage. Heterosexual, homosexual, and bisexual relations, childbearing in and out of marriage, child care by men as well as women, communal living, group marriage, and quasi-extended families not based on kinship are among the alternatives being tried. Those who are experimenting consider it critical to replace the sex-differentiated roles of the conjugal family system. They believe it may be possible to do so by finding a socially acceptable alternative to the conjugal family itself.

The articles on marriage included in this section of the reader treat the husband-wife relationship in the accepted social science perspective; that is, as if it were the critical binding element of contemporary monogamous marriage. Elsewhere in the book, essays consider the marriage relationship in other forms, including ones which could not really be called "marriage" in the traditional sense, since the woman-man relationship exists outside of that context.[1]

In the first reading, Barclay Johnson summarizes the views of Emile Durkheim on womanhood and marriage as these appear in *Suicide* (1897). Durkheim was one of the nineteenth-century founders of sociology, and a source of much twentieth-century sociological thought; this will be apparent to the reader if a comparison is made between the views of Durkheim, Talcott Parsons, Peter L. Berger, and Hansfried Kellner, and the views presented in most texts on the family, courtship, and marriage.[2]

In the second selection, Talcott Parsons, a leading scholar of the functional sociological approach, presents his analysis of the kinship system, woman's place in it, and the relationship of these to the economic system. A division of labor between husband and wife is posited to be necessary for the functioning of the existing economic system; therefore, the division of labor is a necessary component of a family which would be compatible with the economic system. (Parsons indicates some specific reasons why he thinks this is the case.) Parsons considers that harmony in interpersonal relationships, as well as in the social system, and especially in affectionate and emotionally supportive relations, demands that the interests of one member of any such relationship (in his analysis, the wife) be subordinated to the interests of the other (the husband). Thus, while the husband's world is outside of the home, the wife's world is in the home. According to Parsons, the segregation of activities and their unequal prestige—for example, women often say they would like to be doctors, lawyers, and do other of men's work while men rarely say they would like to be housewives—is redressed by the wife participating in humanistic activities. These activities are indicated by Parsons to be the *de facto* equivalence of the man's activities outside the home (work, politics, civic clubs) and avoid a clash of interest between spouses since the woman's activities are

---

[1] See the article by Yonina Talmon in this reader. See also the discussions by Bernhard J. Stern, William J. Goode, and Juliet Mitchell in Part One; by Judd Marmor, Kathleen Gough and Friedrich Engels in Part Two; Mihaly Vajda and Agnes Heller in Part Five.

[2] For examples, see Robert F. Winch, *The Modern Family* (New York: Holt, Rinehart and Winston, Inc., 1963); Norman W. Bell and Egon F. Vogel (eds.), *The Family* (Glencoe: The Free Press, 1960).

ones in which the husband has little interest, involvement, or skill. (Compare this with Durkheim's suggestions of 1897 about the future activities of married women, as discussed in the reading by Johnson.) Parsons himself, however, unwittingly recognizes the lack of *de facto* equality between the activities of women and men outside the home when he notes that women show the strains of the feminine role when they "*give unwarranted importance to such activities,*" without indicating, it should be added, how he came to judge the importance to be "unwarranted." In other writings, Parsons further elaborates on the role strains. The assumption that the family is the natural social unit, and that the division of labor must characterize even an intimate two-person group remains so basic to his views that the recognition of role strains does not lead to a reanalysis of the compatibility of the family and the economy; for example, it is possible that any compatibility is between the man's roles in the family rather than between the family and the economy.

In the next reading, Peter L. Berger and Hansfried Kellner present a social psychological analysis, in contrast to Parsons' structural one, which starts with the problem of *anomie* as posed by Emile Durkheim. They consider the middle-class urban family in the industrial Western world as the place in which its members can develop some sense of order and control they do not experience in society. The husband and wife, they suggest, through sharing their experiences and their thoughts and interpretations, develop a miniature world of their own, providing themselves with order which they actually consider to exist outside of themselves. Both stabilize the sense of who they are, and the couple finds solace in the haven of the domestically constructed social reality. The husband uses the marriage relationship in an additional way: his sense of powerlessness, derived from his everyday experiences in an unfulfilling job, and his cynical view of political action, is mitigated—according to Berger and Kellner—by the sense of control he may feel in the charmed circle of the family, where he can play at being "master."

Several aspects of the Berger and Kellner analysis are especially pertinent to understanding women's roles in the family, as well as to the treatment of women in sociological analysis itself. At first glance, it appears as if Berger and Kellner loosen the marriage relationship somewhat from cultural prescriptions by considering it to be developed, through social interaction by the spouses. This is in contrast to Parsons. He considers marriage, basically, a system shaped by explicit cultural norms, while Berger and Kellner consider cultural norms to effect the marital relationship but not determine it to the same extent. The latter analysis might suggest that less differentiated sex roles could be developed; the process of social interaction would be the means by which the possibly traumatic consequences of deviating from conventional sex-role prescriptions could be avoided. Marriage in the Berger and Kellner conception provides a setting wherein new ways of behaving could be developed and justified.

The second particularly pertinent aspect of their analysis is this: according to Berger and Kellner, marriage is the key relationship within which *men* can construct a social reality with which they can cope, in contrast to the job and politics, and in which they may have a feeling of being in control. Men return to the confines of most American homes, to wives and children over whom they may exert or feign control. Yet, this analysis ignores women who appear to have no comparable context into which they can escape from their own everyday frustrations with politics, and with repetitive household chores, small and demanding children, and the daily isolation in the home from easy contacts with adults. For the 40 percent of married women who work, a job may be an escape from the home, but there, they experience the same problems as their husbands. Women may play "mistress" over small children, domestic helpers, and pets, but this is hardly different from men playing "master" over secretaries and file clerks, receptionists and telephone operators, and cashiers and waitresses whom they encounter on the job and in other daily experiences outside the home. Homemaking and work do not appear to provide the sexes with equivalent structures. The recent diminution in the importance of the "feminine mystique" and of the "work ethic" may be signs that women and men are both becoming aware of their oppression by these socially-prescribed definitions of how they should relate to each other.

Moreover, it is in the Berger and Kellner analysis of the marriage as a haven for the man that the relation between *culture* as a determinant of social behavior and *social interaction* as a determinant of social reality become quite blurred. It is not the idiosyncratic development of social reality which gives the man the chance to bolster his sagging self-esteem and low morale. The cultural norms prescribe that women have more responsibility for their husband's morale than *vice versa;* the cultural norms prescribe that women have less responsibility for certain critical decisions, such as moving from one community to another, than their husbands; the cultural norms prescribe that women have more responsibility than their husbands in the management of the household. These prescriptions long antedate urban, industrial United States, and appear to persist in spite of the middle-class ideology of husband-wife equality.

If social science views of marriage are at best incomplete, often taking male domination and female subordination for granted, what about the views of marriage presented in the mass media to which women may look for help in problem-solving, and for behavioral models? Mary and David Hatch in the next article show that there is a gap between the status and characteristic problems of magazine readership and magazine heroines.

A woman makes two overlooked and important economic contributions to her family's standard of living by the services she renders as a housewife and by the earnings she receives as a worker in the labor force. The sparse attention given to these contributions reinforces both society's attitude towards women and women's views of themselves.[3]

The value of work done by housewives is almost totally ignored by economists and statisticians who exclude it from the calculation of the money value of a nation's output. As a result, women's work is considered of value only when it is done in exchange for money. This is aptly noted by Sylvia Gelber, the director of the Women's Bureau of the Canadian Department of Labor:[4]

> If a number of bachelors who were employing housekeepers in the customary manner of exchanging services for money, decided to marry these housekeepers, then the national dividend would be diminished! Obviously the housekeeper, when assuming the role of a wife, regardless of any additional services she assumed by virtue of her marriage, continued to perform those services which she, as a housekeeper, had been performing previously. In other words, the services continued but the value disappeared!

Because of this lack of systematic calculation of the magnitude of the value of a housewife's services, she is at an economic disadvantage compared with women who work for money. For while workers in the labor force receive such benefits as health insurance, pensions and paid holidays[5] and have access to retraining programs, the housewife receives benefits to a substantially lesser extent, if at all. Employed women may also be affected by the low status given the work of the housewife; by circular reasoning, low value attached to the work of homemaker may reinforce the already low status of most of the paid work done by women rather than men.

The lack of systematic measurements of housewives' services stems, in part, from the theoretical and methodological difficulties involved,[6] but

---

[3] For a detailed discussion, see Sylvia M. Gelber, "The Labor Force; the GNP; and Unpaid Housekeeping Services," an Address to the North American Conference on Labor Statistics, June 8, 1970, in Houston, Texas.

[4] Gelber, "Labor Force", p. 2.

[5] As far as we know, only Swedish housewives get a government-supported holiday from home.

[6] Some attempts have been made to measure the value of housewives' services for inclusion in Gross National Product. See Colin Clark, "The Economics of Housework," *Bulletin of the Oxford Institute of Statistics*, 20 (May 1958), n. 2, 205–211; and Ismail H. Sirageldin, *Non-Market Components of National Income* (Ann Arbor: University of Michigan Survey Research Center), 1969.

attempts to overcome these problems have been made. In the first selection, Chong Soo Pyun provides a method for systematically computing the value of a housewife to her family.

Although the value of women's work in the labor force is recognized, little attention is given to the contribution their earnings make to the economic well-being of families. Generally, women are thought to work for extra money for themselves, but not to make a significant contribution to family income: supporting the family is supposed to be the responsibility of men. However, the increasing movement of married women into the labor force, especially during the past twenty years, has contributed significantly to the rising living standard of families. The article from the Women's Bureau documents the contribution of women's earnings to the level of family income.

In the next reading, Jacob Mincer attempts to explain the sizeable increase in the labor-force participation rate of married women. After first discussing the traditional work-leisure labor supply model, he presents a new model in which work at home is considered an additional alternative (to work outside the home or leisure) for married women. Thus, other family income, the substitution of market goods for household goods, and market wage rates become important explanatory variables. While Mincer's analysis excludes several other relevant variables such as extent and range of job opportunities, and the level of education, these have been incorporated into models derived from his pioneering work.

Mincer's model also fails to provide an explanation for the consistent differences between the labor-force participation rates of black and white women. The data excerpted by the Bureau of Labor Statistics from a study by Father Joseph Fichter provides a partial explanation of this difference in a comparison of the work plans of black and white college-educated women.

THE JOB MARKET

In today's job market, women share many of the same disabilities experienced by other groups with minority status such as low earnings and great job insecurity. Although woman's inferior economic position parallels her general inferior social position, it is her economic disadvantages which cause her the most obvious hardships. It is important to understand the sources and forms of women's disadvantaged position in the job market, if action is to be directed toward improving her position. Thus, the readings in this section focus on: how sex discrimination in the job market limits women's employment opportunities; how sex discrimination in the schools and on the job limits women's ability to obtain training for better paying jobs; how women participate marginally in the labor market; and how federal legislation may reduce sex discrimination.

An important source of discrimination against women can be found in the division of the labor market by sex; there is one for women and one for men, with little interchange and much inequality. According to traditional labor theory, with competition and a homogeneous labor supply (workers are assumed to be perfect substitutes for each other), all workers would tend to receive the same wage. The necessary conditions for this are job mobility and adequate information about job opportunities so workers who want to maximize their wages can easily move from low-pay to high-pay jobs. Some differences that occur in wages are consistent with competitive labor markets. These are "equalizing" wage differentials, compensating for differences in the level of job skills which may vary according to the cost involved in acquiring such skills through additional years of formal schooling and training. However, other "nonequalizing" wage differences persist between groups of otherwise identical workers because of social barriers which prevent mobility. The latter groups of workers are called *noncompeting* groups; for example, men and women are so divided in the labor market that it reduces the range of job opportunities and restricts job mobility for women.

If women are denied entrance into the traditional "masculine" occupations, despite qualifying ability and skills, their efforts are not being used to best advantage by the society. As a result, the output to society is lower than it could be, and all—men as well as women—have fewer goods and services.[7] Among the 250 job categories listed in 1969 by the U.S. Bureau of the Census, one-half of women workers are in 21 job categories, while one-half of men workers are more widely dispersed—distributed among 65 job categories. Moreover, one-fourth of women workers were in five job categories—secretary stenographer, household worker, bookkeeper, elementary school teacher, and waitress.[8] In the first selection, Robert Gubbels surveys the supply and demand factors contributing to existing discriminatory sex-division of jobs so prevalent in noncommunist countries.

Sex-role differentiation begins not with a woman's entrance into the labor force, but early in childhood, and continues to be reinforced throughout the school years. Her first toys are dolls and miniaturized household equipment and the accoutrements thereof so she can be encouraged to develop homemaking skills. Neither in the home, nor later in the schools, is she encouraged to think of herself as entering the labor force as an equal with men. The prevalent cultural attitude is still that woman needs less schooling than man, little technical training, and that she need only to prepare for a job, or at most, a temporary career to fill the years before marriage and after the children are grown. In the next

---

[7] For a general theoretical treatment of this point, see Tibor Scitovsky, *Welfare and Competition* (Chicago, Illinois: Richard D. Irwin, 1951), 98–104.

[8] Janice Hedges, "Women Workers and Manpower Demands in the 1970s," *Monthly Labor Review* (June 1970), 93, p. 19.

selection, John Pietrofesa and Nancy Schlossberg describe the part that school counseling plays in narrowing women's views of their own abilities and of occupational possibilities. Women are discouraged from studying "masculine" fields such as chemistry and mathematics, and from entering "masculine" occupations such as medicine and engineering; they are encouraged to study the "feminine" social sciences, literature, foreign languages and the arts, and to enter social work, secretarial work and nursing, in keeping with their traditional "feminine" role.

In the next reading, the results of Victor Fuchs' empirical investigation of wage differences between men and women reaffirm the importance of the existing sex-role differentiation as a source of women's disadvantaged economic position. His dismissal of the importance of employer discrimination is questionable. He reasons that there is a relationship between competition and employer discrimination, where greater competition means less discrimination.[9] Thus, one would expect to find the wage differential between the sexes to be larger in the noncompetitive market in the government sector, and smaller in the competitive labor markets as in the self-employed sector. Since he finds smaller wage differences in the government sector, and large wage differences in the self-employed sector, he dismisses employer discrimination as a major explanatory variable. While government is a noncompetitive employer, less sex discrimination would be expected because of their explicit policy directed against it. Thus, an accurate evaluation of the relative importance of employer discrimination must be reserved until further evidence is accumulated.

The observed relationship between women's years of schooling and increases in lifetime earnings, presented in the next selection by Fred Hines and associates, is another indication of women's disabilities in the job market. Hines explains the lower rate of return for additional years of schooling for women as compared to men as a probable result of women's casual attachment to the labor force. Hines is in agreement with Fuchs that sex-role differentiation is a major source of women's disadvantaged position in the labor market. However, their results suggest that sex discrimination by employers may be an additional contributing factor, as when newly graduated high school and college women generally are offered lower starting salaries than men graduates and are less likely to obtain positions leading to steady career advancement.

Woman's casual attachment to the labor force also makes her vulnerable to fluctuations in the general level of economic activity. Women have high

---

[9] For a discussion of this point see, Raymond Franklin and Michael Tanzer, "Traditional Microeconomic Analysis of Racial Discrimination: A Critical Review and Alternative Approach," in D. Mermelstein (ed.), *Mainstreams, Readings and Radical Critiques* (New York: Random House, 1970), 117–126.

unemployment rates—like blacks and teenagers, they are among the last to be hired and the first to be fired—and are prone to "hidden unemployment." They are more likely than men to stop looking for work and to drop out of the labor force when jobs become scarce. Betty MacMorran Gray cogently discusses the effects of "hidden unemployment" for women, and the reasons why a full employment, growth economy is necessary for an improvement in women's economic position.

Prior to the 1960s, legislation often had the effect of reinforcing the sex division of the labor market into *noncompeting groups.* Concern with the economic well-being of women took the form of legislation which accentuated differences between men and women; for example, state and local protective legislation for women workers. Although in the short run, some of the legislation created better working conditions, in the long run it reinforced women's inferior economic position. This trend was reversed in 1963, at least in part, by the passage of legislation promoting equal pay. However, passing laws is not enough to insure more than nominal equality, as past legislation on racial equality shows: laws must be enforced. In the last selection, Robert Moran discusses the past problems and future possibilities of enforcing this legislation.

SEX-ROLE DIFFERENTIATION IN AN EQUALITARIAN SOCIETY

YONINA TALMON

The purpose of this paper is an analysis of the emergence of sex-role differentiation in a society originally based on a denial of sex differences. The Kibbutzim in Israel have consciously cultivated a predominantly masculine image of the feminine role in their systems of training and education. The tenet of sex equality still occupies a central place in their proclaimed ideology. Yet, in spite of the systematic efforts to conduct role allocation in accordance with this ideal, a fairly clear-cut though fairly flexible sex-role differentiation has emerged in internal family activities as well as in work assignment and in nomination to committees and central offices. . . .

[Our main foci are:] (a) analysis of the interrelation between differentiation in internal family tasks and differentiation in external activities; (b) analysis of the interrelation between differentiation in role allocation on the one hand and redefinition of sex-role models on the other; (c) analysis of the main institutionalized mechanisms evolved in order to bridge or cover up the gap between the proclaimed ideology and reality in this sphere.

SEX-ROLE DIFFERENTIATION IN THE FAMILY

We shall start our analysis with an examination of the division of labor and sex-role models within the family. The most important determinants of internal sex-role allocation during the initial phases of the movement were the far-reaching limitation of family functions and the equalitarian ideology. Spouses tended their small and simply furnished rooms and looked after their children during their daily reunion, but had few other household responsibilities. Internal relations between members of the elementary family were patterned to a large extent on relations between comembers and emphasized quality and companionship. . . . Spouses had

Excerpts reprinted from Yonina Talmon, "Sex-Role Differentiation in an Equalitarian Society," in Thomas Lasswell, John Burma and Sidney Aronson (eds.), *Life in Society* (Glenview, Illinois: Scott, Foresman and Company, 1965), 145–155.

no right to impose their authority on each other, and there was hardly any differentiation between their spheres of special competence.

An analysis of our data on the families in the Kibbutzim in our sample reveals a gradual increase of family functions and a concomitant increase in sex-role specialization. The family has regained some of its lost functions in the sphere of housekeeping. . . . Housework has become much more time consuming. The typical dwelling unit now consists of a semi-detached flat containing one or two rooms, a kitchenette and private sanitary facilities. . . . The flat requires now more elaborate and more systematic care. Though most clothing still goes to the communal laundry, many families tend to look after their best clothes at home so that there is a little extra washing, mending and ironing now and then. . . . Most important of all changes in this sphere is the partial reversal of functions in the sphere of child care and socialization. Parents take a more active part in looking after their children. There is much closer cooperation between nurses, instructors, teachers and parents. . . . There is considerably more parental supervision of the children's behavior, their choice of friends, and their reading habits. Some of the Kibbutzim have introduced a more radical reorganization. Children in these Kibbutzim no longer sleep in the children's houses. They stay with their age groups during the day but return home every afternoon.

An examination of our data on the families in our sample of Kibbutzim and a more systematic and rigorous observation of the division of labor in a subsample of 60 families indicate that a fairly specialized albeit flexible and fluctuating division of labor has emerged in most families. The husband will usually help his wife clean the flat and prepare the afternoon tea. Few husbands perform these tasks regularly, but all of them do it now and then. A considerable number of the husbands take over household duties only in case of emergency when their wife is either very tired, ill or away. Clothes are exclusively the concern of the wife. The husband does not take much interest in clothes and in almost all cases does not help his wife to look after them at all. In most of the families the wife does most of the housekeeping and it is mainly her responsibility. Her husband is regarded as her assistant or as her temporary stand-in but not as co-worker on equal terms. Budgeting of personal allowances of the whole family is almost invariably the responsibility of the wife. Officially these allowances are personal and not transferable, but in practice this injunction is overruled and the allowances are pooled together and treated as a family allowance. Most men are not very interested in this small-scale budgeting and leave the planning and management of the family "finances" to their wives.

In the sphere of child care, there is considerably more cooperation and interchangeability than in housekeeping. This is clearly the effect of the system of socialization. As parents do not carry the main responsibility for either maintenance or socialization of their children, emphasis is put on affective ties. The main function of the parents is to minister to their children's need for security and love. Both of them interact with their children in much the same way and play a common protective role. Fathers usually take a lively interest in their children and participate actively in looking after them. They play with them, take them for walks and put them to bed about as much as the mothers. Mothers have closer contacts with babies and small children but fathers come into the picture very early. Sex of the children has no marked effect either. Fathers are only a little more concerned with boys. Mothers look after both boys and girls.

In spite of the considerable blurring of differences between the father role and the mother role, there are some signs of differentiation even in this sphere. The mother is as a rule more concerned with the bodily well-being of the children and takes care of them while they are at home. She has usually more contact with the children's institutions and the school and supervises the upbringing of her children there. There is not much routine disciplining in the family but such as there is, is more often than not the mother's responsibility. The source of this responsibility is primarily in her duties as housekeeper and part-time caretaker of her children. The child has to conform to certain standards of cleanliness and order. . . . The father is less involved in these problems and the child may find in him an ally in cases of exaggerated concern with them on the part of the mother. The father's main responsibilities are outside the home—in the yard, on the farm, in dealing with communal affairs which concern the Kibbutz as a whole. Mothers have more say in routine matters and practical problems. Fathers have more say in matters of principle. In the eyes of the growing child, the father emerges gradually as the representative of the Kibbutz and its values within the family, while the mother acts primarily as the representative of the family in the Kibbutz.

. . . The family has remained basically equalitarian and does not enforce an institutionalized position of pivotal authority for either of the spouses. Division of labor is more specialized than decision-making but it is not segregated and rigid either. The pattern of role allocation differs appreciably during different phases of the life cycle in any given family and from family to family.

So far we have dealt with actual division of tasks and authority in the family. The ideological aspect of intrafamilial differentiation was examined by means of four questions included in our interview schedule. . . .

For the classification of the answers given to these questions two cross cutting criteria were used—extent of sex-role differentiation and degree of flexibility postulated by the norms pertaining to internal division of family tasks. Four distinctive ideological patterns emerge from this classification:

(a) An "equalitarian" pattern, based on strict equality and complete interchangeability.

(b) A "joint" pattern, based on close cooperation between husband and wife. This pattern is less equalitarian and more flexible than the equalitarian pattern. It allows for some sex-role differentiation but demands joint activities and mutual help.

(c) A "differentiated" pattern in which specialized activities outnumber shared ones. Most adherents of this pattern are against any rigid general norm and hold that the division of labor within the family should be decided by the spouses. They saw it as a matter of opinion and convenience and not so much as a matter of principle. This pattern is more flexible and considerably less equalitarian than the former patterns.

(d) A "segregated" pattern, based on a clear-cut and rigid sex-role differentiation. Household work and child care are defined as women's work.

The [record] shows that respondents tend to be most equalitarian when dealing with the problem on a high level of ideological generalization but become less equalitarian when dealing with more specific norms. Norms pertaining to child care are more equalitarian than norms pertaining to household duties. Norms of care of clothing are least equalitarian of all. It should be noted that the number of respondents who are undecided, reluctant or unwilling to express their explicit opinion increases progressively when we pass from the general ideological question to the questions pertaining to child care, care of flat and care of clothing. Only seven of the respondents failed to take a definite stand on the general ideological issue whereas the number of uncommitted and undecided respondents rises to 103 when we reach the most specific issue. The decrease in equalitarianism is accompanied by an increase in ambivalence and indecision.

Comparison of the proclaimed ideology and actual practice in our subsample of families indicates that the ideological position is on the whole more equalitarian than the actual practice. While the general ideological position lags far behind there is only a small gap between the more specific norms and actual behavior. There is in fact quite a close fit between the continuum obtained when examining actual practice and the continuum obtained when considering norms—child care is least differentiated; care of the flat comes next in this respect; care of clothes is almost exclusively feminine.

ROLE ALLOCATION AND ROLE MODELS IN THE EXTERNAL SYSTEM

We turn now to the examination of the extent of sex-role differentiation in work assignments and in nomination to committees.

The original ideology postulated that women should participate equally in hard productive work, especially in agriculture. The main emphasis of the ideology pertaining to intrafamilial tasks was on the participation of men in activities traditionally defined as feminine tasks. The main emphasis of the ideology pertaining to work assignment was on the participation of women in masculine tasks. Work assignment was not completely equalitarian even during the initial phases of development but crossing of the line between the masculine and feminine tasks was common. A considerable number of the women were assigned to predominantly masculine occupations and a certain percentage of the men worked in predominantly feminine tasks.

Examination of the work histories of our respondents during the last ten years indicates that there is a gradual but cumulative trend of growing sex-role specialization in work assignment.... [The data] show that a fairly clear-cut division of labor has emerged in this sphere.

Men are concentrated mainly in agriculture, in production services, and in central public offices. Women are concentrated in services and in education. A more detailed analysis of each category indicates considerable sex-role specialization. No woman is assigned to field crops, to fodder, to fishery or to bee keeping, and they are a very small minority in the fruit orchards. Quite a number of them work in the vegetable gardens and in the tree nursery but even in these branches they are only a third of the workers. Women are a small minority in the dairy and flocks. They constitute about half of the workers in poultry. If we take production services we see that women are found only in accountancy. No women are found in either carpentry, electricity, maintenance of machines or construction. When we turn to the predominantly feminine categories we find indications of an even sharper differentiation. Workers in the kitchen, in the clothing shops and stores are almost exclusively women. Workers in the shoe-repair shop and in sanitation are almost exclusively men. There is a fairly sharp differentiation in education, too. Nurses and kindergarten teachers are exclusively women. Women are a majority in teaching but they are concentrated mainly in primary school teaching. Most high school teachers and college instructors are male. To sum up, most occupations are segregated or almost segregated. There are a small number of occupations where a majority of one sex participates with a minority of the other sex. Women participate in predominantly masculine occupations more than men do in predominantly feminine occupations. Interchangeability is thus limited and asymmetrical.

We have examined the ideological aspects of work assignment by means of the following questions: "How in your opinion should the jobs be divided between men and women? Are you for or against sex-role differentiation in this sphere?" Classification of the answers to this question leads us again to the four ideological patterns encountered in the ideological analysis of intrafamilial differentiation. . . .

The main emphasis is on the "differentiated" pattern while the "joint" pattern is second in importance. The gap between ideology and reality is narrower than in the internal system but has not disappeared completely. Ideological acknowledgement of segregation still lags behind reality.

Let us now turn to an examination of *participation in committees* and *overall leadership* of the community. Examination of the membership of committees in the last 10 years indicates that in most Kibbutzim there is a gradual yet cumulative trend towards growing sex-role differentiation. . . .

Men predominate in central offices, in the secretariat which is the most important committee in most Kibbutzim, in the economic committee which is second in importance and is sometimes even more important than the secretariat. The members of the committees for planning and security are exclusively male. Though the educational committee is, as we shall soon see, predominantly female, men predominate in the committee in charge of youth activities.

We find approximately proportional representation in three important committees—in the committee in charge of work assignments, in the committee in charge of social relations and personal needs of the members and in the committee in charge of cultural activities. Joint participation is found also in a number of small committees which are subcommittees of either the social or cultural committees.

Women predominate in the committees in charge of education, health and consumption. They are a majority in the subcommittee in charge of members who serve in the army. Members of the subcommittee in charge of aged parents are exclusively women.

To sum up, there are more exclusively masculine committees than exclusively feminine committees. Men predominate in overall leadership and in central committees. Men predominate in overall planning, in management of economic production and security. Men and women cooperate in the management of social and cultural affairs. Women predominate in committees in charge of consumption, education, health and welfare. Differentiation in this sphere is thus considerable. It should, however, be pointed out that it is neither rigid nor clear-cut. The number of exclusively masculine or exclusively feminine committees is comparatively small. In most committees both sexes are represented. There [are many] committees with proportional or near proportional representation.

The ideological attitudes towards participation in committees were examined by means of the following question: "Should women participate as actively as men in communal affairs? Are you for or against sex-role differentiation in this sphere?" The classification of the answers to these questions leads us again to the four ideological patterns encountered in the examination of attitudes towards familial and occupational division of labor.

The main emphasis is on the "joint" pattern, the "differentiated" pattern coming next. A comparatively high percentage of the respondents adhere to the "equalitarian" pattern. As in the former spheres there is more equalitarianism in theory than in practice.

We conclude our examination of internal and external role differentiation by a comparison of actual and ideal division of labor in the three spheres. Differentiation is most marked in the occupational sphere. It is difficult to compare differentiation in the family to differentiation in committees but it is quite clear that there is less segregation in these spheres than in the sphere of work assignment.

Let us now compare the distribution of the ideological patterns.

Norms pertaining to the occupational system are most differentiated. Next in this respect come the norms pertaining to nomination to committees. Norms pertaining to the family are the most equalitarian.

We have already noted above that ideology lags behind reality in both the internal and external systems. This leads to the conclusion that the main pressures in the process of differentiation are institutional and that ideological reformation follows suit. The original ideology accommodates itself to the changing reality, but lags behind it, conducting a rear-guard action against extreme differentiation. It is perhaps significant that the gap between ideology and reality is narrower in the occupational sphere than in the other spheres. The comparatively sharp occupational sex-role differentiation is sanctioned by the ideology more than the more flexible and more equalitarian sex-role differentiation in the other spheres. This seems to indicate that the pressure towards differentiation is at its strongest in the occupational sphere and that analysis of the process of differentiation in this sphere is of crucial importance.

DYNAMICS OF DIFFERENTIATION

How can we account for the considerable sex-role differentiation revealed by our analysis? Examination of our data on stages of institutional differentiation and scrutiny of the assumptions and considerations which underlie the choice of each of the ideological patterns, indicate that *the sex differentiated role allocation emerges out of an interplay between changes in the internal and external systems.* We shall first examine the development of the interrelations between the family and the occupational sphere and then proceed to analyze the dynamic interplay between these institutional spheres and social participation.

There was very little pressure towards sex-role differentiation in the family at first. The Kibbutzim transferred most of the functions which loom so large in other types of family to communal institutions. All families were young and the birth rate was very low. Since the family unit was small and had very few tasks to accomplish, there was little objective need for a clear-cut division of labor or for a unified command to ensure coordination. Moreover, since the spouses had very few common objectives and tasks, the unity of the family depended primarily on close, affective contacts and companionship. This pattern of companionship operated against differentiation and rigidity. The process of differentiation sets in with the rise of the birth rate and with the overall increase of family functions. The family regains some of its lost functions and becomes more involved in internal activities. Our material indicates that the more task-oriented the family, the more marked is the tendency towards role differentiation within it.

How can we account for the fact that most of the reassumed family responsibilities fall on the wife? Analysis of the interviews reveals that the effects of former socialization and the influence of differentiation in the outside world are not eliminated. The equalitarian ideology does not penetrate very deeply and certain traditional norms persist in spite of it. The attitudes towards care of clothes, to take just one example, indicate clearly the effect of a sex differentiated role prototype. We were surprised to find such a strong and emphatic opposition to interchangeability in this sphere. Many of the respondents who were equalitarian on a high level of generalization stopped short and retracted from their equalitarian position when it came to care of clothes. It was considered as inappropriate, effeminate and slightly ridiculous for men to be engaged in such tasks. Quite a number of the respondents felt that it was somehow "unnatural." Covert conventional role images underlie the attitudes to many other tasks. We should take into consideration also the effects of differentiation of initial training—most wives have had more preparatory experience in performing household tasks and are more competent than their husbands in this sphere.

The initial tendency to differentiation is precipitated by the internal dynamics of family living. The advent of children accentuates the importance of familial roles. The identification with the specifically and typically feminine role of mother undermines the masculine image of the feminine role upheld by the official ideology and weakens the resistance to sex-role differentiations. We observe a gradual process of generalization which leads from childbirth to child-rearing to household duties. The various tasks involved in these responsibilities are correlated and are conceived as parts of a complex yet coherent whole.

A similar though more intense process of differentiation occurs in the sphere of work assignment. During the first phases of development the equalitarian ideology was reinforced by the demographic and economic structure of the Kibbutz. The Kibbutzim put an almost exclusive emphasis on productive labor and the standard of living was kept very low. The simple and small-scale services did not require many workers and a considerable number of the women could turn to productive labor. Most members were young and unattached. Innate biological differentiation was not very noticeable and could be ignored. The primary determinant of the shift in the division of labor is the woman's sex-linked childbearing role which accentuates biological differentiation. Communal institutions replace the mother very early but they cannot completely eliminate her special ties to her baby. Pregnancy and nursing of babies partially incapacitate the woman for hard labor in outlying orchards and fields. Pregnant women are usually transferred to lighter tasks and nursing mothers work only part time. Since they have to nurse and feed their babies every few hours it is more convenient for them to work in one of the communal service institutions which are situated near the children's houses. As long as they look after their babies during work hours they have to resign themselves to taking a leave of absence from productive labor. At first this leave of absence was kept to the bare minimum. Communal institutions took over as soon as possible and the mother, no longer hampered during working hours, returned to productive labor. With the birth of more children and with increasing age mothers usually found it increasingly difficult to return to hard physical labor and the maternity leave grew longer. The recurrent and prolonged interruptions entailed serious discontinuity. Mothers lost touch with their former job and drifted away from it. In the course of time many of them tended to leave agriculture permanently.

The birth of children affects the economic structure of the Kibbutz in yet another way. It entails a growing need for more workers for services and children's care. The balance between productive and nonproductive labor changes considerably. This process is further enhanced by the gradual rise in the standard of living. Nonproductive labor now absorbs about 50 percent of the labor force. Women are only about 45 percent of the total population. The services, child care and education need all the female working power they can get.

The dividing line between masculine and feminine tasks is determined by the ecological seeing and by the economic structure of the Kibbutz. We can discern the effect of the following factors: (a) the extent to which a given job requires considerable physical strength and strenuous exertion; (b) the extent to which it requires specialized technical skill; (c) the extent to which it requires spatial mobility; (d) the extent to which it requires continuity of effort for considerable blocks of time from the point of view of the time rhythm of the working day and from the point of view of the overall work career. Considerations of rationalization and productivization work against the blurring of sex job differentiation. Agriculture in the Kibbutz is becoming increasingly large scale and heavily mechanized. It seems now a waste to assign able-bodied and technically skilled men to the services. Women cannot fully replace them in productive labor because of the limitations that physical disability and childbirth impose on them. Work assigners find it increasingly difficult to allow women to work in agriculture or to draft men to work in the services. When practical considerations of efficiency gain precedence over ideological considerations, sex differentiated job allocation comes to be regarded as inevitable.

Sex differentiation is an outcome of internal pressures within each sphere as well as of an interplay between them. The occupational sphere exercises pressure on the internal division of labor in the family. Productive labor and overall administration draw the men far afield. Women's work does not take them far from their flat and from the children's houses. They find it easier to fit the care of the flat into their timetable. The children's houses are nearby and the mothers can drop in during the day. They take the children to their flat on their way home. As they are concentrated in occupations closely allied to housekeeping and child care, they find it easier to cope with these tasks at home.

Role differentiation within the family in its turn exerts pressure on the occupational sphere. The emergence of an outright feminine prototype of the woman's role precipitates the process of differentiation in work assignment. There is a growing concern with the preservation of a feminine and youthful appearance. Considerations of beauty care are not quite acceptable and are met with ridicule when admitted openly, yet they have a marked effect on work assignment. Women are not as eager as they used to be to work in agriculture and one of the main reasons for this reluctance is the fear that strenuous and exhausting physical labor and work in the open throughout the year will have an adverse effect on their figure and complexion. There is a growing concern with the maintenance of the right balance between external and internal roles. Women tend to avoid work in overall administration because jobs in this sphere are very demanding and preoccupying and do not leave them enough time and energy for their familial roles. Quite a number of members feel that as a rule women should be assigned to jobs that do not interfere with their paramount duties as wives and mothers.

We have already noted that while sex-role differentiation within the family is considerable, it is less clear-cut than in work assignment. This difference is closely related to the division of functions between the family and the occupational sphere. The dividing line between internal family activities and external activities has shifted considerably but this did not entail a radical change in the institutional division of labor. The Kibbutzim put the main emphasis on the occupational sphere and it has remained the major focus of activities for both men and women. The fact that both husband and wife work full time in communal institutions exerts pressure towards sharing of household chores performed after work and obviates the tendency to turn household duties and child care into the wife's exclusive task areas. It should be noted also that the internal pressure towards differentiation within the family is not very strong either. The core of specific family responsibilities has remained comparatively small and most of the tasks involved are not very specialized. These counter-pressures account for the fact that the considerable sex-role specialization in internal family activities did not lead to rigidity and polarization.

The attenuation of the equalitarian ideology and the loosening of communal control over the family lead to a considerable variation in familial role allocation during different stages of the life cycle of any given family, and from family to family. The family has a certain leeway to develop a pattern which suits the personally held values, the needs and interests of its members. A change in the size and in the age and sex composition of the family, a shift to a more or less arduous or time-consuming job, lead to role reallocation. Equally important is the interplay between the personalities of husband and wife and the variation in the nature and intensity of the emotional bonds between them. The tendency to sex-role differentiation is evident in all families, yet each family works out its own dynamic pattern.

How do these processes of differentiation affect the patterns of voluntary participation in the committees and how, in their turn, are they affected by them? Participation in committees serves as an important alternative direction of emancipation from sex differentiation. This outlet for activity and avenue of ascent very often compensates the women for their partial exclusion and for the limitation of their opportunities in the occupational sphere. The sphere of participation is less differentiated than the occupational sphere, but it cannot escape from the pressure towards differentiation. This pressure comes from both directions. Lines of cleavage between the sexes in committees are about the same as in the occupational sphere and in the family. Since women are gradually excluded from production and overall administration they lose touch with these aspects of community life and can contribute very little to the work of committees which deal with production, planning or overall administration. When they are elected to one of these committees they are usually very passive and often drop out after a while. They concentrate in committees in charge of organization, of consumption, of children, of health and of personal problems. Only in these committees can they draw on the experience that they have gained in their jobs and at home and give expert advice. Only in such committees do they feel competent and in their element.

The Kibbutzim realize that joint participation is an indispensable bridge between the sexes and make special efforts to avoid underrepresentation and segregation. These efforts are only partly successful because most women are not very keen on nomination to committees and many of them try to avoid it as much as possible. The reluctance to accept responsibilities in committees is closely related to the limitation of the family sphere in the Kibbutzim. Participation in committees is an important outlet for housewives since it emancipates them from domesticity and isolation. Women in the Kibbutzim work outside their home all day. Work in service institutions entails intensive, constant, and very often strained contacts with many members. By the end of the day they usually crave for their children and for a quiet evening with their husbands at home. The short time spent together in the evening is the main manifestation of the unity of the family. Cutting it short by active participation in committees during off-hours encroaches on family life.

Yet another important determinant of differentiation is the persistence and resurgence of sex-differentiated role stereotypes. Behind the equalitarian façade we find considerable differentiation. The conception of women as reticent, passive and placating has not disappeared. Many feel that a great deal of drive and self-assertion and a strong involvement in public affairs are unfeminine. Attempts of women to make their mark in the general assembly and in the committees are often met with condescension and excessive criticism. Women who hold important leadership positions are treated with a mixture of admiration and vague discomfort. Women tend to be self-conscious and self-deprecating when evaluating their roles in this sphere. The considerable ambivalence concerning feminine social participation reinforces their tendency toward withdrawal.

To sum up, the three spheres are closely interconnected. Division of functions among them has many repercussions on internal differentiation within each of them. Concessions made to segregation in one of the spheres call for similar concessions in the others. The task-determined division of labor undermines the equalitarian ideology and reinforces sex-differentiated stereotypes which persist and develop in spite of it. The redefinition of role models precipitates the tendency to sex-role differentiation.

INSTITUTIONAL MECHANISMS

The discrepancy between the proclaimed equalitarian ideology and the growing differentiation between the sexes is a source of severe strain. Since women are mainly concentrated in occupations and tasks which are closely allied to traditional housekeeping, they very often feel that they might as well perform these tasks within their own home rather than outside it. They retreat to their private sphere and press for a far-reaching redefinition of the relations between the family and communal institutions. Women are, in fact, the main agents of the familistic trend. The Kibbutzim are thus faced with a dilemma. Institutional exigencies and normative pressures lead to growing differentiation. The Kibbutzim cannot yield to segregation since marked inequality between the sexes breeds discontent and disaffection which threatens to overthrow the collective organization of consumption and child care. This dilemma has led to the emergence of ingenious "intermediate" institutional mechanisms which partly bridge and cover up the gap between ideals and reality and check differentiation. These supplementary mechanisms operate in all three systems but they are most prominent in the occupational sphere.

Rationalization and mechanization of service institutions. Until very recently the Kibbutzim have concentrated most of their efforts on improving efficiency in production branches, and the services lagged far behind in this respect. Most service branches operated with a minimal budget and with inadequate and outdated equipment. Their organizational structure was, in addition, very loose and ill-defined. The efficiency drive leads to a certain formalization of communication and control in the work teams and to a far-reaching mechanization of most work processes. This reorganization affects the service branches in many ways. It reduces the number of workers engaged in them so that a certain percentage of the women working power can be assigned to other occupations. It raises the standard of services rendered and enhances confidence in collective institutions. Work becomes easier and more manageable. There is less tension within the team and fewer complaints from "clients."

Professionalization. The Kibbutzim are making a persistent effort to develop scientifically tested techniques in the sphere of housekeeping and child care and to turn these occupations into semiprofessions. Workers in these fields are sent to get professional training in institutions outside the community. The Federations organize seminars and refresher courses in home economics, nursing and child care in which members get some theoretical grounding and practical guidance. The training is kept up and continued by means of extensive reading in semiscientific literature and by occasional lectures. Professionalization makes manifest the hidden potentialities of collectivistic organization of the services. It leads to cultivation of different talents and capabilities by specialization and systematic training. It enables workers to develop high levels of competence and encourages them to perfect their mastery of certain spheres of activity. The professional aura enhances the prestige of jobs in housekeeping and child care and establishes them as full-fledged occupational roles. The specialized training supplies the incumbents of these roles with certain objective criteria of excellence. Their position as competent experts bolsters their status vis-à-vis their "clients" and protects them from excessive criticism.

Diversification of feminine occupations. The occupational opportunities available to women in the Kibbutz are rather limited, but the range of choice open to them can be widened by branching out into new spheres of activity. A recent development in this sphere is the beginning of a training program in social work, psychological therapy and counseling. Training in arts and crafts provides additional openings. A certain increase of suitable employment opportunities results from the development of local industries and crafts.

De-differentiation.

CULTIVATION OF SPHERES OF JOINT ACTIVITY. The Kibbutzim make many efforts to cut the number of exclusively feminine or exclusively masculine occupations. They often develop new branches which are suitable for men as well as for women. They try to achieve proportional or nearly proportional representation in as many committees as possible and pressure is put on the women to accept nomination. The nominating committee will often prefer a female candidate to a male one of equal or even better qualifications. This balancing mechanism serves as an antidote to the limiting effects of occupational sex-role differentiation and overcomes to some extent women's reluctance to accept office. Apprenticeship in a committee enables women to gain experience and to develop new interests and new skills. Quite a number of women who were at first very insecure in their new role have gradually become active and competent participants in the deliberations of their committee. Such an *"equilibrating" system of recruitment* helps to discover untapped energies and hidden talents and opens up new avenues of satisfying activity.

SYMBOLIC DENIAL OF DIFFERENTIATION. The persistence of specifically feminine and specifically masculine roles is partly covered up and neutralized by the *temporary participation of men in specifically feminine roles and vice versa.* The Kibbutzim make a point of assigning a number of men to specifically feminine occupations on a short-term basis. The most important example is participation of men in work in the kitchen and the dining hall. They are drafted by a system of rotation in which each man serves a two- to three-month period. Most of the men serve in the dining hall where everyone can see them every day. Similar mechanisms operate in the family too, particularly in the participation of fathers in taking their children out for their daily walk and in putting them to bed in the children's houses. Their participation in what is regarded as a typically feminine task serves as a *highly visible symbolic denial of segregation.*

Participation of men in feminine tasks has a practical value, but its main significance lies in its symbolic meaning as "atonement" for differentiation. Essentially, it is a token interchangeability. Women participate in masculine tasks much more and for much longer stretches than men in feminine tasks. Girls and young women are assigned to work in masculine occupations for a number of years. When they grow older and have children they leave these occupations and settle down in services and child care. Work in productive labor is regarded as an indispensable *rite de passage* for most women.

A MORE DURABLE CROSSING OF THE LINES OCCURS IN EXCEPTIONAL CASES. The Kibbutzim encourage women who continue to work in productive labor, in overall administration and in central committees, to hold out as long as they can. These exceptions to the rule serve as living proof that there is no deliberate discrimination. The exemplary life stories of such women who have achieved equality in spite of serious difficulties travel far and wide in all Kibbutzim and have become an important part of popular lore. Some of these women have become larger-than-life heroic figures.

In some of the Kibbutzim in our sample we discern signs of the emergence of a *cycle pattern*. This pattern is based on a system of role allocation which combines continuity of career with controlled mobility. It institutionalizes a sequence of changes of occupations during the life cycle coupled with patterned shifts of the center of gravity from one institutional sphere to another. During the first phase of the cycle the main emphasis is on joint participation in the occupational system. As long as they are young and have no children, women tend to concentrate on either predominantly masculine or in joint occupations. When their children come, they settle down in services and child care and become engrossed in family affairs. When the children grow up and the mothers have more free time, they put more emphasis on social participation. The second phase is based on considerable sex differentiation but it is preceded and followed by more equalitarian stages. The cycle pattern is not rigid and allows for many combinations and variations. It does not try to erase sex differentiation completely, but neither does it yield to polarization and segregation. It takes into full consideration the developmental aspects of family life and defines the interrelations between the external systems and the internal family system accordingly. It combines equality and differentiation in an ordered yet flexible and continually changing pattern.

TASK AND SOCIAL BEHAVIOR IN MARRIAGE

GEORGE LEVINGER

The welfare of any human group depends on the fulfillment of two kinds of functions: the performance of tasks for coping with the objective environment and the maintenance of social relationships among the members. From research on five-man problem solving groups, Bales and Slater have concluded that these two kinds of functions tend to interfere with each other. The two functions seemed best carried on by different individuals in the group, referred to as the task and the social-emotional specialist.

Talcott Parsons has drawn on that conclusion in writing about family interaction. He proposed that generally the "husband-father" role is that of task specialist, while the "wife-mother" role is that of social-emotional specialist. Zelditch has tried to substantiate Parsons' generalization. In a review of anthropological essays and field reports, he noted that in the large majority of cultures husbands and wives adhere to a division of roles, in which husband copes mainly with the external environment and wife maintains the home.

In our own culture, the poet Ogden Nash has noted with his typical irreverence that a husband and wife are incompatible, if " ... he has no income and she isn't patible."

Nevertheless, Parsons' and Zelditch's broad generalization must be qualified. It appears largely correct for describing the roles of father and mother in the childbearing nuclear family, a multi-person group. Yet it does not apply as readily to the roles of husband and wife, considered purely in the context of the marriage relationship.

Consider the definitions of task and of social-emotional behavior. *Task behavior* refers to activity that involves " ... the manipulation of the object-world ... for the achievement of goals defined within the system."[1] Such behavior is not necessarily satisfying in itself, but is a means toward

---

Excerpted from George Levinger, "Task and Social Behavior in Marriage," *Sociometry*, 27 (December, 1964), 433–448. Tables and footnotes have been eliminated or renumbered.

[1] Morris Zelditch, Jr., "Role Differentiation in the Nuclear Family," in Talcott Parsons and Robert F. Bales (eds.), *Family, Socialization and Interaction in Process* (Glencoe, Illinois: The Free Press), 1955, p. 310.

attaining a group goal. In principle, task behavior can be performed by any subpart of the group, and even *can be delegated* to persons who are not formal members.

Social-emotional behavior, in contrast, is activity that maintains the relations between the members. Zelditch terms it " . . . the expression of affection . . . and a symbolization of common membership through supportive, accepting behavior."[2] The expression of negative feeling would also, of course, be considered social-emotional behavior with repercussions for group maintenance. Social-emotional behavior is ultimately reciprocal and therefore it *cannot be delegated* to persons outside the group. Thus, while task activity refers to a subject-object relation, social activity represents instead a subject-subject relation.

According to these definitions, task and social behavior differ in their potentiality for delegation. A group's task orientation encourages specialization in its division of labor, particularly when there are many different tasks to be performed and when the members' relations are cooperative. However, social-emotional behavior cannot be delegated in this way, except to the extent that two members' relations to a third party are nominally equivalent.

Social-emotional specialization does occur in groups of *three or more* persons such as in the child–rearing family; the wife's care of children would be considered a social-emotional function.

From the standpoint of the marriage group, however, child care and other aspects of a wife's "inside mastery" must be considered tasks. The two members of a pair may differ in their propensity for *initiating* overt social-emotional interaction, but over the long run the maintenance of a given level of interaction depends on the degree of reciprocation by the less demonstrative partner. Back to Ogden Nash: the importance of the wife's "patibility" derives from the assumption that the husband wants to pat. A marriage where only one partner engages in social-emotional actions breaks down in its *inter*action. The lower its reciprocity, the lower should be the total level of social-emotional behavior.

It is proposed, therefore, that in the marriage group *per se* both spouses are task specialists and neither spouse is a social-emotional specialist. Furthermore, it would seem that an American middle-class husband need not differ substantially from his wife in his marital aspirations.

METHOD

The sample consisted of sixty middle-class couples, all of whom had children, had been married between four and twenty-two years, and lived in

_____
[2] Zelditch, Jr., "Role Differentiation . . ." p. 311.

the area of Greater Cleveland. The average couple was in the late thirties, had been married 13.6 years, had three children, and came from the upper middle occupational-educational index. Thirty-six couples were parents of children in an elementary school; the other 24 couples were clients at a family–service agency, who were comparable in the above-mentioned social characteristics.

Each couple participated in a two- to three-hour long interview and performance session, in which husband and wife were seen first separately and later jointly. Each partner ranked the importance of certain marital goals, and described both spouses' real and ideal performance in the task and social-emotional areas of marriage. Questions about task performance covered ten representative duties such as doing dishes or repairs. Questions about social-emotional matters asked about each partner's supportiveness, the couple's frequency of communication, and the sexual relationship.

Indices of marital satisfaction were derived from questions about general happiness, from those about specific satisfaction areas, and from the discrepancies between statements about real versus ideal behavior.

A laboratory performance part of the session consisted of joint performance on four tests, of which a parallel form had previously been administered individually. The first two group tests required subjects to discuss and rank the importance of two sets of goals; the third was a joint vocabulary test; and the fourth was the Color-Symbol Test, our own special group adaptation of the Wechsler-Bellevue Digit-Symbol Test.

Fifteen months after the first interview, 49 of the 60 couples completed an additional set of instruments, consisting primarily of personality tests.

RESULTS

Findings will be presented under two general headings: (1) specialization versus mutuality in husbands' and wives' task and social behavior; and (2) difference versus similarity in their marital goals, their needs, and their sources of marital satisfaction.

SPECIALIZATION VERSUS MUTUALITY. It is accepted that husbands and wives differ in the kinds of family tasks that they generally perform.

Our own findings . . . show that on eight of the ten family tasks covered in our interview schedule there was significant specialization. On all of the tasks, except getting information about "buying big items" or about "what to do on vacation," it was reported that one spouse took predominant responsibility. The two exceptions, which covered topics not dealt with in previous studies, do not deal with routinized household matters.

On the other hand, in the social-emotional realm, [we find] considerably less contrast between the husband's and wife's activity. There is significantly more inequality on only one of the six items—that is, "talking about one's feelings with [spouse] when one is bothered or upset"; here the wife was usually seen as the more vocal partner. On the remaining five items, there was as much or more mutuality in the spouses' reported behavior as there was specialization.

The results clearly support the present thesis. Forty-nine of the sixty husbands showed a larger percentage of $H = W$ items on the social than on the task set; similarly, 53 of 60 wives reported greater equality on the social-emotional items.

The most convincing evidence in support of the present thesis is drawn from an item-by-item correlational analysis. This analysis is based on the assumption that specialization would be indicated by *negative* correlations between husband's and wife's performance, while mutuality would be shown by *positive* correlations. [The data] show that, indeed, all task items had negative correlations and all social-emotional items had positive correlations.

It seems meaningful that some items, such as making repairs or getting insurance information, produced very high negative correlations; one partner's activity on such items almost precludes the other's activity. Other items, such as doing the dishes or making complaints, do not represent mutually exclusive behavior; it is feasible either to do dishes jointly or to delegate the function almost entirely, and it is possible that neither or both partners may voice their complaints to outside agencies. In the social-emotional realm, "asking the spouse about his daily activities" showed the lowest positive correlation, while kissing behavior showed the highest one, once again a reflection of common sense.

Two other sources of data are pertinent. The spouses' interaction, as observed in the laboratory session, also showed a positive correlation between husband's and wife's social-emotional behavior: (a) acceptance of each other's contributions, $r = .12$, $p = $ n.s.; (b) rejection of each other's contributions, $r = .31$, $p < .02$.

These findings, then, confirm the proposition that while task-oriented behavior in marriage tends to be specialized, social-supportive activity encourages reciprocation. In the latter area, two spouses within the same marriage tend to be more similar than husbands or wives across different marriages.

Similarity in Marriage Goals. Some experts in marriage research claim that American marriage has become predominantly concerned with companionship.

In our study, each respondent ranked a set of nine general marital goals . . . ordering them according to their importance for achieving a good marriage. Two [goals] are primarily social-emotional—Affection and

Companionship—and four are mainly task-oriented—Economic Security, an Attractive Home, Wise Financial Planning, and a respected Place in the Community.

Table 1 indicates that there was no difference between husbands' and wives' ranking of Affection and Companionship. These two goals were ranked at the top, the other four goals near the bottom of the order. Nor was there any difference between the husband and wife groups in their mean ratio of ranks for social versus task goals ($t = .43$, n.s). On rankings of single goals, the only significant differences occurred on Economic Security ($H > W$, $p < .01$) and Religion ($H < W$, $p < .05$).

Companionship marriage is more a reflection of middle or upper-middle than of lower-class position. Evidence from Blood and Wolfe sustains that interpretation: they found that "mean intensity of companionship" was highest for high-status white-collar husbands and lowest for low-status blue-collar husbands. The more a couple is assured of economic security and occupational stability, the more likely it is that the husband will share the wife's concern with social-emotional matters.

Social-Emotional Needs. Another set of findings pertains to the partners' descriptions of their manifest personal "needs." During a follow-up visit 15 months after the first study, 49 of the initial 60 couples completed questionnaires concerning the relative strength of various needs. Data were collected on two forms: a 144-item condensation of the Edwards Personal Preference Schedule, measuring the strength of twelve general

TABLE 1. Relative Importance of Nine Marriage Goals as Ranked by Sixty Couples

Goals in Marriage[a]	Mean Ranks[b]		
	Couples	Husbands[c]	Wives
Affection. Having family members satisfied with the amount of love they give to each other.	1	3	1
Companionship. Having family members enjoy doing things together and feel comfortable with each other.	2	1	3
Happy children. Helping the children to become well-adjusted and to enjoy their lives.	3	2	2
Personal development. Giving each family member the opportunity to develop as an individual.	4	4	4
Religion. Living according to religious principles and teaching.	5	6	5
**Economic security.* Keeping up or improving the family's standard of living.	6	5	8
Attractive home. Having a place which is comfortable and attractive to live in.	7	7	6
Wise financial planning. Making sound decisions in budgeting for present and future purchases, and making intelligent use of money.	8	8	7
A place in the community. Giving family members a respected place in the community.	9	9	9

[a] The goals, which were presented in a different order to the subjects, were introduced somewhat as follows: "... Indicate which of these goals is most important to you, ... second, ... third, ... and so on ...."
[b] The numerals show the mean rank for each goal for each group. On the average, therefore, Affection was seen as first in importance by both the couples and the wives, and third by the husbands.
[c] Rho between husbands' and wives' mean ranks was .83.
* P < .05 (sign test), wives' ranks were higher than husbands'.
** P < .01 (sign test), husbands' ranks were higher than wives'.

needs; and a parallel form of this Schedule, in which Edwards' items for most needs were rewritten to refer specifically to the marital partner as the reference object. [Our analysis] shows that on all four of these needs there were significant differences between the mean scores of husbands and wives on the *general* form of the schedule.

On the *marital* schedule, however, these differences disappeared. In describing their need preferences in marriage, both partners showed markedly lower desire for autonomy, and acknowledged a far higher desire for interdependence, for giving nurturance to and for receiving succor from the spouse. It appears that these latter needs are conventionally suppressed in the general environment, particularly by men; in marriage, though, these needs are given preference by *both* partners over other more achievement-oriented desires.

Marital Satisfaction. The findings on marital goals and needs suggest that these husbands and wives would place a considerably higher value on social-emotional than on task satisfactions in their marriage, and also that husbands and wives would be relatively similar in their profiles. Measures of satisfaction ranged from two indices of global happiness, to ratings of single areas of the marriage, to differences between a partner's reported real and ideal behavior. Satisfaction with either the husband's work or with the couple's division of tasks and decisions was related very little to either spouse's general happiness. In contrast, feelings about affection, use of leisure time, and each other's social supportiveness were rather highly related with general happiness. For husbands, sexual satisfaction was more related to general satisfaction, while for wives, marital communication was of greater importance.

DIFFERENCES BETWEEN HIGH AND LOW SATISFIED COUPLES

Our findings show that marital satisfaction was related far more to social than to task performance. A comparison was made between two groups of fifteen couples, selected from the high and low extremes of the satisfaction continuum. This comparison showed almost no significant differences in task performance, but many differences in social-emotional relations. The *high* satisfied couples reported significantly more socially supportive activity and, in the laboratory, showed less rejecting behavior than the *lows*. The *highs* also reported a higher frequency of marital communication; specifically, *highs* talked with each other more on nine of eleven standard topics, the only exceptions being the discussion of unpleasant feelings and of money matters.

In the task area, though, the only significant difference between the *high* and *low* satisfied couples concerned the husbands' reports of their own decision influence. *Low* husbands reported their influence to be lower than did the *high* husbands, but the *high* and *low* wives' reports did not corroborate this. Also, there was no clear difference between the *high* and *low* groups in the dominance pattern they displayed during the laboratory session.

Contrary to the writer's original hypothesis, the *high* and *low* satisfied groups showed no difference in their joint performance on the two specially designed objective tests: In terms of a ratio of the couple's joint score to the previous average individual score, the *highs* worked together no better than did the *lows*. However, the *highs* tended to exceed the *lows* in their *expected* joint performance when they were asked to predict the couple's score before the first joint trial on the test. This laboratory finding is quite important: it shows that test performance did not, in fact, co-vary with the subjects' mutual feelings. The result adds support to the belief that these couples' marital satisfaction was associated less with their objective task performance than with their subjective evaluation of their relationship.

DISCUSSION

What does one conclude from these diverse findings? They suggest that social-emotional performance is the essence of the marital relationship as seen by both spouses in these American middle-class marriages, and further that it is a mutual rather than a specialized matter.

The findings that show the mutuality of social-emotional behavior have implications for the understanding both of family groups and of other kinds of groups. Concerning marriage, doubt is cast on the stereotype that the wife is principally interested in social-emotional relations while the husband forages merely for the material things in life. If the husband is indeed emotionally absent, the wife's ability to sustain social-emotional relations in the marriage is clearly limited. As mother, she can play a social role regardless of the husband's actions; as wife, she cannot.

BARCLAY D. JOHNSON

Emile Durkheim's main purpose in *Suicide* (1897) is to explain why rates of self-destruction vary among different groups: religious, national, occupational, and sexual. But his book provides more than an explanation of suicide rates. As he presents his theory, he also offers opinions on other topics, among them the nature of women. Scattered through *Suicide* one finds passages which offer doctrines of womanhood which sound rather quaint today, since for the most part they reflect the climate of opinion of nineteenth-century Europe. He consistently portrays men as actively involved in society, which has endowed them with a highly developed intellectual life. Women, in contrast, are not involved in collective existence, and lack the intellectual qualities which social experience provides:

> ... the two sexes do not share equally in social life. Man is actively involved in it, while woman does little more than look on from a distance. Consequently man is much more highly socialized than woman. His tastes, aspirations and humor have in large part a collective origin, while his companion's are more directly influenced by her organism (p. 385).

> Woman's sexual needs have less of a mental character because, generally speaking, her mental life is less developed. These needs are more closely related to the needs of the organism, following rather than leading them, and consequently find in them an efficient restraint. Being a more instinctive creature than man, woman has only to follow her instincts to find calmness and peace (p. 272).

Durkheim invokes this conception of how the sexes differ to account for their dissimilar suicide rates. Since men are more involved in collective life, they are more exposed to the social forces which cause suicide.[1]

The editors thank Barclay D. Johnson for kindly preparing this article especially for this anthology. All references are to Emile Durkheim, *Suicide,* Glencoe: Free Press, 1951.

[1] Anyone familiar with Durkheim's theory may see a possible contradiction here. His theory claims that "egoistic" groups (those low in social integration) will have high

Women, less socially involved, are correspondingly more protected:

> . . . in all the countries of the world women commit suicide much less than men. They are also much less educated. Fundamentally traditionalist by nature, they govern their conduct by fixed beliefs and have no great intellectual needs (p. 166).

> If women kill themselves much less often than men, it is because they are much less involved than men in collective existence; thus they feel its influence—good or evil—less strongly (p. 299).

This kind of thinking also accounts for other relations of sex and suicide. Although the higher suicide rates of men are quite consistent, the picture is complicated by the effects of marital status on suicide. In fact, marriage has opposite effects on the two sexes: it encourages suicide among women, yet inhibits it among men. In almost every age group, married men have lower suicide rates than single men.[2] These lower rates for married men reflect:

> the advantages obtained by a man from the regulative influence exerted upon him by marriage, from the moderation it imposes on his inclinations and from his consequent moral well-being. But at the same time we noted that in the same country the condition of a married woman was, on the contrary, made worse with respect to suicide unless the advent of children corrects the ill effects of marriage for her. We have just stated the reason. Not that man is naturally a wicked and egoistic being whose role in a household is to make his companion suffer. But in France where, until recently, marriage was not weakened by divorce, the inflexible rule it imposed on women was a very heavy, profitless yoke for them. Speaking generally, we now have the cause of that antagonism of the sexes which prevents marriage favoring them equally: their interests are contrary; one needs restraint and the other liberty (p. 274).

Just as marriage benefits men more than women with respect to suicide, so the *loss* of a mate hurts the woman much less than it does the man.

---

suicide rates. However, men are more socially involved than women. This being so, it would seem to follow that they are in a less *egoistic* environment than women. If in fact they are, the prediction generated by Durkheim's theory should be that men will show *fewer* suicides than women. Yet the data consistently show the opposite, that men are *more* inclined to suicide than women. The difficulty might be overcome if (1) social integration and (2) involvement in collective activity could somehow be distinguished, so that they might vary independently of one another. Unfortunately, this issue cannot be pursued further here.

[2] The relation is reversed among males aged 15–20. Very young husbands have higher suicide rates than do single men of the same age. Durkheim says that these husbands suffer from "fatalism," a very high level of social regulation (pp. 275–6, esp. p. 276, ftn. 25).

Thus, the widow is much less prone to suicide than is the widower. This is so:

> because her sensibility is rudimentary rather than highly developed. As she lives outside of community existence more than man, she is less penetrated by it; society is less necessary to her because she is less impregnated with sociability. She has few needs in this direction and satisfies them easily. With a few devotional practices and some animals to care for, the old unmarried woman's life is full. If she remains faithfully attached to religious traditions and thus finds ready protection against suicide, it is because these very simple social forms satisfy all her needs. Man, on the contrary, is hard beset in this respect. As his thought and activity develop, they increasingly overflow these antiquated forms. But then he needs others. Because he is a more complex social being, he can maintain his equilibrium only by finding more points of support outside himself, and it is because his moral balance depends on a larger number of conditions that it is more easily disturbed (pp. 215–6).

Durkheim's theory leads him to conclude that the steady rise in suicide rates during the nineteenth century is partly due to "conjugal anomie," which is his name for a breakdown in the power of the family to regulate its members' conduct.[3] Obviously, this condition is to be found among divorced people. But Durkheim says that in countries in which divorces are common, conjugal anomie afflicts even marriages which remain intact. With such thoughts in mind, he turns from the presentation of this theory to propose a social reform designed to alleviate conjugal anomie:

> The only way to reduce the number of suicides due to conjugal [anomie] is to make marriage more indissoluble.
> What makes the problem especially disturbing and lends it an almost dramatic interest is that the suicides of husbands cannot be diminished in this way without increasing those of wives. Must one of the sexes necessarily be sacrificed, and is the solution only to choose the lesser of the two evils? Nothing else seems possible as long as the interests of husband and wife in marriage are so obviously opposed. As long as the latter requires above all, liberty, and the former, discipline, the institution of matrimony cannot be of equal benefit to both (pp. 384–5).

---

[3] Egoism, and not anomie, is the most common cause of high suicide rates in his time, in Durkheim's opinion. He says this twice, but it is an assertation of which many sociologists today seem to be unaware (pp. 356, 358). Egoism takes the form of a lack of integration of religions, of families, and of political communities. Anomie is a low level of social regulation, and is found in the business world and in some families. For a summary of Durkheim's theory see: Barclay D. Johnson, "Durkheim's One Cause of Suicide," *American Sociological Review,* 30, 1965, 875–886, also issued as Bobbs-Merrill reprint #S 593.

Thus does Durkheim suggest that society be reorganized in a way which will encourage more women to kill themselves.

Surely such a proposal suggests a prejudiced attitude, especially when put forward by a man who has described the woman as "a more instinctive creature than man," whose "mental life is less developed," and who has "no great intellectual needs."

Yet in fact Durkheim seems to be rather mixed up about women. Sometimes he contradicts his usual view, and attributes their position on the margin of society not to organic but to social forces. This being so, perhaps it would be most accurate to say that he has two different doctrines of womanhood, an organic one and a social one. The social one suggests that insofar as society can be changed, women may be able to attain greater self-realization:

> ... it is by no means certain that this opposition [of the interests of the sexes] must necessarily be maintained.
>
> To be sure, we have no reason to suppose that woman may ever be able to fulfill the same functions in society as man; but she will be able to play a part in society which, while peculiarly her own, may yet be more active and important than that of today. The female sex will not again become more similar to the male; on the contrary, we may foresee that it will become more different. But these differences will become of greater social use than in the past. Why, for instance, should not aesthetic functions become woman's as man, more and more absorbed by functions of utility, has to renounce them? Both sexes would thus approximate each other by their very differences. They would be socially equalized, but in different ways (p. 385).

Durkheim pleads for the cause of woman's emancipation with even more fervor in a later passage:

> Only when the difference between husband and wife becomes less, will marriage no longer be thought, so to speak, necessarily to favor one to the detriment of the other. As for the champions today of equal rights for woman with those of man, they forget that the work of centuries cannot be instantly abolished; that juridical equality cannot be legitimate so long as psychological inequality is so flagrant. Our efforts must be bent to reduce the latter. For man and woman to be equally protected by the same institution, they must first of all be creatures of the same nature. Only then will the indissolubility of the conjugal bond no longer be accused of serving only one of the two parties ... (p. 386).

THE FEMININE ROLE AND THE KINSHIP SYSTEM

TALCOTT PARSONS

The isolation of the conjugal unit in this country is in strong contrast to much of the historic structure of European society where a much larger and more important element have inherited home, source of economic support, and specific occupational status (especially a farm or family enterprise) from their fathers. This of course has had to involve discrimination between siblings since the whole complex of property and status had to be inherited intact.

Hence considerable significance attaches to our patterns of inheritance of property. Here the important thing is the absence of any specific favoring of any particular line of descent. Formally, subject to the interests of widows, complete testamentary freedom exists. The American law of intestacy, however, in specific contrast to the older English Common Law tradition, gives all children regardless of birth order or sex, equal shares.

It is probably safe to assume that an essentially open system, with a primary stress on the conjugal family and corresponding absence of grouping of collaterals cutting across conjugal families, has existed in Western society since the period when the kinship terminology of the European languages took shape. The above evidence, however, is sufficient to show that within this broad type the American system has, by contrast with its European forbears, developed far in the direction of a *symmetrically multilineal type*. This relative absence of any structural bias in favor of solidarity with the ascendant and descendant families in any one line of descent has enormously increased the structural isolation of the individual conjugal family. This isolation, the almost symmetrical "onion" structure, is the most distinctive feature of the American kinship system and underlies most of its peculiar functional and dynamic problems.

... There are important upper-class elements in this country for which elite status is closely bound up with the status of ancestry, hence the

Reprinted with permission of the MacMillan Company from "The Kinship System of Contemporary United States," in *Essays in Sociological Theory*, 184–194. Copyright by the Free Press, a Corporation, 1949, 1954.

continuity of kinship solidarity in a mainly patrilineal line of descent, in "lineages." Therefore in these "family elite" elements the symmetry of the multilineal kinship structure is sharply skewed in the direction of a patrilineal system with a tendency to primogeniture—one in many respects resembling that historically prevalent among European aristocracies, though considerably looser.

Finally, there is evidence that in lower-class situations, in different ways both rural and urban, there is another type of deviance from this main kinship pattern. This type is connected with a strong tendency to instability of marriage and a "mother-centered" type of family structure—found both in Negro and white population elements.

In approaching the functional analysis of the central American kinship type, the focal point of departure must lie in the crucial fact that *ego* is a member not of one but of two conjugal families. . . . It acquires a special significance because of the structural prominence of the conjugal family and its peculiar isolation.

The most immediate consequences lie in the structural significance of the marriage relationship, especially in relation to the lines of descent and to the sibling tie. *Ego*, by marriage, that is, is by comparison with other kinship systems drastically segregated from his family of orientation, both from his parents—and their forbears—and from his siblings. His first kinship loyalty is unequivocally to his spouse and then to their children if and when any are born. Moreover, his family of procreation, by virtue of a common household, income, and community status, becomes a solidarity unit in the sense in which the segregation of the interests of individuals is relatively meaningless, whereas the segregation of these interests of *ego* from those of the family of orientation tends relatively to minimize solidarity with the latter.

The strong emphasis for *ego* as an adult on the marriage relationship at the expense of those to parents and siblings is directly correlative with the symmetrical multilineality of the system. . . . In a peculiar sense which is not equally applicable to other systems the marriage bond is, in our society, the main structural keystone of the kinship system. This results from the structural isolation of the conjugal family and the fact that the married couple are not supported by comparably strong kinship ties to other adults.

Our open system . . . tends very strongly to a pattern of purely personal choice of marriage partner without important parental influence. With increasing social mobility, residential, occupational and other, it has clearly become the dominant pattern.

A closely related functional problem touches the character of the marriage relationship itself. Social systems in which a considerable number of individuals are in a complex and delicate state of mutual interdependence tend greatly to limit the scope of "personal" emotional feeling or, at least, its direct expression in action. Any considerable range of affective spontaneity would tend to impinge on the statuses and interests of too many others, with disequilibrating consequences for the system as a whole. . . . The structural isolation of the conjugal family tends to free the affective inclinations of the couple from a whole series of hampering restrictions. . . . In the American kinship system, institutionalized support of the role of marriage partner through its interlocking with other kinship roles is, if not entirely lacking, at least very much weaker. A functionally equivalent substitute in motivation to conformity with the expectations of the role is clearly needed. It may hence be suggested that the *institutional* sanction placed on the proper subjective sentiments of spouses, in short the expectation that they have an obligation to be "in love," has this significance. This in turn is related to personal choice of marriage partner, since affective devotion is, particularly in our culture, linked to a presumption of the absence of any element of coercion.

. . . Since the effective kinship unit is normally the small conjugal family, the child's emotional attachments to kin are confined to relatively few persons instead of being distributed more widely. Especially important, perhaps, is the fact that no other adult woman has a role remotely similar to that of the mother. Hence the average intensity of affective involvement in family relations is likely to be high. Secondly, the child's relations outside the family are only to a small extent ascribed. Both in the play group and in the school he must to a large extent "find his own level" in competition with others. Hence the psychological significance of his security within the family is heightened.

We have then a situation where at the same time the inevitable importance of family ties is intensified and a necessity to become emancipated from them is imposed. This situation would seem to have a good deal to do with the fact that with us adolescence—and beyond—is, as has been frequently noted, a "difficult" period in the life cycle. In particular, associated with this situation is the prominence in our society of what has been called a "youth culture," a distinctive pattern of values and attitudes of the age groups between childhood and the assumption of full adult responsibilities. This youth culture, with its irresponsibility, its pleasure-seeking, its "rating and dating," and its intensification of the romantic love pattern, is not a simple matter of "apprenticeship" in adult values and responsibilities. It bears many of the marks of reaction to emotional tension and insecurity, and in all probability has among its functions that of easing the difficult process of adjustment from childhood emotional dependency to full "maturity." In it we find still a third element underlying the prominence of the romantic-love complex in American society.

The emphasis which has here been placed on the multilineal symmetry of our kinship structure might be taken to imply that our society was characterized by a correspondingly striking assimilation of the roles of the sexes to each other. It is true that American society manifests a high level of the "emancipation" of women, which in important respects involves relative assimilation to masculine roles, in accessibility to occupational opportunity, in legal rights relative to property holding, and in various other respects. Undoubtedly the kinship system constitutes one of the important sets of factors underlying this emancipation since it does not, as do so many kinship systems, place a structural premium on the role of either sex in the maintenance of the continuity of kinship relations.

But the elements of sex-role assimilation in our society are conspicuously combined with elements of segregation which in many respects are even more striking than in other societies, as for instance in the matter of the much greater attention given by women to style and refinement of taste in dress and personal appearance. This and other aspects of segregation are connected with the structure of kinship, but not so much by itself as in its interrelations with the occupational system.

The members of the conjugal family in our urban society normally share a common basis of economic support in the form of money income, but this income is not derived from the cooperative efforts of the family as a unit—its principal source lies in the remuneration of occupational roles performed by individual members of the family. Status in an occupational role is generally, however, specifically segregated from kinship status—a person holds a "job" as an individual, not by virtue of his status in a family.

Among the occupational statuses of members of a family, if there is more than one, much the most important is that of the husband and father, not only because it is usually the primary source of family income, but also because it is the most important single basis of the status of the family in the community at large. To be the main "breadwinner" of his family is a primary role of the normal adult man in our society. The corollary of this role is his far smaller participation than that of his wife in the internal affairs of the household. Consequently, "housekeeping" and the care of children is still the primary functional content of the adult feminine role in the "utilitarian" division of labor. Even if the married woman has a job, it is, at least in the middle classes, in the great majority of cases not one which in status or remuneration competes closely with those held by men of her own class. Hence there is a typically asymmetrical relation of the marriage pair to the occupational structure.

This asymmetrical relation apparently both has exceedingly important positive functional significance and is at the same time an important source of strain in relation to the patterning of sex roles.

On the positive functional side, a high incidence of certain types of patterns is essential to our occupational system and to the institutional complex in such fields as property and exchange which more immediately surround this system. In relatively common-sense terms, it requires scope for the valuation of personal achievement, for equality of opportunity, for mobility in response to technical requirements, for devotion to occupational goals and interests relatively unhampered by "personal" considerations.

But at the same time this small conjugal unit can be a strongly solidary unit. This is facilitated by the prevalence of the pattern that normally only *one* of its members has an occupational role which is of determinate significance for the status of the family as a whole. Minor children, that is, as a rule do not "work," and when they do, it is already a major step in the process of emancipation from the family of orientation. The wife and mother is either exclusively a "housewife" or at most has a "job" rather than a "career."

There are perhaps two primary functional aspects of this situation. In the first place, by confining the number of status-giving occupational roles of the members of the effective conjugal unit to one, it eliminates any competition for status, especially as between husband and wife, which might be disruptive of the solidarity of marriage. So long as lines of achievement are segregated and not directly comparable, there is less opportunity for jealousy, a sense of inferiority, et cetera, to develop. Secondly, it aids in clarity of definition of the situation by making the status of the family in the community relatively definite and unequivocal. There is much evidence that this relative definiteness of status is an important factor in psychological security.

Historically, in Western culture, it may perhaps be fairly said that there has been a strong tendency to define the feminine role psychologically as one strongly marked by elements of dependency. One of the best symbols perhaps was the fact that until rather recently the married woman was not *sui juris*, could not hold property, make contracts, or sue in her own right. But in the modern American kinship system, to say nothing of other aspects of the culture and social structure, there are at least two pressures which tend to counteract this dependency and have undoubtedly played a part in the movement for feminine emancipation.

The first, already much discussed, is the multilineal symmetry of the kinship system which gives no basis of sex discrimination, and which in kinship terms favors equal rights and responsibilities for both parties to a marriage. The second is the character of the marriage relationship. Resting as it does primarily on affective attachment for the other person as a concrete human individual, a "personality," rather than on more objective considerations of status, it puts a premium on a certain kind of mutuality and equality. There is no clearly structured superordination-subordination pattern. Each is a fully responsible "partner" with a claim to a voice in decisions, to a certain human dignity, to be "taken seriously." Surely the pattern of romantic love which makes his relation to the "woman he loves" the most important single thing in a man's life, is incompatible with the view that she is an inferior creature, fit only for dependency on him.

In our society, however, occupational status has tremendous weight in the scale of prestige values. The fact that the normal married woman is debarred from testing or demonstrating her fundamental equality with her husband in competitive occupational achievement, creates a demand for a functional equivalent. At least in the middle classes, however, this cannot be found in the utilitarian functions of the role of housewife since these are treated as relatively menial functions. To be, for instance, an excellent cook, does not give a hired maid a moral claim to a higher status than that of domestic servant.

This situation helps perhaps to account for a conspicuous tendency for the feminine role to emphasize broadly humanistic rather than technically specialized achievement values. One of the key patterns is that of "good taste," in personal appearance, house furnishings, cultural things like literature and music. To a large and perhaps increasing extent the more humanistic cultural traditions and amenities of life are carried on by women. Since these things are of high intrinsic importance in the scale of values of our culture, and since by virtue of the system of occupational specialization even many highly superior men are greatly handicapped in respect to them, there is some genuine redressing of the balance between the sexes.

There is also, however, a good deal of direct evidence of tension in the feminine role. In the "glamor girl" pattern, use of specifically feminine devices as an instrument of compulsive search for power and exclusive attention are conspicuous. Many women succumb to their dependency cravings through such channels as neurotic illness or compulsive domesticity and thereby abdicate both their responsibilities and their opportunities for genuine independence. Many of the attempts to excel in approved channels of achievement are marred by garishness of taste, by instability in response to fad and fashion, by a seriousness in community or club activities which is out of proportion to the intrinsic importance of the task. In all these and other fields there are conspicuous signs of insecurity and ambivalence. Hence it may be concluded that the feminine role is a conspicuous focus of the strains inherent in our social structure, and not the least of the sources of these strains is to be found in the functional difficulties in the integration of our kinship system with the rest of the social structure.

MARRIAGE AND THE CONSTRUCTION OF REALITY

PETER BERGER
HANSFRIED KELLNER

Ever since Durkheim it has been a commonplace of family sociology that marriage serves as a protection against anomie for the individual. Interesting and pragmatically useful though this insight is, it is but the negative side of a phenomenon of much broader significance. If one speaks of *anomic* states, then one ought properly to investigate also the *nomic* processes that, by their absence, lead to the aforementioned states. If, consequently, one finds a negative correlation between marriage and anomie, then one should be led to inquire into the character of marriage as a *nomos*-building instrumentality; that is, of marriage as a social arrangement that creates for the individual the sort of order in which he can experience his life as making sense.

The process that interests us here is the one that constructs, maintains, and modifies a consistent reality that can be meaningfully experienced by individuals. In its essential forms this process is determined by the society in which it occurs. Every society has its specific way of defining and perceiving reality—its world, its universe, its overarching organization of symbols. This is already given in the language that forms the symbolic base of the society. Erected over this base, and by means of it, is a system of ready-made typifications, through which the innumerable experiences of reality come to be ordered. These typifications and their order are held in common by the members of society, thus acquiring not only the character of objectivity, but being taken for granted as *the* world *tout court*, the only world that normal men can conceive of. The seemingly objective and taken-for-granted character of the social definitions of reality can be seen most clearly in the case of language itself, but it is important to keep in mind that the latter forms the base and instrumentality of a much larger world-erecting process.

The socially constructed world must be continually mediated to and actualized by the individual, so that it can become and remain indeed *his*

Excerpted from Peter L. Berger and Hansfried Kellner, "Marriage and the Construction of Social Reality," *Diogenes*, 46. Copyright 1964 by Diogenes.

world as well. The individual is given by his society certain decisive cornerstones for his everyday experience and conduct. Most importantly, the individual is supplied with specific sets of typifications and criteria of relevance, predefined for him by the society and made available to him for the ordering of his everyday life. This ordering or (in line with our opening considerations) nomic apparatus is biographically cumulative. It begins to be formed in the individual from the earliest stages of socialization on, then keeps on being enlarged and modified by himself throughout his biography.

This order, by which the individual comes to perceive and define his world is discovered by him as an external datum, a ready-made world that simply is *there* for him to go ahead and live in, though he modifies it continually in the process of living in it. Nevertheless, this world is in need of validation, perhaps precisely because of an ever-present glimmer of suspicion as to its social manufacture and relativity. This validation, while it must be undertaken by the individual himself, requires ongoing interaction with others who coinhabit this same socially constructed world. In a broad sense, *all* the other coinhabitants of this world serve a validating function. Every individual requires the ongoing validation of his world, including crucially the validation of his identity and place in this world, by those few who are his truly significant others. Just as the individual's deprivation of relationship with his significant others will plunge him into anomie, so their continued presence will sustain for him that *nomos* by which he can feel at home in the world at least most of the time. In everyday life, however, the principal method employed is speech. In this sense, it is proper to view the individual's relationship with his significant others as an ongoing conversation. As the latter occurs, it validates over and over again the fundamental definitions of reality once entered into, not, of course, so much by explicit articulation, but precisely by taking the definitions silently for granted and conversing about all conceivable matters on this taken-for-granted basis. Through the same conversation the individual is also made capable of adjusting to changing and new social contexts in his biography. In a very fundamental sense it can be said that one converses one's way through life.

If one concedes these points, one can [then] state a general sociological proposition: The plausibility and stability of the world, as socially defined, is dependent upon the strength and continuity of significant relationships in which conversation about this world can be continually carried on. Or, to put it a little differently: The reality of the world is sustained through conversation with significant others. This reality, of course, includes not only the imagery by which fellow men are viewed, but also includes the way in which one views oneself. The reality-bestowing force of social relationships depends on the degree of their nearness; that is, on the degree to which social relationships occur in face-to-face situations and to which they are credited with primary significance by the individual.

With these preliminary assumptions stated we can now arrive at our main thesis here. Namely, we would contend that marriage occupies a privileged status among the significant validating relationships for adults in our society. Put slightly differently: Marriage is a crucial nomic instrumentality in our society. We would further argue that the essential social functionality of this institution cannot be fully understood if this fact is not perceived.

We can now proceed with an ideal-typical analysis of marriage; that is, seek to abstract the essential features involved. Marriage in our society is a *dramatic* act in which two strangers come together and redefine themselves. The drama of the act is internally anticipated and socially legitimated long before it takes place in the individual's biography, and amplified by means of a pervasive ideology, the dominant themes of which (romantic love, sexual fulfillment, self-discovery, and self-realization through love and sexuality, the nuclear family as the social site for these processes) can be found distributed through all strata of the society. The actualization of these ideologically predefined expectations in the life of the individual occurs to the accompaniment of one of the few traditional rites of passage that are still meaningful to almost all members of the society. It should be added that, in using the term "strangers," we do not mean, of course, that the candidates for the marriage come from widely discrepant social backgrounds—indeed, the data indicate that the contrary is the case. The strangeness rather lies in the fact that, unlike marriage candidates in many previous societies, those in ours typically come from different face-to-face contexts—in the terms used above, they come from different areas of conversation. They do not have a shared past, although their pasts have a similar structure. With the dramatic redefinition of the situation brought about by the marriage, however, all significant conversation for the two new partners is now centered in their relationship with each other—and, in fact, it was precisely with this intention that they entered upon their relationship.

It goes without saying that this character of marriage has its root in much broader structural configurations of our society. The most important of these, for our purposes, is the crystallization of a so-called private sphere of existence more and more segregated from the immediate controls of the public institutions (especially the economic and political ones), and yet defined and utilized as the main social area for the individual's self-realization. It cannot be our purpose here to inquire into the historical forces that brought forth these phenomena, beyond making the observation that these are closely connected with the industrial revolution and its institutional consequences. The public institutions now confront the individual as an immensely powerful and alien world, incomprehensible in its inner workings, anonymous in its human character. If only through his work in some nook of the economic machinery, the individual must find a way of living in this alien world, come to terms with its power over him, be satisfied with a few conceptual rules of thumb to guide him through a vast reality that otherwise remains opaque to his understanding, and modify its anonymity by whatever *"human relations"* he can work out in his involvement with it. It ought to be emphasized, against some critics of "mass society," that this does not inevitably leave the individual with a sense of profound unhappiness and lostness. It would rather seem that large numbers of people in our society are quite content with a situation in which their public involvements have little subjective importance, regarding work as a not too bad necessity and politics as at best a spectator sport. It is usually only intellectuals with ethical and political commitments who assume that such people must be terribly desperate. The point, however, is that the individual in this situation, no matter whether he is happy or not, will turn elsewhere for the experiences of self-realization that do have importance for him. The private sphere, this interstitial area created (we would think) more or less haphazardly as a by-product of the social metamorphosis of industrialism, is mainly where he will turn. It is here that the individual will seek power, intelligibility and, quite literally, a name—the apparent power to fashion a world, however Lilliputian, that will reflect his own being: A world that, seemingly having been shaped by himself and thus unlike those other worlds that insist on shaping him, is translucently intelligible to him (or so he thinks); a world in which, consequently, he is *somebody*—perhaps even, within its charmed circle, a lord and master. What is more, to a considerable extent these expectations are not unrealistic. The public institutions have no need to control the individual's adventures in the private sphere, as long as they really stay within the latter's circumscribed limits. The private sphere is perceived, not without justification, as an area of individual choice and even autonomy. This fact has important consequences for the shaping of identity in modern society that cannot be pursued here. All that ought to be clear here is the peculiar location of the private sphere within and between the other social structures. In sum, it is above all and, as a rule, only in the private sphere that the individual can take a slice of reality and fashion it into his world. If one is aware of the decisive significance of this capacity and even necessity of men to externalize themselves in reality and to produce for themselves a world in which they can feel at home, then one will hardly be surprised at the great importance which the private sphere has come to have in modern society.

It is on the basis of marriage that, for most adults in our society, existence in the private sphere is built up. It will be clear that this is not at all a universal or even cross-culturally wide function of marriage. Rather has marriage in our society taken on a very peculiar character and functionality. It has been pointed out that marriage in contemporary society has lost some of its older functions and taken on new ones instead. This is certainly correct, but we would prefer to state the matter a little differently. Marriage and the family used to be firmly embedded in a matrix of wider community relationships, serving as extensions and particularizations of the latter's social controls. There were few separating barriers between the world of the individual family and the wider community, a fact even to be seen in the physical conditions under which the family lived before the industrial revolution. The same social life pulsated through the house, the street, and the community. In our terms, the family and within it the marital relationship were part and parcel of a considerably larger area of conversion. In our contemporary society, by contrast, each family constitutes its own segregated subworld, with its own controls and its own closed conversation.

Unlike an earlier situation in which the establishment of the new marriage simply added to the differentiation and complexity of an already existing social world, the marriage partners are now embarked on the often difficult task of constructing for themselves the little world in which they will live. To be sure, the larger society provides them with certain standard instructions as to how they should go about this task, but this does not change the fact that considerable effort of their own is required for its realization. The monogamous character of marriage enforces both the dramatic and the precarious nature of this undertaking. Success or failure hinges on the present idiosyncracies and the fairly unpredictable future development of those idiosyncracies of only two individuals (who, moreover, do not have a shared past)—as Simmel has shown, the most unstable of all possible relationships.

Every social relationship requires objectivation; that is, requires a process by which subjectively experienced meanings become objective to the individual and in interaction with others become common property and thereby massively objective. The degree of objectivation will depend on the number and the intensity of the social relationships that are its carriers. A relationship that consists of only two individuals called upon to sustain by their own efforts an on-going social world will have to make up in intensity for the numerical poverty of the arrangement. This, in turn, accentuates the drama and the precariousness. The later addition of children will add to the, as it were, density of objectivation taking place within the nuclear family, thus rendering the latter a good deal less precarious. It remains true that the establishment and maintenance of such a social world makes extremely high demands on the principal participants.

The attempt can now be made to outline the ideal-typical process that takes place as marriage functions as an instrumentality for the social construction of reality. The chief protagonists of the drama are two individuals, each with a biographically accumulated and available stock of experience. As members of a highly mobile society, these individuals have already internalized a degree of readiness to redefine themselves and to modify their stock of experience, thus bringing with them considerable psychological capacity for entering new relationships with others. Also, coming from broadly similar sectors of the larger society (in terms of region, class, ethnic and religious affiliations), the two individuals will have organized their stock of experience in similar fashion. In other words, the two individuals have internalized the same overall world, including the general definitions and expectations of the marriage relationship itself. Their society has provided them with a taken-for-granted image of marriage and has socialized them into an anticipation of stepping into the taken-for-granted roles of marriage. All the same, these relatively empty projections now have to be actualized, lived through, and filled with experiential content by the protagonists. This will require a dramatic change in their definitions of reality and of themselves.

In other words, from the beginning of the marriage each partner has new modes in his meaningful experience of the world in general, of other people and of himself. By definition, then, marriage constitutes a nomic rupture. In terms of each partner's biography, the event of marriage initiates a new nomic process. Now, the full implications of this fact are rarely apprehended by the protagonists with any degree of clarity. There rather is to be found the notion that one's world, one's other-relationships and, above all, oneself have remained what they were before—only, of course, that world, others, and self will now be shared with the marriage partner. It should be clear by now that this notion is a grave misapprehension. Just because of this fact, marriage now propels the individual into an unintended and unarticulated development, in the course of which the nomic transformation takes place. What typically *is* apprehended are certain objective and concrete problems arising out of the marriage—such as tensions with in-laws, or with former friends, or religious differences between the partners, as well as immediate tensions between them. These are apprehended as external, situational, and practical difficulties. What is *not* apprehended is the subjective side of these difficulties, namely, the transformation of *nomos* and identity that has occurred and that continues to go on, so that all problems and relationships are experienced in a quite new way, that is, experienced within a new and ever-changing reality.

Take a simple and frequent illustration—the male partner's relationships with male friends before and after the marriage. It is a common observation that such relationships, especially if the extramarital partners are single, rarely survive the marriage, or, if they do, are drastically redefined after it. This is typically the result of neither a deliberate decision by the husband nor deliberate sabotage by the wife. What rather happens, very simply, is a slow process in which the husband's image of his friend is transformed as he keeps talking about this friend with his wife. The process, if commented upon at all within the marital conversation, can always be explained by socially available formulas about "people changing," "friends disappearing," or oneself "having become more mature." This process of conversational liquidation is especially powerful because it is one-sided— the husband typically talks with his wife about his friend, but *not* with his friend about his wife. Thus the friend is deprived of the defense of, as it were, counter-defining the relationship.

Marriage thus posits a new reality. The individual's relationship with this new reality, however, is a dialectic one—he acts upon it, in collusion with the marriage partner, and it acts back upon both him and the partner, welding together their reality.

The reconstruction of the world in marriage occurs principally in the course of conversation, as we have suggested. The implicit problem of this conversation is how to match two individual definitions of reality. By the very logic of the relationship, a common overall definition must be arrived at—otherwise the conversation will become impossible and, *ipso facto,* the relationship will be endangered. Now, this conversation may be understood as the working away of an ordering and typifying apparatus—if one prefers, an objectivating apparatus. Each partner ongoingly contributes his conceptions of reality, which are then *"talked through,"* usually not once but many times, and in the process become objectivated by the conversational apparatus. The nomic instrumentality of marriage is concretized over and over again, from bed to breakfast table, as the partners carry on the endless conversation that feeds on nearly all they individually or jointly experience.

This process has a very important result—namely, a hardening or stabilization of the common objectivated reality. It should be easy to see now how this comes about. The objectivations ongoingly performed and internalized by the marriage partners become ever more massively real, as they are confirmed and reconfirmed in the marital conversation. The world that is made up of these objectivations at the same time gains in stability.

Furthermore, it is not only the ongoing experience of the two partners that is constantly shared and passed through the conversational apparatus. The same sharing extends into the past. The two distinct biographies, as subjectively apprehended by the two individuals who have lived through them, are overruled and reinterpreted in the course of their conversation. Sooner or later, they will "tell all"—or, more correctly, they will tell it in such a way that it fits into the self-definitions objectivated in the marital relationship. The couple thus constructs not only present reality but reconstructs past reality as well, fabricating a common memory that integrates the recollections of the two individual pasts. Similarly, there occurs a sharing of future horizons, which leads not only to stabilization, but inevitably to a narrowing of the future projections of each partner. Before marriage the individual typically plays with quite discrepant daydreams in which his future self is projected. Having now considerably stabilized his self-image, the married individual will have to project the future in accordance with this maritally defined identity. The wife, having "found herself" as a liberal, an agnostic and a "sexually healthy" person, *ipso facto* liquidates the possibilities of becoming an anarchist, a Catholic, or a lesbian. At least until further notice she has decided upon who she is—and, by the same token, on who she will be. The stabilization brought about by marriage thus affects the total reality in which the partners exist.

It cannot be sufficiently strongly emphasized that this process is typically unapprehended, almost automatic in character. The protagonists of the marriage drama do *not* set out deliberately to recreate their world. Each continues to live in a world that is taken for granted—and keeps its taken-for-granted character even as it is metamorphosed. The new world that the married partners, Prometheuslike, have called into being is perceived by them as the normal world in which they have lived before. Reconstructed present and reinterpreted past are perceived as a continuum, extending forwards into a commonly projected future.

We have analyzed in some detail the process that, we contend, entitles us to describe marriage as a nomic instrumentality. It may now be well to turn back once more to the macrosocial context in which this process takes place—a process that, to repeat, is peculiar to our society as far as the institution of marriage is concerned, although it obviously expresses much more general human facts. The narrowing and stabilization of identity is functional in a society that, in its major public institutions, must insist on rigid controls over the individual's conduct. At the same time, the narrow enclave of the nuclear family serves as a macrosocially innocuous "play area," in which the individual can safely exercise his world-building proclivities without upsetting any of the important social, economic, and political apple carts. Barred from expanding himself into the area occupied by those major institutions, he is given plenty of leeway to "discover himself" in his marriage and his family, and, in view of the difficulty of this undertaking, is provided with a number of auxiliary agencies that stand ready to assist him (such as counseling, psychotherapeutic, and religious agencies). The marital adventure can be relied upon to absorb a large amount of energy that might otherwise be expended more dangerously. The ideological themes of familism, romantic love, sexual expression, maturity, and social adjustment, with the pervasive psychologistic anthropology that underlies them all, function to legitimate this enterprise. Also the narrowing and stabilization of the individual's principal area of conversation within the nuclear family is functional in a society that requires high degrees of both geographical and social mobility. The segregated little world of the family can be easily detached from one milieu and transposed into another without appreciably interfering with the central processes going on in it. Needless to say, we are not suggesting that these functions are deliberately planned or even apprehended by some mythical ruling directorate of the society. Like most social phenomena, whether they be macro or microscopic, these functions are typically unintended and unarticulated. What is more, the functionality would be impaired if it were too widely apprehended.

There now exists a considerable body of data on the adoption and mutual adjustment of marital roles. Nothing in our considerations detracts from the analyses made of these data by sociologists interested primarily in the processes of group interaction. We would only argue that something more fundamental is involved in this role-taking—namely, the individual's relationship to reality as such. Each role in the marital situation carries with it a universe of discourse, broadly given by cultural definition, but continually reactualized in the ongoing conversation between the marriage partners. Put simply: Marriage involves not only stepping into new roles, but, beyond this, stepping into a new world. The *mutuality* of adjustment may again be related to the rise of marital equalitarianism, in which comparable effort is demanded of both partners.

The purpose of this article is not polemic, nor do we wish to advocate any particular values concerning marriage. We have sought to debunk the familistic ideology only insofar as it serves to obfuscate a sociological understanding of the phenomenon. We wanted to show that it is possible to develop a sociological theory of marriage that is based on clearly sociological presuppositions, without operating with psychological or psychiatric categories that have dubious value within a sociological frame of reference. We believe that such a sociological theory of marriage is generally useful for a fully conscious awareness of existence in contemporary society and not only for the sociologist.

PROBLEMS OF MARRIED WORKING WOMEN AS PRESENTED BY THREE POPULAR WORKING WOMEN'S MAGAZINES

MARY G. HATCH
DAVID L. HATCH

The purpose of this inquiry has been to discover to what extent articles appearing in magazines designed to serve the interests of working women, present a constructive approach to the recognition and solution of the problems of the married woman with regular paid employment outside the home.

Articles were drawn from the three leading magazines which appeal primarily to the working woman: *Mademoiselle, Glamour,* and *Charm.* . . . Over a period of a year, 1956–57, all issues of these three magazines were analyzed for articles dealing primarily with the problems of the married woman employed outside the home. . . .

Thirty-five articles were found which dealt primarily with the problems of the married working woman. The particular problem dealt with was recorded, together with the solution proposed by the author of the article. The problems were then classified in three general groups: problems involving conflict among objects of striving, problems involving vagueness of goals, and problems due to failure of the objects of striving. The general attitude of the writer of the article toward the possibility of achieving a satisfactory solution was also noted.

The basis for classification of problems was derived from Alexander Leighton's outline for a frame of reference contained in his article "Psychiatric Disorder and Social Environment." Leighton lists what he considers to be the ten principal patterns of striving with the acknowledgement that the list is somewhat arbitrary, objects of striving change with age of the individual, and some degree of tension and frustration is not only inevitable but desirable. The ten essential patterns of striving for the maintenance of the essential psychical condition of the individual are: for physical security, for sexual satisfaction, for expression of hostility, for the expression of love, for the securing of love, for the securing of recognition, for the expression of a positive force called spontaneity or creativity, for

Excerpted from Mary G. Hatch and David L. Hatch, "Problems of Married Working Women as Presented by Three Popular Working Women's Magazines," *Social Forces,* 37 (December 1968), 148–159.

orientation in terms of one's place in society, for the securing of membership in a definite human group, and for a sense of belonging to a moral order.

Of the 35 articles, 31 dealt with conflict in some form; three were found to deal exclusively with vagueness of objects of striving; no article was found which dealt only with failure of object. Seven articles dealing primarily with conflict also raised questions of vagueness of objects. Two articles mentioned failure of the object as a secondary concern.

In no case was a problem left unsolved, and in all but two articles, the attitude of the author was one of unquestioning optimism and hope for the happy solution of the varied problems of the married working woman. In fact, many articles reveal an aggressively crusading spirit, which tends to emphasize the need for women to fight prejudice against married women workers.

In consideration of the structure of the American family as an isolated conjugal system, the following questions might be raised as relating to conflict in the struggle of the married woman to carry on a career outside the home.

1. Problems relating to the woman herself:
   a. The woman still has the primary responsibility for the care of the home and children. For how many individuals, and under what conditions, will it be possible to maintain two major careers both demanding time, energy, and emotional balance?
   b. The married woman with a job is a member of two minority groups. Among workers, as a married women, she is usually in the minority. As a wife, she is also a member of the minority group carrying on outside jobs. This may result in a kind of social isolation which might be expected to give rise to emotional strains.
2. Problems relating to the husband of the working woman:
   a. What happens to the wife's career when the husband is transferred to a new locality?
   b. What is the attitude of the husband's employer toward the employed wife? (Many corporations discourage employment of wives of employed men.)
   c. What is the effect upon the husband's efficiency as a wage earner if he is obliged to assume extensive household obligations?
3. Problems relating to children:
   a. What about an honest attempt to appraise the needs of children at all ages for supervision and support of parents?
4. Problems relating to financing of the home and family:
   a. Under what conditions may the wife's job contribute to the financial security of the family? Under what conditions may the wife's job be a luxury which actually costs the family money? (One article only suggested that: "Too often, after subtracting taxes, carfare, lunches,

office clothes, and household help, there is just enough money left to buy headache pills.")

One article, only, makes an attempt to face honestly the element of permanence in the woman's choice of jobs. The length of time the woman plans to work, the author suggests, should determine choice of jobs. If she intends to make the combination of job and marriage a life-time undertaking, she might better take the job with lower income and greater personal satisfaction.

Three articles on education and professional training fail entirely to make a meaningful connection between the woman student and her eventual working plans. One article simply points out that we have come a long way in one hundred years to provide graduate training for women. Another points out that it is difficult for the woman graduate student to meet eligible men, but that if the woman graduate student does succeed in finding a husband and consequently gives up a professional career, she will at least continue to frequent her local public library. Only one ("Occupation: Housewife") asks without apology, what is the connection between academic training and housework?

Notably deficient are the inquiries into the collapse of ambitions because of lack of definition of goals for women. The implication is: any woman can combine marriage and an interesting career outside the home if she cares enough, and the proof is that certain individuals seem to do it. An editorial statement in *Mademoiselle* introducing a survey of educational advance for women is typical of the blurring of goals: "To this department's reader—the girl who wants or has a college education, a husband and babies, a job that's more than a pay check, we present her opposite number of a century earlier, when college and careers were chiefly reserved to men."

The following questions associated with lack of clarity of goals are never touched upon:
1. What types of work for women lend themselves best to enforced geographic mobility?
2. What vocations for women lend themselves best to periods of enforced unemployment because of obligations to home and children?
3. How can the prospective career wife pick a husband who will cooperate wholeheartedly with her working plans?
4. How can the woman who must withdraw for periods of months or perhaps years keep up her working competence?

CONCLUSIONS

It is true that opportunities for women in business and the professions in this country have expanded in the last hundred years. Whereas objects of striving associated with the attainment of recognition, creative expression, and security were formerly identified with marriage and home, they may now be linked with paid employment outside the home. However, marriage and children still give women the satisfactions associated with giving and receiving affection, sexual satisfaction, membership in a group, and security. The conflicts and confusion resulting from the attempt to reconcile the desired objects of marriage and children with equally desired recognition and creative expression through occupation outside the home have given rise to some suggested solutions and a considerable expression of emotion.

The articles purporting to promote the well-being of the married woman worker recognize certain of the strains in her position. Strains arising from the need to reconcile child care with absence from home receive the greatest attention, but solutions are confined to suggested techniques for dealing with children accompanied by reassurance to the working mother. Techniques for doing housework are offered as the solution to the problem of managing a home after working hours. Basic conflicts between the husband as worker and the wife as worker are not recognized, nor are conflicts properly evaluated which arise from physical and emotional strain upon the woman herself. The attitude of the writers of the articles, and certainly of the editorial staffs of the publications, is unduly optimistic.

Equally striking is the failure of spokesmen for women workers to deal realistically and effectively with the lack of clarity of goals. No attempt is made to recognize need for early choice of vocational training which will lend itself to the exigencies of family life. Nor is there any reasonable attempt to point out the need for agreement of husband and wife concerning working objectives of the wife. The problems of maintaining working skills during periods of enforced unemployment, the loss of seniority, the discouragement resulting from slowness of advancement due to uneven employment are all passed over.

As William Inge states in an interview which is conspicuously noted at the end of an article on the changing status of women: "Since Ibsen's *Doll's House,* women have been wondering who they are, where they belong. Some are still trying to find themselves. They express dissatisfaction, defiance in many ways."

THE MONETARY VALUE OF A HOUSEWIFE

CHONG SOO PYUN

... The purpose of this paper is twofold: (1) to develop a reasonable synthesis of a theoretical and methodological frame of reference which will render a workable basis for *estimating* the monetary value of replacement costs of a housewife, the purpose of the estimation being to aid judicial decision, and (2) to elicit enlightening comments and criticism on the issues discussed in the note from the wider quarter of the economics profession, so that "expert testimony" on the replacement cost of a housewife can be based on a standard professional consensus ...

PROBLEMS AND THE CONVENTIONAL METHODOLOGY

The monetary value of a housewife's services to the household is an imponderable. First, the prevalence of nongainful employment among most housewives poses a vexing problem in estimating the probable earning power of the housewife before her death. Even if a consensus is assumed to have been reached as to how the probable earning power should be measured, there remains the formidable problem of estimating the *real* value of a housewife to the household in terms of her want-satisfying capacity, for her money income, if any, has to be converted to want-satisfying means. Within our institutional setting the values of housewives' activities in the household are not susceptible to objective and empirical economic measurement; aside from the fact that their services are not generally offered in the market for exchange, neither their motivation nor the rewards they are seeking in household activities can be quantified for pecuniary measurement. . . .

Certain conceptual obscurities as well as methodological flaws are contained in the several methods that have been used in the courts to prove the extent of economic loss arising from the death of a housewife to the

Excerpts reprinted from Chong Soo Pyun, "The Monetary Value of a Housewife: An Economic Analysis for Use in Litigation," *American Journal of Economics and Sociology*, 28, July 1969, 271–284.

household. All of these methods share affinity in that they break down the average housewife's usual household activities into four to 16 discernible occupations, for example, governesses, cooks, domestic servants, and then they use the average going market wage rates for these occupations as statistical bases for estimating the replacement cost of the deceased housewife. If one follows these methods he is, in fact, tacitly assuming that all housewives are identical as to ability in home management, mental and physical capacity, and that housewives and those in labor markets, such as governesses, cooks, and servants, are readily interchangeable. Thus, the replacement cost of a housewife's services computed on these methods will *always* be equal to any deceased woman's unrealized contribution to family income for some specified, normal life span.

This method of computation may be justifiable at best for macro-economic analysis and only if the purpose is to determine the imputed value of services rendered by nonpaid housewives. It should be pointed out that the monetary value so computed, aside from the question of irrational processes involved in imputation, is nothing more than an *imputed* value which has no substance in and of itself so far as the question of the value of a particular individual housewife is concerned. Consequently, when critically evaluated, the monetary value of the replacement cost estimated on the basis of the imputed value concept renders little rational basis for judicial decisions which involve a human being whose identity as the wife (and/or the mother) is at stake. . . .

PROPOSED METHODOLOGIES

This writer proposes to estimate the replacement cost of a deceased housewife on the basis of "estimated prospective earning capacity" properly adjusted to the most probable market value of the replacement costs at going wage rates paid for the usual household occupations. More specifically, the proposed methodology requires, first, the estimation of the housewife's probable earning capacity through statistical methods. Then, the estimated earning capacity is adjusted to reconcile a divergence between her earning capacity and her utility creating capacity for the household; for, in general, the housewife's earning capacity is less than the amount required to replace the housewife's services by hiring the similar services at the market wage rates.

Estimation of Prospective Earning Capacity. . . . One of the important conditions that have to be met in using the statistical technique is the condition that there exists some uniformity of the system of facts to which certain premises and the conclusion which is about to be drawn from the statistical inference are related. In our case, as it is proposed to project the probable earning capacity of the housewife on the basis of statistical inference, it is imperative for the investigator to substantiate a set of facts through which her earning capacity may be statistically estimated. Then, given a set of pertinent facts, for example, labor-market conditions, her educational background, experience, and demonstrated skill and talent, statistical technique will enable us to obtain a good first approximation of the most probable amount of earning she could have made under certain assumptions. . . .

Estimation of the Replacement Cost. The adjustment of the divergence between the housewife's prospective earning capacity and her utility-creating capacity is made by the indifference-curve approach. A word of caution seems to be in order. The indifference-curve approach and the utility concept are applied in this study without the pretence that one is able to measure "utility" or to register his preference in numerical values. Nor are they used here without awareness that certain shortcomings are inherent in the indifference-curve approach. Rather they are used as analytical devices showing changes of the set of variables used in this study.

In Figure 1, the household's total money-income position is measured

FIGURE 1. EQUILIBRIUM OF HOUSEHOLD

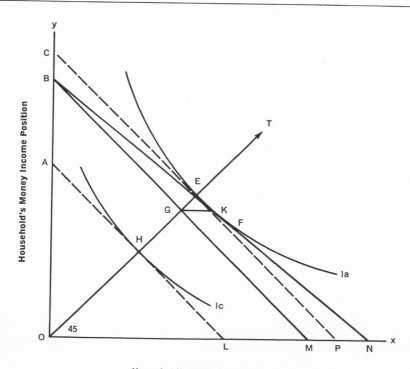

Household's Utility Income Position

in dollars on the Y axis while the household's total utility-creating capacity expressed also in dollars is measured on the X axis. Thus, LN on the X axis represents the housewife's utility-creating capacity expressed in terms of monetary value of her services computed on the basis of going wage rates for her various services in the household. The X axis will be termed the household's utility-income position. OA on the Y axis represents the husband's share of the household money income and AB the estimate of the housewife's prospective earning. AB equals the value of $\overline{X}$ explained in the preceding section. ... Note that $\triangle OAL$ is isosceles. Thus, the household's total money income Y_t is

$$Y_t = OA + AB,$$

and the household total utility income X_t is

$$X_t = OL + LN.$$

BN is the family's income restraint line before the death of the housewife. Indifference Curve I_a, which is asymptotic to the X and Y axes, is the behavior line of the household as a whole toward the total utility derived from the combination of the X and Y income sources, that is, the slope of the curve is the marginal rate of substitution.

Since $I_a = \dfrac{\Delta Y}{\Delta X}$ and, since $\Delta Y \cdot MU_y = \Delta X \cdot MU_x$, $\dfrac{\Delta X}{XX} = \dfrac{MU_x}{MU_y}$. If we let the slope of BN equal $\dfrac{Q_x}{Q_y}$, at point F, $\dfrac{MU_x}{MU_y} = \dfrac{Q_x}{Q_y}$, which means the equilibrium position of the household prior to the death of the housewife. The result of her death will force the household's behavior line down to the I_c line, and if no substitutes for the housewife are employed, the household will eventually settle at point H.

Since $\triangle OBM$ is isosceles, and since $\overline{AB} < \overline{LN}$, there exists MN amount of divergence between the housewife's money-income earning and her utility-creating capacity expressed in terms of market value of her services. This divergence may be logically reconciled by an adaptation of the Hicksian approach to the income and substitution effects, that is, by drawing a straight line in such a manner that it is parallel to the line AL and yet tangent to the curve I_a. The new line is indicated by line CP. Since the curve I_a is convex to the origin, and since the slope of CP is steeper than that of BN, line CP will be tangent to the curve I_a to the left of the point F, that is, the initial equilibrium position. If we let $CP = \dfrac{Q_x}{Q_y}$, at the point K, $\dfrac{MU_x}{MU_y} = \dfrac{Q_x'}{Q_y'}$, and, thus $\dfrac{MU_x}{Q_x'} = \dfrac{MU_y}{Q_y'}$.

Therefore, the household's economic well-being measured by the total utility is not affected in any way. The cost required to replace the service previously performed by this particular housewife will be at least LP. If the line OT is assumed to be the ideal path for the behavior line to move in (since one can inscribe the largest rectangular area inside of the isosceles by following the midpoint cut by line OT), the loss of the housewife's service in terms of her total utility-creating capacity is represented by HE. Since $HG : HE = LM : LP$, the monetary value of replacement cost of the deceased housewife for the base year period, R_o, will be

$$R_o = LM + MP$$

Geometrically, $\overline{MP}$ can be computed by solving for $\overline{GK}$. That is

$$\overline{GK} = \frac{\overline{MN}\ \overline{BG}}{\overline{MB}} \text{ , because } \frac{\overline{MB}}{\overline{MP}} = \frac{\overline{BG}}{\overline{GK}} \text{ and } \overline{GK} \cdot \overline{MB} = \overline{MN} \cdot \overline{BG}.$$

The value of R_o may be projected for a number of years to obtain the total replacement cost of the housewife. However, the length of the projection used must be justifiable on the basis of the demonstrated needs of her services by the household.

A HYPOTHETICAL EXAMPLE

As a hypothetical case, take the death of a housewife whose personal data reveals the following predicates.
a. She was white, 41 years old, mother of three sons whose ages were 14, 13, and 11.
b. She and her husband were killed at the same time and the three sons are the only surviving members of the household.
c. No special substitute was employed after her death; the grandmother of the boys assumed the custody of these surviving children.
d. She graduated from a liberal arts college in the Eastern part of the United States.
e. She was not gainfully employed at the time of her death, and a substantial time span had elapsed since she had been employed. She once worked, before her marriage, as a secretary.

In any statistical investigation which involves projection, certain basic assumptions are necessary. It is assumed:
a. That there will be no drastic change in social and economic conditions.
b. That the economy will grow at an average rate of 4 percent per annum with a relatively high level of employment.
c. That the average earnings of occupations included in the computation of the housewife's probable earnings represents symmetrical distribution of the population.
d. That the housewife had general aptitude and educational background making her eligible for consideration for employment in the occupation selected for the computation of her earning power.
e. That she would seek full-time employment, if she were sufficiently motivated to do so for any reason, and would accept an average salary rate represented in occupations selected for her by the investigator.

For the purpose of estimating the probable earning power of the house-wife, 24 occupations that a woman with a four-year college education would be likely to consider were first selected and earning statistics for these occupations were obtained from data compiled and published by reliable agencies such as the Bureau of Labor Statistics, U. S. Department of Labor, Civil Service Commission, and the National Educational Association.

The five occupations randomly selected included the following occupations and annual earnings:

Identification Number	Occupation	Annual Earning
16	Public School Teacher I	$6,184
6	Keypunch Operator II	4,957
12	Typist II	4,623
21	Librarian (Inexperienced)	5,365
10	Tabulating Machine Operator	5,390

The arithmetic mean of these five occupations, that is, her prospective annual income in the base year, $\bar{x}$, was found to be $5,300. The prospective annual income was adjusted to obtain the primary replacement cost of the housewife (that is, $R_o = LM + MP$).

Since we have now the household's total money income, Y_t, and the household's total utility income, X_t, as:

$$Y_t = AO + AB = \$10,000 + \$5,300 = \$15,300$$
$$X_t = OL + LN = \$10,000 + \$8,200 = \$18,200$$

where: OA and OL represent the husband's money income ($10,000 is a hypothetical figure in this case),

AB is the housewife's prospective annual income estimated above. (Note that AB is equal to LM. See Figure 1 in text), and

LN represents the monetary value of the housewife's service computed on the basis of going wage rates for her various services in the household. It was estimated that at least $159 per week is required to hire substitutes for various tasks normally performed by a housewife. $159 times 52 weeks is $8,268, in round numbers, $8,200.

MP is found by estimating $\overline{GK}$, and $\overline{GK}$ in turn is estimated by the formula:

$$d = \sqrt{(x_1 - x_2)^2 + (y_1 - y_2)^2}$$

where: (x_1, y_1) and (x_2, y_2) are coordinates for G and K respectively.

In order to operate this formula, we let coordinates of M, B, and N be as follows:

$$M = (a_1, b_1)$$
$$B = (a_2, b_2)$$
$$N = (a_3, b_3).$$

Then,

$$G \begin{bmatrix} x_1 = \tfrac{1}{2}(a_1 + a_2) = \tfrac{1}{2}(15,300 + 0) = 7,650 \\ y_1 = \tfrac{1}{2}(b_1 + b_2) = \tfrac{1}{2}(0 + 15,300) = 7,650 \end{bmatrix}$$

$$K \begin{bmatrix} x_2 = \tfrac{1}{2}(a_3 + a_2) = \tfrac{1}{2}(18,200 + 0) = 9,100 \\ y_2 = \tfrac{1}{2}(b_3 + b_2) = \tfrac{1}{2}(0 + 15,300) = 7,650 \end{bmatrix}$$

and

$$\overline{GK}: d = \sqrt{(7,650 - 9,100)^2 + (7,650 - 7,650)^2}$$
$$= \sqrt{(-1,450)^2}$$
$$= 1,450.$$

Adding $1,450 to the prospective annual income of the housewife, her primary replacement cost, R_o, was found to be $6,750 (that is, $1,450 + $5,300). An annual increment factor at the rate of 4.5 percent was added to this figure and the minimum supplement factor of 13 percent was further added to the adjusted primary replacement cost in order to arrive at the total annual replacement cost of the housewife. Then the total annual replacement cost was discounted at the rate of 4 percent per annum compounded.

To illustrate her total replacement costs and the present cash value of the total replacement cost for the first and second year period:

First year = $6,750 + $877 (that is, 13 percent of the adjusted primary replacement cost) = $7,627. (Note that the adjusted primary replacement cost in the first year is equal to the primary replacement cost, as no annual increment factor is applicable in the first year.) The present cash value of $7,627 discounted at 4 percent per annum is $7,334.61

Second year = $6,750 (adjusted primary replacement cost for the first year) + $303 (4.5 percent of $6,750) + $917 (13 percent of $7,054 which is the adjusted primary replacement cost in the second year) = $7,970. The present cash value of $7,970 discounted at 4 percent per annum compounded for 2 years is $7,380.35.

Repeating the above calculations for the remainder of 11 years, the total replacement cost computed for the 11-year period, before discount, is found to be approximately $105,500. When an annual discount of 4 percent is applied, the present cash value of the total replacement cost is about $82,640.

Nearly half of all women 18 to 64 years of age work in any one month. About 3 out of 5 of these women are married and living with their husbands. Almost all of these wives contribute to family income. It is often the wife's earnings that raise family income above poverty levels.[1] In other families the wife's contribution raises the family's income from low- to middle-income levels. In fact, it is at the middle-income level that the largest proportion of wives are in the labor force.

There were 42.6 million husband-wife families in the United States in March 1967.... In 15 million of these families, the wife was in the paid labor force. In the husband-wife families where the wife was an earner, the median family income in 1966 was $9,246 a year. In those families where the wife did not work, the median family income was $7,128.

The likelihood of escaping poverty is much greater among husband-wife families when the wife is an earner than when she is not. Nearly 5 million husband-wife families had incomes of less than $3,000 in 1966. Only 5 percent of all husband-wife families fell into this income group when the wife was in the paid labor force; 15 percent, when she was not.

Another 1.4 million husband-wife families, in which the wife was an earner, had incomes between $3,000 and $4,999 in 1966. Many of these families might have fallen into the poverty group except for the wife's contribution to family income.

An income of about $7,000 in 1966 dollars was considered a modest but adequate income for an urban family of four. Twenty-nine percent of all husband-wife families had incomes below this mark when the wife was a worker; 49 percent, when she was not. Another 2.8 million husband-wife families in which the wife was an earner had annual incomes of $7,000 to $8,999. A large proportion of these families might have received incomes

Excerpts reprinted from "Working Wives—Their Contribution to Family Income," (Washington: U.S. Department of Labor, Wage and Labor Standards Administration, Women's Bureau, November 1968), WB 69–63.
[1] For purposes of this study, families with incomes of less than $3,000 a year were considered to be living in poverty.

below the modest but adequate level if the wife had not been a worker.

The higher the annual family income (up to $15,000), the greater is the likelihood that the wife is in the labor force. The labor force participation of wives, in March 1967, was lowest (13 percent) in families with 1966 incomes of less than $2,000, and highest (53 percent) in families with incomes of $12,000 to $14,999.

The contribution of working wives to family income is even more significant among Negro husband-wife families. There were 3.2 million such families in the United States in March 1966. . . . In 1.5 million of these families, the wife was in the paid labor force. The median family income in 1965 was $5,709 when the wife was an earner and $3,785 when she was not.

Only 19 percent of the Negro husband-wife families had incomes of less than $3,000 in 1965 when the wife was an earner. In contrast, when the wife did not work outside the home, almost twice as many (37 percent) were poor.

Nearly 900,000 Negro husband-wife families had incomes at or below the poverty level in 1965. They might have been joined by many of the 340,000 families with incomes between $3,000 and $4,999, where the wife was an earner, if it had not been for her contribution to family income.

Another measure of the contribution of working wives is the number and distribution of husband-wife couples according to the income of the husband alone. There were 43.2 million husband-wife couples in March 1967. . . . About one-fifth, or 8 million, of the husbands had own incomes of less than $3,000 in 1966. Another 17 percent had own incomes of $3,000 to $5,000 when only 5 percent of husband-wife families had family incomes of less than $3,000 and only 14 percent had family incomes of less than $5,000 when the wife was in the paid labor force . . . the real contribution made by the working wife is evident.

The picture is similar among nonwhite husband-wife couples who are nonfarm residents. There were 3.4 million such couples in March 1966. . . . Nearly two-fifths, or 1.3 million, of the husbands had own incomes of less than $3,000 in 1965; 68 percent had own incomes of less than $5,000. But when the wife was an earner, less than one-fifth of all Negro husband-wife families had 1965 incomes of less than $3,000 and about two-fifths had incomes of less than $5,000.

Just how much do working wives contribute to family income? According to a study made by the Bureau of Labor Statistics, the median percent of family income in 1966 accounted for by the wife's earnings was 22.2 percent [see Table 1, p. 197]. However, when the wife worked full time year round, it was 36.8 percent. It was a little greater among nonwhite than white nonfarm families: 24.5 percent and 23.0 percent, respectively.

It should be noted, however, that in 22 percent of all husband-wife families where the wife worked at some time during the year, she accounted for 40 percent or more of the family income in 1966. In 38 percent of such families, her contribution was 30 percent or more.

The proportions were even higher among comparable nonwhite nonfarm families. In 25 percent of these families, the wife accounted for 40 percent or more of the family income in 1966; in 41 percent, her contribution was 30 percent or more.

The median percent of family income accounted for by the wife's earnings was highest (28 percent) in families with incomes between $10,000 and $15,000 and lowest (6 percent) in families with incomes of under $2,000.

TABLE 1. EARNINGS OF MARRIED WOMEN (HUSBAND PRESENT) AS A PERCENT OF FAMILY INCOME IN 1966, BY SELECTED CHARACTERISTICS, MARCH 1967[1]

Selected Characteristics	Median percent of family income accounted for by wife's earnings	Total	Percent distribution of wives by percent of family income accounted for by wife's earnings				
			Less than 20.0	20.0 to 29.9	30.0 to 39.9	40.0 to 49.9	50.0 and over
Total wives with work experience	22.2	100.0	46.7	15.2	16.1	11.7	10.2
Nonfarm	23.2	100.0	45.0	15.8	16.8	12.2	10.2
White	23.0	100.0	45.2	15.8	16.9	12.1	9.9
Nonwhite	24.5	100.0	42.8	15.8	16.3	12.8	12.1
Farm	4.6	100.0	69.3	8.2	7.0	5.3	10.3
Year-round full-time workers	36.8	100.0	14.5	17.1	27.1	22.4	18.9
Family income:							
Under $2,000	6.0	100.0	66.8	6.9	5.8	3.8	16.7
$2,000 to $2,999	12.2	100.0	61.4	7.0	7.4	6.4	17.7
$3,000 to $4,999	14.4	100.0	58.2	9.8	7.5	6.4	18.0
$5,000 to $6,999	15.8	100.0	55.3	11.8	10.2	9.3	13.4
$7,000 to $9,999	23.0	100.0	45.4	15.5	17.5	12.4	9.3
$10,000 to $14,999	28.1	100.0	35.2	18.4	23.1	16.6	6.8
$15,000 and over	22.9	100.0	43.5	22.3	18.7	11.0	4.5
Median income		$8,767	(²)	$9,993	$10,322	$9,973	(²)

¹ Data relate to the civilian noninstitutional population.
² Not Available.

Source: U. S. Department of Labor, Bureau of Labor Statistics: Special Labor Force Report No. 94.

LABOR FORCE PARTICIPATION OF MARRIED WOMEN: A STUDY OF LABOR SUPPLY

JACOB MINCER

INTRODUCTORY: STATEMENT OF THE PROBLEM

On the assumption that leisure time is a normal good, the standard analysis of work-leisure choices implies a positive substitution effect and a negative income effect on the response of hours of work supplied to variations in the wage rate. An increase in the real wage rate makes leisure time more expensive and tends to elicit an increase in hours of work. However, for a given amount of hours worked, an increase in the wage rate constitutes an increase in income, which leads to an increase in purchases of various goods, including leisure time. Thus, on account of the income effect, hours of work tend to decrease. In which direction hours of work change on balance, given a change in the wage rate, cannot be determined a priori. It depends on the relative strengths of the income and substitution effects in the relevant range. The single assumption of a positive income elasticity of demand for leisure time is not sufficient to yield empirical implications on this matter.

An empirical generalization which fills this theoretical void is the "backward-bending" supply curve of labor. This is the notion that on the average the income effect is stronger than the substitution effect, so that an increase in the wage rate normally results in a decreased amount (hours) of work offered by suppliers of labor. Extreme examples of such behavior have been repeatedly observed in under-developed countries. On the American scene, several kinds of empirical evidence apparently point to the same relationship: the historically declining work week in industry; historically declining labor force participation rates of young and old males; an inverse relation between wages of adult males and labor force participation rates of females by cities in cross sections; an inverse relation between incomes of husbands and labor force participa-

Excerpts reprinted from Jacob Mincer, "Labor Force Participation of Married Women: A Study of Labor Supply," in a report of the National Bureau of Economic Research, *Aspects of Labor Economics* (Princeton, New Jersey: Princeton Un. Press, 1962), 63–68.

tion of wives, by husbands' incomes, in budget studies. Similar phenomena have been reported from the experience of other modern economies.

The secular negative association between the length of the work week, participation rates of males, and rising real incomes is clearly consistent with the backward-bending supply curve. Whether this is also true of cross-sectional data on males is a question which has as yet received little attention. Superficially, the cross-sectional behavior of females seems similarly capable of being rationalized in terms of a backward-bending supply response, or at least in terms of a positive income elasticity of demand for leisure. Such views, however, are immediately challenged by contradictory evidence in time series. One of the most striking phenomena in the history of the American labor force is the continuing secular increase in participation rates of females, particularly of married women, despite the growth in real income. Between 1890 and 1960 labor force rates of all females fourteen years old and over rose from about 18 percent to 36 percent. In the same period rates of married women rose from 5 percent to 30 percent, while real income per worker tripled.

The apparent contradiction between time series and cross sections has already stimulated a substantial amount of research. The investigation reported in this paper is yet another attempt to uncover the basic economic structure which is, in part, responsible for the observed relations.

The study starts from the recognition that the concepts of work, income, and substitution need clarification and elaboration before they can be applied to labor force choices of particular population groups, in this instance married women. The resulting analytical model, even though restricted to two basic economic factors, seems capable of explaining a variety of apparently diverse cross-sectional behavior patterns. It also, in principle, reconciles time series with cross-section behavior, though further elaboration is needed for a proper explanation of the former. . . .

CONCEPTUAL FRAMEWORK

Work. The analysis of labor supply to the market by way of the theory of demand for leisure time viewed as a consumption good is strictly appropriate whenever leisure time and hours of work in the market in fact constitute an exhaustive dichotomy. This is, of course, never true even in the case of adult males. The logical complement to leisure time is work broadly construed, whether it includes remunerative production in the market or work that is currently "not paid for." The latter includes various forms of investment in oneself, and the production of goods and services for the home and the family. Educational activity is an essential and, indeed, the most important element in the productive life of young boys and girls. Work at home is still an activity to which women, on the average, devote the larger part of their married life. It is an exclusive occupation of many women, and of a vast majority when young children are present.

It is, therefore, not sufficient to analyze labor force behavior of married women in terms of the demand for leisure. A predicted change in hours of leisure may imply different changes in hours of work in the market depending on the effects of the causal factors on hours of work at home. Technically speaking, if we are to derive the market supply function in a residual fashion, not only the demand for hours of leisure but also the demand for hours of work at home must be taken into account. The latter is a demand for a productive service derived from the demand by the family for home goods and services. A full application of the theory of demand for a productive service to the home sector has implications for a variety of socioeconomic phenomena beyond the scope of this paper.

Family context. The analysis of market labor supply in terms of consumption theory carries a strong connotation about the appropriate decision-making unit. We take it as self-evident that in studying consumption behavior the family is the unit of analysis. Income is assumed to be pooled, and total family consumption is positively related to it. The distribution of consumption among family members depends on tastes. It is equally important to recognize that the decisions about the production of goods and services at home and about leisure are largely family decisions. The relevant income variable in the demand for home services and for leisure of any family member is total family income. A change in income of some family member will, in general, result in a changed consumption of leisure for the family as a whole. An increase in one individual's income may not result in a decrease in *his* hours of work, but in those of other family members. The total amount of work performed at home is, even more clearly, an outcome of family demand for home goods and for leisure, given the production function at home. However, unlike the general consumption case, the distribution of leisure, market work, and home work for each family member as well as among family members is determined not only by tastes and by biological or cultural specialization of functions, but by relative prices which are specific to individual members of the family. This is so, because earning powers in the market and marginal productivities in alternative pursuits differ among individual family members. Other things equal (including family income), an increase in the market wage rate for some family member makes both the consumption of leisure and the production of home services by that individual more costly to the family, and will as a matter of rational family decision encourage greater market labor input by him (her). Even the assumption of a backward-bending supply curve would not justify a prediction of a decrease in total hours of work *for the particular earner,* if wages of other family members are fixed.

Recognition of the family context of leisure and work choices, and of the home-market dichotomy within the world of work, is essential for any analysis of labor force behavior of married women, and perhaps quite important for the analysis of behavior of other family members, including male family heads. For the present purpose of constructing a simple model of labor force behavior of married women it will be sufficient to utilize these concepts only insofar as they help to select and elucidate a few empirically manageable variables to represent the major forces of income and substitution contained in the market supply function.

Work choices. Let us consider the relevant choices of married women as between leisure, work at home, and work in the market. Income is assumed to have a positive effect on the demand for leisure, hence a negative effect on total amount of work. With the relevant prices fixed, increased family income will decrease total hours of work. Since the income effect on the demand for home goods and services is not likely to be negative, it might seem that the increased leisure means exclusively a decrease in hours of work in the market. Such a conclusion, however, would require a complete absence of substitutability between the wife and other (mechanical, or human) factors of production at home, as well as an absence of substitution in consumption between home goods and market-produced goods. Domestic servants, laborsaving appliances, and frozen foods contradict such assumptions. Substitutability is, of course, a matter of degree. It may be concluded therefore that, given the income elasticity of demand for home goods and for leisure, the extent to which income differentially affects hours of work in the two sectors depends on the ease with which substitution in home production or consumption can be carried out. The lesser the substitutability the weaker the negative income effect on hours of work at home, and the stronger the income effect on hours of work in the market.

Change in this degree of substitutability may have played a part in the historical development. At a given moment of time, the degree of substitutability is likely to differ depending on the content of home production. Thus substitutes for a mother's care of small children are much more difficult to come by than those for food preparation or for physical maintenance of the household. It is likely, therefore, that the same change in income will affect hours of market work of the mother more strongly when small children are present than at other times in the life-cycle.

While family income affects the total amount of work, the market wage rate affects the allocation of hours between leisure, the home, and the market. An increase in the real wage rate, given productivity in the home, is an increase in prices (alternative costs) of home production as well as of leisure in terms of prices of wage goods. To the extent of an existing substitution between home goods and wage goods such a change will lead to an increase in work supplied to the market. Again, the strength of the effect is a matter of the degree of substitution between wage goods and home production.

TEMPORAL DISTRIBUTION OF WORK

In a broad view, the quantity of labor supplied to the market by a wife is the fraction of her married life during which she participates in the labor force. Abstracting from the temporal distribution of labor force activities over a woman's life, this fraction could be translated into a probability of being in the labor force in a given period of time for an individual, hence into a labor force rate for a large group of women.

If leisure and work preferences, long-run family incomes, and earning power were the same for all women, the total amount of market work would, according to the theory, be the same for all women. Even if that were true, however the *timing* of market activities during the working life may differ from one individual to another. The life cycle introduces changes in demands for and marignal costs of home work and leisure. Such changes are reflected in the relation between labor force rates and age of woman, presence, number and ages of children. There are life-cycle variations in family incomes and assets which may affect the timing of labor force participation, given a limited income horizon and a less than perfect capital market. Cyclical and random variations in wage rates, employment opportunities, income and employment of other family members, particularly of the head, are also likely to induce temporal variations in the allocation of time between home, market, and leisure. It is not surprising, therefore, that over short periods of observation, variation in labor force participation, or turnover, is the outstanding characteristic of labor force behavior of married women. . . .

MARRIAGE AND MOTHERHOOD OF BLACK WOMEN GRADUATES

FATHER JOSEPH H. FICHTER

Since marriage and child rearing are significant aspects of the female role and must be considered in relation to both occupational careers and postgraduate study, it seems important to look at the racial contrasts in this regard. At the point of college commencement, the female graduate of a predominantly Negro college is somewhat more likely than the southern white woman or other American female graduates to be single and have no definite marriage plans. Yet those who are married are significantly less likely than the two other categories to be childless. The average number of children is 1.20 for female graduates of predominantly Negro colleges, 0.71 for southern whites, and 0.86 for other female graduates.

... The woman graduate of a predominantly Negro college is about one-half as likely as the southern white woman and the other female graduates to say that marriage would make it difficult for her ever to go to graduate or professional school.

This is a clear indication of a fact for which we have further overwhelming evidence: That the educated Negro woman either does not want, cannot afford, or is culturally conditioned against the notion of marriage and family to the exclusion of other roles. Only 4 percent of the Negro women estimate that marriage would make it difficult for them to have any kind of a career at all. Furthermore only one-tenth of the Negro women, as compared with about one-fourth of the other female graduates, say that marriage "would enable me to be the homemaker I really want to be instead of working."

Practically no one of either race wants a career to the exclusion of marriage, and hardly any of these women would prefer to have a marriage which excludes children completely. The significant differences in preference occur in the two responses on combining marriage and child rearing

Excerpted from "Career Expectations of Negro Women Graduates," *Monthly Labor Review*, 90 (Washington: Bureau of Labor Statistics, November 1967), 36–42. From Father Joseph H. Fichter's report on his study of 1964 graduates of predominantly Negro colleges, prepared for the National Institutes of Health with the joint sponsorship of the U.S. Department of Labor and the National Science Foundation.

with either a professional career or steady employment. Here we find that almost one-half (47 percent) of the Negro women, compared with one-fourth (24 percent) of the southern white women and even fewer (21 percent) of the others, would really prefer to combine the familial role with the occupational role. The response that is most popular with the white women of both categories is to be employed before children are born and only after children are grown.

The large difference is the work orientation of the Negro college woman, who is more than twice as likely (40 percent) as the southern white woman (19 percent) and the others (14 percent) to say that she realistically expects to combine marriage, child rearing, and gainful employment. In contrast to their preference to work only until children are born, the percentage of Negro women decreases and that of white women increases in their expectation of realizing this end.

It is clearly demonstrated that the great majority of American women college graduates of both races expect, and would prefer, to have some gainful employment after marriage, at least at certain times and under certain conditions. . . . The general impression is that these female respondents tend to state a preference for that which they realistically expect to experience, and this seems to be the case more with the Negro women than with the white women. Statistics of the Department of Labor reveal that a larger proportion of Negro married women than of white married women are actually in the labor force. Our data reveal that three-fifths (59 percent) of the Negro female graduates expect to work occasionally or regularly throughout their married life, and the same proportion (58 percent) say that this is what they want. Only about one-third of the white female graduates have this expectation and preference.

What [do] these women think their husbands or fiances prefer for them, compared with what we have seen they prefer for themselves(?) . . . What (do) the male respondents to this survey . . . prefer for their wives (?) In the first place, all three categories of female graduates believe that their men prefer less employment for them than they prefer for themselves. But there is still a significant racial difference, in that many more of the Negro women (42 percent) than of the southern whites (23 percent) or of the other female graduates (18 percent) say that their men prefer them to work regularly or occasionally throughout their married life.

The fact is that the male graduates have an even greater preference that their wives have a minimum of outside employment than the female graduates realize. In this matter, the racial contrast also persists, with a much larger proportion of male Negroes (39 percent) than of male southern whites (14 percent) or other male graduates (15 percent) saying they prefer that their wives work regularly or occasionally throughout their married lives.

. . . These data show that the attitudes on marriage, child rearing, and wife's occupational role are most dissimilar between male and female whites and most similar between male and female Negroes. Here again, the male Negro's preferences may well be much closer to the realities of the female Negro's role than are those of the male white to those of the female white.

CHANCES OF FINDING A HUSBAND

... We asked a series of questions about women in relation to dating, marriage, and children. The educational discrepancy between the races seems to be reflected in the fact that more Negroes than whites agree with the statement that a single woman who gets an [advanced] degree will have a hard time finding a husband.

... More Negroes of both sexes than whites feel that the [advanced] degree does lessen a woman's chances of finding a husband. Since marriage is a principal goal of practically all these women, of both races, we would suspect that they would want to avoid experiences—like going to graduate school—that might make it difficult to get married. The reverse of this question, whether marriage hinders graduate study, we have already discussed. On that matter, we found a significant racial difference in opinion: The Negro woman was much more confident than the white woman that she could go on, even though married, to postgraduate study and professional training. We also saw that the female Negro college graduate was much less interested than the white college graduate in being "merely" a homemaker.

We can draw from these various data the generalization that men want their women to stay home and out of the labor market more than the women want to do so. This seems to be reflected in the fact that more men than women, of both races and both regions, want the woman to avoid an occupation that would be difficult to combine with childbearing. The racial difference, however, seems more significant than the sex difference in this regard. A larger proportion of Negro men (66 percent) and women (60 percent) than of whites of either sex want to be sure that they have children. They say this in spite of the fact that the Negro woman is more likely than the white woman to combine child rearing and gainful employment.

WORKING MOTHERS

... When women of ability, talent, and interest get into gainful employment, do they have smaller families? ... Neither the amount of schooling nor the extent of employment has the negative effect on childbearing for

Negro women that it has for white women. Putting this in another way, we may suggest that trained and talented Negro women, even though married, are more likely than their white counterparts to make a contribution to society through the professions and occupations.

Certain other questions . . . about women and careers elicited responses with an expected difference in opinion by sex, the largest of which concerns the statement that a woman should not seek advanced degrees unless she expects to work in her field almost all her adult life. Men favor this statement more than women, but the difference in opinion between white men and women is much greater than that between Negro men and women. The statement that a man can make long-range plans for his life but a woman has to take things as they come gets agreement from one-fifth of the men of both races.

"FEMININE" CAREERS

. . . There is a sharp sex differential both in the major areas of college study these graduates choose and in the occupational fields they enter. For example, women are more likely to go into social work and into grade school and high school teaching, while men are more likely to go into business fields, the physical sciences, medicine, and law. What is of immediate interest at this point, however, is the racial comparison of female graduates in these areas. [There is] a remarkable similarity in the general fields of major academic preparation among female respondents.

. . . In the most general terms, what we are finding is that, regardless of the occupational field they enter, women around the country and across racial lines tend to have the same distribution of work activities on the job itself.

YES, I CAN

One of the more significant finds of our study . . . is . . . that the female Negro with a college education has a great deal more confidence in her own abilities than does the female white graduate. Using . . . (a) . . . list of eight selected occupations, we asked them to weigh the statement: "I don't have the ability to do this kind of work." On every one of these occupations the proportions of Negro women who say that they do not have the necessary ability are lower than those of white women.

We asked further whether the respondent felt she had an unsuitable personality for work in each of the eight occupations. In most instances, the female white graduates are about twice as likely as the Negroes to think they do not have a suitable personality for the occupation.

... The ranking of the eight occupations, from those for which most have a suitable personality to those for which least have it is roughly the same across racial lines. The large difference is still in the percentage of Negro women compared with the whites who feel they have a suitable personality for these jobs. ...

In making comparisons with southern and nonsouthern female whites, we found that there were always smaller proportions of female Negroes who were ready to admit that they did not have the ability to do the work. This seems to imply great self-confidence in their own abilities in spite of the demonstrably poorer schooling of Negroes and in spite of a lack of broad experience in many of these occupations.

An even more telling difference in occupation self-appraisal between Negro and white female college graduates had shown up in the question whether they felt they had an unsuitable personality for the selected occupations. In every instance, a significantly higher proportion of female whites than of Negroes admitted they had an unsuitable personality for the work. In every instance except law, a higher proportion of Negro women from the better-educated families admit they do not have a suitable personality for the particular occupation. The percentage differences are not large (except for the job of high school teacher), but they tend to support the hypothesis that lower-class Negroes—even those with a college education—express an unusual amount of confidence in themselves.

ASPIRATIONS AND EXPECTATIONS

These findings provide a broad insight into the peculiar position of the educated Negro woman in the American society. Probably because of various occupational pressures, Negro women are more educated than Negro men and are more likely than white women to be gainfully employed. From the point of view of both family and career, they come to prefer that which they have learned to expect; that is, to combine marriage, child rearing, and gainful employment.

The class comparisons among women within the Negro group do not show much difference in orientation toward marriage and career. It appears that the employment preferences and expectations of Negro women emerge from traditional patterns which are not greatly altered by class position.

THE SUPPLY AND DEMAND FOR WOMEN WORKERS

ROBERT GUBBELS

QUALIFICATIONS DEMANDED AND THE TYPES OF APPLICANT

It is no easy task to determine the qualifications demanded; the situation in these matters is always fluid, and varies both in time and space. The situation may differ from one country to another, for many reasons, ranging from the degree of technical development to social habits and prejudices. The qualifications demanded may also vary in time, since women workers occupy a very special place on the labor market. In most countries they are still largely marginal and constitute an "emergency reserve" to be called upon in periods of full employment or over-employment.

For the last ten years or so, as a result of full employment, the number of women workers has increased in most industrialized countries.

But if we started to head for a contraction in the volume of employment, if appreciable unemployment were to manifest itself, the employment of women workers would no doubt decline substantially. There are very few people who find it natural that "women should work while men are idle." This is true both of employers and workers and of the women themselves.

These reservations must be kept well in mind and it must be recognized that they underlie all discussion of the subject: an economic crisis would reopen the whole issue.

With this premise, it can be said that, for some years past, the main characteristics of demand have been the following:

AN INCREASE IN VOLUME. The demand for labor has been expanding almost permanently over the last ten years or so.

Thus, over the last decade (1951–1961) the proportion of women in the total work force has increased in all OECD countries, except France, Portugal and Turkey.

Excerpts from Robert Gubbels, "Characteristics of Supply and Demand for Women Workers on the Labour Market," *Employment of Women*, Regional Trade Union Seminar, Paris, 26–29 November, 1968 (Paris, France: Organization for Economic Cooperation and Development, 1970), 99–111.

One of the essential features in this trend is the increase in the number of married women going out to work. In the old days, the working woman was essentially a woman on her own, unmarried, widowed, divorced or separated. Nowadays, a constantly increasing number of married women are found in the working world. In the United States, for example, they account for about 60 percent of the female work force, and one-fifth of them have one or more children aged five or under.

Married women also form a majority of the female work force in Canada, France, the United Kingdom and Sweden.

GREATER INSISTENCE ON TRADE SKILLS. This is true of the whole work force, men as well as women. A job which was filled twenty years ago, without calling for trade certificates, would now be reserved for candidates who could prove a certain amount of theoretical knowledge. It is true to say that, except for pure laborers' jobs, the insistence on trade skills has increased very appreciably.

This trend is no doubt linked up with technical development and the perfection of production methods. This shift in the qualifications required of manpower in general has been less marked in the case of women, but it is nevertheless perceptible, and it is reflected in particular in the establishment of a certain number of training courses under the auspices either of the authorities, or of firms themselves.

Simultaneously, the implementation of an active manpower policy and full employment imply a fall in *unemployment through maladjustment* represented by the conjunction of unfilled manpower requirements of firms and a mass of workless without the required type or standard of skill.

Assuming that the industrialized countries experience no grave economic crisis, it can be expected that the reduction of unemployment through maladjustment will be the main social objective for the next few years.

It is along these lines that we must consider the fairly widespread idea that the future solution is a division of labor between men and women, the men specializing in the "blue collar" jobs and the women in the "white collar" jobs.

To some extent, this trend seems in line with the present position. There are obviously far more men in industrial jobs in the strict sense, while women are mainly employed in the tertiary sector, in offices, shops and the like.

It is impossible to exaggerate the disadvantages and dangers of a solution of this kind, which would introduce a factor of rigidity into the labor market. Furthermore, technical evolution, and the long term lightening of tasks which it entails, should throw open to constantly increasing numbers of women a certain number of industrial jobs from which they are at present virtually excluded. The objection will no doubt be raised against this view that the women themselves prefer "white collar" jobs in the tertiary sector. But this is largely the result of the marginal position accorded to them in industry. We shall revert to this point in the second part of this paper.

It is clear that the lack of vocational training among women, which condemns most of them to unskilled jobs and confines them to a certain number of trades, is precisely a barrier to that interchangeability which is so desirable.

If women have always constituted a reserve on the labor market, the whole nature of that reserve has changed, since it is increasingly the result of a cleavage in vocational training; *women nowadays are no longer only economically marginal, they are also technically marginal.*

THE BARRIERS TO INTERCHANGEABILITY

If, therefore, total interchangeability is the ideal to be aimed at, it is in the interest, not only of the women themselves, but also of the economy in general. The aim is that the division of labor in society should no longer coincide with the division of the sexes.

We must therefore inquire into the barriers to this evolution. This will lead us to consider in turn a certain number of factors of different kinds which contribute towards creating or maintaining the cleavage.

The physical barriers. The first objection which obviously leaps to the mind is the physical differences between men and women.

It is nevertheless important to make it clear that most of the studies undertaken in this field fail to show any essential difference between them from the point of view of work.

There are no grounds for attributing to either sex special aptitudes or characteristics which would make them a different economic unit. The only really unquestionable difference in aptitude relates to muscular strength.

Researches conducted by the International Labor Office indicate that the muscular strength of women is about 65 percent of that of men.

It must nevertheless be clearly recognized that, in industrial societies, muscular strength is becoming less and less important, particularly because, in general, technical progress lightens the tasks and does away with the heavier jobs; the mechanical excavator has driven out the navvy.

A more serious obstacle is obviously the impediments arising from pregnancy and childbirth. And this means not only the stoppages of work involved—since men may also experience similar stoppages, for example for military reasons—but a certain number of counter-indications in the case of pregnant women, such as vibrations, toxic fumes and the like.

Less essential, though still real, are the various arrangements, particularly sanitary, resulting from the segregation of the sexes. If a manufacturer, for example, introduces women into a factory previously occupied by men only, he will have to provide separate conveniences in the form of lavatories, showers, cloakrooms and the like, which may involve considerable expense and, in some cases, may be enough to deter the engagement of women.

The legal barriers.   For many years past we have witnessed the elaboration of a whole body of legislation designed to protect women workers and safeguard them from some of the particularly harmful consequences of working life.

The practical effect of this legislation is to bar women from a certain number of jobs. Examples are the legislation on nightwork or the prohibition of underground employment of women in mines. In the same category may be ranged a certain number of special provisions, which vary widely from one country to another, governing the employment of women in certain jobs. The most typical case is the driving of lorries and heavy vehicles, which is subject to regulations which are extremely variable in different countries.

The justification for these various protective measures is a highly controversial issue which hinges on the meaning to be attached, in this context, to the word "progress"; is progressive legislation that which protects women and by so doing introduces discrimination or is true progress to be found in absolute and complete equality subject to the special reservations noted above in the matter of pregnancy and childbirth?

Whatever the answer may be there seems little doubt that, in their day, the various protective enactments represented substantial progress.

Since then, however, it is clear that there has been an evolution and the line of approach for the future is now to strengthen protective measures for *all workers,* men and women alike. This will gradually make the special protection for women workers superfluous. It may be emphasized in this connection that Sweden, for example, has recently repealed its legislation prohibiting women from night work and underground work in the mines, and has replaced it with very strict regulations on these two types of work for all workers It is, moreover, worth noting that, contrary to widespread opinion, the most troublesome shift is not the night shift but what is called the afternoon shift, which generally runs from about 2:00 p.m. to about 10:00 p.m. This is the most inconvenient shift because it rules out any possibility of social life and introduces the greatest upsets into family life.

But the objection will no doubt be raised that the prohibition of night work for women is also based on moral reasons and is designed to protect them against the "dangers" they may encounter both at work and on the way to and from work.

The technical barriers.   A third category of barriers is connected with machine and tool design. Machines and tools are very generally designed and constructed to be handled by men and not by women. Many of the difficulties in transferring a job from a man to a woman arise out of this fact.

It is obviously difficult to put a woman behind a machine which has been designed to fit the size of a man's hand, a man's height, and so forth.

These difficulties are obviously overcome in theory. The fact nevertheless remains that, in practice, they often have serious consequences.

Cultural and technical barriers.   Among the factors which militate against interchangeability, a large place must be allotted to all those connected with habit and prejudices. Habits and prejudices which are all the harder to eradicate since they always purport to be based on reason and "experience."

Among these, pride of place must obviously be given to discrimination in the matter of vocational training, It is, for example, quite exceptional for parents to attach the same importance to the education of their daughters and of their sons. The girls are brought up and educated to be wives and housewives rather than for any professional occupation; even when they do follow a course of study, a great many of them are very naturally channelled to schools which offer quite negligible career possibilities, such as schools of dressmaking or domestic science and the like. Even when they go on to higher education, there is still a certain segregation; girls are, for example, extremely rare in the polytechnic faculties.

On the same plane may be placed the relative absence of social infrastructure which makes it so problematical for a mother to go out to work unless she has the benefit of quite exceptional circumstances (relations, neighbors, et cetera).

This lack of social infrastructure, in addition to the practical difficulties it involves, also has moral and psychological consequences; a mother who is obliged to go out to work will often have a feeling of guilt because she is not giving her children the care and attention they are entitled to expect from her.

All these factors frequently lead to the abandonment, or at least the interruption, of work outside the home if some mishap upsets the precarious arrangements made for looking after the children, or as soon as family circumstances make the woman's wages less vital.

It is clear that this risk will always make the employer hesitate. He knows that everything may be upset until the woman reaches middle age when the children become independent and she can at last experience a certain occupational stability.

The barriers to interchangeability resulting from what may be called "the image of woman" or the idea of "womanliness" can be placed on the same footing.

In our society, only too often, a man does not regard himself as a real man, unless he is doing "a man's job." A woman is only "a real woman" if she is doing "a woman's job." These ideas flow from a purely man-made traditional image of woman.

The same can be said of the traditions which reserve a certain number of jobs for women or exclude them from certain others.

Examples are very numerous. It is only relatively recently that women have been admitted to plead at the bar or deal on the stock exchange. Even today, a woman engineer is an exception. Similarly, certain jobs and certain trades are still closed to women. A woman crane-driver is unheard of and, with one outstanding exception, we know of no ship-building yard in which women are accepted. And yet, during the War, we found women doing these jobs from which they are excluded and, when all is said and done, they did no worse than their male counterparts. And, furthermore, the work in no way lessened their attraction. But once the War was over everything reverted to normal.

It may be noted, in passing, that in nearly all cases, these jobs which are deemed "unwomanly" are highly paid.

The prevailing conception continues to be that of the division of labor and of functions; the man is the breadwinner, the woman contributes "a little extra" which allows for some luxuries or tiding over temporary difficulties, and this pattern is made to fit all women, even those who live on their own and have no other resource except that "little extra."

The sociological barriers. A last category of barriers is connected with social habits and behavior. An example is the hostility of the male workers themselves, who will often be opposed to the transfer to women of jobs previously "reserved" for them.

To this must be added the fears or feeling of inferiority of the women themselves, who often acquiesce in this state of affairs.

Yet other factors come into play, and in a recent paper at the 62nd Congress of the American Sociological Association, the sociologist Cynthia Epstein clearly demonstrated the extremely complicated mechanism which results in maintaining the existing cleavage. An instance is what she calls the "protégé system" under which top management is generally co-opted; a man will train his assistants, initiate them into his work and brief them, to such an extent that, if one day the question of his succession arises, whoever has the power of appointment is in practice left with very little latitude; the decision has been ready-made for them. But in practice, and for many reasons, a department head, for example, would hesitate to take on a woman as his direct assistant. In the first place because he can never be certain that she will not one day quit her job for family reasons, and secondly because working in such very close collaboration might raise psychological problems between a man and a woman, who may, moreover, each have his own marriage partner.

Family obstacles. Among the factors of discrimination, mention must also be made of a certain instability which may arise out of family circumstances; in general, a woman is constrained to work in the same region as her husband. If he is transferred away, or has to move, she has to give up her job and look for another. This is an additional factor in arousing a certain apprehension among employers and creating a definite reluctance to take on women workers.

THE CLEAVAGE

This whole combination of factors leads in practice to a veritable cleavage. Women are restricted to a certain number of jobs and trades with common characteristics. It is perfectly possible to typify women's jobs and to define the work generally done by women as follows:

1. Women's work is unskilled or almost unskilled work, calling for:
   (a) great resilience;
   (b) manual dexterity, generally acquired in other trades.
2. Women's work is fragmented and purely operative.
3. Women's work is poorly paid.
4. Women's work involves no responsibilities.

It is important to emphasize at the outset that in practice manual dexterity is an element which is generally undervalued in all job-evaluation systems.

Muscular strength, in contrast, is always highly prized. The out-and-out application of the principle "equal pay for equal work" inevitably means a revision of trade classifications. But it must be borne well in mind that modern technical evolution is calculated to lessen the role of physical strength while dexterity and concentration are becoming more and more important. In this sense, it could be said that industrial work is tending to become more and more "women's work." It should also be emphasized that another reason for low pay is the exclusion, already referred to, of any work involving responsibility, either for material, or for the work of others. Thus, for example, in the clothing industry, traditionally a favored sector for women workers, with some exceptions, it is men who are cutters, thus assuming great responsibility for the material. The women are merely makers-up, "apprentices" or "improvers."

All this boils down to the fact that, in practice, segregation is the rule. The statistics, moreover, bear this out; in nearly every trade where they are represented, women are in the majority.

SOME CONCRETE CASES

A certain evolution is, however, beginning to take shape. Investigation brings to light a certain number of transfers, which we shall first list and then analyze.

MOTOR REPAIR AND MAINTENANCE. Women service-station attendants have been fairly common for some years. What is less common, but is nevertheless found, is the employment of women for garage work proper, both the maintenance and repair of vehicles.

DRIVING BUSES, TAXIS, TRUCK-LIFTS AND TRAVELLING CRANES. Another sphere in which women workers are tending to take a considerable place is everything to do with vehicle driving. An example is the truck-lifts used to transport goods and supplies inside a factory. In several countries a fairly large number of women are beginning to be employed on this work. A similar case is that of travelling cranes; women operators are found, especially in Sweden and France. On the other hand, there are no women crane drivers proper.

ARC WELDING. This job was commonly done by women during the War, but the old practice was resumed after the War. A certain tendency can be noted to bring women back to this work, especially in Sweden, Japan and Canada.

WOMEN MACHINISTS IN GENERAL. The woman machinist is, of course, nothing new, but the evolution which is taking place relates mainly to the type of work done. So far, women machinists have done purely repetitive work, calling for nothing but simple manual dexterity.

Women are now sometimes found assigned to creative work, such as working to plans. There are, however, two limitations on this evolution; first of all, women are excluded from work which involves lifting heavy objects. Secondly, they are excluded from work on the machine itself; a woman machinist is only very rarely authorized, at any rate officially, to adjust and maintain her own machine. But this is often a decisive criterion in trade qualifications, as well as affecting wage rates.

WORKING TO PLAN. Wiring, assembly, welding, molding, et cetera, have traditionally been women's work, but so far the work done has been purely repetitive work. Women are now sometimes entrusted with working to plans.

OPERATING AUTOMATED PROCESSES. Examples are found of women controlling automated processes. In Sweden there is a chemical plant and an automatic rolling mill entirely operated by women.

POLICE, SURVEILLANCE, ET CETERA. Women in posts of authority, marked for example by a uniform and, where appropriate, the use of weapons, have hitherto been limited to very special jobs, such as Customs searchers, vice squads, et cetera. The situation is tending to change in this respect and armed women surveillance officers, women detectives and women traffic police are becoming relatively numerous.

A LAST, AND VERY IMPORTANT, EXAMPLE IS THAT OF PROGRAMMERS. The increasingly intensive use of electronics in the form of computers, ordinators, electronic brains, et cetera, has meant the creation of new jobs, among which women have carved themselves an appreciable place. This is not a question of punched card operators, whose work is similar to shorthand typing, but various jobs of a mathematical character involved in the operation of the equipment.

This is a very important development since these jobs are quite foreign to the conventional definition of women's work, especially in the matter of remuneration.

NEW JOB OPENINGS

The typology set out above, corresponding to the conventional characteristics of women's work, is therefore in the process of evolution. This evolution has, moreover, impressed public opinion, since it is manifest in everyday life in the form of women taxidrivers, tram drivers, policemen and so forth. But the visible character of the evolution under way might induce an error of judgment as to its true scope and character. It is therefore important to emphasize that in practice this evolution has two aspects. There is, first of all, a transfer to women of traditionally masculine activities, or in other words, as the result of a certain number of factors, in the forefront of which we must place technical progress, there are jobs whose characteristics have changed and which have evolved so as to conform to the type outlined above. This case is relatively frequent. The most typical case is the job which used to be done by highly skilled workers, but which is considerably simplified by the introduction of new apparatus. It thereby loses its "masculine" characteristics and thus quite naturally becomes open to women. In other words, it becomes "a woman's job."

In this case, it can be said that the line of cleavage shifts but does not disappear.

A traditionally masculine job becomes a woman's job; this does not necessarily mean any fundamental evolution in the matter of cleavage. Nor can it be regarded as a feminine "conquest." In practice, nothing fundamental is changed by an evolution of this kind. Simultaneously, however, a much more profound, but also much slower, evolution is also taking place towards the disappearance of the cleavage, or to use a word which is not yet in established usage, but which is evocative, in the direction of "mixity." In this case, and in this case only, we can talk of a fundamental evolution. It exists, but we must recognize quite clearly that it is infinitely less clear-cut and less decisive than might be imagined. One woman cosmonaut does not mean that the condition of women as a whole has evolved.

Nevertheless, tenuous as it is, this evolution unquestionably exists and we can see women doing totally new jobs which were formerly closed to them.

This evolution is the result of various factors, the first of which, already referred to, is technical progress, which normally lightens the task and thus breaks down the main physical barrier to the "mixity" of jobs. In any event, this phenomenon is well known, and there is no need to dwell on it further.

On the contrary, it would be much better to emphasize that what is believed to be a quite general rule, is nevertheless subject to a certain number of exceptions. It may happen that technical progress makes a job heavier. In the textile industry, for example, certain entirely new machines are fitted with reels which are so heavy that they cannot be handled by the women who traditionally did this work. As a result, jobs previously done by women have had to be transferred to men. Similarly, in general, the perfecting and improving of tools sometimes means an increase in their weight. An example recently noted is that of multiple head screwdrivers, which have become so heavy that most women workers have had to be replaced. No doubt all these are only exceptions, but it is as well to bear clearly in mind that the lightening of jobs by technical progress is no more than a general rule which may be subject to a certain number of exceptions.

Another factor which has contributed towards creating new job openings for women has been the labor shortage in recent years. This is obviously the decisive factor: the business chief who needs labor to meet his commitments to his customers will override tradition, prejudice or any other similar consideration. The labor shortage has unquestionably been the driving force behind the evolution in countries where it has been particularly marked, such as Sweden and Japan. It is, moreover, significant to note the strange similarity in this respect between countries which are otherwise so different; not only are the jobs transferred substantially the same, but in addition, when business chiefs are questioned about their projects, the experiments contemplated are also largely similar. This convergence of evolution is obviously not merely due to hazard. It is partly the result of identical technical evolution (sometimes, even, the equipment is purely and simply standardized internationally). Account must also very probably be taken of contacts within the world of employers, exchange of experience, et cetera.

But another factor, of a more sociological character, has contributed towards the launching of interpenetration; outlooks are changing. Women, especially among the younger women, no longer find it quite natural that some jobs should be reserved for men. A minority among them are beginning to recognize their capabilities. Men, for their part, are slowly beginning to accept the evolution.

Furthermore, the well-known phenomenon of middle-aged women going back to work has also played its part. It is common knowledge that, for some years past, there has been a very marked tendency for women who have passed the age of child-bearing to return to work. The presence of these middle-aged women on the labor market has a great many consequences, especially in our present context. In practice they have generally very little geographical mobility, their life is organized, their home well established, the husband in a steady job. For this reason, if they want work, they must adapt themselves to the local openings. Where appropriate, they will therefore be candidates even for jobs which are not "women's jobs," if only they are open.

Experience in fact shows that there is a substantial proportion of middle-aged women among the cases of transfer.

All the factors summarized above constitute what might be called the components of sociological determinism, or in other words, they will all take effect, in the absence of any external influence. They represent "the force of events."

If, as is probable, the rate of technical progress continues and if, at the same time, the rate of economic development is maintained (or in other words, if we succeed in staving off unemployment), it can be said that the evolution, which is still only in its first infancy, will gain momentum. But we must not burke the fact that this evolution will be slow, extremely slow. The question whether this slowness is acceptable and whether a gradual painless evolution is preferable to a rapid evolution, which by its very speed involves numerous upheavals, is essentially a question of policy. It is therefore outside the competence of the economist and the sociologist, who can do no more than formulate it, and analyze its components and its applications. But in the last analysis, the decision will depend on an option, and that option will depend on the overall view which is taken of society. We reiterate that this means that the problem is a political one.

This being said, it is clear that if a rapid evolution is desired, it would be illusory to rely purely and simply upon social and economic determinism. A rapid evolution calls for measures of compulsion such as those recently taken in the United States, where the Civil Rights Act prohibits outright any discrimination based on sex and forbids employers to exclude women from any job whatsoever.

COUNSELOR BIAS AND THE FEMALE OCCUPATIONAL ROLE

JOHN J. PIETROFESA
NANCY K. SCHLOSSBERG

Even though a large percentage of women work, and a large percentage of workers are women, the startling fact is the decline in their position in recent years. [Women's] representation among professional workers has actually declined from 40 percent in 1950 to 37 percent in 1966. Furthermore, women receive proportionately fewer Master's degrees and Doctorates today than in the 1920s, and women hold proportionately fewer technical and professional positions today than in 1940. . . . Complicating the picture is the fact that each sex occupies different levels on the status hierarchy and the sexes are unevenly distributed as to field of endeavor. It has been substantiated that:

> American education is blighted by a sex-split in its curriculum. At present the whole field of knowledge is divided along tacit but well-understood sex lines. Those subjects given the highest status in American life are 'masculine'; those given the lowest are 'feminine' . . . thus math, the sciences . . . business administration . . . are men's subjects . . . and the humanities are relegated . . . 'suitable to women.'[1]

Since many high school and college women discuss their choice of major and occupation with counselors, the question arises—what do counselors feel the role of women should be? In discussing this question with counselors-in-training, they voice a partial egalitarian view—women should do whatever they want to do. Since actions speak louder than words, it was decided to study actual interviews of counselors-in-training with a female client who was deciding between a "feminine" and "masculine" occupational role. The assumption was that through careful analysis of verbatim interviews, the degree of counselor bias would be revealed. Thus, this study was conceived as an investigation of the counselor's bias in the total process of role stereotyping of women. If counselors do dis-

---

Reprinted from an unpublished paper by John J. Pietrofesa and Nancy K. Schlossberg, "Counselor Bias and the Female Occupational Role."

[1] K. Millett, *Token Learning: A Study of Women's Higher Education in America* (New York: National Organization for Women, 1968), p. 14.

play bias, the ramifications of such a fact would have to be taken into account in counselor-education programs.

The data suggest that counselors do hold bias against women entering a so-called "masculine" occupation. Female counselors, interestingly enough, displayed as much bias as did their male counterparts. The results tend to suggest that male and female counselors both display more statements "biased against females" than "biased for females." The three ratings combined showed a significant difference at the .01 level of confidence. Percentage results strongly reinforce the conclusion that counselors are biased against women entering masculine fields. Of the total bias statements, 81.3 percent are against women, whereas only 18.7 percent are biased for women.

A content analysis of the 79 biased statements made by the counselors in this study reveals that most negatively biased statements emphasized the masculinity of the field. Working conditions and promotional opportunity were a far second and third.

In order to tabulate the statements 10 categories were devised so that negative bias (NB) and positive bias (PB) statements could be classified as to content. The following examples of bias statements will give the flavor of the kinds of pressures counselors imposed.

Salary—Amount of monetary return
      (NB) "Money isn't everything."
      (PB) "You could make much more money as an engineer."

Status—Perception of self in vocation
      (NB) "The status of a woman is higher in the field of teaching."
      (PB) "There is more prestige in becoming an engineer."

Marriage and Family—Family Attachment
      (NB) "Would your husband resent you being an engineer?"
      (NB) "You would only be gone from home during school hours if you taught school."
      (PB) "Being an engineer would not interfere with you becoming married."

Parents—Parental Support
      (NB) "How do your parents feel about you entering engineering instead of education?"
      (PB) "I am glad your parents want you to become an engineer."

Educational Time—Amount of time necessary for preparation to enter the vocational field

(NB) "Engineering would take five years and elementary education would be four years. . . . These are things you might want to consider."

(PB) "It may take longer to become an engineer but it is well worth it."

Educational Preparation—Classes one must take to enter the field and the kinds of classes already taken

(NB) "The course work in engineering would be very difficult."

(PB) "Your classwork up to now shows that you would do well as an engineer."

Promotional Opportunities—Advancement in position

(NB) "There might be a holding back of you because you are a woman."

(PB) "Your chances of promotion would be good in engineering."

Hiring—Opportunity to enter field

(NB) "They are not supposed to discriminate against women, but they still get around it."

(PB) "The opportunities for a woman in engineering are good."

Working conditions—Where, with whom, what kind of work, and/ or under what conditions work is done

(NB) "Engineering . . . it is very, you know, technical, and very, I could use the term 'unpeopled'."

(PB) "You could work at a relaxed pace as an engineer."

Masculine Occupation—Identification of occupation as masculine

(NB) "You normally think of this as a man's field."

(PB) "There is no such thing as a man's world anymore."

The implications of the study are quite clear—counselors, both male and female hold biases against female counselees entering an occupation characteristically associated with males. Counselor-education programs must take this into account in their programs and attempt to bring into the open such biased feelings, so that counselors are able to control them, or better yet, remove them from their counseling and human encounters.

Women should have an equal opportunity to compete in the world of work with their male counterparts. Yet, discriminatory practices still exist. Further subtle pressures and influences against entering so-called "masculine" occupations by parents, as well as teachers and counselors, may do more harm than discriminatory practices by employers. Self-fulfillment for women is not an insubstantial and irrational dream; it can be achieved.

DIFFERENCES IN HOURLY EARNINGS BETWEEN MEN AND WOMEN

VICTOR R. FUCHS

The fact that men earn more than women is one of the best established and least satisfactorily explained aspects of American labor-market behavior. The lack of satisfaction does not stem from a dearth of hypotheses, but rather the reverse. It is claimed that men are stronger than women; that they invest more in themselves (in on-the-job training, apprenticeships, and so on) after formal schooling is completed; that they are more firmly attached to the labor force; that women place more importance on the nonmonetary aspects of a job than do men; and last, but not necessarily least, that women suffer from discrimination at the hands of employers, fellow employees, customers, and society at large. . . .

The principal focus [of this paper] is on determining the size of the sex differential in hourly earnings for all nonfarm employed persons and on analyzing how this differential varies across industries, occupations, and other subgroups. The assumption underlying the research strategy is that the *pattern* of variation can shed some light on the *causes* of the differential. . . .

The basic source of data is the One-in-One-Thousand sample of the 1960 *Census of Population and Housing*. . . .

Total annual earnings in 1959 are calculated for workers in each classification. Total hours are estimated by multiplying (for each worker) the weeks worked in 1959 and the hours worked in the Census week in 1960 and summing across all the workers in a classification. Average hourly earnings for each classification are obtained by dividing total earnings by total hours. When there are only a few workers in a classification the estimates of hourly earnings are subject to considerable sampling error; therefore, results for groups containing fewer than 50 observations are usually omitted or are marked accordingly.

The differential is expressed in the form of female earnings as a percent-

Excerpts reprinted from Victor R. Fuchs, "Differences in Hourly Earnings between Men and Women," *Monthly Labor Review*, 94 (Washington: U.S. Department of Labor, Bureau of Labor Statistics, 1971), 9–15.

age of male earnings. These percentages are based on comparison of group means using simple and multiple regressions on dummy variables.

DISCRIMINATION AGAINST WOMEN

For nonfarm employed, average female hourly earnings were 60 percent of male earnings in 1959 (see Table 1). Adjustment for color, schooling, age, and city size has very little effect on this differential. Adjustment for length of trip to work, marital status, and class of worker raises the ratio to 66 percent. The length-of-trip variable is of particular interest because it reflects the different pressures on women that cut into their market earnings. It is well known, and confirmed by this study, that jobs located in residential areas pay less on average than do comparable jobs not located in residential areas. Regardless of sex, employed persons who work at home or walk to work earn about 26 percent less than do those who must travel to their jobs, other things being equal. Women typically have greater responsibilities in the home, and we might expect them to seek employment nearer home.

The variation in the size of the differential by marital status is quite large and suggests some of the processes that contribute to differences in earnings. The differential is largest for men and women who are married

TABLE 1. FEMALE AVERAGE HOURLY EARNINGS RELATIVE TO MALE FOR ALL NONFARM EMPLOYED AND SELECTED SUBGROUPS, 1959[1]
(in percent)

Characteristic	Unadjusted	Adjusted for color, schooling, age, and city size	Adjusted for color, schooling, age, city size, marital status, class of worker, and length of trip
All	60	61	66
Length of trip to work:[2]			
Short trip	64	63	65
Medium trip	63	63	66
Long trip	59	62	65
Marital status:			
Married, spouse present	58	59	61
Never married	88	82	83
Other	69	67	68
Class of worker:			
Self-employed	41	45	58
Private wage and salary	58	59	64
Government	81	77	79
Age:[3]			
Less than 25	83	82	82
25–34	69	69	73
35–44	58	59	62
45–54	58	57	61
55–64	57	54	61

[1] The source of all tabular material is the One-in-One-Thousand sample of the 1966 Census of Population and Housing. All calculations are by the author.
[2] Short trips = work at home or walk to work. Long trips = place of work in different county or city than place of residence. Medium trips = all other.
[3] Whites only.

with spouse present. In such cases the man's incentive and ability to devote himself to work in the market is greatest, and that of women is usually the smallest.

Analysis of earnings for different classes of workers also helps to shed some light on the nature and extent of discrimination against women. Consider first the hypothesis that the employer or supervisor is the principal source of discrimination. If so, we would expect the male-female differential in earnings to be smallest for the self-employed, because no discrimination of this type is possible. Also, a smaller differential might be expected for private wage and salary workers than for government workers because the competitive pressures for profits and survival would tend to exert more discipline in the private sector.

The results presented in table 1 strongly reject this hypothesis. The male-female differential in earnings is definitely largest for the self-employed and smallest for government employees. The data could be interpreted as saying that there is less employer discrimination in government, but this fails to explain why the differential is larger for the self-employed than for private wage and salary workers. The observed pattern of earnings differentials and employment distribution *is* consistent with the hypothesis of discrimination by customers. (For example, customers at an auto repair shop may not be willing to let a female mechanic work on their cars, regardless of her training and experience. Or, many customers in expensive restaurants often prefer waiters to waitresses.) Government could be expected to be least sensitive and the self-employed most sensitive to that type of discrimination.

EFFECT OF AGE AND MARITAL STATUS

The sharp decrease in the female-male earnings ratio with increasing age is one of the most striking findings of this study. It supports the hypothesis that much of the overall differential is related to the more casual attachment of women to the labor force and to sex differences in post-school investment. This interpretation is confirmed if we look at the differentials by age and marital status. . . . Women who have never married—who are much more likely to stay in the labor force and who have more incentive to invest in themselves after formal schooling is completed—have an age-earnings profile which is very similar to that of men. At young ages there is not much variation in the size of the sex differential by marital status, but for married women with spouse present (and "other" women to a lesser extent), the differential increases with age. The pattern of differentials in average annual hours shows clearly the way marital status (and its concomitant demands on women for work outside the market) affects their earnings potential.

DIFFERENCES ACROSS INDUSTRIES

The male-female differential in hourly earnings varies considerably across industries . . . analysis of this variation may help to shed light on the differential itself. For instance, a finding that the differential is related to institutional industry characteristics such as unionization or establishment size would tend to support the employer discrimination hypothesis. If, however, differences in the differential can be explained primarily by differences in worker characteristics such as schooling and age, the discrimination hypothesis tends to be refuted.

In order to avoid considering atypical situations, the analysis is restricted to industries with at least 50 males and 50 females in the One-in-One-Thousand Sample. These 46 industries account for 81 percent of all women and 54 percent of all men. Most of the excluded industries employ very few women; some employ fewer than 50 (thousand) of either sex.

In the regressions . . . the dependent variable is female hourly earnings as a percentage of male. The most significant independent variable, in either the simple or multiple regressions, is female "expected" earnings as a percentage of male ["expected" hourly earnings based on all industries earnings ratios for 168 color, age, sex, and schooling classifications and the distribution of employed persons in each group]. This tells us that the pattern of the differential across industries is highly correlated with the pattern of differences in mix of schooling, age, and color. Furthermore . . . the differential is *not* related to extent of unionization or size of establishment. If employer discrimination was a major factor in the sex differential, we might expect that it would vary across industries in an erratic fashion or be related to such institutional variables as unionization and establishment size.

The age-profile variable is also significant. This is a measure of the extent to which earnings of white males rise with age, and I interpret it as revealing the extent to which there is labor-market-relative post-school investment in human capital. The sex differential in earnings is higher in industries with steep age profiles because men are more likely than women to undertake such investment.

The higher the percentage of female employment the lower are earnings, but this is true for men as well as women. There is no support for the hypothesis that men dislike working in the same industries as women and must, therefore, be given special compensation to do so.

DIFFERENCES ACROSS OCCUPATIONS

When sex differentials across occupations are examined, one of the most striking findings is how few occupations employ large numbers of both sexes. Most men work in occupations that employ very few women, and a significant fraction of women work in occupations that employ very few men.

Although there are significant differences in schooling between white men and black men, their occupational distributions are much more alike than are those of white men and white women.

It should not be thought that the difficulty in finding many occupations that employ both large numbers of men and women is attributable to the small size of the average occupation. There are 100 occupations that employ over 100,000 persons, but only 46 of them employ as many as 35,000 of each sex.

The results of regressions across these occupations are in general similar to those reported for industries. One new variable, which measures the extent of variation of earnings of individual males, proves to be highly significant. This variable can be interpreted as a measure of the heterogeneity of the occupational classification. The more homogeneous the occupation, the smaller will be the individual variability. We find that women's earnings are particularly depressed in occupations in which there is great individual variability among males. This suggests that the more detailed the occupational classification the smaller would be the observed sex differential in earnings. Indeed, I am convinced that if one pushes occupational classification far enough one could "explain" nearly all of the differential. In doing so, however, one merely changes the form of the problem. We would then have to explain why occupational distributions differ so much.

SUMMING UP

The difference in hourly earnings between men and women has been and is very large. When most jobs required heavy labor, the difference might have been explained by differences in physical strength, but, given the present occupational structure, it is implausible to attribute a 40 percent differential to inherent differences in physical or mental ability.

In my opinion, most of the 40 percentage points can be explained by the different *roles* assigned to men and women. Role differentiation, which begins in the cradle, affects the choice of occupation, labor-force attachment, location of work, post-school investment, hours of work, and other variables that influence earnings. Role differentiation can, of course, result from discrimination. We have not found, in this preliminary study, evidence that employer discrimination is a major direct influence upon male-female differentials in average hourly earnings. Discrimination by consumers may be more significant.

Given the changes that have been and are occurring in our society—such as the reduction in infant mortality, the improvements in family planning and the shift from an industrial to a service economy—it appears to many (including this writer) that some reduction in role differentiation is desirable. Such reduction would require the combined efforts of men and women at home and in school, as well as the marketplace, and probably would result in a narrowing of earnings differences over the long run.

SOCIAL AND PRIVATE RATES OF RETURN
TO INVESTMENT IN SCHOOLING

FRED HINES
LUTHER TWEETEN
MARTIN REDFERN

It is now widely recognized that formal schooling has contributed significantly to growth in income, both for the nation and for individuals. But major gaps still exist in our knowledge of the economic productivity of schooling. . . . Gaps also exist in knowledge of the private rates of return from schooling investment for the U.S. as a whole and for groups classified by race, sex, and region. This report fills some of these gaps in our knowledge of the economic payoff from formal schooling. . . .

Our research employs the 1959 cross-sectional age-earnings data of the *One-in-One-Thousand Sample of the 1960 Census of Population.* The direct public costs of schooling for each race-sex group and region are derived from data found in the *Statistical Abstract of the United States.* School enrollment data from the 1960 *U.S. Census* are used to weight the seven "marginal" social rates of return to obtain the total social rate of return on schooling as a weighted average for all persons enrolled in school during the 1959–60 school year.

BENEFITS FROM SCHOOLING

The 1/1,000 sample of the 1960 Census of Population includes more than 107,000 persons 14 years of age and over (not enrolled in school). These cross-sectional earnings data by 12 age categories and eight schooling levels are used to compute the age-earnings profiles for U.S. white males, males of other races, white females and females of other races and also for the aggregate of these four race-sex groups in the Northeast, North-central, South, and West Census Regions. The reliability of each age-earnings profile tends to increase with a larger sample size and with a considerable number of observations within each age category. By this measure the white profiles are more reliable than the profiles of other

Excerpted from Fred Hines, Luther Tweeten, Martin Redfern, "Social and Private Rates of Return to Investment in Schooling, by Race-Sex Groups and Regions," *The Journal of Human Resources,* 5, 1970, n. 3, 318–340.

races—the total white sample is approximately ten times as large as the sample for other races. Reliability of the profiles for the elementary schooling levels over all race, sex and regional groups suffers from a small sample in the lower age brackets. Over schooling groups, the high school profiles are the most reliable. While there are substantial numbers of high school graduates in each age category, results presented later will show considerable bias in estimates of returns to this investment in secondary education.

The age-earnings profiles provide the basis for computing benefits from schooling for each race-sex and regional group. The benefit derived from an additional year of schooling is the present value of the difference in earnings between two adjoining schooling groups over all age groups.

COSTS OF SCHOOLING

Direct and indirect costs comprise total schooling costs. Direct schooling costs include public and private expenditures, whereas indirect costs here include only the foregone earnings of persons receiving schooling. . . . For elementary and secondary schooling, the Northeast had the highest combined current costs of $471 per student and the South had the lowest current costs of $281 per student. Total direct college costs per student ranged from $2,121 in the Northeast to $1,823 in the South. Combined current costs per pupil in elementary and secondary schooling were $329 for U.S. whites and $304 for students of other races. College costs were assumed to be equal for whites and students of other races.

Social costs of schooling include all public and private costs. Social costs are paid by taxpayers, parents, and students, and include teachers' salaries, administrative expenses, and building expenses as well as earnings foregone by students while in school. . . .

Private costs, or all costs of education to the individual, are considered to be equal to earnings foregone while in school. Foregone earnings by students are taken as equal to the earnings of people of the same age and schooling level but not enrolled in school. Miscellaneous expenses of students are assumed to be equal to student earnings; that is, expenses paid by students for school supplies, tuition, et cetera, are considered to be exactly offset by the earnings of students during the school year and vacation periods.

SOCIAL AND PRIVATE RATES OF RETURN TO SCHOOLING

The social rate of return to investing in any marginal year of schooling is that interest (discount) rate which makes the present value of net social benefits from schooling equal to zero. The overall total social rate is defined as the rate that sets the aggregate of all net social benefits over all schooling groups equal to zero. The overall rate, R, is computed as:

(1)
$$\sum_{i=1}^{7} \sum_{n=b}^{75} \frac{P_i(NB_{in})}{(1+R)^{n-b}} = 0$$

where:

$n =$ age.
$i =$ the marginal schooling group under question.
$b =$ age of beginning the marginal schooling.
$P_i =$ total number of persons receiving the marginal schooling.
$(NB_i) =$ net social benefits from the marginal year of schooling where costs are treated as negative benefits and positive benefits are the additional earnings of the schooling group.

Based on age-earnings profiles for all persons within the designated schooling group within each region, the total U.S. rate of return over all regions is calculated as:

(2)
$$\sum_{j=1}^{4} \sum_{i=1}^{7} \sum_{n=b}^{75} \frac{P_{ij}(NB_{ijn})}{(1+R)^{n-b}} = 0$$

where j is the region. The rate of return, R, from equation (2) is that interest rate at which the nation could afford to borrow funds and just break even on its investment in schooling over all schooling levels for all race-sex groups and regional locations. Alternatively, the rate, R, may be considered a measure of the overall economic payoff from formal schooling.

Rates of Return for Race-Sex Groups. Table 1 presents social rates of return for four U.S. race-sex groups as well as the overall total social rate for each group. The private rates of return are shown in parentheses. The diagonal elements of Table 1 are marginal rates (they deal with one schooling increment and adjoining schooling groups) and the off-diagonal elements are average rates (they are based on more than one schooling increment).

The overall total social rate, shown in the lower right corner, may be confused with the average rate, shown in the lower left corner. The latter represents the average return on dollars spent on 16 years of schooling of the typical individual from the point of view of that individual (the private rate) and the point of view of society (social rate). These rates indicate what interest rate could be paid by individuals or society on money borrowed to finance education (16 years) of the typical individual and break even on that investment. The total social rate, from equation

TABLE 1
SOCIAL AND PRIVATE (IN PARENTHESES) RATES OF RETURN TO FORMAL SCHOOLING, BY RACE-SEX GROUP, UNITED STATES, IN PERCENT, 1959

Higher Schooling Level	Lower Schooling Level							Total Social Rate
	0	1–4	5–7	8	9–11	12	13–15	
White Males								
1–4	15.6 (a)							
5–7	17.4 (a)	20.5 (a)						
8	17.8 (155.1)	20.3 (117.1)	19.8 (48.7)					
9–11	17.6 (80.9)	19.3 (56.3)	18.1 (32.2)	16.9 (25.4)				
12	16.7 (56.1)	17.4 (38.8)	15.5 (24.4)	14.0 (19.5)	11.3 (14.5)			
13–15	14.9 (40.8)	14.6 (28.6)	12.5 (19.4)	11.2 (16.1)	9.4 (13.0)	8.3 (12.1)		
16	14.7 (33.4)	13.7 (24.6)	12.1 (18.1)	11.2 (15.8)	10.6 (14.4)	9.7 (13.6)	11.0 (15.1)	
Total social rate								15.1
Males of Other Races								
1–4	4.0 (a)							
5–7	12.2 (a)	20.7 (a)						
8	9.7 (78.8)	12.5 (46.2)	7.2 (8.8)					
9–11	10.6 (53.1)	13.2 (38.0)	9.4 (14.0)	15.6 (30.8)				
12	11.9 (40.8)	14.2 (32.5)	11.9 (17.7)	16.7 (27.3)	17.5 (24.6)			
13–15	8.5 (23.7)	9.4 (20.3)	7.2 (12.0)	7.2 (14.4)	5.6 (10.3)	0.6 (2.2)		
16	7.9 (20.3)	8.5 (16.9)	6.8 (11.4)	6.7 (12.6)	5.7 (10.2)	3.0 (6.0)	5.8 (10.1)	
Total social rate								10.2
White Females								
1–4	8.9 (a)							
5–7	5.6 (a)	3.1 (a)						
8	5.6 (37.8)	4.0 (9.8)	5.8 (13.3)					
9–11	6.3 (33.7)	5.3 (14.4)	7.3 (18.9)	8.7 (28.0)				
12	7.7 (39.0)	4.4 (23.7)	10.1 (27.7)	13.0 (39.8)	21.0 (56.2)			
13–15	6.1 (26.7)	5.5 (16.4)	6.4 (19.0)	4.9 (21.7)	5.8 (19.1)	2.3 (6.9)		
16	6.0 (23.3)	5.6 (15.6)	6.2 (17.4)	6.2 (18.7)	5.8 (17.0)	4.2 (9.9)	5.8 (13.4)	
Total social rate								6.4
Females of Other Races								
1–4	12.9 (a)							
5–7	10.3 (a)	6.5 (a)						
8	7.6 (76.0)	4.1 (8.7)	1.6 (3.1)					
9–11	8.6 (83.7)	6.2 (18.8)	6.0 (12.9)	16.0 (98.6)				
12	9.9 (66.4)	8.6 (23.6)	8.6 (18.8)	9.5 (57.7)	16.4 (32.8)	16.6		
13–15	8.3 (53.0)	6.8 (21.8)	6.9 (18.3)	9.1 (39.2)	7.6 (24.6)	0.2 (16.7)		
16	10.2 (50.8)	9.6 (25.9)	10.2 (22.8)	12.6 (41.0)	11.8 (30.1)	11.0 (29.1)	16.6 (41.4)	
Total social rate								10.3

a Infinite private rate of return resulting from assumption of no private costs in the form of foregone earnings below 14 years of age.

(2), indicates what interest society could afford to pay on money borrowed to finance the education of the entire group in question (in the mix of schooling levels actually completed) and break even on that investment.

Several inferences follow from Table 1.

1. Rates of return in 1959 were highest for white males. The largest single social rate of return, 20.5 percent, was for white males completing five to seven years of school over those who completed only one to four years. The overall social rate of return was 15.1 percent for white males. For this group, the average rate of return for completion of 16 years over no schooling was 33.4 percent for the individual and 14.7 percent for society. Few uses of private or public funds are as productive. All levels of schooling in Table 1 appear economically attractive for white males.

2. Social and private rates of return for males of other races were substantially lower than those for white males despite less foregone earnings and less direct schooling costs for nonwhite males. These lower rates of return stem from job discrimination and other factors reflected in lower workforce participation and lower earnings received by males of other races than by white males in the workforce. Social investment in males of other races enrolled in grades 5 to 7 yielded the highest marginal rate of return, 20.7 percent. Investment in high school yielded a favorable 16.7 percent return, but rates of return at the college level were not high. Social investment in college for males of other races yielded only a 3.0 percent return whereas the private investment yielded only a 6.0 percent return (see column headed 12 and row 16).

The average private return for four years of college makes higher education appear to be only marginally attractive to persons of other races, especially if they must borrow money. This conclusion can be very misleading. Workforce participation tends to be low among males of other races, reducing the rate of return over all persons. For those on the job, the payoff from schooling will tend to be substantially higher than that of the average male of other races. Furthermore, discrimination also reduces rates of return for alternative investment opportunities among persons of other races—making even the low rates in Table 1 attractive in many instances.

3. Social and private investment in the schooling of white females yielded a relatively low rate of return as compared with the other race-sex groups. The highest marginal social rate was incurred for those in the 12th year of schooling (21.0 percent). The 12th year of schooling also yielded the highest marginal private rate of return of 56.2 percent. The lowest marginal social and private rates for white females were incurred from investments in college dropouts. Marriage, family responsibilities, and attendant low workforce participation go far to explain the low overall social rate of return, 6.4 percent, to white female education. The private

rate of return on schooling investment is likely to be high for the female (white or of other races) who uses education to prepare for a lifetime business career (or alternatively uses education to attract a high-earning marriage partner) or who remains in the world of work.

4. The overall social rate of return for females of other races, 10.3 percent, is surprisingly high. Returns for completion of college exceed those of any other race-sex group. One explanation for the high return is statistical error. Other more reasonable explanations are the small supply and large demand for school teachers and high rates of workforce participation.

High workforce participation rates are characteristic of females of other races. The proportion of females reporting some wages and salaries and/or self-employment income in 1959 was 51.4 percent for females of other races and 39.2 percent for white females. This participation coupled with low schooling costs helps to explain the sharply higher returns for females of other races than for white females.

The family unit makes schooling a joint male-female resource with attendant social costs and returns, and it would be desirable to compute rates of return for the husband and wife as a family unit. The high workforce participation and payoff from schooling among white males enables white females to have low workforce participation and low rates of return while rearing socially productive children. In contrast, the low workforce participation and payoff from schooling among males of other races leads to high workforce participation and rates of return for females of other races. This in turn may lead to inadequate parental guidance and supervision of children, and to juvenile delinquency and to high unemployment in the new generation. Consideration of this social cost and the potential benefits from a more stable family engendered by higher male earnings may suggest greater schooling investment in males than females of other races, even though rates of return appear to be higher for females.

The social and private rates of return discussed in Table 1 have not been adjusted for (1) secular growth in earnings, (2) mortality, (3) ability, and (4) taxes. They also are based on the assumption (also used in other studies) that the opportunity cost of capital invested in the schooling plant and equipment is 6 percent. [Using] the costs and benefits of white males to illustrate the effects of these factors . . . [we find] the private and social rates of return for elementary schooling and college are only slightly affected, but both private and social rates for high school are affected substantially. . . .

SUMMARY

Although the average social costs in 1959 of schooling were 43 percent higher for white males than for males of other races, the resulting social rate of return was approximately 50 percent higher for whites. On the other hand, social rates of return between white females and females of other races suggest that investment in females of other races is substantially more profitable than investment in white females, partly because of the lower level of social investment in females of other races (which totaled $507 per student in 1959) but largely because of their greater workforce participation.

Private rates of return by race-sex group indicate that private schooling investment is economically justified for all race-sex groups at all schooling levels. The highest private rates were computed for white males in elementary schooling, and the lowest private rates were computed for males of other races in college. Obtaining higher workforce participation rates for persons of other races through breaking down discrimination and through other means would likely raise the *social* rate of return for all groups to levels that would provide very attractive growth prospects for private and public funds.

SEX BIAS AND CYCLICAL UNEMPLOYMENT

BETTY MACMORRAN GRAY

... How does capitalism, unable to use an increasing quantity of women workers, systematically disuse women workers? Unemployment is awkward, especially when it spirals up against the background of the American dream. During busts, the numbers of unemployed rise to embarrassing highs. However, what might be called the "statistical-industrial complex" comes to the rescue of capitalism. Often it can obscure the awkward highs as effectively as a cloud can obscure the top of the Empire State Building. The statistical-industrial complex defines the labor force as being made up of people who are *at work, or eligible for and actively seeking work.* Consequently, it counts only those people as being either employed or unemployed. The logic is faultless, but the reality behind it—the reality of the definition itself—is awry. Economists estimate that the number of people who want jobs and don't have them at any given time is considerably higher than the official reports—how much higher depends on which economist you read.

Who are the workers who don't make the official reports—the hidden unemployed? In the main, they are the woman (sometimes called "married," sometimes "adult"), the teen-ager, the old man and the old woman—almost a group, a rather touching one, from a Faulkner novel. It is easy for the statistical-industrial complex to count them, *at will,* as either in or out of the labor force. It is easy to hide them, for they come from and go to some place—presumably, the home, the school, retirement.

It is difficult to hide white adult males and increasingly difficult to hide black adult males. Either they are working or they are hanging around, visibly and embarrassingly. During booms, the woman, the teen-ager, the old man and the old woman can be counted in; they are dubbed "Madam" and "Sir," the "emergency labor force," the "secondary labor force," the "peripheral labor force." During busts, they can be counted out. When

Excerpted from Betty MacMorran Gray, "Economics of Sex Bias," *The Nation,* 1971, 742–744.

they are counted out, not only are they not being used in increasing numbers but they are being systematically *disused:* the counting out compensates in large part for a major defect in the system of capitalism—for its cyclical fluctuations which lead to cyclical unemployment.

How do we know that, during a bust, the woman, the teen-ager, the old man and the old woman don't go back, happily, to cooking the chicken in the pot, to the Bunsen burners and the playing fields, to Florida? How do we known that their numbers are significant? We don't know about them all, but we have many clues about many. Here are three, from diverse years and sources.

(*1*) In 1944 and 1945, as the full employment years of World War II were coming to an end; the Women's Bureau surveyed 13,000 women who were employed in war-production areas and who represented all occupations, except domestic service. The bureau found that more than half of the women who had been housewives at the time of Pearl Harbor, and three-quarters of the girls who had been students, wanted to stay, after the war, on the job or on another job; wanted to stay within the labor force.

In 1947, however, J. Frederic Dewhurst, explained in the Twentieth Century Fund's semiofficial, indeed semibiblical, *America's Needs and Resources,* that "Reemployment of returning servicemen and of workers laid off by munitions industries has been facilitated by the withdrawal of emergency war workers from the labor market." Indeed, 6 million of the 7 million members of the emergency labor force—which, according to Dewhurst, was made up of married women, young people of from 14 to 19, and superannuated-retired-marginal workers—"withdrew" within a year after the war's end.

(*2*) In 1955, the Bureau of the Census experimented with a new definition of unemployment. The bureau believed that the new definition might prove more objective than the existing one and more in accord with the actual labor force behavior of jobless people; that it might include, in addition to those actively seeking work, the inactive (people who wanted work, but who judged there was no point in trying—at Macy's, at the machine shops).

The bureau turned up one million inactive unemployed. And the bureau stated, "Most of the additional persons who would be classified as unemployed under the proposed new definition were *teen-agers and adult women.* (Emphasis added.) If those million had been added to 1955s officially unemployed, they would have raised the total by one-third. The statistical-industrial complex failed to adopt the new definition; it is still using the old one.

(*3*) The woman, the teenager, the old man and the old woman, according to multitudinous reports, are forever "withdrawing from," "leaving" or "dropping out of" the labor force—at moments convenient for capitalism. A random example: "Last month's improvement [in unemployment] was due to a drop in unemployed women, presumably because they had left the labor force," wrote *The New York Times* on December 2, 1962. Another: "49,000 people, many of them students and housewives, dropped out of the work force [of Massachusetts] after the Christmas holidays," *The Boston Globe* reported almost a decade later, on February 25, 1971.

In such observations, the woman, the teen-ager, the old man and the old woman sound, in their labor-force behavior, as obliging as Fielding's Sophia who "took the first Opportunity of withdrawing with the Ladies," as content as baseball fans leaving a doubleheader, as ready as pears to drop out of a tree. It is likely, however, that the terminology of the statistical-industrial complex is as slippery as that of the Pentagon; that, for instance, "withdrawing" resembles "Vietnamization." A general comment (in a·"Crisis of Confidence" editorial): "The Bureau of Labor Statistics is suddenly stopped from explaining its data when such an analysis might remind the American public that all is not well with the economy," from *The New York Times* of April 13, 1971.

REDUCING DISCRIMINATION: ROLE OF THE EQUAL PAY ACT

ROBERT D. MORAN

Significant steps have been taken in recent years in an attempt to end discrimination against women in employment. Laws and regulations have been placed on the books requiring that women be paid at the same rate as men for equal work and that equality of job opportunity be available to all, regardless of race, color, religion, sex, national origin, and age.

Although much has been accomplished in this field at the State level, this article is limited to actions taken by the Federal Government and concentrates on the activity under the Equal Pay Act of 1963.

Federal measures to bar discrimination in employment, which are of particular interest to women, include the following: (1) The Equal Pay Act of 1963, which requires equal pay for equal work, regardless of sex; (2) Title VII of the Civil Rights Act of 1964, which states that discrimination on the basis of race, color, religion, sex or national origin is an unlawful employment practice; (3) Executive Order 11246, as amended by Executive Order 11375 of October 13, 1967, which bars discrimination on the basis of race, color, religion, sex, or national origin by Federal contractors; and (4) The Age Discrimination in Employment Act of 1967, which protects most individuals over age 40 until they reach the 65th birthday, regardless of sex.

Since its scope is limited to sex-based wage differentials, passage of the Equal Pay Act in 1963 was regarded by many as only the beginning of a long battle to achieve equality in employment between the sexes. Nevertheless, when the equal pay provisions became law, the action marked the culmination of persistent efforts to establish the principle of equal pay that began soon after the Civil War. In 1868, the National Labor Union Convention was the first organized group to demand equal pay for government workers. Subsequently, the Congress passed an appropriation bill to

---

Reprinted from Robert D. Moran, "Reducing Discrimination: Role of the Equal Pay Act," *Monthly Labor Review*, 1970, 30–34.

give "female employees in the Departments the same compensation as male clerks when they perform similar service." However, equality of the sexes with respect to pay did not become a legal requirement in all Federal employment until the Classification Act of 1923 established the present day system, under which the salary for each job is determined solely according to the duties and responsibilities involved. Thus, the Federal Government was the first among major employers to establish the principle of equal pay for equal work.

THE EARLY CAMPAIGNS

Efforts to apply the equal pay concept to jobs in the private sector also occurred in the 19th century. In 1868, the Knights of Labor made equal pay for both sexes one of their major objectives. The first serious implementation of the principle, however, had to await the wartime economies during the first half of the 20th century. The National War Labor Boards in World War I and World War II, and the Wage Stabilization Board in the Korean War, adopted the equal pay principle as guiding policy during the periods when they had the power to set labor standards for American business and industry. In 1919, Michigan and Montana enacted equal pay legislation, but it was not until almost 25 years later that equal pay laws began to appear on the books of other States, during and following World War II.

Chief among the early supporters of the equal pay principle was the Women's Bureau of the U.S. Department of Labor which, since its establishment in 1920, consistently promoted the concept of "a rate for the job" regardless of sex. In one of its first publications, issued in 1920, the Women's Bureau set forth the provision that "[w]ages should be established on the basis of occupation and not on the basis of sex."

As the number of women in the labor force substantially increased, the major women's organizations, joined by employer, labor, and civic groups, continued to press for adoption of a Federal equal pay standard. In the year 1952, some of these organizations grouped together at the national level to establish the National Committee for Equal Pay, for the purposes of conducting a concerted campaign for Federal equal pay legislation.

The first comprehensive equal pay bill was introduced in the 79th Congress in 1945. Neither this nor the many similar measures proposed in each Congress during the next 18 years received favorable action, despite the efforts of their bipartisan proponents and the support from both the public and the Government. Success came in 1963, when the 88th Congress incorporated the provisions of the Kennedy Administration's equal pay proposal into the Fair Labor Standards Act as the Equal Pay Act of 1963.

However, in making the equal pay bill a part of the Fair Labor Standards Act, the congressional action also had the effect of making equal-pay coverage generally coextensive with the minimum wage coverage. As a result, today equal pay is required for only about half of the jobs in the United States. The major exclusions from the equal pay coverage include numerous jobs in State and local governments, domestic employment, outside salespersons, and all of the higher paying jobs that are exempted from the wage and hour law as bona fide executive, administrative, and professional positions. Recently bills have been proposed to close the gap for the high paying jobs and make it possible to equate them for equal pay purposes. At least three such bills are currently pending in Congress.

In brief, the Equal Pay Act provides that where men and women are doing "equal" work on jobs which require equal skill, effort, and responsibility, and which are performed under similar working conditions in the same establishment, they must receive equal pay. The jobs under comparison must be of a closely related character, but the Congress made it clear that they do not have to be identical; as Senator McNamara, one of the bill's sponsors, put it, "such a conclusion would be obviously ridiculous." Certain exceptions are permitted where differences in pay are found to be based on any "factor other than sex," such as a bona fide seniority or merit system or payment of wages under a piecework plan.

In enacting the 1963 equal pay amendment, Congress also took the precaution of preventing pay reductions by employers in order to effect compliance with the equal pay requirements. It specifically prohibited the reduction of the wages of any employee for the purpose of eliminating an improper wage differential. The law also prohibits a labor organization from causing or attempting to cause an employer to discriminate against an employee in violation of the statute.

The language of the Equal Pay Act was drafted so as to require the elimination of wage discrimination on the basis of sex, regardless of whether a man or a woman worker is the victim. The vast majority of lower pay workers are women but, in rare cases where a woman may be paid more for equal work than a man, the protection of the act is available to the man. In one case, 11 men employees of a bank in San Francisco benefited by obtaining overtime compensation which had been paid only to women pursuant to the requirements of a California State law.

The scope of Title VII of the Civil Rights Act of 1964 and of Executive Order 11246, as amended, is in many respects broader than that of the equal pay provisions of the Fair Labor Standards Act. Their provisions bar sex discrimination in most aspects of employment, not simply in compensation. Their scope is, in fact, broad enough to bar discriminatory pay practices based on sex even in the higher-pay executive, administrative, and professional jobs.

ENFORCEMENT

Offsetting the more restricted scope of the Equal Pay Act, however, is the considerable advantage of the much stronger administrative and enforcement procedures of the Fair Labor Standards Act which were made applicable to the equal pay amendment. Also, complaints under the Equal Pay Act are treated in strict confidence and, unless court action ultimately becomes necessary, the name of an aggrieved employee need not be revealed.

The Wage and Hour Division of the Department of Labor, which administers the law, has uncovered substantial violations of the Equal Pay Act to date. By the end of April 1970, over $17 million in underpayments had been found owed to more than 50,000 employees, nearly all of them women. During the same period, the Department of Labor's legal staff filed over 140 equal pay cases in court; about one-third of these have been decided. Even a cursory glance at the decisions so far rendered reveals that legal actions under the act are rapidly developing a body of principles that may have far-reaching effect on job structuring and pay practices throughout the country.

Jobs that never before were thought to be equal within the meaning of the Equal Pay Act are now being closely scrutinized. A Federal district court in Dallas, for example, has held that the traditionally all-male job of orderly in a hospital was equal to the all-female job of nurse's aide. Courts elsewhere have followed this principle, causing hospitals in many parts of the United States to begin paying their nurse's aides at a rate equal to that of their orderlies.

As the body of equal pay laws continues to grow, it is probable that many other jobs will be found to be equal under the act. Investigations have been conducted to determine whether the work of tellers and clerks in banks, insurance companies, and similar institutions is equal. Similar questions arise in manufacturing regarding inspectors, assemblers, and other types of production line jobs; in retail trade, concerning sales clerks and cashiers, tailors and fitters; in food service establishments, regarding cooks, chefs, and a number of other jobs; and in various other types of establishments, as regards custodians, janitors, and security agents. The list could be extended much further.

VIOLATIONS TOO COSTLY

Employers cannot afford to take these equal pay developments lightly, for the cost of inequality in compensation practices for jobs held to be equal under the act can be high. It is estimated that as the result of a single court decision, a glass container manufacturer in New Jersey may have to pay more than a quarter million dollars in back wages to 230 women selector-packers in the bottle inspection department for the period during which they were paid less per hour than were male employees doing work which, the court found, was equal. In addition, each of these women will have to be paid a 21.5-cent-an-hour increase in wages, to bring them to their male counterparts' level of compensation.

In this particular case, Chief Judge Abraham Freedman, speaking on behalf of the appellate court, observed that the Equal Pay Act was intended "as a broad charter of women's rights in the economic field" and "sought to overcome the age-old belief in women's inferiority and to eliminate the depressing effects on living standards of reduced wages for female workers and the economic and social consequences which flow from it."

Among the principles established by *Wheaton Glass* are these: Jobs must be only "substantially equal," not "identical," to permit job comparisons under the act; there must be a rational explanation for the amount of a wage differential, and it is the employer's burden to provide it; and the employer's past history, if any, of unequal pay practices is an important factor in determining whether there is a violation of the act.

Another important principle, established by an earlier court ruling, is that job comparisons under the Equal Pay Act may not be made on a group sex basis, that is, that wage differentials based on alleged differences between the average cost of employing women as a group and that of employing men as a group do not qualify as a "factor other than sex" within the meaning of the statute. In that situation, the employer had paid all his women employees 10 cents an hour less than he paid the men, claiming higher costs for women on the basis of certain selected fringe benefits.

A particularly difficult question to resolve under the Equal Pay Act has been the extent to which lifting of heavy objects ("heavy-lifting") on the job might be used to justify a wage differential. An early court decision established a rule that occasional or sporadic performance of a function requiring such lifting would not render unequal the jobs that were otherwise equal. In that situation, men and women employees were doing essentially the same work but the men, from time to time, had to lift much heavier glass plates than any of their women coworkers were able to lift. Of course, where male employees are actually engaged in heavy-lifting for a considerable portion of their worktime, and such lifting is not done by their women coworkers, the jobs cannot be equated for equal pay purposes.

The heavy-lifting claim has been used more frequently than any other reason, by unions and employers alike, for the perpetuation of a lower wage rate for women workers who are otherwise doing substantially the same work as men. Investigations have revealed, however, that although some male employees in an establishment seldom, if ever, do any heavy-lifting, they still are paid at the same wage rate as those who actually do a good deal of it. Situations of this kind indicate that the heavy-lifting is not the reason for the higher rate.

Another pretext often used to justify sex-based wage discrimination are alleged training programs. A number of banks and department stores maintain a so-called trainee system which is invariably restricted to men as a basis for paying a higher rate to the male employees. The employer will claim, for example, that he is paying women bank tellers less money because the male tellers are being primed for eventual promotion to positions of bank officers. But a closer investigation often reveals that, in fact, there is no training being given to the men. This phenomenon can probably be traced to the employer's stereotyped view that bank officers are traditionally men, hence, male tellers have promotional potential and should be paid more in order to keep them from going elsewhere. In the absence of any visible ongoing training program which is open to both sexes, this practice cannot be justified and is considered a violation of the Equal Pay Act. This position of the Wage and Hour Division has recently been upheld by a Federal court of appeals, which ruled that the exclusion of women from a training program was based on "subjective assumptions and stereotyped misconceptions regarding the value of women's work."

There are a number of other methods employed in covered establishments to frustrate the purposes of the Equal Pay Act. They are rapidly being examined and exposed. Of course, it isn't always easy to arrive at a determination as to whether certain jobs are "equal" within the meaning of the statute, particularly in large plants or firms employing hundreds or thousands of workers.

THE COST OF ENFORCEMENT

The cost in man-hours of investigating and determining equal pay questions can be exceedingly high. Litigation is equally—if not even more—expensive. Since this type of court action is becoming increasingly necessary to penetrate the long-standing discriminatory pay systems, larger appropriations for the equal pay program will most certainly be necessary in the future. The results to date, however, have been well worth the expense. Discernible progress is being achieved. The mandate of a pay rate for the job regardless of sex is beginning to be fulfilled.

While Government enforcement activities have played an important role in securing equal pay for women over the past several years, many employers have voluntarily adjusted their practices to comply with the Equal Pay Act. Many labor unions also have contributed to that result. Nevertheless, in a wide variety of establishments, women continue to be paid less than men, even while working on jobs that are "equal" within the meaning of the statute. One may only hope the situation will change soon.

PART FOUR: MYTHS ABOUT WOMEN

Some ideology accompanies a society's departure from a general principle of social justice to which it claims fidelity. The ideology which justifies women's inferior position in American society has long abandoned notions of innate evilness, sexual corruptness, and the sanctity of motherhood and marriage—the divorce rate alone belies a serious acceptance of that—for supposedly hard facts. Though actual studies of relevant subjects are made infrequently, the hard facts contradict the ideology. In this part of the book, each selection presents some empirical data which dispute a common assertion used to justify particular political and economic acts of discrimination against women.

POLITICAL POWER

Women have little political power as office-holders. No woman has ever been President of the United States, and only two have even occupied major cabinet posts; Madame Frances Perkins was Secretary of Labor during the Roosevelt administration and Oveta Culp Hobby was Secretary of Health, Education and Welfare during the early Eisenhower years. No woman has ever been appointed to the Supreme Court; few women are elected to the Congress, or to state legislatures, or to the office of governor or mayor. The listing is seemingly endless, and probably continues to the local dog-catcher.

According to many political theorists, office-holding may be less important than access to an organized pressure group. The United States, to these theorists, is a pluralist society—characterized by multiple-interest groups each of whom work for their own interests in part, through the voluntary association. Not all voluntary associations represent an interest group that has any particular relevance to politics, for associations include poker clubs as well as conservation clubs, golf clubs as well as peace groups, and drinking clubs as well as businessmen's associations. Nevertheless—aside from the validity of this conception, and its validity can be seriously questioned—since many middle-class American women frequently join voluntary associations and work in political campaigns, they are asserted to be politically powerful. This is contended in spite of the obvious political deficit of being nearly absent from political offices or bodies.

In the first reading, Nicholas Babchuk and his colleagues examined voluntary associations in a large Northwestern city, and concluded that women's organizations have too little prestige and control too little money to participate in the more important community decisions. Hence, the contention that membership in voluntary associations means political power is questionable. Furthermore, Talcott Parsons' suggestion (discussed in Part Three) that men's jobs and political activity, and women's club activity are *de facto* equivalents becomes questionable: if women's clubs are not even important in decision-making about social-welfare services (supposedly, this could be considered compatible with women's nurturing roles), then one wonders where her powers may be exerted.

ECONOMIC POWER

According to traditional labor theory, workers who perform the same job should be paid the same wage. This assumes that workers are equally productive and their costs to the firm are the same. If firms pay some workers less than others for doing the same work, this is economically justifiable only if those workers are less productive than others, or the cost of employing them is greater than for others. Such costs occur when workers tend to be more frequently absent from their jobs than others, and thereby raise the firm's labor costs due to a reduction in output; similarly, workers who frequently leave their jobs increase the firm's costs because of the cost of rehiring and retraining. A popular myth used to justify paying women less than men for doing the same work is that women are absent more often and leave their jobs more often than men. The reading by the Women's Bureau surveys a number of studies concerning these occurrences to find that the data do not support this popular belief.

The social norms say a woman ought to marry and to stay married.

Therefore, a man will support her. The divorce rate contradicts the norms while the pay rate reflects a belief that the norms are followed. In the United States, 10 percent of the households are headed by women, with responsibilities for children and other dependents. One of every three families headed by a woman live at the poverty level.[1] For black families, the poverty is even more frequent: one of every two families is poor. In the second reading, Robert Stein discusses the problems facing these poverty families headed by women and the inadequacies of the present government-aid programs.

Since the 1920s, many reports have circulated in magazines and newspapers to the effect that women are the majority of shareholders in some corporations or are the main beneficiaries of many large estates,[2] and thus, women must be in control of great wealth. Perhaps that is the symbolism of giving the post of the United States Treasurer to a woman! Some recent studies show that women do not have quite the wealth attributed to them: women, for example, retain control over their wealth less often than men do by delegating management of their assets to others. A study by the New York Stock Exchange concluded that although shareholders are evenly divided between men and women, much of the stock is simply put in a woman's name because men frequently put shares in their wives' names to limit their liabilities and taxes, and to avoid certain aspects of community-property laws.[3] In the final reading, Robert Lampman presents other data to suggest that women are not as wealthy as popular belief makes them.

---

[1] In 1970, nonfarm households where total money income was less than $1954 for an unrelated individual, $2525 for a couple, and $3963 for a family of four were classified as poor.

[2] R. Barlow, H. Brazer, and J. Morgan, *Economic Behavior of the Affluent* (Brookings Institution: Washington, D.C., 1966).

[3] New York Stock Exchange, "Shareownership—1970: Census of Shareowners New York Stock Exchange."

MEN AND WOMEN IN COMMUNITY AGENCIES:
A NOTE ON POWER AND PRESTIGE

NICHOLAS BABCHUK
RUTH MARSEY
C. WAYNE GORDON

This report examines the role played by women in the power structure of a community. The study focuses on persons affiliated with civic organizations as represented by all board memberships of the Council of Social Agencies in a large northeastern city, as well as the Council itself and the Community Chest. Women participate extensively as members of these boards; of the 1,937 memberships, 522 are held by women. There are 88 agencies affiliated with the Council and 73 of these have board memberships selected on a voluntary basis. These boards are charged with the responsibility for administering a total budget of well over four million dollars. Studies dealing with community power structure indicate a relationship between membership in civic organizations and economic or political dominance on both. Clearly, one way in which women wield power in the community is through membership or boards of social agencies, rather than through association in economic and political structures.

Board memberships have power implications that can be evaluated in a number of ways. The function of the agency is one such criterion. For example, services provided by a hospital are essential to all segments of a community and have considerable potential for control; as an agency the hospital's function is primarily instrumental. Since the board of the hospital has control over it, the board members exercise vital power in the community. On the other hand, to the extent that the board of a scouting organization controls activities not especially vital to the community, its members wield less power. A further clue to the power component is the control of money indicated by the size of the agency budget. Still another criterion bearing on power is the individual's general status in the community: the higher the prestige, the greater the potential access to board memberships. A related criterion is that of differential status and power based on sex roles. These criteria constitute the basis for analyzing the relationship between board membership and power.

Excerpted from Nicholas Babchuk, Ruth Marsey and C. Wayne Gordon, "Men and Women in Community Agencies: A Note on Power and Prestige," *American Sociological Review*, 25, 1960, 399–403.

Of central concern are the roles played by women on boards of agencies and the relationship of these memberships to the community power structure. Most boards recruit members on a voluntary basis; they can be viewed as voluntary associations. There are 15 agencies, however, whose boards are not wholly selected voluntarily; in these cases the boards include paid personnel whose jobs, in part, entail board membership (as in the case of the Sisters who administer a Catholic hospital) or personnel selected through political appointment or public election (as with the Board of Education and the Board of Supervisors of the Department of Social Welfare). In order to insure comparability, only the 73 agencies whose boards are wholly voluntary are included in the present analysis.

It is hypothesized that the more vital the function of an agency to the welfare of a community, the higher will be the rank of the board and the status of its members. Size of budget and the sex composition of the board are additional variables related to the agency function. For example, women are more likely to serve on boards of agencies functioning primarily as expressive organizations than on essentially instrumental agency boards.

PROCEDURE

A number of techniques were employed to test the hypothesis. The agencies were classified according to their functions, as instrumental, instrumental-expressive, or expressive. Instrumental agencies, as a type, may provide a service, produce a product, or serve as organizations designed to maintain or to create some normative condition or change (for example, the Council of Social Agencies or a hospital). Expressive agencies provide a framework within which activity for the participants is immediately gratifying (for example, a settlement house). Instrumental-expressive agencies provide a framework within which both instrumental and expressive activities are self-consciously exercised (for example, the Jewish Home and Infirmary).

The sex composition of the individual boards was determined from a list of all board members. Records pertaining to agency budgets were also utilized. Several persons who were both knowledgeable concerning agencies and boards and active in them were used as judges to rank all of the agencies studied. Included were the presidents of the local Chamber of Commerce and the Council of Social Agencies, a prominent lawyer active in community affairs, two women representing the social elite, and two professional women prominent in community activities. The judges ranked the agencies into four equal divisions, ranging from those which they believed to be most vital to those least vital to the community welfare. In addition, the informants designated the boards on which they would most like to serve. Their board preferences reflected their own evaluations of the agencies' function in serving the needs of the community, their desire to associate with boards whose members were socially prominent, or both.

One criterion employed to determine the status of the individual board members was occupation, classified as follows: director of a large industrial, commercial, or financial enterprise; professional; entrepreneur; and so on. (In the case of women members, their husbands' occupations were used.) Directorships are taken to indicate economic dominance. The second criterion used was membership in the most exclusive private clubs, listing in the social register, or both—as an index of social prominence.

INSTRUMENTAL AND EXPRESSIVE AGENCIES

Consistent with the central hypothesis, it was posited that agencies with instrumental functions would not only be more vital to a community but would be more highly valued than expressive agencies. This would be reflected in the relative status of the boards. Furthermore, since men rather than women are economic and political dominants, it was expected that they would dominate the boards of philanthropic agencies with instrumental functions; and that, generally, such agencies would have the largest budgets. On the other hand, it was expected that women more likely would be members of boards of agencies with expressive functions, and with smaller operating budgets.

Of the 73 boards whose membership was voluntary, 40 represented instrumental agencies, 18 instrumental-expressive agencies, and 15 expressive agencies. Eight organizations, including the YMCA and the Boy Scouts, required that all board members be of the same sex; their exclusion left 38 instrumental, 16 instrumental-expressive, and 11 expressive agencies.

Of the 38 instrumental agencies, 33 were directed by boards having a majority of male membership, of which six were entirely male, 11 more than 80 percent male, and 11 others between 70 and 79 percent male. Only five agencies classified as instrumental had boards with a majority of women members: the Society for the Prevention of Cruelty to Children, the City Maternal and Adoption Service, the City Guidance Center (for children), the County Chapter of the Muscular Dystrophy Association, and the Convalescent Hospital for Children. The fact that these agencies provide services for children is consistent with the traditionally defined role expectations for women; they constitute an exception—if numbers are used as a measure of dominance—to the expectation that men will dominate vital instrumental agencies.

Instrumental agencies vary in the degree to which they are vital and controlling. For example, the Community Chest conceivably is more highly ranked than others because it controls funds for all participating agencies, instrumental and expressive. The board of the Community Chest is one of the six whose membership is entirely composed of men. (The other five are boards of the following agencies: three hospitals, a dental dispensary, and the County Medical Society.) Thus, men dominate the boards of most of the instrumental agencies, and the boards of the most vital of such agencies.

Further confirmation for the hypothesis is provided by the board memberships of the 16 instrumental-expressive agencies. Fourteen of these had a substantial male majority, over 70 percent in 11 cases. Moreover, the more instrumentally oriented of the instrumental-expressive agencies had a greater proportion of men on their boards (for example, the Salvation Army, 87 percent; the Jewish Home and Infirmary, 92 percent.)

More women are found on the boards of expressive agencies, although the board memberships remain predominantly male. The services provided by these agencies relate to the needs of children and young people. The percentages of women on the boards of the three types of agencies are: instrumental 23, instrumental-expressive 32, and expressive 39 percent.

THE RANKING OF BOARDS

As noted above, seven civic leaders ranked the agencies according to how vital they are to the community's welfare. The judges agreed strongly on the ranking of eight agencies considered most vital and eight agencies considered least vital. The "most vital" include five hospitals, the Community Chest, the Council of Social Agencies, and the Visiting Nurse Service of the city and county. Following the ranking, the judges were asked to explicate the criteria they had used, which were named as (a) the agency served a large segment of the community, (b) it controlled considerable funds, and (c) the agency dealt with a crucial problem. The eight agencies (of quite different types) ranked as being least vital include among others, the local USO, the Lutheran Inner Mission, the St. Elizabeth Guild House, and the local Traveler's Aid. These "least vital" agencies serve a limited clientele, have little money, and deal with relatively minor problems.

Of the 222 board members of the agencies ranked as most vital, 198, or 89 percent, were men. Only 147 of the 240 members, or 61 percent, of the boards of agencies ranked as least vital were men. Thus, while men tend to dominate the boards of both types, they are more likely to be represented on boards of agencies ranked as most vital. This finding supports the hypothesis that the higher the board's rank, the greater will be the proportion of male members. In addition, all of the agencies ranked as "most vital" are instrumental. The evidence confirms the hypothesis that men are more likely to be on the boards of instrumental agencies, and indirectly provides further support to the proposition that more highly ranked boards are more likely to be predominantly male.

The operating budgets of the eight agencies ranked as most vital totalled 2,916,622 dollars. This figure contrasts with a budget of 276,982 dollars for agencies ranked as least vital. These budgets include the Community Chest allotments to the agencies for a fiscal year. The difference in Chest allotment to the most vital and least vital agencies reflects a pattern similar to that of the operating budgets. Furthermore, the least vital agencies are among those having the smallest budgets of all organizations affiliated with the Council and Chest.

To test the hypothesis that the higher the rank of the board, the higher will be the status of its members, random samples of 25 persons were selected from the total board memberships of agencies ranked as most vital and least vital. The status of the board members was determined by their degree of economic and social dominance, indicated by occupation (several were directors of industrial or banking enterprises), and by their memberships in the most exclusive clubs or inclusion in the social register or both. Most women on boards derive their status from their husbands or families; exceptions are to be found among professionally trained women. The status characteristics of the members of the boards of the most and the least vital agencies were compared. Eleven of the persons associated with the most vital agencies were listed in *Who's Who in America*; none associated with the least vital agencies was so listed.

Occupations were classified into four categories: (a) directorships—officers of large industries and banks, (b) professionals—limited to physicians, lawyers, and top educators (for example, school superintendent, university president), (c) entrepreneurs of medium-sized businesses, and (d) others—including ministers, nurses, engineers, and sales personnel. Eighteen of the 25 board members of the most vital agencies, but only three of the least vital, held directorships, and these 18 held a total of 61 such directorships. Several of these prestigeful and powerful persons were associated with each other as directors in the same enterprises.

There were no board members from the most vital agencies in the lowest occupational category (of the four listed above) as compared with 11 board members from the least vital agencies in this category. Thus, persons with high occupational status are more likely to be members of boards which are highly ranked.

The sex composition of the boards ranked as most vital and least vital further differentiates the role of the woman in community power. Of the 25 members of the most vital boards only one was a woman (a person of social prominence and the wife of the superintendent of schools). In contrast, 13 of the 25 members of boards ranked as least vital were women. Except for two professional women on these boards, the husbands' occupations, used as an index of economic dominance, were mainly in the lower occupational categories (entrepreneur and others).

Seventeen of the 25 board members of the agencies ranked as most vital, but only 11 of the 25 board members of the least vital agencies, were socially prominent. Of the first 17, 15 were also directors. The 11 board members of the least vital agencies were distributed among all four of the occupational categories. Thus, the hypothesis that the higher the rank of the board the higher the status of its members is supported by interlocking evidence on economic dominance and social prominence.

THE ECONOMIC STATUS OF FAMILIES HEADED BY WOMEN

ROBERT L. STEIN

One of the important domestic problems facing the Nation in the 1970s is how to improve the economic status of families headed by women. According to the latest estimates—for March 1970—5.6 million families in the United States are headed by women, or more than 1 family in 10.

The number has been increasing more rapidly than the total of all families. Between 1960 and 1970, for example, it rose by 24 percent, whereas total families increased by 14 percent.

Historically the employment and income situation of such families has generally been bleak. Most of the women are ill-equipped to earn an adequate living. Many suffer from one handicap or more to successful competition in the labor market—lack of sufficient education or training, irregular and unstable work histories, sex or racial discrimination in hiring, ill health, and the difficulty of arranging for satisfactory child care. As a result, these women have not been able to share fully in the Nation's economic growth, with its associated expansion in jobs and advances in earnings. During the 1960s, the income of families headed by men remained more than double the income of families headed by women. While the number of families headed by men with incomes below the poverty line ($3,700 for a family of four in 1969) was reduced by one-half between 1959 and 1969, the number of poor families headed by women remained virtually unchanged at about 1.8 million. Employment growth, the most powerful weapon in the antipoverty arsenal, has not significantly reduced the number of poor families headed by women.

Public assistance, a primary source of income for many of the families headed by women, has been expanding in coverage and in benefit levels, but payments are still generally very low—in most States below the poverty line.

The welfare system has been caught in a crossfire of public criticism. The target for most of the hostility is the AFDC program—Aid to Families

Excerpted from Robert L. Stein, "The Economic Status of Families Headed by Women," *Monthly Labor Review*, 93 (December 1970), 3–9.

with Dependent Children—designed to provide income assistance to the families of children whose fathers have died or deserted or are absent for a variety of other reasons. On the one hand, welfare programs are criticized because their payment levels are considered too low to provide economic security to families in need. On the other hand, the programs are criticized on the grounds that work, as well as need, should be a requirement for eligibility. The welfare system has also been faulted because of the widely disparate State benefit levels, because it may discourage some women from seeking employment, and because it may induce some families to break up.

The attacks have become sharper in recent years because of steady growth in the welfare population during a period of rapid economic growth and very low unemployment. By March 1970, about three-fifths of the 3.4 million families with children headed by women were already on welfare and the rolls were still rising. These developments were placing a growing burden on the already hardpressed taxpayer. One result of the resistance to the rising welfare bill has been a heightened interest in the possibility of employment for welfare mothers. One important aspect of welfare reform involves the development of training and job placement programs for able-bodied adult welfare recipients. The manpower provisions of the Administration's proposed Family Assistance Act of 1970 include a training and work requirement for mothers of school-age children.

SCOPE OF THE PROBLEM

In March 1970, 5.6 million women were heads of families (table 1); 2.4 million of these women (43 percent) were widows and 2.6 million (46 percent) were divorced or separated from their husbands. The remaining 600,000 had never been married. About a third of these single women had children under 18.

From the standpoint of society, foremost concern is centered on the status of those families with dependent children. The environment in which these children are growing up is inevitably affected by the stresses and strains on the mother who must take over the responsibility for the discipline, training, and guidance of the young as well as their financial support. In March 1970, there were 3.4 million such families, comprising 8 million children under 18 years of age (an average of 2.4 per family) and 13 million persons altogether.

The remaining 2.2 million—women without children under 18—were nearly all past the age of 45. Two-thirds were widows, and all but a few were heads of small families consisting of only two or three persons. These older family heads were not without employment and income problems.

TABLE 1. SELECTED CHARACTERISTICS OF FAMILIES HEADED BY WOMEN

Characteristic	Thousands of families		Percent of families in each category	
	March 1970	March 1960	March 1970	March 1960
ALL RACES				
Total, all families	5,580	4,494	11	10
With children	3,363	2,542	11	9
Below the poverty line	1,803	1,916	36	23
With children	1,488	1,525	47	28
In central cities of metropolitan areas	2,269	1,764	15	12
Below the poverty level	738	585	50	29
WHITE				
Total, all families	4,185	3,545	9	9
With children	2,255	1,834	9	8
Below the poverty line	1,063	1,233	30	20
With children	831	948	40	25
In central cities of metropolitan areas	1,418	1,240	12	10
Below the poverty line	337	303	39	24
NEGRO AND OTHER RACES				
Total, all families	1,395	949	27	22
With children	1,108	708	31	25
Below the poverty line	739	683	53	32
With children	657	577	59	35
In central cities of metropolitan areas	851	524	29	23
Below the poverty line	402	282	66	38

By and large, however, their situation was less serious than that of younger families with children since they had more freedom to accept employment, they had more income from other sources, and they had fewer dependents. Half had fully grown children in the household who could contribute to the family's income. In 1969, the median income of families headed by women 45 to 64 years of age who had no children under 18 in the household was $7,000, whereas the income of families headed by women 24 to 44 years of age who did have children was only $4,000.

Between 1960 and 1970, the number of women heading families with children rose by 800,000. Roughly one-third of this increase could be attributed to general population growth. There has been considerable speculation that rising welfare benefits in the large industrial States of the North have contributed to the breaking up of poor families. However, it would be extremely difficult to isolate this factor from the entire complex of forces that leads to family disorganization. (One-third lived in the South where welfare payments are still comparatively low.)

The proportion of families headed by women is highest among poorly educated and low income groups, among minority groups, and among city residents. On the other hand, the group is also more heterogeneous than might be supposed. Among women 25 and over, most of whom have completed their formal schooling, one-third of the family heads have no more than an elementary school education (compared with one-fourth of other women), but 13 percent have some college education. Although one-third have incomes below the poverty line, a small minority (nearly 300,000) have incomes of $15,000 or more. These are mainly older white families without children.

Among the black urban poor, the proportion of families headed by women was 66 percent in March 1970. Here, as in the Nation as a whole, the proportion has been increasing; the trend is much more pronounced among the urban poor.

Even among the 3.4 million families with children, the situation is uneven. About 65 percent have only one or two children and their incomes are somewhat higher than the incomes of larger families. However, those with few or no children tend to be at the extremes of the age scale. Among women family heads age 25 to 44, presumably the prime candidates for training and employment, nearly half had three children or more. The problems confronting women with many children are compounded by the fact that they are also the least educated and therefore the least equipped to find employment.

FAMILY INCOME

The relationship between income and family stability is complex. When a breadwinner dies or leaves his family, the loss or reduction of financial support may be only partly offset by the wife's earnings and Social Security, private pensions or insurance, welfare payments or other benefits. Poverty or low income may itself create tensions leading to family breakup. Or the fact that a man does not have a steady job at good pay may induce him to leave so that his family can obtain public assistance. These situations are not easily quantified. In any case, the data show a very strong correlation between income and the presence or absence of fathers.

As table 2 shows, the percentage of families headed by women moves down steadily as family income rises. The proportion starts out at 63 per 100 families with incomes under $2,000, and then moves down progressively to reach 2 per 100 families with incomes of $10,000 and over.

Negro families with children are much more likely than white families to be headed by a woman—1 in every 3 Negro families is in this category, compared with 1 in every 10 white families. The difference in family structure is one reason for the lower average income of Negro families. Although the proportion of black families without husbands and fathers is higher than for whites at every income level, it moves down sharply and continuously from about 3 in 4 among the lowest income families to about 1 in 20 among the higher income families.

The median income of the families of 8 million children who were being brought up by their mothers—or other female relatives—was $4,000 in 1969. This contrasts with a median family income of $11,600 for the 61 million children living with both parents.

Only 38 percent of the families headed by women had incomes over $5,000 and only 9 percent had incomes over $10,000. By contrast, 55 percent of the husband-wife-children families had incomes over $10,000. Although husband-wife families tend to be larger than families headed by women, the differences in income between the two types of families far exceed any differences in need.

Families headed by women account for a large and growing proportion of the remaining poverty in the United States. In 1969, 47 of every 100 poor families with children were headed by women. In 1959, the proportion was 28 out of 100.

The poverty line takes account of both family income and family size. In 1969, the line was set at $3,700 for a nonfarm family of four headed by a woman. It goes up (or down) by roughly $700 for each additional person (or each person less) in the family.

The poverty thresholds as used in this discussion are not intended to provide a measure of income adequacy; that is, it should not be inferred that those with incomes above the poverty line have necessarily achieved a minimally adequate level of living. The cutoffs do provide a useful device for measuring the prevalence of, and trends in, very low income levels among various family-type and family-size groups, and are more realistic

TABLE 2. INCOME IN 1969 OF FAMILIES WITH CHILDREN, HEADED BY WOMEN

Family income	All races	White	Negro and other races
Total: Number (in thousands)	3,363	2,255	1,108
Percent	100	100	100
Under $2,000	21	18	26
$2,000 to $2,999	15	13	18
$3,000 to $3,999	14	12	18
$4,000 to $4,999	12	12	11
$5,000 and over	38	45	27
$5,000 to $5,999	10	10	10
$6,000 to $6,999	8	9	6
$7,000 to $7,999	5	6	3
$8,000 to $8,999	3	4	3
$9,000 to $9,999	3	5	1
$10,000 and over	9	11	4
Median income	$4,008	$4,523	$3,327
Families headed by women as percent of all families with children	11	9	31
Under $2,000	63	57	74
$2,000 to $2,999	54	48	67
$3,000 to $3,999	40	33	56
$4,000 to $4,999	28	26	36
$5,000 to $5,999	20	17	31
$6,000 to $6,999	14	12	22
$7,000 to $7,999	8	7	12
$8,000 to $8,999	5	4	14
$9,000 to $9,999	5	5	6
$10,000 and over	2	2	5

than are fixed dollar amounts of income (for example, families with incomes under $3,000) because they are graduated by family size. They are varied over time to reflect annual changes in the average price level as measured by the Consumer Price Index.

The poverty statistics point up the importance of family size. If a family headed by a woman has only one or two children, it has about a 2 out of 3 chance of staying above the poverty line. However, as the number of children increases, the probability that the family's income is under the poverty line rises sharply. Among those families with four children or more, over two-thirds are poor.

Additional children might have been economically helpful to poor families in an earlier era. But in modern urban society with its complex technology and its unrelenting emphasis on education and skill, each additional child diminishes the woman's prospects for economic independence and security through employment. The bearing and rearing of children may interfere with the completion of her education, and most certainly will interfere with the continuity of her employment. Unless a woman can acquire at least a high school education or can acquire mean-

TABLE 3.   EXTENT OF POVERTY IN 1969 AMONG FAMILIES HEADED
BY WOMEN, BY NUMBER OF CHILDREN
(Numbers in thousands)

Race and number of children under 18[1]	Total number of families	Poor families		
		Number	Percent of total	Median deficit between total income and poverty line[2]
ALL RACES				
Total	5,580	1,803	32	$1,200
No children under 18	2,218	315	14	700
One child	1,211	360	30	1,100
Two children	960	386	40	1,200
Three children	545	279	51	1,500
Four children	303	202	67	1,700
Five children or more	344	262	76	2,400
WHITE				
Total	4,185	1,063	25	1,200
No children under 18	1,931	232	12	700
One child	906	227	25	1,100
Two children	702	258	37	1,300
Three children	353	163	46	1,700
Four children	163	97	60	1,700
Five children or more	130	86	66	2,400
NEGRO AND OTHER RACES				
Total	1,395	739	53	1,400
No children under 18	286	83	29	700
One child	306	133	43	1,100
Two children	258	128	50	1,100
Three children	191	116	61	1,500
Four children	140	105	75	1,600
Five children or more	214	174	81	2,400

[1] Own or related.
[2] Based on data for 1968.

ingful job training and job experience, and unless she can work full time most of the year, it is unlikely that her annual earnings alone would be sufficient to lift the income of a family of four above the poverty line. Additional children tend to reduce her earning power, while raising family expenses. The extra welfare allowance for each additional family member is too small to prevent the gap from widening. The situation is illustrated statistically in table 3. On the average, poor families headed by women had total incomes in 1969 which were $1,200 below the poverty threshold, but this income deficit increased with each child added to the family. The median difference between income level and the poverty line (the "poverty gap") was $1,100 for those with one child, $1,500 for those with three children, and $2,400 for those with five children or more.

One-quarter of all families headed by a woman are black. For these families, the rate of poverty is greater than for white families irrespective of the number of children. Moreover, large families are more common among blacks; one-third of the Negro families headed by women has four children or more compared with only one-eighth of the white families.

Among families with children, nearly two-thirds had only one child or two children. But when the children themselves are considered by family size, a different picture emerges—three-fifths lived in families with three children or more. These are the families where the poverty rate ranged from 51 to 76 percent and the poverty gap averaged from $1,500 to $2,400.

EXTENT OF EMPLOYMENT

The proportion of women holding paid jobs outside the home has been climbing steadily for 25 years and by March 1970, 43 of every 100 women 16 years of age and over were in the labor force (that is, either employed or seeking work).

The typical pattern has been for a woman to enter the labor force after completion of her education and prior to marriage, to leave after starting a family, and to reenter the labor force as family responsibilities diminish. During the last 10 years, however, there has been some modification of this pattern with the increasing entry into the labor force of mothers with young children. Their participation rate, although still comparatively low, has increased much faster than the rate for other mothers. From 1960 to 1969, the rate for mothers with children under 6 years of age increased from 20 percent to 30 percent, while for mothers with children 6 to 17 years of age it increased from 43 to 51 percent.

The data indicate that the labor force participation of mothers responds to economic need. In March 1969, divorced, separated, or widowed women with young children under 6 had a participation rate of 47 percent, compared with 29 percent for married women with children under 6. The higher rate for women without husbands reflects in part an insufficiency of income from sources other than employment (alimony, child support, welfare, and Social Security).

From the standpoint of developing programs geared to assist women to earn their way off welfare, these labor force trends appear somewhat encouraging. However, the statistics on labor force participation of women can be misleading because they reveal nothing about the duration of employment. It is readily apparent that there is a high rate of turnover in the female work force. During 1968, an average of 28 million were employed, but 37 million different women were employed at some time during the year. For insight into the duration of employment, it is necessary to turn to data on work experience during the entire calendar year rather than in an average survey week. Because of concern with the capacity of women not merely to hold jobs but to support their families on the basis of their earnings, it is particularly important to examine the extent of full-time and part-time labor force activity, and the extent of year-round work compared with seasonal or temporary work.

Special tabulations of data on work experience in 1967, compiled for the Manpower Administration of the U.S. Department of Labor, were summarized for female heads of families age 16 to 44 years. These are women who still have many years of potential working life remaining and for whom job training is a realistic possibility. They are also the ones, however, who are most likely to be prevented from working steadily by the presence of children. Altogether, 70 percent worked at some time during the year, but only 38 percent worked throughout the year at full-time jobs.

. . . Working only part of the year is not enough to enable many female family heads to support their families at a level of living above the poverty line. Of the families headed by women who were employed only part time or part year, about half were poor. On the one hand, where the mother was employed year round full time, only 16 percent were poor. Of course, supplementary income was a factor in some cases, but the mother's earnings were clearly the most decisive factor. On the other hand, three-fourths of the families headed by nonworkers were poor.

If a woman can hold a professional, managerial, or clerical job, her chances of keeping her family above the poverty line are very good; only 16 percent of these families were poor. Over two-fifths of the mothers who worked at all had a job in one of these white-collar occupations.

Half of all female heads of poor families did not work at all during the year so that any skills or experience they might have were not being used. Of those who did work, nearly half had low-paid service jobs such as kitchen helpers, maids, hospital attendants and aides, and laundry workers. A fifth held semiskilled factory jobs. Only one-fifth of those with any employment experience (one-tenth of the overall total) worked at some time during the year in the better-paid white-collar occupations.

WEEKLY EARNINGS OF WOMEN

Data on the usual weekly earnings of wage and salary workers in full-time jobs reveal that in general the median earnings of women full-time workers are not very high. . . . The overall median weekly earnings for all women full-time workers in May 1969 were $87. Even among white woman with high school diplomas, who were employed mainly in clerical jobs, usual weekly earnings were only $88.

The data by educational attainment (years of formal schooling completed) and occupation from the May 1969 earnings survey are instructive. They reveal that only among the college-educated professional and managerial groups did a majority of women working full time earn over $100 a week. Among those with no college attendance (three-fourths of the total), only 3 out of every 10 white women and 2 out of every 10 black women earned $100 a week or more.

The earnings potential of women heading poor families is even more restricted because of limited formal education. Nearly 70 percent of the 1 million in the 16- to 44-year age bracket never completed high school; 300,000 never went beyond elementary school. More than half of the least educated are black. Negro women with less than a high school education were earning only $60 a week in the spring of 1969, even working at full-time jobs. Many were working in domestic and other service activities not covered by minimum wage legislation and where hourly pay scales are still comparatively low.

If all women heading poor families were to become employed at jobs with weekly earnings commensurate with their education levels, and assuming that they would be subject to prevailing practices of racial and sex discrimination in hiring and pay scales, they would earn an average of about $74 per week (as of the spring of 1969). Data from the Work Incentive Program show that the average WIN graduate in a followup sample was earning about $2 an hour or roughly $80 a week. A woman who earned that much, and who worked every week of the year, would make enough to support herself and her family above the poverty standard if she had no more than three children.

Women who can be trained to fill clerical, technical, and lower grade professional jobs, and who stay on those jobs on a regular year-round basis, could expect to earn between $5,000 and $7,500 a year, on the average. On the other hand, average earnings are much lower in semiskilled manual occupation and in service (excluding domestic) occupations, where about two-fifths of the female heads age 16 to 44 who work at all are clustered. Year-round work in these occupations would yield annual earnings of about $4,500 and $3,500, respectively.

PROGRAMS TO UPGRADE EMPLOYABILITY

Paid work would appear to be a logical solution to the income problems of many welfare mothers. However, the data point up several constraints operating against any employment strategy. If employment is to be effective in raising family standards, it must be full time and year round. Even for the mother of a small or average-sized family, the cost and difficulty of finding adequate child care, and the lack of sufficient education and job training, are formidable barriers to steady work at good wages. For mothers of large families, these problems are compounded because their family responsibilities are greater, and their income needs are larger.

In an effort to overcome these barriers to employment, Federal programs such as the Work Incentive Program (WIN) and the proposed Family Assistance Act (FAP) have been developed in recent years. Both of these programs have training, job placement, and child care provisions which are designed to enable employable adult members of poor families to find jobs and gain economic independence.

The benefit and tax rate schedules under FAP provide some idea of how much a mother would have to earn to get off welfare completely. If a four-person family received $3,920 or more in earned income, its Federal income supplement would be eliminated entirely. The earnings equivalent of that annual income would be roughly $2 an hour for 2,000 hours of work, or $80 a week for at least 50 weeks. The head of a six-person family would have to earn more than $2.50 an hour or over $100 a week all year long before the income supplement would phase out completely. In many northern States (Connecticut, Massachusetts, New Jersey, New York, Pennsylvania, Minnesota, in particular), where AFDC payments are relatively high, the woman's earnings would have to be considerably higher to equal welfare payments, since State welfare benefits would not be reduced under the proposal.

Of course, any increase in a woman's earning power would at least reduce her welfare subsidy. It would be important, therefore, to take account of trends in the average payment per family, in addition to the total number of beneficiaries, if an integrated income support and employability program were to go into effect.

The main issue in any employment strategy is whether the incentives can be made strong enough to induce welfare recipients to accept training and jobs. In the recent controversy over the Family Assistance Program, proponents of the bill pointed to the provisions for child care, training, job counseling, and job placement, and to the flexibility in program design to meet the individual needs of each beneficiary. They stressed that the poor in this country are imbued with a strong work ethic, needing only the opportunity to exercise it. They emphasized that the act was so designed that the tax and benefit provisions would always make it more profitable for a recipient to work than not to work. For the small minority who might otherwise reject the opportunity, the act includes a provision requiring adults to register with the U. S. Employment Service unless exempted because of illness, age, or in the case of female family heads, the presence of children under 6. Opponents of the act raised a number of questions about the appropriateness and effectiveness of the work requirement in the case of mothers. Skepticism was voiced about the availability of jobs; about the cost-effectiveness of child care and training; and, above all, as to whether the monetary incentives would be strong enough to offset the loss of welfare payments and in-kind benefits (food stamps, Medicaid, etc.) associated with increased earnings.

Perhaps some answers will be forthcoming from experimentation with income-maintenance programs which is now under way in several communities. In the meantime, the data available on the work experience, occupational and educational backgrounds, and, particularly, the earnings of women family heads do give some useful perspective on the feasibility of providing employment as a substitute for welfare.

FACTS ABOUT WOMEN'S ABSENTEEISM AND LABOR TURNOVER

FOREWORD

Interest in the comparative costs of employing men and women workers has been heightened by recent efforts to extend and enforce the principles of equal pay and equal opportunity in employment. Allegations of differences in costs are made to justify differential treatment.

This report summarizes the latest facts available about certain factors affecting labor costs; namely, absenteeism, labor turnover, job tenure, and labor mobility. The cost differentials are shown to be insignificant. The favorable findings for women workers emphasize the importance of judging work performance on the basis of individual achievement rather than of sex.

Women workers have favorable records of attendance and labor turnover when compared with men employed at similar job levels and under similar circumstances. This conclusion is supported by a careful analysis of various impartially collected statistics on absenteeism and labor turnover which also indicates that the skill level of the job, the age of the worker, the worker's length of service with the employer, and the worker's record of job stability—all provide better clues to an understanding of differences in work performance than does the mere fact that the worker is a man or a woman.

These data contradict some generalizations about the comparative labor costs of men and women. However, such generalizations are based on studies which point to the sex of the worker as the major determining factor in situations where numerous other factors have much more influence.

Before examining details of studies that consider comparable characteristics of workers, however, it is pertinent to cite the overall averages of data compiled by official or independent agencies. Even these show smaller net differences in the work records of men and women than frequently are suggested.

Reprinted from U.S. Department of Labor, Wage and Labor Standards Administration (Washington, D.C.), Women's Bureau, August 1969.

OVERALL AVERAGES OF ABSENTEEISM

A Public Health Service study of worktime lost by persons 17 years of age and over because of illness or injury shows an average of 5.6 days lost by women and 5.3 days lost by men during the calendar year 1967. Significant differences were noted between men and women in the amount of time lost because of acute or chronic illness. Women lost an average of 3.7 workdays because of acute illness, whereas men averaged just 3.3 days away from work for this reason. On the other hand, men were more likely than women to be absent because of chronic conditions such as heart trouble, arthritis, rheumatism, and orthopedic impairment.

Another analysis also has indicated that women's illnesses usually keep them away from work for shorter periods than men's illnesses do. The Health Information Foundation of the University of Chicago studied the total loss to the American economy from work absences that occurred because of illness or injury between July 1959 and June 1960. Since women lost more worktime because of acute conditions and men because of chronic conditions, the study found that the total financial loss caused by women's absences was about the same as that caused by men's.

The Bureau of Labor Statistics, in its monthly survey of the labor force, records the incidence of illness but not its duration. During an average week in 1968, 1.7 percent of women workers and 1.5 percent of men workers were absent from work because of illness. In addition, an average of 1.2 percent of the women and 1 percent of the men did not report to work for other reasons, excluding vacations. This survey does not give the full story, of course, since women have, on the average, shorter periods of absences than men.

Available statistics on labor turnover also indicate that the net differences in job-leaving of men and women are generally small—even when considered on an overall basis.

Labor turnover rates, which refer to the movement of employees among firms, consist of both hiring and separation rates. The average turnover rates for men and women factory workers in 1968, collected by the Bureau of Labor Statistics on a quarterly basis are:

(Rate per 100 employees)

Type of labor turnover	Women	Men
Accessions (hires)	5.3	4.4
Separations (total)	5.2	4.4
Quits	2.6	2.2
Layoffs and other involuntary separations	2.6	2.2

Comparison of these quit rates with those analyzed in an earlier study shows a narrowing of the gap between the rates of men and women. The fact that women have become relatively less inclined to quit their jobs than they were formerly is due probably to the higher proportion of older women in the work force and the increased interest of women in continuous employment.

A study of occupational mobility by the Bureau of Labor Statistics indicates that men are more frequent occupation changers than women. According to that study, only 7 percent of the women but 10 percent of the men held a different occupation in January 1966 than in January 1965. Movement between occupations was greater among young workers than among mature ones. In the 18- and 19-year-old group, more than 1 out of 4 girls and almost 1 out of 3 boys had worked in more than one occupation in 1965. Among those workers 35 years or older, fewer than 4 percent of the women and 6 percent of the men had changed occupations.

The seeming inconsistency between the labor turnover rates and the occupational mobility percentages of the two studies made by the Bureau of Labor Statistics is explained by their different coverage. The study of turnover rates referred to job changes of factory workers only. The study of mobility rates, on the other hand, measured all occupational changes but not job changes within the same occupational classification. In addition, the latter figures exclude workers who left jobs in 1965 and had not obtained new ones by January 1966, either because they were unsuccessful in their jobhunting or had voluntarily left the labor force. Since there are relatively more women than men in this category, the figures for women's occupational mobility tend to be slightly understated.

Geographic labor mobility was also found to be somewhat less among women workers than men workers in a study made by the Social Security Administration. Between 1957 and 1960, an average of 6.3 percent of women workers but 7.7 percent of men workers changed the region of their main job. The extent of regional movement among white women workers (6.4 percent) and Negro women workers (5.3 percent) was exceeded by both white men workers (7.8 percent) and Negro men workers (7.3 percent).

Another indication of women's increasing stability in the work force is revealed in trend figures on the worklife expectancy of women, as compiled by the Department of Labor. These figures show that the average number of years a woman works had more than tripled from 1900 to 1960 and had increased by almost one-third in the decade 1950–60. Worklife expectancy for those women born in 1900 averaged 6.3 years; in 1940, 12.1 years; in 1950, 15.2 years; and in 1960, 20.1 years. In each case, the percentage increase in women's average worklife expectancy far exceeded that of their average life expectancy.

The expected worklife of a woman is closely related to her marital status and the number of children she has. In the large group of women who enter the labor force by age 20, the relatively small number who never marry have a worklife expectancy of 45 years. This is about 10 years longer than for those women in the group who marry but have no children and about 2 to 3 years longer than for those who become widowed or divorced. For the large number of married women with children, worklife expectancy declines with the higher number of children and the later timing of the last child. A woman marrying at age 20 has a worklife expectancy ranging from 25 years if she has just one child to 17 years if she has four or more children.

STUDIES OF COMPARABLE CHARACTERISTICS

Several studies provide insight into the job stability of men and women by comparing those who hold similar jobs or have similar employment characteristics. These studies present a much more favorable picture of women's worklife than frequently is realized and support the contention that hiring decisions of employers generally are based on factors other than the relative labor costs of men and women.

JOB TENURE. In its study of the job tenure of American workers, the Bureau of Labor Statistics found that continuous employment in the current job as of January 1966 averaged 2.8 years for women and 5.2 years for men. In comparable age groups, job stability was as great for single women as for all men. In fact, among those 45 years of age and over, single women averaged more time on the same job (15.5 years) than all men in the same age group (13.1 years).

Workers with the shortest job tenure were typically youth and married women. Young workers 14 to 19 years old—boys as well as girls—had spent an average of less than 1 year on their current job. The average job tenure of married women was generally shorter than that of single women in all age groups except the youngest (14–24 years). The job attachment of married women was greater for each age group, with the longest period (6.4 years) reported for those 45 years of age and over.

ILLNESS ABSENTEEISM. Detailed statistics of illness absenteeism were provided by the Bureau of Labor Statistics to the U.S. Public Health Service from the monthly survey of the labor force for the period July 1959 to June 1960. The analysis compared men and women employed as civilian wage and salary workers by major occupational group, industry, type of employment, and type of manufacturing industry. On an average workday during that year, when illness rates were adjusted for age, relatively more women (1.6 percent) than men (1.3 percent) were absent from work because of illnesses lasting a workweek or more. However, among certain groups—for example, clerical workers and government workers—women had a lower rate of illness absence than men.

When sick absence days for the period July 1959 to June 1961 were analyzed by the U.S. Public Health Service and adjusted to eliminate the effects of marital status as well as age on sickness absences, they showed fewer sick days per year for single women (3.9 days) than for single men (4.3 days). Within comparable age groups, single women used more sick leave than single men below 35 years of age but used less sick leave at 35 years and over.

Among "ever married persons," however, there were more days of sick absence for women (6.1 days) than men (4.7 days) when compared by the total age-adjusted data as well as by individual age groups. It was thought that women's greater responsibility for childrearing and probably their lesser dependency on their own jobs for economic support might explain the relatively higher sick absence of the "ever married women."

LABOR TURNOVER. A private study conducted among 65 large chemical and pharmaceutical laboratories revealed only moderate differences in the labor turnover of men and women chemists when they were grouped by type of degree required for the grade of work performed. A majority of the surveyed laboratories reported that in comparisons made on this basis, women's turnover rates were "about the same" as men's. No more than 10 percent of the laboratories reported them "much higher." The overall turnover rates were much less favorable for women than for men "mainly because women are disproportionately represented at the lowest level, where turnover is highest for both sexes." It is significant that directors of many of the largest laboratories said that differentials in turnover were not sufficiently great to be a deciding factor in employment of women.

Two studies have focused attention directly on factors which might explain the consistently high turnover rates of hospital nurses. One study, published by the Industrial Relations Center of Iowa State University, surveyed staff registered nurses in several large general hospitals to learn specifically about their turnover, their propensity to leave, and their absenteeism. This investigation indicated that inadequate definitions of the nurses' role in the organization, poor communication and coordination, and unreasonable work pressures all had an adverse influence on the nurses' turnover and, to a lesser extent, on their absenteeism.

The second study of nurses also suggested that hospitals might look more closely at their methods of operation to learn some of the reasons for nurses' high turnover rates. Nurses leaving one sample hospital over a 15-month period were mailed exit questionnaires by three researchers at Western Reserve University. The majority (69 percent) of reasons given for leaving were not related to job situations and in most cases were involuntary ones, such as pregnancy, illness, retirement, or moves to another city. The primary reasons cited for quitting voluntarily were: nature of work (10 percent), lack of promotion (7 percent), supervision and human relations (6 percent), to get new experience (4 percent), and other reasons (4 percent).

The survey report of the Western Reserve researchers contained these comments on the lack of job challenge felt by the nurses who had voluntarily quit their jobs:

> Some of the respondents, dissatisfied with what they were doing as a result of not using their experience and ability, left their jobs. Others left because their work was not appreciated or recognized, because of lack of advancement possibilities, or to get new experience somewhere else. These individuals did not find a chance to achieve what they expected. Their work did not satisfy their needs for what may be called self-actualization and psychological growth.

FEDERAL EMPLOYEES' ABSENTEEISM. A Public Health Service analysis of the number of absences reported because of illness by a sample of employees in one large Federal agency corroborated the theory that employees in high-level jobs generally had fewer absences than those at lower levels, regardless of the sex of the worker. Thus, the generalization made in the report that women employees had more absences than men employees was based on the overall data, which did not take account of the fact that relatively more women than men were employed in the low grades. In addition, it was found that women employees with children generally had a greater number of absences than those without children. As a result, differences in the incidence of illness absenteeism varied much more among the women employees than among the men employees.

Since this report did not include statistical data concerning the length of each absence period—generally found to be longer for men than women—it presented only a partial story of the illness absenteeism of Federal employees in one agency.

A U.S. Civil Service Commission study of sick leave records in 1961 showed relatively small difference in the total amount of sick leave averaged by women and men Federal workers—9.6 days for women and 7.9 days for men. But even this difference narrowed in most instances when comparisons were made of women and men with similar salaries, ages, or years of service. For example, in 1961 among those earning $9,000 to $10,000 a year, 6.9 days of sick leave was the average for women and 6.3 days for men.

The highest average numbers of sick days occurred among those in the lowest salary levels—the levels where women workers are concentrated. Two groups of women had less sick leave, on the average, than their male counterparts: those 60 years of age and over (10.5 days for women, 11 days for men) and those with more than 30 years of Federal service (10.7 days for women and 11.3 days for men).

A study made by the Civil Service Commission especially for the President's Commission on the Status of Women covered voluntary separations of full-time career employees between December 16, 1962, and February 2, 1963. On an overall basis, the relative separation (turnover) rate was about 2½ times greater for women than for men. The higher rate for women can be explained by the larger proportion of women than men who are under 25 years of age, who have lower grade clerical jobs, and who have fewer years of Federal service—all factors associated with high turnover. When the data for men and for women were compared separately by age group, by broad occupational group, and by length of service, differences in their relative turnover rates decreased.

FRENCH WORKERS' ABSENTEEISM. The importance of considering job levels and other factors in any study of absenteeism is further emphasized in an international report on women industrial workers in Paris, France. The following quotation is from that report:

> Detailed study of absentee figures for large numbers of employees of both sexes and at all levels of skill discloses that the comparatively high proportion of women at the lower levels of the occupational scale (even in countries where the employment of women is a long-standing tradition) goes a long way towards explaining their frequent irregularity at work. Highly trained women occupying responsible and skilled positions are seldom absent, even if they have several children to bring up.

CONCLUSION. Meaningful comparisons of absenteeism and labor turnover of women and men workers must take into consideration similar job levels as well as other factors such as age and length of service. Many of the critical generalities frequently voiced not only exaggerate overall differences but also compare dissimilar groups of men and women.

ROBERT J. LAMPMAN

CHARACTERISTICS OF TOP WEALTH-HOLDERS

The median age of the 1953 top living wealth-holders was 54 years (Table 1). Over half of the number were between 40 and 60 years of age. While top wealth-holders made up only 1.04 percent of the total population and only 1.6 percent of the adult population they accounted for 3.5 percent of the men over 50.

Approximately 1.4 million of the 1.7 million top wealth-holders are heads of households, the 0.3 million being (according to our estimate) the number of married women and dependent children in the group. We find that a minimum of 2.28 percent of households and 2.35 percent of married couples have at least one member owning $60,000 of gross estate (Table 2). This compares closely with the Survey of Consumer Finances finding that 3 percent of spending units in 1950 had $60,000 or more of total assets.

The association of age and size of estate is quite clear for men; that is, average estate rises with age and median age rises with estate size.... (The latter association is remarkably slight, however. See Table 3.) For women, on the other hand, this relationship is much more irregular.

Women top wealth-holders have gradually increased, both in numbers and in wealth, relative to men so that they comprised one-third of all top wealth-holders in 1953 (while only one-fourth in 1922) and held 40 percent of the wealth of the group (Table 1). Women have a larger

TABLE 1. SELECTED CHARACTERISTICS OF TOP WEALTH-HOLDERS, 1953

Characteristic	Both Sexes	Men	Women
Number of persons	1,659,000	1,144,000	514,000
Median gross estate size ($)	112,800	116,800	105,200
Average gross estate size ($)	182,000	162,400	220,500
Share of top wealth (percent)	100	60	40
Median age (years)	54	52	57

Excerpted from Robert J. Lampman, *The Share of Top Wealth-Holders in National Wealth, 1922–56* (Princeton, New Jersey: NBER, Princeton University Press, 1962), 17–20.

	Top Wealth-Holders		
	Both Sexes	Men	Women
All persons	1.04	1.44	0.64
Adults (20 and over)	1.60	2.26	0.98
Persons (65 and over)	3.00	4.00	2.50
Married persons	1.40	2.30	0.70
Widowers and widows	2.69	3.10	2.60
Households with at least one top wealth-holder	2.28		

average estate size than men, although within most age groups there is no clear difference by sex, and although men have a higher median estate size than women.

The information on top wealth-holders furnishes little support for the popular idea that women own the greater part of American wealth. The type of property in the holding of which women come closest to men is corporate stock. While men, it is estimated, held $63 billion worth of stock, women held $54 billion worth. This was the case for the basic variant wealth, but in the total wealth variant, which takes into account personal trust funds, it is probable that women have over half the corporate stock.

One factor that contributes to the increasing importance of women as wealth-holders is the relative population growth in community property states, which now include Arizona, California, Idaho, Louisiana, Nevada, New Mexico, Texas and Washington. In these eight states ownership is, in many cases, divided by law between husband and wife. Hence, the executor of the estate of the first spouse to die must report for estate tax purposes only half the property acquired after the marriage. Despite this legal provision, this group of eight states has almost exactly the share of top wealth-holders to be expected from its population, that is 18 percent of the wealth-holders and 18 percent of the population. They have somewhat less of the estate tax wealth than would be expected from their per capita income rank, however. A disproportionate number of the married female top wealth-holders are in community property states. This finding would suggest that if the family were the wealth-holding unit rather than the individual, considerably more than 18 percent of the top wealth-holding families would be found in community property states.

TABLE 3. MEDIAN AGE OF MALE TOP WEALTH-HOLDERS IN
NON-COMMUNITY PROPERTY STATES, BY GROSS ESTATE SIZE, 1953

Gross Estate Size (thous. dollars)	Median Age (years)
60 to 100	54
100 to 200	53
200 to 500	53
500 to 2,000	56
2,000 and over	67

Source: Table 48.

PART FIVE: TOWARD SEX EQUALITY

What do American women want? There is no one answer. Social class, ethnicity, race, education, religion, and politics are some factors which make it unlikely that women readily share one view of their own condition, or degree of contentment with their lives. Women also vary in their acceptance of women's rights movements, and even those who want changes disagree about what those changes ought to be.

Alice Rossi[1] proposes several models of sex equality which are useful for thinking about the current movement. Rossi suggests three models: pluralism, assimilation, and hybrid, which derive, like Hacker's analyses in Part One, from theories of minority group relations.

In the *pluralist* model, groups which are different from the mainstream of the society—blacks from whites, women from men, Catholics from Protestants—are encouraged to develop and maintain their distinctiveness. In this view, women may be considered different from men on any number of grounds; certain social roles and behaviors are considered appropriate for women but not men. Rossi suggests there are too many barriers (for example, white Anglo-Saxon men dominate the economic and political systems) for this model to mean equality—sexually, racially, or ethnically. In addition to Rossi's observations of limitations, one might ask whether the pluralist model including ideas such as the "feminine mystique" may not really be an ideological justification of *in*equality.

---

[1] Alice Rossi, "Sex Equality: The Beginning of Ideology," *Humanist* (Fall, 1969). See also Alice Rossi, "Equality Between the Sexes: An Immodest Proposal," *Daedalus* 93 (Spring 1964), 607–652.

The *assimilation* model of equality essentially conceives of women being allowed to do what men do. Hence, the life-styles of men—in sex, work and play, politics and civic affairs, clothing and grooming—must be open to adoption by women. Rossi suggests that this style is both uncritically accepted as an ideal and is impossible for women to adopt. The life-style of men, which women wish to imitate, depends on the existence of a wife who carries out all of the background activities which make that life-style possible. The wife accepts responsibility for the children, the home, the everyday chores inside and outside of the household; she coordinates family activities and makes sure these do not conflict with any of her husband's obligations; she plans appropriate entertainment and carries out the necessary attendant duties. All of these leave her husband free to pursue a career, or an interest in politics or civic affairs. Women cannot achieve this life-style, notes Rossi, until they, too, have "wives."

Finally, there is the *hybrid* model, the least developed and most provocative approach to sex equality. This model rejects both the assumptions that women and men are basically different and ought to retain the social differences, and that present social organization and the present life-style of men are the most desirable. Rather, the model proposes a society in which the sexes live similar lives, but lives which are markedly different from the ones either lives now. The intense devotion of American men to career advancement, their preoccupation with the sexual exploitation of women, and with making money are among the themes which are being critically questioned, and believed by some to be socially undesirable. What the new society would be is not clear, aside from offering both sexes relief from the burdens of their sex-defined roles.

Many reactions to the contemporary women's movement and the demands now being made for social changes can be clarified by a comparison with these three models.

First, not all women are involved, even in minor ways, in demanding changes in their current social position. Pluralism is the model of sex equality used by women who accept the traditional homemaker role and may even consider changes in women's roles to be distasteful and undesirable. Some of these women may believe that they are inferior to men, and that it is men, not women, that society discriminates against.[2]

Black women may also accept the pluralist model when they contend that the recent women's movement, from the National Organization of Women to women's communes, weakens the more important struggle for human rights. If they see racism and black matriarchy as having prevented

---

[2] See the testimony of Mrs. Lynne S. Grace, Housewife, Chevy Chase, Maryland, *Hearings on the Equal Rights Amendment*, S.J., Res. 231, Committee on the Judiciary, U.S. Senate (Washington: Government Printing Office, 1970), 352–363.

black men from achieving manhood, then they may believe that black women must work for the improvement of blacks and black men, in particular, rather than for women. While the Black Panthers, Black Muslims, and the National Alliance for Business differ widely from each other in their political visions, their programs appear, in effect, to lower the status of the black woman. Their implied ideal marriage seems very close to the white Anglo-Saxon Protestant relationship of a dominating male breadwinner and a dependent, supportive female childbearer and homemaker: black manhood vindicates black womanhood, too, as men can now be relied on for protection and economic support.

Second, politically radical women sometimes believe that the current women's movement weakens the efforts to establish a new society. A new society supposedly would bring the necessary preconditions for developing sex equality or it would bring sex equality itself; the implied content of sex equality, in much radical political thought, fits within the assimilation model for though social organization is radically altered, there is no indication that sex roles would be. The argument that a radical change in social organization means sex equality persists, even though socialist countries have only lessened rather than eliminated inequality between women and men. Radical men who also protest that women's liberation deflects from "real" problems and who are eager to be democratic and just (except often in their relations with women) seem to be supporting some version of a pluralist model.

Arguments which advise women to wait are familiar: women repeatedly are urged to step aside, for the general good of their husbands and children, and for the benefit of special causes such as the enfranchisement of black men after the Civil War, and unionization of men during the nineteenth and twentieth centuries. Must a gain in competence and stature for men require an absolute loss in competence and stature for women? Has the women's rights movement retarded other rights movements? No evidence can be shown to support either of these objections to an improved status for women.

Third, the hybrid model is advocated by many kinds of women. The issues of personal and sexual fulfillment, frequently discussed in the "consciousness-raising" groups of the Women's Liberation movement sometimes lead to the issues of the reorganization of sex roles and the reorganization of social institutions. Some politically radical women have come to see that social policies specifically directed at women's social condition are explicit needs in any program of radical social change.

What social changes are advocated by women? Some resist all changes except those which would broaden the traditional protective legislation such as alimony laws which favor women, or labor laws which limit the hours women may work. Others advocate changes ranging from legislation for equal economic rights through social equality in interpersonal relations to broad institutional reorganization. Nearly all women share a concern—usually formulated in terms of the assimilation model—for economic problems such as little job opportunity, low earnings, and little training opportunity for women, even though the current movement originated among white, college-educated, middle-class women rather than among working-class, poor, or black women.

In sharp contrast, there are some women who believe that women do not readily think of themselves except in terms of their relationships to men, since unlike other oppressed minorities, women live with rather than apart from their oppressors. For this reason, some women favor a separation of the sexes, hoping that they can use it as other minorities have—to develop a positive identity. While the model of sex equality is pluralist, it may be a precursor for the development of a hybrid model, for some women favor the separation only partly and/or temporarily, in politics and the classroom, for example. Others see a temporary need to separate themselves from men in sexual relations and living arrangements; still others support a total separation from men, at least until women are, in fact, equal to men.

The readings in this last part of the book represent some contemporary proposals related to the demands women make.

In the first selection, the Women's Platform of the New Democratic Coalition presents a range of demands which combines aspects of the assimilation and hybrid models of sex equality, though without changes in social organization that are probably necessary for the realization of the latter model. Much of the platform is probably acceptable to women seeking changes, though some Catholic and black women may disagree with the demands about abortion and contraception. Catholics argue that abortion and contraception are violations of natural law. Black women raise another issue: since sterilization or contraceptive use is sometimes required of poor, black women receiving financial aid, they regard these policies as racial genocide.[3]

In the next selection, Kate Millett discusses a hybrid model of sex equality when she explores the political nature of sex relations, the processes by which these develop, and the benefits for both sexes of their elimination. Then, Pat Mainardi, in a personal essay, discusses a particular

---

[3] While one may sympathize with this view because many social policies seem aimed primarily at making the black movement ineffective, a rejection of birth control may not be a useful response. The danger is not distinguishing between present social action and the possibilities of action in some distant future by the babies now being born. The possible cultural roots of such reasoning are captured in the statement by the black woman and lawyer, Florynce Kennedy: ". . . breeding revolutionaries is not too far removed from a cultural past where black women were encouraged to be breeding machines for their slave masters." Diane Schulder and Florynce Kennedy, *Abortion Rap* (New York: McGraw-Hill Book Company, 1971).

aspect of the hybrid model in her analysis of the power relations between a working wife and her working husband in a struggle about housework.[4]

In the last selection, the Hungarian sociologists Mihaly Vajda and Agnes Heller present the most systematic hybrid model in their discussion of how changes in sex roles are limited by the conventional nuclear family. They are especially interested in the political relations between men and women, and between parents and children; they suggest the broad outlines for an alternative life-style and living arrangements for a socialist society.

---

[4] See also Agnes Heller, "On the Future of Relations Between the Sexes," *International Social Science Journal*, 4, 1969, 535–544.

PLATFORM ON WOMEN'S RIGHTS, NEW DEMOCRATIC COALITION, NEW YORK STATE, ADOPTED MARCH 10, 1970

EQUAL EMPLOYMENT OPPORTUNITY

Women, who are over a third of the State's workforce, have for years been condemned to the lowest paid, least rewarding jobs, and have been denied the opportunity to advance according to their abilities. Men college graduates are welcome in executive training programs; women are asked if they can type.

A 1968 study by the U.S. Equal Employment Opportunity Commission revealed that in 100 major New York corporations, women held only 3.8 percent of the management posts, and 4.7 percent of professional jobs. Almost 70 percent of the City's women workers are in clerical jobs; men got higher pay than women for identical work.

Women in this country no longer work as a diversion, if they ever did. Labor Department studies show that 85 percent work because they have to, and that the typical worker is 41 and married. Nonetheless, women earn under 60 percent of what men do. Nationally, women with 4 years of college earn less than half of what men with equivalent training are paid.

Federal, state and city laws outlaw job discrimination against women, but these laws are honored more in the breach than the observance. Even the agencies charged with enforcement have given little emphasis to fighting bias against women.

The New Democratic Coalition calls for a substantial increase in all government efforts to end employment discrimination against women, beginning with hearings by Federal, State, and City Human Rights Commissions into the nature and extent of job bias in the major industries. We also call for widespread publicity campaigns to inform women of their

---

Excerpts reprinted from *Discrimination Against Women,* Hearings before the Special Subcommittee on Education of the Committee on Education and Labor, House of Representatives, 91st Congress, second session, Part I (Washington: U.S. Government Printing Office, Committee on Education and Labor, 1970), 177–180.

rights and to encourage complaints by those who suffer discrimination. Finally, we urge the government to withhold contracts and deposits from firms found guilty of discrimination against women.

Women have always assumed the burdens that go with bearing children in order to carry on our civilization. They are the ones who sacrifice their own dreams and careers to stay home and care for their babies. Even when women find ways to go on with their work, society sets up artificial obstacles and penalties to make their lot more difficult.

Pregnant women can be fired and have no rights to guarantee their rehiring after childbirth. There are no maternity benefits to reflect the contributions of women to the economy and to the companies and institutions for which they work.

We call for laws to make maternity leaves and maternity benefits available to working women. Women should not be barred from employment or fired because of pregnancy, and they should be guaranteed the right to return to their jobs after childbirth.

ABORTION LAW REPEAL

There are over a million abortions performed in the United States every year. Under 1 percent of them are legal, 25 percent of all women in America have had illegal abortions, according to some statistics—one for every four live births, 500 to 1000 women die each year from illegal abortions or suffer brutalizing and degradation at the hands of amateurs and hacks.

The poor suffer most: in New York City, 80 percent of the women who die are Black or Puerto Rican. The abortion death rate in the U.S. is 50 to 100 per 100,000, far greater than the 3 per 100,000 in countries where abortion is legal. (The death rate from pregnancy and childbirth is over 29 per 10,000 live births.)

In New York state, abortions may be performed only to save the life of the mother. Proposed reforms would help, at most, 15 percent of the cases, as 85 percent of abortions are performed because the woman does not want the child.

The New Democratic Coalition affirms a woman's right to control her own body and to decide whether or not to bear a child. The State Abortion Law denies a woman's right to privacy in her personal and sexual relations, imposes on her the religious beliefs of others, discriminates against the poor, and endangers a woman's right to life. Hospitals which receive government funds or tax benefits should be required to give medically safe abortions to all women who request them. Personnel in schools, hospitals, welfare centers and other government-supported institutions should be required to let all women know of the availability of abortion.

The New Democratic Coalition supports the Cook-Leichter Bill.

HOUSING AND PUBLIC ACCOMMODATIONS

It is illegal to bar people from housing or public accommodations on the basis of race, creed, color or national origin—but not on the basis of sex. Women suffer serious economic consequences from the policies of landlords and rental agents who have convinced themselves that women are undesirable tenants.

Women also suffer disadvantages in business from the practice of barring women from numerous restaurants, eating clubs, and other places of public accommodation.

The New Democratic Coalition believes that discrimination against women in housing and public accommodations is archaic and unfair, and that it should be illegal.

UNIVERSAL CHILD CARE

Almost 40 percent of the women who work are mothers, and 40 percent of them have children under 6. Over a quarter of all mothers with children under 6 work. However, nationally, only 2 percent of the children of working mothers receive group day care. The rest are watched by relatives or look after themselves.

In New York City, over 150,000 children under 5 have working mothers, yet the City's day care centers have space for only 8,000 youngsters from 3 to 5 years old. This crisis situation exists throughout the State, and the few private centers that exist are expensive and inadequate to handle the need.

The government spends billions of dollars in subsidies and experimentation for farmers, in management assistance and technical development for businessmen and industrialists, in research and training grants for academics, and in countless other programs that help certain groups of Americans earn their livings. However, it does not spend a fraction of that sum to give women the most basic assistance they require to earn theirs.

The New Democratic Coalition believes the government should provide child care centers as a matter of right to all children whose mothers need it. These centers should be educational or recreational, or a combination of the two: as the mothers of the children in the community want them to be. We call now for a massive expansion of child care facilities, with priorities for admission given to the children of mothers who are working, looking for work, or enrolled in schools, colleges, or training programs.

It is amazing that working mothers are not allowed to deduct child care expenses, while tax laws recognize the generous deductions claimed for "entertainment" and the ever popular "businessman's lunch." A woman may be unable to work at all without undertaking the expenses of baby-sitting or nursery school. The New Democratic Coalition believes that this inequity in the law should be remedied on all levels—and applied to widowers and divorced or separated men in similar circumstances.

EQUALITY IN EDUCATION

It is illegal for schools and colleges receiving Federal funds to discriminate against students on the basis of race, color, creed or national origin—but nothing stops them from discriminating against women. This practice is particularly onerous in the professions, where women who would be lawyers, doctors, and college professors are faced with long-standing graduate school quotas. However, even secondary schools discriminate: in New York City there are 31 high schools restricted according to sex.

More girls than boys graduate from high school in this country, but more men than women enter college. A quarter of the men aged 20 to 24 are in school, compared to only a tenth of the women. There is also sex discrimination in training programs financed by the government. For example, the State University of New York Urban Center in its Brooklyn Data Processing Program restricts machine operator trainees to men, and keypunch operators to women—again limiting women to the lowest paying jobs.

Millions of dollars of City, State, and Federal money support teachers' salaries, construction, research projects, and operation of schools that deny their opportunities to women, or restrict them to a small quota of the enrollment.

The New Democratic Coalition supports total equality of opportunity in education for women, and favors Federal, State, and City legislation to bar discrimination in education and training programs on the basis of sex, which would make it illegal to grant government funds to schools that discriminate.

The history of women in this country and the rest of the world has been virtually ignored. When women are discussed at all, it is generally because they are famous men's wives. The suffragettes are ridiculed, and the battle to win the vote, which took over seven decades, is passed over with brief comment.

Numerous women who freed themselves from the limiting stereotypes that trapped other women in those times have made great contributions to this country and the development of man. Students barely learn that they existed at all. School guidance teachers continue the stereotypes by shunting girls into secretarial courses; directing them towards the traditional female occupations, and discouraging them from so-called men's jobs. Boys are encouraged to become doctors; girls are told to be nurses.

It is important that girls and boys grow up with the knowledge that sex is no barrier to achievement, and that women have been kept back by discrimination and social convention, not by their lack of ability.

We call for a new emphasis in the schools on the contributions of women in history and culture. We call for new guidance policies that encourage girls to break the barriers that keep them from the more satisfying, better paying jobs and professions. Shop and homemaking classes should be required for all students, and should be integrated.

WOMEN'S RIGHTS AMENDMENT

"Equality of rights under the law should not be denied or abridged by the United States or by any State on account of sex." This amendment to the U.S. Constitution has been introduced in the Senate by Eugene McCarthy and John Tower, and in the House by Martha Griffiths (D-Mich.) and Catherine May (R-Wash.). It seeks to overturn laws that restrict the rights of women in business, employment, marriage, divorce, and political activity in virtually every state of the union. (Five states, for example, require court approval before a married woman can go into business on her own. A woman may be refused unemployment insurance if she leaves her job to follow her husband to another city, but she can be divorced for desertion if she fails to go with him.)

The Equal Rights Amendment is a small beginning in the continuing struggle for feminine equality. The New Democratic Coalition endorses it as a necessary protection, and as a statement to Americans that we can no longer afford to limit the opportunities and achievements of more than half of our population.

Legislation has also been proposed to amend the State Charter to prohibit discrimination on the basis of sex. NDC endorses this goal.

WOMEN IN PARTY AND GOVERNMENT OFFICE

There are 62 counties in New York state—but only one woman County Chairman (Jean Angel of Tompkins County), and only one woman Acting County Chairman (Catherine Blintz of Oneida County). Traditionally women are made Vice-Chairman—a powerless job given as reward for years of canvassing and envelope stuffing.

Reform Democratic clubs have claimed to be different, with women District Leaders often exerting as much power and influence as men. Yet, with a few exceptions, women are not nominated for public office by local, county, or state Democratic organizations—including those that belong to the NDC.

In the recent New York City elections, there were 85 Democratic candidates for City-wide office, judgeships, City Council, and other posts. Of these only five were women (they all won election).

The position of women in government is nearly as bleak. Only 29 of the 401 top jobs in New York City government are held by women. All of the 12 superagency administrators, and the 17 presidents of boards and commissions are men. All but three of the thirty commissioners are men. Government, which should be setting an example to private industry on equal employment opportunity laws, is itself guilty of denying women the right to hold the jobs they earn by merit of their talents.

The New Democratic Coalition pledges to encourage more women to seek nomination for public and party office, and to press government officials to hire more women in major administrative and policy-making capacities.

CONTRACEPTION

Last year, there were nearly 2,500 reported pregnancies among New York City high school students; others doubtless went unreported. The Board of Education has a policy of not providing information about contraception to students, and State law forbids prescribing contraceptive devices to anyone under 16. This policy is senseless. It does not prevent young girls from engaging in sexual activity: it only makes it almost inevitable that those who do will become pregnant. Among the general population, many women are unaware of the availability of contraceptive devices; unwanted pregnancies become a special burden for poor women who find themselves trapped even more firmly in the vise of poverty. The New Democratic Coalition urges the repeal of laws that restrict the availability of contraceptives, and calls on the government to make low cost contraceptives available to women who want them. We also call for a public education campaign on contraceptives by the State government which is liberally financed.

FINANCIAL DISCRIMINATION

Existing laws and policies regarding taxes, insurance, credit and pension, health, life and other public and private welfare benefits often discriminate on the basis of sex or marital status. Such discrimination should be made illegal.

ALIMONY

When equal employment opportunity, child care and programs for preparing women for re-entry into the work force at an equal level with men become realities, the alimony laws should be revised to reflect the changed conditions and needs of women.

PROSTITUTION

Prostitution is almost always a result of severe economic and social deprivation. Some 90 percent of the prostitutes in New York are drug addicts. Nevertheless, instead of rehabilitation, the emphasis in the law and the courts has been on punishment. The real victims of prostitution are the women who pass through the revolving doors of the cities' jails.

We call for a revision of the whole approach to the problem of prostitution, starting at once with the end of entrapment by police (who could be better employed fighting crimes that have victims). We call for changes in the laws that punish women but do not punish men. We call for the end of the cynical sacrifice of women by a society which punishes them to assuage its own guilt.

SEXUAL POLITICS: A MANIFESTO FOR REVOLUTION

KATE MILLETT

When one group rules another, the relationship between the two is political. When such an arrangement is carried out over a long period of time it develops an ideology (feudalism, racism, et cetera). All historical civilizations are patriarchies: their ideology is male supremacy.

Oppressed groups are denied education, economic independence, the power of office, representation, an image of dignity and self-respect, equality of status, and recognition as human beings. Throughout history women have been consistently denied all of these, and their denial today, while attenuated and partial, is nevertheless consistent. The education allowed them is deliberately designed to be inferior, and they are systematically programmed out of and excluded from the knowledge where power lies today—for example, in science and technology. They are confined to conditions of economic dependence based on the sale of their sexuality in marriage, or a variety of prostitutions. Work on a basis of economic independence allows them only a subsistence level of life—often not even that. They do not hold office, are represented in no positions of power, and authority is forbidden them. The image of woman fostered by cultural media, high and low, then and now, is a marginal and demeaning existence, and one outside the human condition—which is defined as the prerogative of man, the male.

Government is upheld by power, which is supported through consent (social opinion), or imposed by violence. Conditioning to an ideology amounts to the former. But there may be a resort to the latter at any moment when consent is withdrawn—rape, attack, sequestration, beatings, murder. Sexual politics obtains consent through the "socialization" of both sexes to patriarchial policies. They consist of the following:

1) the formation of human personality along sterotyped lines of sexual category, based on the needs and values of the master class and dictated by what he would cherish in himself and find convenient in an underclass:

aggression, intellectuality, force and efficiency for the male; passivity, ignorance, docility, "virtue," and ineffectuality for the female.

2) the concept of sex role, which assigns domestic service and attendance upon infants to all females and the rest of human interest, achievement and ambition to the male; the charge of leader at all times and places to the male, and the duty of follower, with equal uniformity, to the female.

3) the imposition of male rule through institutions: patriarchal religion, the proprietary family, marriage, "The Home," masculine-oriented culture, and a pervasive doctrine of male superiority.

A Sexual Revolution would bring about the following conditions, desirable upon rational, moral and humanistic grounds:

1) the end of sexual repression—freedom of expression and of sexual mores (sexual freedom has been partially attained, but it is now being subverted beyond freedom into exploitative license for patriarchal and reactionary ends).

2) Unisex, or the end of separatist character-structure, temperament and behavior, so that each individual may develop an entire—rather than a partial, limited, and conformist—personality.

3) reexamination of traits categorized into "masculine" and "feminine," with a total reassessment as to their human usefulness and advisability in both sexes. Thus if "masculine" violence is undesirable, it is so for both sexes, "feminine" dumbcow passivity likewise. If "masculine" intelligence or efficiency is valuable, it is so for both sexes equally, and the same must be true for "feminine" tenderness or consideration.

4) the end of sex role and sex status, the patriarchy and the male supremacist ethic, attitude and ideology—in all areas of endeavor, experience, and behavior.

5) the end of the ancient oppression of the young under the patriarchal proprietary family, their chattel status, the attainment of the human rights presently denied them, the professionalization and therefore improvement of their care, and the guarantee that when they enter the world, they are desired, planned for, and provided with equal opportunities.

6) bisex, or the end of enforced perverse heterosexuality, so that the sex act ceases to be arbitrarily polarized into male and female, to the exclusion of sexual expression between members of the same sex.

7) the end of sexuality in the forms in which it has existed historically—brutality, violence, capitalism, exploitation, and warfare—that it may cease to be hatred and become love.

8) the attainment of the female sex to freedom and full human status after millenia of deprivation and oppression, and of both sexes to a viable humanity.

THE POLITICS OF HOUSEWORK

PAT MAINARDI

> Though women do not complain of the power of husbands, each complains of her own husband, or of the husbands of her friends. It is the same in all other cases of servitude; at least in the commencement of the emancipatory movement. The serfs did not at first complain of the power of their lords, but only of their tyranny.
> —John Stuart Mill, *On the Subjugation of Women*

Liberated women—very different from Women's Liberation! The first signals all kinds of goodies, to warm the hearts (not to mention other parts) of the most radical men. The other signals—*housework*. The first brings sex without marriage, sex before marriage, cozy housekeeping arrangements ("You see, I'm living with this chick") and the self-content of knowing that you're not the kind of man who wants a doormat instead of a women. That will come later.

On the other hand is Women's Liberation—and housework. What? You say this is all trivial? Wonderful! That's what I thought. It seems perfectly reasonable. We both had careers, both had to work a couple of days a week to earn enough to live on, so why shouldn't we share the housework? So I suggested it to my mate and he agreed—most men are too hip to turn you down flat. You're right, he said. It's only fair.

Then an interesting thing happened. I can only explain it by stating that we women have been brainwashed more than even we can imagine. Probably too many years of seeing media-women coming over their shiny waxed floors or breaking down over their dirty shirt collars. Men have no such conditioning. They recognize the essential fact of housework right from the very beginning. Which is that it stinks.

Here's my list of dirty chores: buying groceries, carting them home and putting them away; cooking meals and washing dishes and pots; doing the

Excerpts reprinted from Pat Mainardi, "The Politics of Housework," *Discrimination Against Women*, Hearings before the Special Subcommittee on Education of the Committee on Education and Labor, House of Representatives, 91st Congress, second session, Part I (Washington: U.S. Government Printing Office, Committee on Education and Labor, 1970), 265–268.

laundry; digging out the place when things get out of control; washing floors. The list could go on but the sheer necessities are bad enough. All of us have to do these jobs, or get someone else to do them for us. The longer my husband contemplated these chores, the more repulsed he became, and so proceeded the change from the normally sweet considerate Dr. Jekyll into the crafty Mr. Hyde who would stop at nothing to avoid the horrors of—housework.

So ensued a dialogue that's been going on for several years. Here are some of the high points:

"I don't mind sharing the housework, but I don't do it very well. We should each do the things we're best at."

Meaning: Unfortunately I'm no good at things like washing dishes or cooking. What I do best is a little light carpentry, changing light bulbs, moving furniture. (How often do you move furniture?)

Also meaning: Historically the lower classes (Blacks and women) have had hundreds of years doing menial jobs. It would be a waste of man-power to train someone else to do them now.

Also meaning: I don't like the dull stupid boring jobs, so you should do them.

"I don't mind sharing the work, but you'll have to show me how to do it."

Meaning: I ask a lot of questions and you'll have to show me everything, every time I do it because I don't remember so good. Also, don't try to sit down and read while I'm doing my jobs because I'm going to annoy hell out of you until it's easier to do them yourself.

"I've got nothing against sharing the housework, but you can't make me do it on your schedule."

Meaning: passive resistance. I'll do it when I damn well please, if at all. If my job is doing dishes, it's easier to do them once a week. If taking out laundry, once a month. If washing the floors, once a year. If you don't like it, do it yourself oftener, and then I won't do it at all.

"Women's Liberation isn't really a political movement."

Meaning: The Revolution is coming too close to home.

Also meaning: I am only interested in how I am oppressed, not how I oppress others. Therefore the war, the draft and the university are politi-cal. Women's Liberation is not.

POSTSCRIPT

Participatory democracy begins at home. If you are planning to implement your politics there are certain things to remember.

1. He is feeling it more than you. He's losing some leisure and you're gaining it. The measure of your oppression is his resistance.

2. Most men are not accustomed to doing monotonous, repetitive work which never issues in any lasting let alone important achievement. This is why they would rather repair a cabinet than wash dishes. If human endeavors are like a pyramid with man's highest achievements at the top, then keeping oneself alive is at the bottom. Men have always had servants (you) to take care of this bottom stratum of life while he has confined his efforts to the rarefied upper regions. It is thus ironic when they ask of women: "Where are your great painters, statesmen, etc." Mrs. Matisse ran a millinery shop so he could paint. Mrs. Martin Luther King kept his house and raised his babies.

3. It is a traumatizing experience for someone who has always thought of himself as being against any oppression or exploitation of one human being by another to realize that in his daily life he has been accepting and implementing (and benefiting from) this exploitation: that his rationalization is little different from that of the racist who says "Niggers don't feel pain" (women don't mind doing the———work), and that the oldest form of oppression in history has been the oppression of 50 percent of the population by the other 50 percent.

4. Arm yourself with some knowledge of the psychology of oppressed peoples everywhere and a few facts about the animal kingdom. I admit playing top wolf or who runs the gorillas is silly but as a last resort men bring it up all the time. Talk about bees. If you feel really hostile, bring up the sex life of spiders. After sex, she bites off his head.

The psychology of oppressed peoples is not silly. Blacks, women, and immigrants have all employed the same psychological mechanisms to survive. Admiring the oppressor, glorifying the oppressor, wanting to be like the oppressor, wanting the oppressor to like them.

5. In a sense all men everywhere are slightly schizoid—divorced from the reality of maintaining life. This makes it easier for them to play games with it. It is almost a cliche that women feel greater grief at sending a son off to war or losing him to that war because they bore him, suckled him, and raised him. The men who foment those wars did none of those things and have a more superficial estimate of the worth of human life. One hour a day is a low estimate of the amount of time one has to spend 'keeping' oneself. By foisting this off on others, man has seven hours a week—one working day—more to play with his mind and not his human needs. Over the course of generations it is easy to see whence evolved the horrifying abstractions of modern life.

6. With the death of each form of oppression, life changes and new forms evolve. English aristocrats at the turn of the century were horrified at the idea of enfranchising working men, were sure that it signalled the death of civilization and a return to barbarism. Some working men even fell for this line. Similarly with the minimum wage, abolition of slavery, and female suffrage. Life changes but it goes on—don't fall for any crap

about the death of everything if men take a turn at the dishes. They will imply that you are holding back the Revolution (their Revolution). But you are advancing it.

7. Keep checking up. Periodically consider who's actually doing the jobs. These things have a way of backsliding so that a year later once again the woman is doing everything. Use timesheets if necessary. Also bear in mind what the worst jobs are, namely the ones that have to be done every day or several times a day. Also the ones that are dirty—it's more pleasant to pick up books, newspapers, et cetera, than to wash dishes. Alternate the bad jobs. It's the daily grind that gets you down. Also make sure that you don't have the responsibility for the housework with occasional help from him. "I'll cook dinner for you tonight" implies that it's really your job and isn't he a nice guy to do some of it for you.

8. Most men had a bachelor life during which they did not starve or become encrusted with crud or buried under the litter. There is a taboo that says that women mustn't strain themselves in the presence of men—we haul around fifty pounds of groceries if we have to but aren't allowed to open a jar if there is someone around to do it for us. The reverse side of the coin is that men aren't supposed to be able to take care of themselves without women. Both are excuses for making women do the housework.

9. Beware of the double whammy. He won't do the little things he always did because you're now a "Liberated Woman, right?" Of course, he won't do anything else either. . . .

I was just finishing this when my husband came in and asked what I was doing. Writing a paper on housework. Housework? he said. *Housework?* Oh my god how trivial can you get. A paper on housework.

FAMILY STRUCTURE AND COMMUNISM

MIHALY VAJDA
AGNES HELLER

The abolition of private property and the destruction of alienated collective authority, which are recurring themes of Marxian communism, are a function of ... positive value presuppositions. Neither is a goal in itself. Both are means and processes meant to bring about a "humane" society, since the end of private property and the state are fundamental preconditions for the elimination of (1) the fetishization of human relations into relations among things, (2) the subordination of men to other men (social division of labor), and (3) the relation of men to other men as mere means. ...

Does the process of total social transformation automatically satisfy the preconditions which would permit the realization of its goal; that is, the positive and non-alienated regulation of human relations? Does purely political and economic activity create the types of men necessary for a really *free* society? The communist transformation of the relations of production and the transformation of alienated power structures into "social," local governing structures can be accomplished only if *our conscious revolutionary intentions* are also directed toward transforming everyday life. Indeed, all these factors are mutually conditioning. The transformation of production relations and the dissolution of power relations are unimaginable without the conscious revolutionary reconstruction of everyday life, and *vice versa*.

Engels posed this problem in his *Origin of the Family, Private Property, and the State*. According to him, the destruction of private property and the withering away of the state must necessarily accompany the dissolution of the monogamous family. Engels argued that in a communist society the monogamous family would turn into a marriage partnership but added that nothing certain can be said in advance about this development since the new forms are yet to be worked out.

It has been suggested that within communism it is possible to separate the task of bringing up new generations from the constant framework of

Excerpts reprinted from Mihaly Vajda and Agnes Heller, "Family Structure and Communism," *Telos*, 7 (New York: *Telos*, Spring 1971), 99–111. This essay was originally written in Hungarian. English translation by Andrew Arato.

intimate relations between men and women (that is, in the form of child care centers organized by the state or by the whole of society as the basic units for forming new generations). This notion is not only utopian but also implies the impoverishment of human life in at least one essential respect. Thus, it stands in opposition to the value presuppositions of communism: it would eliminate from life the internal connections of adults and children as organic parts of universal human relations. Furthermore, it implies the introduction of a new division of labor, the separation of a stratum of educators. The rejection of this view, however, is also connected with the rejection of the alternative that the children's upbringing must always take place within the framework of the monogamous bourgeois family.

The original structure of both types[1] of bourgeois family is in a state of transition. Today, as a result of changes in the structure of modern capitalism, the majority of bourgeois families are no longer organized around production but around consumption. Thus, even within capitalism, the economic function of the family is diminishing. The phenomena usually described as the "dissolution of the family" or "crisis of the family form" are probably connected to this change. What are these phenomena? (1) The end of monogamy in the strict sense. Divorce *de jure* (or at least *de facto*) is universally accepted, although some attention has been paid to its socially negative characteristics. The most dramatic manifestation of this phenomenon was the suggestion in Sweden and Denmark to legally abolish marriage as an institution. (2) The almost complete *de jure* elimination and the *de facto* reduction of male authority in marriage. This is connected to so-called women's emancipation, the gradual widening of the circle of occupations open to women, the achievement of political equality by women, et cetera. (3) The transformation of moral norms relating to sexuality, which improves the situation of women and is connected to the increase in divorces. (4) The practical disappearance of the multi-generational family: the narrowing of the family to the "nuclear family."

From the viewpoint of the basic value of free choice of human ties, this process must be considered positive even if it leads to insoluble conflicts which society is powerless to solve even when it seeks to eliminate them in an organized manner. One such basic conflict flows from the contradiction between the freedoms of divorce and raising children. The financial problems involved are easily solved if the society is sufficiently affluent. This is not as serious a problem as the disruption brought about by divorce in the lives of many children.

Another basic problem resulting from this disintegration is loneliness.

---

[1] The petit bourgeois family function was that of a *productive unit;* the upper bourgeois family was as a property holding unit.

The nuclear family reduces the possibility of intensive, many-sided relationships (in societies where, almost without exception, human ties outside the family are merely functional). This problem is all the more serious in the case of old people who are left alone. In many families, if the old people live with the nuclear family, they either serve it or become a burden for it; and if they do not live with the family, they are abandoned to complete loneliness. The same problem arises with divorced people, especially women who must raise children. Such a task obviously interferes with entering into new relations.

Sexual revolution as a slogan and as a movement expresses and stimulates this process of disintegration, although its main aim is the formation of free human relations. For the sake of this aim, the "sexual revolution" strives toward the complete dissolution of the bourgeois family. Naturally, as in all human relations, the free choice of sexual relations and the freedom to choose them again and again is a basic precondition for the development and universalization of individuality. At the same time, the sexual revolution restricts the program of establishing human ties to the free choice of sexual partners. It fails to analyze the relationship between sexuality and other types of intense ties: first and foremost, the relations between adults and children. The sexual revolution offers no solution toward the formation of the basic units of a new society. It is one-sided even in terms of its restricted analysis of sexual relations. Beginning with the assumption that the historically available types of sexual relations are not free, it prefers promiscuity and disregards the fact that the most substantial, intense, and many-sided human relations (for example, love, friendship, et cetera) originate in the lives of couples. . . . The solutions to the two problems of sexuality and family must be sought together, but it would be regressive to seek the solutions in some new type of bourgeois family.

Independently of its economic function, the basic social function of the bourgeois family is to shape a type of personality that guarantees the frictionless operation of bourgeois society. The Marxist theory of society presupposes an immediate connection between the structure of personality and the totality of social relations. It assumes as natural that the transformation of the production and property relations, political structures, et cetera, of a given society will produce the type of man adequate to the new society. The theory does not examine the concrete mechanisms which shape character types corresponding to social conditions. As a result, it ignores that family which plays no basic role in the organization of production; it examines the relations between family structure and society only as a moment of production or of property relations. . . .

Because of inborn characteristics, a basic human personality is formed and fixed in early childhood. We will call this "psychic character." The belief that the whole human personality can go through *perceptual* and *radical* changes during the entire life-span is implicitly or explicitly present in Marxism. However, this is an unfortunate inheritance from sensualism. What can and often does change is *moral character,* and even this does not change independently of the psychic character: for example, a negative psychic character precludes a radical moral catharsis. Accordingly, psychic character is primarily formed in the family, which also transmits basic moral preferences to the child. Later on, however, these moral preferences can be modified through choice, unlike psychic character, which cannot.

The bourgeois family must guarantee that the psychic character of the men who grow up within it are adequate to the demands of bourgeois society. This, of course, need not be accomplished consciously. Indeed, in most cases the task is accomplished even if the dominant family ideology is openly *anti-bourgeois.* . . .

The two parents constitute the basic environment of the small child. Upbringing in the nursery and in the day care center always relates back to the family. It is "natural" for the child to love his parents before anyone else. Indeed, parents "must" be loved and honored: society expects it. Until the moment of adulthood, the child's deepest emotional ties are with his parents, and he must seek his moral ideals in them. The day care center, and later the school, provide other moral ideals, but never in relation to everyday life and activity and never with such immediacy that they can direct the child in his activities. . . . Without going into situations where one or both parents have generally negative moral character yet society demands that the child love *these* parents (although in extreme cases of blatantly brutal or criminal parents society does not demand it), it suffices to point out that in this situation the child becomes totally homeless: he belongs nowhere.

The bourgeois family is authoritarian: it is not a community. Even today in the great majority of families, because of tradition and his social situation, the man is the authority independently of the means to exercise this authority. There are families where, because of her place in society or the strength of her personality, the woman has authority. This does not change the fact that the family is authoritarian. As a result, the contemporary family is not adequate to teach the child how to live and act in a community. . . . Second: a real community cannot be formed because of the small number of children. Even in those unusual cases where the family has many children, they are not of the same age and the age-difference creates a kind of "natural hierarchy." This happens because older children often become the representatives of parents. The children's authoritarian social conduct is prepared by this structure. . . .

Within the family, the instinct of self-preservation becomes a desire to own or to have. Even when it is not a unit of production and does not have private property that provides an income, the bourgeois family is based on community of property. Because of its authoritarian structure, the use of the family's property is a function of the decision of the family authority. This can lead to a struggle for the use of property within the family and at the same time to a defense of the family's material interests against every other family and group. . . .

Originally, the proletarian family was *not* a bourgeois family. It was not bourgeois even in Marx's time, when the material conditions of the proletariat prevented it from developing the preconditions for a "normal" bourgeois family life. . . . The gradual improvement of the conditions of the proletariat permitted the "bourgeoisification" of its family structure and encouraged the development of the predominant family type: the monogamous bourgeois family. Bernstein saw this well and approved of it: everyone must be brought up as a *Bürger*. He also correctly saw the connection between this process and the development of reformist tendencies within the working class movement. Those who live in a bourgeois way do not wish to fundamentally change bourgeois society but instead try to reform it so as to guarantee higher standards of living. Even in great economic crises, the proletarian who grows up in a petit bourgeois family becomes a rebel, not a revolutionary. . . .

Naturally, the negative role of the bourgeois family in the formation of psychic and moral character does not seem to be entirely a function of the family structure. This restriction applies specifically to the "possessive orientation" and the particular "collective unconsciousness." But, in the first place, there seem to be factors which cannot be transcended within the given family structure, for example, the essentially authoritarian relationship between child and parent and the absence of community in everyday life. Secondly, and this is the crucial point, certain habitual norms and value preferences have historically become attached to the contemporary family in such a way that their elimination from the family structure as it is seems almost impossible. Thus, a revolutionary transformation of the family structure aimed at the denial of these habitual norms and value preferences seems more promising.

The Marxism of the Second International considered the total social process and the formation of psychic character to be immediately related: it was convinced that the transformation of the former leads mechanically to the transformation of the latter. Originally, Bolshevism did the opposite. Thus, in the period immediately following the October Revolution it seemed natural that decisive changes must occur in the relations between man and woman and in the basic forms of communal living, since the creation of proletarian authority and the liquidation of the ruling classes does not automatically imply these changes. There were fundamental changes in family law, along with decisive attempts to completely transform everyday life. . . .

The ideology that became predominant in the 1930's and restored many theoretical conceptions of the Second International also restored Social

Democratic conceptions of family structure. Conscious steps were taken to restore or to strengthen the bourgeois family structure. Although they might have felt it instinctively, they were not conscious that this tendency strengthened the authoritarian character of the whole system. When other socialist countries came into being, the transformation of the family structure was definitely not on the agenda. There was concern only with those aspects of the bourgeois family which were directly connected with all of society, while the family ideal itself remained untouched. . . .

In the history of Marxist theory, however, a different conception has been developed which now plays an important role in Western European Leftist movements. This conception does not consider the shaping of a "new man" merely as a result of ideological "influences" nor does it view this aim simply as the mechanical result of the transformation of the total social structure. Rather, it considers the development of a new psychic character in relation to the democratic transformation of the *units of social production*. . . . Naturally, the democratic transformation of the structure of the workshop is also one of the basic preconditions of communism. However, even this provides no answer to our problem. That is: (1) The more developed a society, the later an individual enters production. Thus, the young increasingly begin work with a fixed psychic and moral character. (2) The more developed a society, the less time is spent in production. Indeed, the reduction of working time is a goal, although the formation of many-sided relationships is also related to production. (3) Even if professions and skills are freely chosen, it is still impossible to determine production from the individual viewpoint. Democracy at the level of production can become natural and free from manipulation only if democratic life and norms of action have *already* become natural for the individual entering production. . . .

A solution to this problem is possible only through a *radical transformation of the family*. What criteria must be met by the new family structure? (1) It must be a democratically structured community which allows the early learning of democratic propensities. (2) It must guarantee many-sided human relations including those between children and adults. (3) It must guarantee the development and realization of individuality. The basic precondition of this is the free choosing and re-choosing of human ties even in childhood. (4) It must eliminate both the conflicts originating in monogamy and those originating in its dissolution. This is the type of solution to be sought in the new type of family, which we will call the *commune*.

The following will outline how we conceive of family structure in communist society. It is useless to work out details since, as always, the organizations of the future cannot be realizations of prior "plans." Furthermore, in the same way that there are many different types of monogamous families, the "collective family," or the commune, will also take on a variety of guises. In fact, since it is a matter of putting together a much more complicated structure than the monogamous bourgeois family, it is likely that the number of variations will be greater.

This commune is the "successor" of the bourgeois family. Thus it is not the basic economic or political cell of communist society. The whole organization of society is completely independent of the commune, which is the *organizational center of everyday collective life*.

Thus, our commune has nothing in common with Fourier's phalanx or other similar plans for communes functioning as productive units or communities based on the sharing of the same living space. Since it functions *only* as a family, the realization of our commune is *not* independent of the socio-political situation and of the *over-all* realization of communism. This commune would help bring about communist transformation by producing the type of men and frameworks needed for such transformation. Although its immediate function is the solution of the conflicts discussed, the commune creates the preconditions for communist changes in the economic and political structure so that they become *irreversible*. This does not mean that the organization of communes "must wait" at least *until* the beginning of communist social transformation. On the contrary, the two processes must begin together. If the situation favors this solution, it may be possible for the transition to communes to precede the full process.

The commune is a freely chosen community. Its members choose to be in it and are accepted by *all* other members of the community. Individuals enter the commune: every adult member of the entering families becomes a commune member as an individual. Of course, the membership must be small enough to guarantee that the affairs of the commune can be conducted through immediate democracy. In the commune, all forms of personal individuality must be respected. Three conditions are necessary for the functioning of the commune. These are: (1) the obligation to work (all able members of the commune must work and participate in the social division of labor). Thus, even in the present context, it is not permissible within the commune that a high-earning man supports a woman with whom he has a stable attachment. (2) No one is relieved of collective tasks within the commune. (3) Everyone must be somehow engaged with the commune's community of children, regardless of whether or not he has children of "his own." Aside from this, the community does not interfere in the life of its members, their occupation, free time, and human relations. Of course, as in every community, there will be preferred forms of human conduct. Except in extreme cases, however, moral preferences will not become moral imperatives. In extreme cases, the commune will expel the member.

According to our notion, the commune does not have value preferences concerning sexual relations. Until now in civilized societies, value preferences relating to sexuality had their main source in two factors. The first is the consciousness of property or ownership: the woman is the man's private property or, in a more modern version, the man and the woman are each other's property. The second factor is the need to take care of children. Since the commune is based on the denial of private property relations, the first factor is naturally dropped. In relation to the second, the solution lies in the commune, which will take care of children born in or belonging to it even if their parents choose a different partner, or if one or the other leaves the commune. What is the concrete meaning of the absence of value preferences regarding sexuality in the commune? It means that both life-long relations of couples and promiscuity are possible within the confines of the same commune. The commune does not make promiscuity obligatory. This is important, because in past years similar organizations have not only opted for promiscuity, but have been directly built on it. This, however, entails as much limitation of the individual's free self-development as does monogamy. Under these conditions, the dissolution of the relations of couples not only leaves the children's life unchanged, but also reduces the negative aspects of contemporary divorce for adults. Here, it is not a question of the reduction of pain, since it is not a question of life. Rather, it is a question of the possibility that after the end of a relation, the divorced partners can stay in their original community without remaining alone.

The commune solves the problem of loneliness in cases other than those involving divorce. Unattached people can find a community with married people since, given the present family structure, marriage partners can also be lonely. Because of lack of time, spatial separation, et cetera, married people can lack varied and many-sided human relations even if there are other people with whom they would gladly associate. Naturally, the loneliness of the old and their feeling of superfluousness disappears in the commune.

Communal living reduces human relations based on mere habit and routine. Within the context of the contemporary family, people often continue living with each other because they are used to it, cannot imagine a better solution, and want to avoid the problems brought about by divorce. These problems disappear in the commune.

The commune is not a closed unit which hinders the formation of rich human ties outside of it. External ties will develop spontaneously, since the commune is neither a productive nor a political unit. To the extent that there are many communes, fluctuation of membership among them will be natural.

Obviously, the commune will hold no "officially" declared ideology. But it is also obvious that a community of people who have freely chosen each other will have some common ideological outlook, especially in view of the fact that, at least in the present context, the commune implies the *revolutionary* transformation of life in one fundamental respect. As a result, ideological problems in the commune are likely to generate internal conflicts.

"Liberation" from housework does not seem possible in the foreseeable future, and the service industry, in spite of its growth, is not a solution. The modernization of the household helps, but it does not solve the problem. Within the commune, however, it is possible to substantially reduce the time spent running the household, even under present economic and technological conditions: larger households are much more economical and conducive to the use of machines. This alone increases the amount of free time which, in the commune, can also be used in radically different ways. Whereas in the monogamous family parents with small children are tied to the house, such is not the case in the commune, and the "house" itself allows a *diversified* use of free time. Even "within the house," free time should not be restricted to consumption but should be active, cultural, and conducive to personal development. Of course, the forms this development will take cannot be determined in advance, but within such a cultural context a community is likely to advance. This is shown by historical examples such as the cultural effects of the trade union communities of the old working class movements. This advancement, of course, occurs only when the community does not restrict the unfolding of individuality, which we have postulated in principle.

As already mentioned, the commune's most basic advantage concerns children. Everything discussed so far concerns "finished" persons for whom the commune guarantees the solution of already existing problems. But the destruction of the bourgeois family is fundamental because it eliminates many negative factors determining the formation of psychic character. Before investigating this problem, however, it is important to outline the commune's community of children. In the commune, children are not "collectively" raised, but they belong to a real *community of children*. The judgment of children's conduct, their entrance into the division of labor, and the bestowing of reward and punishment, that is, the regulation of children's relations, is a function of age levels and should be not an adult task but one of the community of children. This does not mean that the relations between adults and children are not close and diversified; but they are not unambiguously authoritarian as in the bourgeois family. Children should be aware that they decide their fate in many ways. This leads to the early development of democratic inclinations so that children can become full members of the community of adults at a relatively early age. Even with very small children, for whom the authoritarian aspect of adult-child relations cannot be eliminated, it is crucial that *every* adult and older child in the commune, rather than just their "biological parents," be somehow occupied with them. Thus, from birth, they lack fixed emotional preferences. While growing, the child increasingly chooses adults to whom he is more attracted and to whom he feels connected by fundamental inner ties. The opposite is also true. The commune's adult members are not necessarily most strongly attracted to their "own" children. Thus, they can choose the children whose temperament, character, and intellect are "nearest" or most "attractive" to them. Both adults and children do not *have to* love anyone, nor *must* one love anyone *the most*. As with every other emotion, *love* also is a function of choice. This lessens the "mine"/"yours" dichotomy on the emotional level.

Of course, unlike the case of children born within the commune, free choice of emotional ties is illusory for members entering the commune with children. This can result in conflicts for people brought up in the old family structure. Yet, we should recall the common experience of people who feel they could love a child as "their own" if the child had been brought up in their environment. On the other hand, parents often cannot confront their children's faults, since they are afraid that exposure of these faults would leave them with nothing. The latter is not always the case today in families with many children.

The commune's community obviously makes demands on the children's community: there are the *same* demands made on adults, for example, the obligation to work (study) and obligatory participation in the community's common work. In this context, even if the adult community is forced to appear authoritarian, it is not in the sense of "family head," since the adults require the performance of obligations similar to their own. In addition to deemphasizing the "mine"/"yours" dichotomy, the child community also hinders the development of private property psychology in other contexts. In the children's world, unlike the adults' world, all personal property is eliminated. Many existing child communities show how this can be accomplished.

The psychic character of children who grow up in these circumstances will be conducive to democratic life. They will *never accept as natural* a situation in which they do not have a voice in determining their fate. At the same time, they will not develop a need to oppress other men. It could be argued that existing children's communities are characterized by cruelty. These communities, however, consist of children who grew up in bourgeois families and who want to "live out" power instincts that were developed and at the same time repressed in the family. A more serious objection is that children's communities might hinder the development of individuality. To avoid this, the commune must create the preconditions to enable children as well as adults to follow their own wishes and tastes after satisfying their communal obligations. Each child must be able to play as he wants, read what he wants, and spend his free time as he wishes.

On the other hand, the development of free individuality is greatly enhanced by children confronting a large number of adults. If adults are basically of positive moral character, as in the case of the nuclear family, the children have the opportunity to choose as the ideal of everyday conduct those adults whose psychic and moral character is adequate to their particular gifts. Thus, communes which satisfy their social functions will have definite material preconditions. First, the commune cannot be closed: each individual member must be free to leave the commune at any time. Second, the community must have the right to expel a member if necessary. The preconditions of this must be assured: society must guarantee available apartments which can be occupied by departing members at any time. Also, the normal functioning of the commune requires a certain level of material prosperity. "Communes based on misery," at least under European conditions, necessarily dissolve. Yet no great "affluence" is necessary for the establishment of the commune, especially since housekeeping, common library, collective child education, et cetera, substantially reduce individual expenses. As long as the commune operates within a commodity-producing society, material problems must be carefully regulated so that they create as few conflicts as possible. Since the commune cannot be isolated from society at large, this problem can be solved only by reduction of income differences. As long as the communist solution to the problem of income is not completed, the commune can only reproduce in itself the larger problems in this area.

The commune can also change or dissolve as a result of other conflicts. Since the commune is the organizational center of the everyday life of communist society, existing noncommunist societies hinder the development of communes and aim at their dissolution. The ideal type of commune described is also laden with conflicts; but these are not the conflicts of a society built on possession. They are "truly human" conflicts. However, the influence of existing societies can result in the reproduction of old conflicts and structures. Thus, the development of a very strong particular identity within individual communes is to be expected. This identity can be the cause or effect of competition or even of animosity among communes. Other important problems can result from the fact that individual communes would probably consist of people occupying the same position in the social division of labor. This can cause significant differences in the standards of living of the various communes and results in the preservation of cultural differences.

It is utopian to believe that the commune *alone* can solve the most basic social problems. No isolated political or economic transformation can be final or prevent the reproduction of old social structures. Thus, for example, workshop democracy can easily be deformed and transformed into manipulated democracy. An isolated solution to the problem of the family is no exception and, if it remains isolated, the commune will definitely be deformed. Thus, a basic social task of commune members is to assist in communist transformation in *every* social sphere. Similarly, without the revolution of the family, structural changes in a communist social direction cannot become irreversible. The formation of a new psychic character can take place only within the revolutionized family. This is the only locus of mass education for individuals who are to take an active part in the direction of social affairs, not only in times of great social crises but "every day."

as block to mother's education and employment, 259
decrease in years spent on, 9
of educated working Black women, 205–6
Child care
as factor in woman's subordination, 3
as factor of household production, 121, 126
as task behavior, 158
for working mothers, 263–64
in commune, 300
in Israel's Kibbutzim, 144
socialization of, 118
tax deductions for cost of, 283
under socialism, 105
Child-care centers
as substitutes for home, 294, 296
need for, 282–83
Child development, new studies in, 81
Children
aggressive or antisocial behavior of, 94–95
and working mothers, statistics, 37
in commune, 301–2
protection and maintenance in primitive societies, 115
psychological problems of, 92, 94–95
rearing of, as responsibility of society, 126, 127
socialization of, 17, 20, 22, 48
China, today's woman, role in, 46
Chivalry, Southern male, 43
Chong Soo Pyun, 138, 187–93
Civic organizations, women in, 248–49
Civil Rights Act of 1964
and job discrimination, 218, 238
Civil rights movement, women in, 6, 11
Clans (gentes), women's place in, 100–101
Clitoris-vagina shift, 62–63
Clark, Alice, 3 (footnote)
Cohen, Mabel Blake, 55, 79–88
Commune
as collective family, 289–99
child care in, 300
conflicts in, 303
criteria for, 298
housework load in, 301
ideology of, 301
sexual relations in, 300
work obligations in, 299
Communism
and family structure, 293–99
household, supremacy of women in, 100, 104
Community agencies
classified as to functions, 249

female role in, 248–49, 250–51
board memberships, 248
male dominance on vital boards, 251–53
status and board membership, occupational and social, 250, 252
voluntary associations, 249
Community-property laws, states having, 273
Companionship marriage, 161
Comparative primatology, 111
Conjugal family
affective involvement in, 170
and social scientists, 133
as basic social unit, 12
development of, 5
economic base of, 171
ego as member of two types
family of orientation, 169
family of procreation, 169
ideology of, 20
lower-class mother-centered emphasis, 169
sex-differentiated roles in, 133–34, 171
structural isolation of, 169–70
symmetrically multilineal, 168
unique role of mother in, 168–69
upper-class patrilineal emphasis, 168–69
Consumption, organization of today's family around, 16, 294
Contraception
and maternal deaths, 8
and natural law, 278
and pregnancies, 8–9
free access to, 18, 118
in China, 46
state provision for, 51
women's attitudes toward, 18
Cook-Leichter bill, 282
Courtly love and sex love, 109

Day care. *See* Child care
Day-care centers. *See* Child-care centers
Dependency in marriage
as historical feminine role, 172
imbalance in, 86
Deutsch, Helene, 70, 72
Dexter, Elizabeth A., 3
Discrimination
against stigmatized individuals, 97–98
as identifying factor in minority groups, 39
by customers, 224, 226
in job market, sex factors in, 139
race-sex, in hiring and pay scales, 262
Discrimination against women
elimination of material basis for, 126

Friedan, Betty, 8
Fuchs, Victor R., 140, 222–27

Gang system of female labor, 23
Gelber, Sylvia, 137
Genetic sex, 63
Gentes (clans), origins of, 117
Gilman, Charlotte Perkins, 132
Girls
　aggressive and competitive behavior
　　of, 82
　genital sexual interest of, 55
　tomboy behavior of, 80
Goffman, Erving, 56, 96–99
Goode, William J., 10, 17–22
Gordon, C. Wayne, 248–53
Gough, Kathleen, 57, 107–18
Gray, Betty MacMorran, 141, 235–37
Great Depression
　effects on women, 7
　women's activities during, 6
Greeks and the monogamous family, 104
Gross National Product [GNP]
　exclusion of household work from, 131
Group marriage, 100, 108, 111, 113, 116,
　117
Group sex, in primeval times, 107
Gubbels, Robert, 139, 208–18
Guilds, 3

Hacker, Helen Mayer, 10, 275
Hamilton, Henry, 3, 4
Hartley, Ruth, 80
Hatch, Mary and David, 136, 183–86
Havighurst, R. J., 93
Heller, Agnes, 279, 293–99
Hetaerism, 103, 110
Hines, Fred, 140, 228–34
Hobby, Oveta Culp, 245
Home production, alternative forms of,
　127
Homosexuality, 51, 60, 75, 90, 288
Horney, Karen, 55, 74–78
Household production
　as function of women, 121
　distinguished from "real work," 121
Household work and GNP, 124, 137
Housewives
　decrease in work and social-service
　　duties, 8
　economic disadvantages of, 137
　low status of, 137
　monetary value of, 187–93
　　computing, 188–89
　working, economic value to family,
　　138
Housework
　capitalization of, 128

need to industrialize, 122
politics of, male excuses, 290
time spent on
　effect of immigrant labors on, 8
　effect of technological improvements
　　on, 8
Human rights
　and family system, 17
　changed or changing ideas about
　　abortion, 19
　　bride price or dowry, 18
　　contraception, 18
　　control by elders and other kin, 18
　　divorce, 19
　　egalitarianism in family, 19
　　inheritance, 18
　　intercaste and interclass marriage,
　　　18
　　mate choice, 17–18
　of women and children, 20
Husband-father, role as "task specialist,"
　157

"Ideal, typical marriage,"
　active-passive balance in, 85
Identification
　defined, 89
　development of, sex differences in, 89
　vs. sex-role adoption, 89
　vs. sex-role preference, 89
Identity
　personal
　　defined, 79
　　conflict, as persons and sexual be-
　　　ings, 79
　　in pregnant wives, 83–84
　　problems in marriage, 86
Identity, social, stigmatization and, 97–
　98
Ideology
　"cult of the home," 125
　feminine mystique and inequality, 275
　justifying woman's inferior position,
　　245
　man's traditional image of woman,
　　213
　of the commune, 301
　of the conjugal family, 20
　of male supremacy, 287
　of marriage, themes of, 176, 182
　religion and woman's inferiority, 4
　stigma theory, 97
　term explained, 2
Illegitimacy, abolition of, as a legal no-
　tion, 51
Incest prohibitions, 114, 116
Inductor theory of sexual differentiation,
　63–64

Male supremacy, and sexual freedom, 103
Mandel, Ernest, 119–20
Mannheim, Karl, 2
Marcuse, Herbert, 49
Marginal workers, women as, 210, 224
Marital disharmony, types of, 86–87
Marital roles, adoption and adjustment, 16, 182
Marital satisfaction, social performance and, 162
Market economy, shift from household, 4
Marmor, Judd, 68–73
Marriage
    and community relationship, 178
    arranged vs. love, 110
    as private sphere, 176
    as significant instrumentality, 176
    as sign of successful woman, 130
    as social elevator for women, 43
    as small-world haven, 135
    as social reality, 174, 180
    concretized through marital conversation, 180
    cultural stereotypes in, 81
    current alternatives to, 133
    division of labor in, 80
    husband-wife relationship as binding element in, 134
    functional, 134
    ideal-typical analysis of, 176
    inequality in, 166, 167
    in macrosocial context, 181
    in tribal societies, 117
    legal equality in, 104
    morale of men in, wife's role, 136
    nomic-building process in, 179, 181
    role of men in, 130
    relationship of husband and male friends, 180
    satisfaction in, social performance and, 162–63
    sibling-rivalry relationship in, 87
    similarity of goals in, 160–61; table, 161
    social distance in, 41–42
    social-emotional needs in, 161
    social-emotional satisfactions vs. task, 162
    specialization vs. mutuality in, 159–60, 163
    subordination of wife's interest in, 134
    task vs. social-emotional behavior in, 157–58
Marriage and motherhood of black vs. white women graduates, 203–7
    aspirations and expectations, 207

attitudes of husbands, 205
    attitudes toward career plus marriage, 203
    attitudes toward graduate study, 205
    children, 203
    labor-force work patterns, 204
    marriage as goal, 205
    occupational choices, 206
    self-identity stabilized in, 181
    single vs. married, 203
Marriage relationship as keystone of U.S. kinship system, 169
Married women
    labor-force participation of
        factors affecting, 202
        historical trends, 3, 25
        today, 31, 32, 199, 209
        turnover as characteristic of, 202
        white vs. Negro, 34–35
    loss of economic independence, 26
    work choices of, 201
Married working women, survey of magazine articles about
    educational and professional training of, 185
    lack of clarity of goals in, 185
    problems covered in, 184
    sex-role conflicts in, 186
    women's role in, 184
Marx, Karl and Marxism, 45, 56, 57, 102, 103, 111, 119, 293, 295–96, 297–98
    abolition of private property, 293
    destruction of alienated collective authority, 293
    formation of psychic character, 297–98
    social position of women in, 56
    theory of classes, 57, 119
    theory of personality changes, 295–96
Marx and Engels
    on division of labor in family, 103
    on exploitive nature of capitalism, 15
Mary-cult, 4
Masculinity and femininity
    invalidity of "accepted" roles, 87–88
    masculine ideal, typical, 85
    masculinity complex, 58
    traditional concepts of, 79–80
Masochism and passivity in women, 70, 72–73
Massey, Ruth, 248–53
Masters and Johnson research program, 65–66
Mate choice, freedom of, 17–18
Maternal behavior, effects on children, 82
Maternal law and inheritance, 101–2

Maternal estrogens, **64**
Matriarchy
 among Blacks, 276
 as kinship pattern in U.S. lower class,
 169
 concept of, a fantasy, 117
 freedom of women in, 115
 male dominance in, 115
Matrilineal, matrilocal communist household, 108
Matrilineal descent
 and female dominance, 115
 and inheritance, 117
Matrilocal *vs.* patrilocal residence, 114
Meadian social psychology, 99
Men
 compulsion to prove manhood, 77
 propensity to debase love-object, 77–
 78
 secret dread of women, 74–78
Millett, Kate, 278, 287–88
Mincer, Jacob, 10, 138, 198–202
Minority groups
 defined, 10
 self-concept of, 39
 theory of, application to women's
 status, 11
Mitchell, Juliet, 10, 11, 45–57, 122
Mixed economy, 98
MMPI, 93
Monogamy
 and subjugation of women, 103
 end of, in strict sense, 294
 in "civilized" societies, 118
 origin of, 103
 serial, 108
Monolithism of marriage and family, 51
Moral character, family as molder of,
 296
Moran, Robert D., 141, 238–44
Morgan, Lewis Henry, 107, 111
Moss, Howard A., 79, 82
Mowrer, O. H., 90, 93
Myths about women
 of economic power, 246–47
 of female asexuality, 67
 of political power, 67
 sex, 84

Narcissism, phallic, 77
Negroes
 abortion among, 281
 attitudes of women toward sterilization, contraception, 278
 castelike status, 42–43
 childbearing of educated working
 women, 205–6
 earnings, 232–34; table, 231

matriarchy and, 276
wives in labor force, 32–33, 34, 195
women and pluralism, 276–77
women as heads of families
 earnings, 232–34
 percentages, 260
 tables, 256, 258
women graduates, problems of marriage and motherhood, 203–7
working women, turnover, 267
young women in labor force, 34
Neocapitalism, 124, 127
New Democratic Coalition (New York)
 platform of women's rights, 280–
 86
Nottingham, Elizabeth K., 7
Nuclear family
 alternatives to, 279
 and neocapitalism, 127
 as consumption unit, 125
 loneliness and, 294–95
 male dominance in, 117
 roots, in colonial America, 15

Occupational mobility
 age as factor in, 267, 268–69
 of men *vs.* women, 267
 studies of job tenure and absenteeism,
 268–71
 white *vs.* Negro, 267
Occupations
 distribution of women in, 139
 division of labor in, 33, 209–10
 functional equivalents for women, 134
 growth in, open to women, 294
 of woman heads of families, 261–62
Oedipal complex, 70
Oedipal situation, girls, 59
 part- *vs.* full-time, 34
 women in professions, decline, 219
Oppression of women, 45, 103, 289, 291.
 See also Subordination

Parsons, Talcott, 47, 48, 50, 54, 90, 132,
 134–35, 157, 168–73, 246
Patriarchal family
 nuclear concept, 109
 paternal authority in, 102
 polygamy in, 102
 supremacy of men in, 102
Patrilineal descent, 14
Penis envy, 58, 70, 71, 88
Perkins, Frances, 245
Phallic narcissism, 77
Phallic phase in boys, 75
Piercy, Marge, 6
Pietrofesa, John, 140, 219–21
Pinchbeck, Ivy, 10, 23–29

in occupational and political spheres, 155

suggested models of
  assimilation, 276
  hybrid, 276
  pluralist, 275

Sex identity, problems of, 55–59
Sexism *vs.* racism, 10
Sex mythology, 84
Sex revolution and dissolution of family, 295
Sex-role adoption, defined, 89
Sex-role assimilation, 171
Sex-role concepts, stereotypes, 287–88
Sex-role differentiation
  and biological capabilities, 132
  from childhood on, 139
  in family, 132, 142
  in Israel's Kibbutzim, 132
Sex-role identification
  age and, 92
  child-parent similarity as factor, 93
  development of, in boys, 91
  development of, in girls, 91–92, 95
  shift of, in boys, 90
  with mother, 90
Sex-role preference, defined, 89
Sex roles, clichés about, 53
Sex-role stereotypes, nineteenth century, 164
Sex traits, categorized, 288
Sex traits, parental efforts to ascribe, 21
Sexual frustration, in boys, 75
Sexuality
  evolution in, today, 48
  female
    dual nature of, 62
    Freudian theory of, 54
  noncreative, 49
  production-and-work *vs.* consumption-and-fun ethos, 49
  repression in China, 46
Sexual differentiation, inductor theory of, 63
Sexual-identity problems, in marriage, 85–88
Sexual inequality of oral contraception, 47
Sexual inhibition, in girls, 58
Sexual love, nonrole in origin of monogamy, 100
Sexual morality, double standard of, 109
Sexual revolution, results predicated for, 288
Shaftsbury, Lord, 27
Sherfey, Mary Jane, 10, 55
Sibling rivalry in marriage, 87
Simmel, Georg, 178

Single women
  and the Industrial Revolution, 26–27
  historical role in labor force, 3
Slavery
  abolition of, women's role in, 6
  and class society, 109
Smuts, Robert W., 5
Social class
  and marriage, 110
  bourgeoisie and women's work, 14
  stigmatization, 97–98
Social-emotional behavior
  defined, 158
  mother as specialist in, 157
  need for interaction in, 158
  specialization in, 158
Social fatherhood, origins, 114–15
Social identity
  vs. social status, 96
  virtual *vs.* actual, 96
Social infrastructure, 212
Socialism, limits of, for women's liberation, 57
Socialization
  alternatives to family, 52
  and stigma labels, 56
  defined, 55
  effect on family system, 48
  in modern socialist societies, 118
  of children, need for, 17, 20, 21, 48
  of domestic work and child care, 118
  prolonged, results of, 298
  theoretical perspectives on, 55
  through social politics, 287
  women's sense of inferiority, 129
Social mobility
  as factor in U.S. kinship system, 169
Sociological determinism, 218
Social position of women, 6, 9
Social reality and sex roles, 136
Social revolution [Engels' predictions], 105–6
Socioemotional tasks, 132–33
Sopchak, A. L., 93
Stalinism, women under, 46
Stein, Robert, 247, 254–64
Stem families, 113
Stern, Bernhard J., 9–10, 13–16
Stigma
  acceptance of, 98
  and social contacts, 98–99
  as excuse, or blessing, 98
  defined, 96
  individual's response to own, 98
  types of, 96
Stigmatization, social-interaction effect, 99
Strong Vocational Interest Blank, 93

Structural differentiation, 50
Subordination
    of women
        Judeo-Christian doctrine of, 54
        physical strength as factor in, 3
    of women and Negroes, relation be-
        tween, 42
Suicide, male *vs.* female, 164–66
Superego, in women, 59, 73
Symbolic interaction
    and the world-erecting process, 174
    in marriage relationship, 135–36, 176
    language as base for, 174
    socialization of individual, 175

Talmon, Yonina, 132, 142–56
Task behavior, 157
Technology
    automation and jobs, 8
    bureaucratization and jobs, 8
    differentiated from *type of economy*, 2
Training programs and sex-based wage
        discrimination, 243
Tribal societies
    group-type marriage in, 117
Tweeten, Luther, 228–34

Unemployment
    of women, categories of, 36
    "hidden" unemployed, 235
    sex bias and, 235–37
    women *vs.* men, 36
Unisex, defined, 288
Use-value *vs.* exchange value, 57, 120

Vaginal orgasm, 63
Vajda, Mihaly, 279, 293–99
Victorian middle-class women, role of,
    28
Voluntarism, and exploitation of women,
    49

Wage differentials
    employer discrimination as factor in,
        140
    equalizing *vs.* nonequalizing, 139
Wage labor, slavery, and prostitution,
    103
Waldman, Elizabeth, 10, 30–38
Wealth, U.S. top holders of, 272–73
Welfare system, criticisms of, 255
Wirth, Louis, 39
Woman
    as slave of man, 100, 102
    family as her universe, 45
    her "place," 3, 27
    her role, Old Testament concept, 1

her status
    effects of dominant ideology on, 13
    in early bourgeois society, 14
her subordination
    in family, 2
    origins of, 3
"Woman's world," 40
Womb envy, 55, 72
Women
    "acceptable occupations for," 131
    "anatomy as fate," 70–71
    and marriage, nineteenth century, 134
    and men, career contrasts, 131
    as heads of U.S. households, 260–64
    as marginal beings, 44, 236
    as minority group, 40, 45
    as "natural" beings, 50
    as reserve labor force, 125, 140–41
    as sex objects, 9
    as top wealth-holders, 272–73
    as wage earners in early New En-
        gland, 15
    castelike status of, 42
    conflict between class and caste status,
        43
    discrimination against. *See* Discrimi-
        nation against women
    domestic slavery of, 105
    doubts and fears of, 129–30
    dual role of, 9, 126
    early socialization, effects of, 129
    economic contributions of, 137
    economic oppression of, 104
    economic role in family, 70
    effects of passivity and dependence
        on, 88
    egalitarianism in occupational sphere,
        19
    employment patterns, 38
    everyday frustrations of, 136
    exclusion from production, 104–5
    exclusion from voluntary associations,
        15
    exploitation in capitalist society, 128
    exploitation, slave and sexual, 109
    factors keeping at home, 127
    household work not counted as wage
        labor, 122
    humanistic-cultural role of, 173
    in competition with men, 43
    inferior status of, 125
    inferiority of, Freudian theory, 54
    integration in four structures, 45–49
    in voluntary associations, 246, 248
    legal rights *vs.* social and economic,
        118
    Marxian class-structure analyses, 119
    other women, attitudes toward, 40, 91

Printed in U.S.A.